IFIP Advances in Information and Communication Technology 356

IFIP – The International Federation for Information Processing

IFIP was founded in 1960 under the auspices of UNESCO, following the First World Computer Congress held in Paris the previous year. An umbrella organization for societies working in information processing, IFIP's aim is two-fold: to support information processing within its member countries and to encourage technology transfer to developing nations. As its mission statement clearly states,

> *IFIP's mission is to be the leading, truly international, apolitical organization which encourages and assists in the development, exploitation and application of information technology for the bene t of all people.*

IFIP is a non-profitmaking organization, run almost solely by 2500 volunteers. It operates through a number of technical committees, which organize events and publications. IFIP's events range from an international congress to local seminars, but the most important are:

- The IFIP World Computer Congress, held every second year;
- Open conferences;
- Working conferences.

The flagship event is the IFIP World Computer Congress, at which both invited and contributed papers are presented. Contributed papers are rigorously refereed and the rejection rate is high.

As with the Congress, participation in the open conferences is open to all and papers may be invited or submitted. Again, submitted papers are stringently refereed.

The working conferences are structured differently. They are usually run by a working group and attendance is small and by invitation only. Their purpose is to create an atmosphere conducive to innovation and development. Refereeing is less rigorous and papers are subjected to extensive group discussion.

Publications arising from IFIP events vary. The papers presented at the IFIP World Computer Congress and at open conferences are published as conference proceedings, while the results of the working conferences are often published as collections of selected and edited papers.

Any national society whose primary activity is in information may apply to become a full member of IFIP, although full membership is restricted to one society per country. Full members are entitled to vote at the annual General Assembly, National societies preferring a less committed involvement may apply for associate or corresponding membership. Associate members enjoy the same benefits as full members, but without voting rights. Corresponding members are not represented in IFIP bodies. Affiliated membership is open to non-national societies, and individual and honorary membership schemes are also offered.

Mike Chiasson   Ola Henfridsson
Helena Karsten   Janice I. DeGross (Eds.)

Researching the Future in Information Systems

IFIP WG 8.2 Working Conference
Turku, Finland, June 6-8, 2011
Proceedings

 Springer

Volume Editors

Mike Chiasson
Lancaster University, Management School
Department of Management Science
LA1 4YX Lancaster, UK
E-mail: m.chiasson@lancaster.ac.uk

Ola Henfridsson
Chalmers University of Technology
Department of Applied Information Technology
41296 Göteborg, Sweden
E-mail: ola.henfridsson@chalmers.se

Helena Karsten
Åbo Akademi University
Department of Information Technologies
20520 Turku, Finland
E-mail: ekarsten@abo.fi

Janice I. DeGross
University of Minnesota
Carlson School of Management
Minneapolis, MN 55455, USA
E-mail: degro003@umn.edu

ISSN 1868-4238   e-ISSN 1868-422X
ISBN 978-3-642-21363-2   e-ISBN 978-3-642-21364-9
DOI 10.1007/978-3-642-21364-9
Springer Heidelberg Dordrecht London New York

Library of Congress Control Number: 2011927857

CR Subject Classification (1998): K.4.3, K.6, J.0, H.0, H.1, H.4

Typesetting: Camera-ready by author, data conversion by Scientific Publishing Services, Chennai, India

Printed on acid-free paper

Springer is part of Springer Science+Business Media (www.springer.com)

Preface

This book contains the collection of papers, panels and a workshop presented at the IFIP WG8.2 Working Conference "Researching the Future." The conference took place during June 6–8, 2011 at the Åbo Akademi University in Turku, Finland.

We thank the authors and the Program Committee for their efforts in ensuring, again, an excellent WG8.2 conference. The impeccable book you have now in your hands is due to the skillful editing by Jan DeGross and the very experienced Springer team, with Erika Siebert-Cole.

We had the honor of hosting three experienced creators of the future, our keynote speakers, Yrjö Neuvo, Judith Gregory and Youngjin Yoo. The Cultural Capital of Europe 2011, Turku, provided a colorful setting for them and for all the conference participants.

The following organizations supported the conference through financial or other contributions and we would like to thank them for their engagement:

International Federation for Information Processing
Åbo Akademi University
Copenhagen Business School
Turku Centre for Computer Science
Turku Science Park
Turku 2011 Cultural Capital of Europe
Stiftelsen för Åbo Akademi (Foundation for Åbo Akademi University)
Tieteellisten Seurain valtuuskunta (Federation of Finnish Learned Societies)

Many individuals contributed to the successful conference. Our General Chairs Michael Myers and Jacob Nørbjerg worked behind the scenes, using their influence and contacts. The WG8.2 Chair Nancy Russo and secretary Kevin Crowston kept us on the narrow path. Our liaison to TC8, Juhani Iivari, brought the TC8 business meeting participants to Nauvo for the weekend before the conference, and then navigated them to the conference get-together. The annual ECIS conference was held in Helsinki, right after ours. Matti Rossi and Virpi Tuunainen at the Aalto University Business School were vital in coordinating our actions.

Barbro Back offered her experience and contacts for getting financial support for the conference, in her role as the head and deputy head of the department of Information Technologies at Åbo Akademi University. The conference could not have had a better hosting organization.

Tiina Haanila and Anna von Haartman took care of the income and expenditure. Andrea Hynynen coordinated our actions before and during the conference. Magnus Dahlvik provided the Web pages and computer support. Attia Zainab designed the look of the conference. Their skilful, quick and accurate work is much appreciated.

Mike Chiasson
Ola Henfridsson
Helena Karsten

Conference Organization

Conference Chairs

Michael Myers	University of Auckland Business School
Jacob Nørbjerg	Copenhagen Business School

Program Chairs

Mike Chiasson	Lancaster University
Ola Henfridsson	Chalmers University of Technology

Program Committee

Margunn Aanestad	University of Oslo
Michel Avital	University of Amsterdam
Michael Barrett	University of Cambridge
Richard Baskerville	Georgia State University
Nicholas Berente	University of Michigan
Tina Blegind Jensen	Copenhagen Business School
Richard Boland	Case Western Reserve University
Elisabeth Davidson	University of Hawaii
Robert Davison	City University of Hong Kong
Philip Dobson	Edith Cowan University
Uri Gal	Copenhagen Business School
Matt Germonprez	University of Wisconsin - Eau Claire
Jonny Holmström	Umeå University
Helena Holmström	Olsson IT University of Göteborg
Debra Howcroft	Manchester Business School
Juhani Iivari	University of Oulu
Netta Iivari	University of Oulu
Matthew Jones	University of Cambridge
Michael Gallivan	Georgia State University
Karl Kautz	Copenhagen Business School
Julie Kendall	Rutgers School of Business - Camden
Ken Kendall	Rutgers School of Business - Camden
Lynette Kvasny	Penn State University
Allen Lee	Virginia Commonwealth University
Rikard Lindgren	IT University of Gothenburg
Kalle Lyytinen	Case Western Reserve University
Lars Mathiassen	Georgia State University
Kathy McGrath	Brunel University

Catherine Middleton	Ryerson University
Emmanuel Monod	Paris Dauphine University
Eric Monteiro	NTNU, Norway
Bonnie Nardi	University of California, Irvine
Björn Niehaves	University of Muenster
Peter Axel Nielsen	Aalborg University
Jan Pries-Heje	Roskilde University
Sandeep Purao	Penn State University
Jeremy Rose	Aalborg University
Alain Ross	Athabasca University
Matti Rossi	Helsinki School of Economics
Nancy Russo	Bosnia/Northern Illinois University
Johan Sandberg	Umeå University
Suprateek Sarker	Copenhagen Business School
Chad Saunders	University of Calgary
Steve Sawyer	Syracuse University
Ulrike Schultze	Southern Methodist University
Susan Scott	London School of Economics and Political Science
Gamila Shoib	Griffith University
Lucy Suchman	Lancaster University
Fredrik Svahn	Viktoria Institute
Eileen Trauth	Penn State University
Duane Truex	Georgia State University
Tuure Tuunanen	University of Auckland
John Venable	Curtin University of Technology
Geoff Walsham	University of Cambridge
Edgar Whitley	London School of Economics and Political Science
Youngjin Yoo	Temple University

Organizing Chairs

Helena Karsten	Åbo Akademi University, Turku, Finland
Barbro Back	Åbo Akademi University, Turku, Finland

Local Organizers

Anna von Haartman	Åbo Akademi University, Finland
Andrea Hynynen	Åbo Akademi University

Webmaster

Magnus Dahlvik	Åbo Akademi University, Finland

Table of Contents

Section 4: The Future of Information Technology and Work-Related Practices in Health Care

Section 5: The Future of Industrial-Institutional Practices and Outcomes through Information Technology

Section 6: The Future of Critical Realism in IS Research

Section 7: Panels and Workshop

Researching the Future: The Information Systems Discipline's Futures Infrastructure

Mike Chiasson[1] and Ola Henfridsson[2]

[1] Department of Management Science, Management School,
Lancaster University, United Kingdom
m.chiasson@lancaster.ac.uk
[2] Department of Applied Information Technology,
Chalmers University of Technology, Sweden
ola.henfridsson@chalmers.se

1 Introduction

This proceedings for the IFIP 8. 2 working conference on Researching the Future is an attempt to pull together some of our research community's best ideas about how to research the future. The choice of conference theme should be seen as a way to solicit work that can help in building the information system discipline's futures infrastructure. Such an infrastructure is one that provides an initial and developing set of intellectual structures from which IS research can respond to the needs of our future society.

Researching the future is important. As researchers within a discipline focused on the design, adoption, utilization, and effects of information and communication technologies (ICT), we should be well-positioned to contribute to the future shaping of ICT-based practices. If anticipating and influencing the future is something qualitatively different than immediate research relevance, we must then ask whether and how our approaches to inquiry can affect our ability to do so. Such reflection would be valuable in shaping a discipline that is progressive and confident about its role in dealing with questions about the future. Drawing on a healthy debate about research relevance, it is now time to explore, develop, and substantiate how our field can shape and influence the future of ICT-based practices.

The papers covered in this volume are the result of such reflection. Reflecting differences in philosophical foundation, theoretical orientation, and topical emphasis, each deals with the future of ICT in both traditional and novel ways, in illustrating the process and outcomes of ICT applications in contemporary and emerging social settings, as individuals, collectives, firms, and institutions seek to change their future worlds.

2 Toward a Futures Infrastructure for IS Research

Some of the ongoing digitally enabled transformations in business, institutions, and societal practices dazzle us with possibilities for improving social welfare, while others suggest that social inequality may be increasing and preserving the status quo.

M. Chiasson et al. (Eds.): Future IS 2011, IFIP AICT 356, pp. 1–7, 2011.

Still, there is little doubt that we live in a time when anticipating the future is becoming increasingly difficult. Technologies converge (Lyytinen and Yoo 2002); product life cycles shrink (D'Aveni 1994); institutions evolve (Porter and Teisburg 2006); new learning cultures are born (Thomas and Brown 2011). The multitude of ongoing and parallel changes is vast, which makes the governance of not only enterprises but also some of our society's basic institutions, such as the educational and healthcare systems, increasingly challenging. There are many indications that this complex web of socio-technical changes will continue to evolve as digital technology becomes ever more woven into the fabric of everyday life.

As a result, successful businesses of our time are shifting attention from decision-making, planning, and control toward enactment, improvisation, and empowerment. This shift is manifested in attempts to build platform-centric strategies (Ciborra 1996; Tiwana et al. 2010), where the focus is on creating and nurturing the socio-technical capabilities needed for being responsive to emerging opportunities. Such capability-creation seems doubly distributed across two dimensions: control and knowledge (Yoo et al. 2010). First, the control over innovation resources is increasingly distributed across actors and stakeholders. Second, the heterogeneity of knowledge sources is increasingly apparent, where digital technology multiplies the space of possible pockets of innovation.

In this period of social transformation, it seems increasingly important for our research discipline to be more than by-standers as our object of study changes the world. To be participants in this change, learning how to research the future is a key ingredient.

Just as the businesses of our time are becoming increasingly infrastructure- centric, it may be time to reflect upon the futures infrastructure of IS research—the practices, logics, and approaches to our research which enable our ability to contribute to the future of IS practice. Important questions arise from this reflection. What can we do in order to be more aware, resilient, and capable of responding and prompting changes in and through our research? How can we adopt infrastructural thinking for making us capable of enacting, improvising, and empowering futures that are responsive to the future needs of our society?

While these are issues partly covered in this book, there are at least three issues that are worth exploring further as we seek to research the future. First, as manifested in the papers included in this volume, we need new conceptual and practical resources for IS research to help us understand what lies ahead. Some argue that our best chance to understand the future lies in understanding the past. Others propose that the adoption of new research methods, especially tailored for future studies, is important. Without a coherent and unambiguous road ahead, a first step toward a futurology of IS is to expand and treat common and unusual positions as resources to engage in the conceptualization, design, and execution of our research.

Second, an IS futures platform would possibly investigate and use the boundary resources of other disciplines. Just as the meanings of a smartphone multiply with infrastructural thinking (not just a phone, but also a navigation system, remote, camera, blood pressure instrument, and so on), it seems likely that the research ecosystem is enriched through the concepts and practices of unrelated disciplines. Neuroscience (Dimoka 2010) and ecological sustainability (e.g., Watson et al. 2010) are recent examples. Moreover, in affecting the future, an IS futures infrastructure also offers its boundary resources to emerging knowledge bodies, making it possible for them to tap into our ecosystem (e.g., recent eHealth special issues in IS journals).

Third, an IS futures infrastructure rethinks the prevalent assumption about the individual research hero and the increasing subspecialization prompted by small and isolated collectives. Just as infrastructure owners deal with numerous and emerging networks of stakeholders, a resilient research infrastructure would increasingly be ready to respond to the increasing diversity and changing configuration of the research participants and stakeholders in the future, while still preserving a distance and level-headedness that isn't swept along by fashions and fads. In our view, this suggests the need to think about how to prepare IS researchers for this future, and how the infrastructure for IS research may be able to foster both theoretical stability and practical application as research–participant collectives regroup around important issues emerging in the wake of increasing societal change.

3 The Review Process

A total of 36 papers were submitted. The papers were submitted from all three AIS regions, with 7 papers from region 1 (Americas), 24 from Region 2 (Europe, Middle East, and Africa), and 5 from region 3 (Asia and the Pacific). Using a three-tier review structure, all papers went through a rigorous review process where feedback was provided by at least four independent referees including the editorial by one of the program cochairs. While the program chairs managed the 38 papers together, any conflicts-of-interest with a cochair was managed by assigning sole responsibility to the other program chair.

Considering the reviews of members of the program committee, we accepted 16 papers. We also accepted three panels and one workshop presentation on methods for studying the future. The program also includes three plenary sessions with invited speakers.

4 Overview of the Book

4.1 Keynotes

We would like to show our appreciation of the efforts of our three invited keynote speakers.

Yrjö Neuvo's topic is "Unfogging the Future." He was vice president and chief technology officer for Nokia during the years it was establishing itself as the world's leading mobile phone manufacturer. For many decades, he has been a very influential voice in European research initiatives. Now retired from Nokia, he is based at Aalto University.

The topic of Judith Gregory presentation is "Design for Participation and Negotiation across Logics and Knowledge Communities." She is, and for over 30 years has been, a key figure in the participatory design community. In other words, she engages in making the future together with others. With a very international past, she is currently based at the Illinois Institute of Technology.

Our third keynote speaker is Youngjin Yoo, with a topic "After the Promised Land: What Do We Do Now?" He is an associate professor in Information Systems and an IBIT Research Fellow at the Fox School of Business and Management at Temple University. His research and teaching interests include digital innovation, experiential computing, design, knowledge management, and virtual teams. You can read his reflections on technology, design, and innovation in everyday experiences in his blog at youngjinyoo.com.

4.2 Papers

We wish to thank the authors for the range of approaches taken to the topic of researching the future of information systems. We grouped the articles—somewhat imperfectly—into particular methodological, theoretical, and/or practical approaches to the theme.

We grouped a number of paper focused specifically on **how the future and the past are connected and inter-related**. Sewchurran and Brown explore the importance of metaphor and analogy across theory and as-lived experience, in transforming the future of IT project management theory and practice, and IS research generally. In a complementary contrast, Aanestad considers how the durability of the past and present is important in understanding and anticipating what the future may hold, and which futures we may wish to hold. Finally, Wynn examines how the future is made "present-at-hand" in corporate projects, and how the future is produced from revisiting the past and realizing its presence within the present. All three papers provide an interesting starting point for thinking about the issues that research about the future may conceptually need to consider.

Another grouping of papers focused on a **critical view of the future**. Stahl examines discourses emerging from 11 discussions about future ICTs and, by highlighting particular assumptions in the discourse, goes on to critique the implied assumptions in each. In doing so, he provides a basis for examining the unrealized futures beyond these assumptions, which we may wish to pursue instead. Brown examines and explores the people who anticipate and shape the future in organizations—forecasters—and how the supposed foolishness of their activities, as defined within the mathematical forecasting literature, may be seen as an alternative rationality of dealing with the uncertainties of the future in organizations.

Another group of papers examines particular **technological futures**. Stahl examines the difficulty (if not impossibility) of anticipating specific technological futures, and moves on to consider the need and possibility for participation in shaping the collective future of technology, through approaches such as participatory technology assessment. In contrast to Stahl's epistemology, Andreev, Duane, and O'Reilly examine how perceptions of trust and ease-of-use in m-payment systems affect individuals' willingness to pay and transact using m-payment systems. By examining a future technology using more traditional research approaches, the paper provides an important point of contrast to the open-ended possibilities of Stahl's critique. In a similar vein, Ou, Leung, and Davison examine the growing use of instant messaging tools used in organizations for knowledge management and team performance. Again, as a specific example of researching the future about an important information technology using traditional research methods, the paper provides an important and complementary perspective on futures research about particular types of IT, complementing and adding to the debate in this session on the shaping and co-shaping of information systems.

A group of papers examines **the future of information technology and work- related practices in health care**. Litchner and Venters lead off the health care session using science fiction—a relatively rare approach to researching the future in IS research. They employ science fiction to make a futuristic sense of the evaluation of an electronic prescription system implementation in the national health service (NHS) in the United Kingdom. Pedersen, Ellingsen, and Monteiro consider how the future is standardized through the enactment of both top–down and bottom–up processes in nursing work, and the performativity of standardization beyond the traditional dichotomous view of top-down or futile (bottom-up) views of standardization. Finally, Petrakaki, Cornford, Hibberd, Lichtner, and Barber propose a framework for considering how ICT could affect worker's professional standing in terms of both increasing and decreasing autonomy and capability depending on the effect of ICT on professional roles, work practices, and jurisdictions.

A group of papers examines **the future of industrial–institutional practices and outcomes through information technology**. Nylén and Holmström consider how latent capabilities in the computing in forestry machinery could transform it into a service sector organization, through the possibilities of open innovation. They make a general claim that open innovation possibilities in an embedded ICT could enable transformation in a number of industrial settings. Crowston examines how insights from the open source community and their use of ICTs may tell us something general about the future of knowledge work—the organization and incentives produced through ICT. Kautz, Bunker, Rab, and Sinnet consider the relations and actions among various companies involved in the production, standardization, and customization of a CRM system, and their use of various open and proprietary positions in producing various niches. They illustrate the range of organizational positions needed to create a rich interorganizational ecosystem around a technological platform, and point to the future of the software industry.

A final group of papers examines **the future of critical realism in IS research**. Vega and Brown employ critical realism to examine the production and effects of government programs on the diffusion of IT in small and medium sized companies. They illustrate how the social complexity of IS diffusion in the future can be better understood through critical realism (CR). Carlsson explores the past, present, and future use of critical realism in information systems research. Given the position of fallibility in any particular method and study, CR opens the door to many current and future approaches to IS research, and to a never-ending future for IS research practice. A more than fitting conclusion to a special issue on researching the future in IS research.

4.3 Panels and Workshop

We have three panels and one workshop in the conference. The first panel by Sawyer, Iivari, Venkatesh, Light and Urquhart examines how our conceptual apparatus for systems design needs to be changed to consider the future of building social software (e.g., online communities) as opposed to role-based software within a single organization. Two questions considered in their panel and discussion are: How do designers deal with the tensions of developing more socially complex users of social software versus traditional role-based users, and how do designers grapple with the need to design systems to address social needs versus only functional work activities? Our second panel by Carmel, Avital, Gray, Kallinikos, and King focuses on the importance and relevance of teaching foresight and futuristic thinking in a university curriculum. Their panel focuses on particular controversies in attempting to do so. Our final panel, with Alter, Korpela, Petkov, and Russo, considers the viability of revisiting and reinfusing socio-technical principles and practices in systems development. The panel, through its various questions about the strengths and weaknesses of current approaches, possible extensions, and the current and future trends and issues in design, considers the future form and application of socio-technical approaches in systems development. Our workshop with Gray and Hovav considers three rigorous approaches to futures research in information systems that move beyond simple extrapolation of the present. A fitting conclusion to our volume on the future of IS research about the future.

5 Conclusion

In responding to the future of information systems research about the future, the comprehensive and creative response to the call is represented in this volume. However, as a project to produce the infrastructure for futures research in information systems, it is only a beginning within other attempts to tackle the IS researcher's role in shaping the future. Whether it is speculating on particular technological futures, exploring the philosophical foundations for futures research, or critiquing the limited possibilities in visions of the future, the future of IS practice is both potentially limitless and unnecessarily limited. Our only enduring role in the future may be the unstable mixing of observing and understanding what we think is endurable, critiquing what we come to realize is unnecessarily durable, and considering and prompting the IS futures worth having. Our infrastructure for thinking, observing, writing, and participating in dealing with the future may, therefore, be open to continuous exploration and experimentation—a wonderful future indeed!

References

Ciborra, C.: The Platform Organization: Recombining Strategies, Structures, and Surprises. Organization Science 7(2), 103–118 (1996)

D'Aveni, R.: Hypercompetition: Managing the Dynamics of Strategic Maneuvering. Free Press, New York (1994)

Dimoka, A.: What Does the Brain Tell Us About Trust and Distrust? Evidence from a Functional Neuroimaging Study. MIS Quarterly 34(2), 373–396 (2010)

Lyytinen, K., Yoo, Y.: Research Commentary: The Next Wave of Nomadic Computing. Information Systems Research 13(4), 377–388 (2002)

Porter, M.E., Teisburg, E.O.: Redefining Health Care: Creating Value-Based Competition on Results. Harvard Business School Press, Boston (2006)

Thomas, D., Brown, S.B.: A New Culture of Learning: Cultivating the Imagination for a World of Constant Change (2010)

Tiwana, A., Konsynski, B., Bush, A.A.: Platform Evolution: Coevolution of Platform Architecture, Governance, and Environmental Dynamics. Information Systems Research 21(4), 685–687 (2010)

Watson, R.T., Boudreau, M.-C., Chen, A.J.: Information Systems and Environmentally Sustainable Development: Energy Informatics and New Directions for the IS Community. MIS Quarterly 34(1), 23–38 (2010)

Yoo, Y., Henfridsson, O., Lyytinen, K.: The New Organizing Logic of Digital Innovation: An Agenda for Information Systems Research. Information Systems Research 21(4), 724–735 (2010)

Section 1. How the Future and the Past Are Connected and Inter-related

Toward an Approach to Generate Forward-Looking Theories Using Systems Concepts

Kosheek Sewchurran and Irwin Brown

University of Cape Town, South Africa
Kosheek.sewchurran@uct.ac.za

Abstract. The need to generate original theory about information systems phenomena and ensure that such outputs are forward looking is an important concern. The paper gives examples of how IS project management practice and theories remain underpinned by concepts which do not map to experienced realities. The paper makes the case to use systems thinking approaches to unearth new theories to offer better explanations. In the pursuit of this goal, the paper first provides insight into the as-lived condition that makes human beings prone to being imprisoned by theories of yesteryear. This is done by discussing the role of language in cognition and theory development. In the IS literature, such discussions are limited despite the considerable attention to on types of theories and anatomies of theories. The paper claims and demonstrates why debate on theory cannot take place without explicit attention to aspects of cognition and as-lived existence. In the context of these discussions, the paper puts forward the suggestion that theoretical contributions rooted in systems concepts could allow for the emergence of forward-looking theory about IS phenomena. As a means of illuminating how to go about developing such theories, the paper provides a brief overview of how soft systems methodology and work systems method concepts can be used in a theorizing framework to achieve this. The main contributions to knowledge are two-fold. First, there is the inter-contextual coherence which is established by creating coherence between as-lived human experience, embodied cognition, theory, and language. Second, within such a context, we are able to demonstrate a pragmatic approach to generate better explanations about IS phenomena using systems concepts.

Keywords: Systems thinking, research, project management.

1 Introduction and Background

Human existence is caught in a cycle that Peter Checkland described as the never-ending dance of theory and practice (Checkland 1999; Checkland and Holwell 1998; Checkland and Scholes 1999). Theory can be defined as "a set of welldeveloped concepts related through statements of relationship, which together constitute an integrated framework that can be used to [describe], explain, predict, [and prescribe] phenomena" (Strauss and Corbin 1998, p. 15). Concepts are the basic building blocks of theory, and are abstract representations of some reality (Strauss and Corbin 1998).

M. Chiasson et al. (Eds.): Future IS 2011, IFIP AICT 356, pp. 11–26, 2011.
© IFIP International Federation for Information Processing 2011

Phenomena refer to the central ideas or events of interest related to a substantive area of study (Strauss and Corbin 1998).

At a societal level the cycle of theory informing practice and vice versa can be experienced as controlling systems of knowledge as well as aspirations to evolve knowledge paradigms. The effects of controlling systems of knowledge are constantly at play, either individually or in combination, but the effects are not always known. If we consider how current research affects or can affect the future, then we may conjecture that what we know in the present sets an organizing trajectory for what we can know in the future. Human beings, therefore, cannot know anything anew; all knowledge has some connection to the past and thus does influence the future. Research plays a key role in understanding the present in order to shape the future.

As researchers in Information Systems, we are interested in explaining the interaction between information technology and human beings. Often these interactions arise as a result of background effects (culture) that cannot be directly observed. The effects of culture can be estimated by referring to theorists such as Heidegger, Bourdieu, Latour, and Giddens. Heidegger (1962) speaks of the *leveling* effect of culture until it evades any questioning. Similarly, Bourdieu (1975) speaks of *habitus* and Latour (1999) speaks of *enrolment* and *actor-networks*. All these theorists note that cultural effects are mostly below the consciousness level. Appropriately, John Maynard Keynes suggested that people often turn out to be the intellectual prisoners of theoreticians of yesteryear (Winter and Szczepanek 2009).

As information technology permeates daily existence more and more, research in the IS field is challenged to explain more complex and abstract phenomena related to human existence and human enterprise. Scholarship in IS has long been concerned with relevance and rigor to ensure that there is acculturated progress in providing better explanations (Banville and Landry 1989; Benbasat and Zmud 2003; King and Lyytinen 2004; March and Story 2008; Niederman et al. 2009). Recently there have been concerns raised by many IS scholars about the need to develop original theory about IS phenomena. One specific call by Grover et al. (2008) and others is to build better explanations and more forward-looking theories. The purpose of this paper is to respond to this call and to prescribe how systems thinking concepts can be used in developing forward-looking theory about IS phenomena. To understand the pragmatic needs that can be served with our proposed framework we look at problems being faced in IS project management.

1.1 IS Project Management: The Need for New Metaphors

An IS project is commonly understood as an orchestrated process initiated by a project manager, stakeholders, and project workers on behalf of an owner to deliver a valued outcome that is unique and needs to be achieved within predetermined constraints which can include time, scope, quality, and cost (Hughes and Cotterell 2006; Richardson and Butler 2006; Schwalbe 2007). In this area, there have been sustained research efforts to improve the unacceptably high failure rates rom which IS projects tend to suffer (Hoving 2003). Frequently, IS project implementation failures are explained in the IS research literature by a lack of proper project planning, poor project management, poor project leadership, or incorrect application of project management practices (Kappelman et al. 2006; Kent 2006; Nelson 2007). Nelson (2007) tried to explain failures by conducting project retrospectives on 99 projects undertaken in North America. Nelson claimed that in more than half the projects, success could have been improved if there had been more attention paid to better use of best- practices in estimating, scheduling, stakeholder management, and risk management.

On the other hand, Reich et al. (2008) state that successful IS managers learn how to bravely step away from traditional "thou-shalt" forms of project practices to deliver value early by constantly reaffirming and reviewing the value being delivered with the sponsors. This suggestion of what seems to work in practice is different than the plan-driven, role separation, deterministic processes assumed in many textbooks used to train IS project practitioners and graduates (Dalcher and Brodie 2007; Fuller et al. 2008; Richardson and Butler 2006; Schwalbe 2007). In these texts the project management body of knowledge (PMBOK), a popular practice, is often epitomized as the central core that comprises project management. The same assumptions are reflected in IS research literature where contributions tend to explicitly or tacitly accept that the core basis of project management is PMBOK. It seems researchers are locked into an incorrect image of what a project is by frequently explaining that a lack of proper project planning, poor project management, poor project leadership or incorrect application of project management practices (Kappelman et al. 2006; Kent 2006; Nelson 2007) is primarily responsible for project failure.

If we look deeper, we see that the metaphorical image that gives rise to the expectations of what a project is conjures up expectations that the project has a predetermined universal form; hence it is reasonable to expect a fixed life cycle and to be diligent with application of the project life cycle (Cicmil 2006; Cicmil et al. 2006). Project participants and many researchers in Information Systems often see projects in this way and hence exclude or marginalize other explanations.

In general, what does get defined as a project is a "non-normal" set of unique tasks that are highly uncertain in total, but can be composed of relatively known stages. The extant research literature on IS project management does give a sense that there is considerable confusion about the true nature of IS project management, but this is where the debate has been for a few years. A project-driven culture has since emerged but better explanations are required to help understand the dynamics of IS projects. To allow for newer understandings to emerge, metaphors or analogies could be useful.

1.2 Focus and Outline of the Paper

In this paper, we argue that such abstract knowledge can be built analogically from more experience-based knowledge. We encourage an approach to develop analogical extensions from richer, more experience-based domains (Boroditsky and Ramscar 2002). We specifically argue that metaphorical conceptual structures that draw from systems concepts and ideas provide a means of addressing the call for forward-looking theory. Metaphorical representation, we argue, allows for the presentation of abstract knowledge through more commonly understood concepts. It is claimed by some that metaphors are pervasive in everyday life, not just in language but in thought and action as well. So there is some acceptance that the conceptual systems affecting how we think and act are metaphoric in nature (Murphy 1996). We hope to awaken researchers to this reality by offering an approach to theorizing that encourages the generation of forward- looking theory about IS phenomena using systems concepts.

A discussion of how research does and could affect the present and future has to be premised on the nature of human as-lived daily existence and cognition. Only with such an understanding can an attempt to understand how the theories we develop enable or disable particular ways of knowing be realized. In this paper, we will draw on the works of Heidegger, Bourdieu, Maturana, and Varela to give a characterization of daily as-lived experience. Once such an understanding is established, we will then explore the role of theory development in enabling and disabling further understanding. Thereafter the paper will give an account of theorizing that takes cognizance of the need to develop forward-looking theory about IS phenomena using systems concepts. We will present an approach using soft systems methodology as an example of a research framework to show how to undertake the development of better forward-looking theories.

2   As-Lived Human Behavior

Martin Heidegger cryptically proclaimed in his letters on humanism in 1947 that language is the house of *being*. In the same letter, he went on to also claim that "in its home man dwells." This is cryptic, but it points to the central role language plays in constructing reality and allowing for learning and evolution. As social creatures, human beings cycle through knowledge systems by representing (signification), reproducing (interacting), and legitimizing (observing) various types of knowledge systems. Since the beginning of time, human beings have been subjected to an on-going trajectory of being constructed by controlling systems of knowledge.

Heidegger, Maturana, Varela, and others claim that human beings embody understanding of their environments and this allows for human beings to undertake their daily activities without necessarily being conscious of their involvement. Heidegger and others claim that human beings are not always reflective while they undertake daily mundane activities. These researchers also go on to qualify that, at times, human beings are reflective; in this mode of existence they can observe themselves undertaking the various tasks or look back and reflect on various interactions. Because human beings develop a pre-reflective sense or grasp of their environments, they thus bring to bear habituated expectations in their perceptions.

All perceptions are, however, formulated while *being-in-the-world* and the process is not rational nor does it present a view from nowhere (Guignon 1983). There are thus no complete or all-encompassing perspectives or facts in themselves. Human beings embody their environments and contexts, and there is always the danger of knowledge systems becoming controlling systems of thought. Human beings are thus historically conditioned to provide responses they have become socialized into; often they cannot step back from these responses and rationally alter them. As a result of this, cognition is not something that is rational and engaged with consciously. The environment is observed through the retina where images are processed by the mind during a cognitive process to compute understanding of the phenomena, together with adequate behavior for the given situation. Maturana and Varela (1998) explain that in the area of the retina, to which the visual image is transferred, there are hundreds of neurons from other zones of the nervous system. The retina, therefore, should not be understood as a relay station that transfers visual images as retinal stimulation to the visual cortex. Instead, the transfer to the visual cortex needs to be understood as a confluence of the visual stimulation and other stimulation coming continuously from the rest of the body (Maturana and Varela 1998).

Maturana and Varela believe that cognition is an ongoing process subservient to existential concerns. They cryptically say that "all knowing is doing; and all doing is knowing" (p. 27). Matrurana and Varela claim that the nervous system is the means by which human beings learn and store knowledge of their interactions with the environment. The human nervous system is said to interconnect the sensory and motor surfaces via the brain, providing a dynamic system of coordination between sensory and motor surfaces that is ongoing, and tied to existential concerns. Further, according to Merleau-Ponty (2002), the human being as an organism is tied to its environment in a dialectic manner such that the recurrent interactions are stored by the nervous systems as sensory-motor coupling of particular phenomena.

Phenomena, concepts, or theories that make up the reality human beings experience are said to be brought about by an act of distinction, either promoted by researchers or by human beings themselves as they learn and cope in daily existence. For the rest of the paper, the terms *phenomena*, *concepts*, and *theories* will be referred to collectively as a *phenomenal domain*. The experience of *human* consciousness is considered to only be possible through such phenomenal domains made possible by language. Through the use of concepts, theories, metaphors, and analogies, human beings are able to interact with their consciousness (Maturana and Varela 1998). Language, therefore, provides for the definition of various states of consciousness where individual words become tokens for linguistically coordinating actions representing bodily responses that can be triggered by the nervous system.

Consequently, linguistic behavior can be seen as a form of orienting behavior. Through linguistic means a human being can orient others and/or themselves to a phenomenal domain. Accordingly, language is said to be connotative or symbolic instead of denotative of individual entities (Maturana and Varela 1980). Because the nervous system produces coherent behavior through the generation of sets of neuronal activity that anticipate a pre-given world (Maturana and Varela 1998); the nervous system is said to always already be in a specific state, which presents a unique context for each human being. Reality is, therefore, a unique disclosure for each human being.

Since human beings largely exist with language, the acquisition of knowledge or mastery of a domain of interactions is achieved by expanding the nervous system through learning how to interact with various phenomenal domains. Such evolution then becomes constrained by the anatomical organization of the human being and language available to identify the states relevant for facilitating interaction with the phenomenal domain. Although the nervous system expands the domain of interactions of human beings, the nervous system remains subservient to the existential concerns of the human being. For this reason Maturana and Varela (1998) say the nervous system operates by structural determination because the environment triggers reactions from the human being, yet the environment cannot specify the reactions. Consciousness and mind can consequently be seen as constructions that arise from social interaction that human beings are capable of with themselves, other beings, and/or their environment.

As a result of this biological nature, cognitive structures are created and re-created in an infinite cycle through recurrent practices within a phenomenal domain. Heidegger believes that human beings are in a state of continual *becoming* until death. Given this context, his cryptic statement that language is the home of *being* within which man lives becomes more appreciable. From the above, it is also evident that language is central to learning and evolution in a cultural sense because phenomenal practices get stored and enriched in the nervous system throughout an individual's existence (Llewelyn 2003; Raelin 2007; Varela et al. 1993). With such a view we accept that language is both the means and median of constructing the future.

3 Theorizing

In accordance with the above discussion on learning and cognition, this section will present a view on how knowledge claims can generally be structured, crafted, and positioned to maximize utility and learning, and to facilitate cultural evolution. Cultural evolution occurs naturally and theoretical development should facilitate such evolution to enable human beings to mediate their changing environments with more relevant practices.

Research contributions can be defined as the development and use of theoretical concepts as a means to understand, observe, act, or bring forth a world with which to talk and interact. It is through theoretical concepts that human beings bring forth an understanding of the world. The assimilation of new concepts, therefore, depends on the ease with which they can be assimilated by the nervous system given the constraints of the existing nervous system structure. Alternatively, learning may need to dislodge conceptual phenomena already embedded in the nervous system (Llewelyn 2003). It can be inferred that there is a logical architecture to structure the phenomenal schema of the nervous system. Similarly, Varela et al. (1993) claim that a basic activity in cognition is categorization of the concepts that appear to come from the structured nature of bodily and social experiences.

In this paper, we attempt to give insight into the architecture of knowledge that human beings embody. The lens provided by Llewelyn (2003) is useful in this regard. There is also a taxonomy presented by Gregor (2006) that is widely cited in the IS literature. For our purposes, Llewelyn's work is more useful in providing a framework that gives insight into the architecture of how phenomenal domains evolve. Gregor's work classifies theories according to purpose (i.e., analysis, explanation, prediction, explanation and prediction (EP), design, and action). These are descriptions of the utility and almost assume a rational and reflective human being. This taxonomy, while useful, does not consider the nature of human understanding from the perspective of both researchers and those being researched.

It is widely established in the IS research culture that new theories have the potential to bring new phenomena into being. In IS research, there is a rich history of using theoretical lenses to emphasize particular aspects of a research problem space. Theories also serve a more mundane and practical purpose in daily interaction. For the most part, the extent to which theories are influencing reality is not consciously known because they serve as a resource base to provide understanding of situations or provide a basis to acquire more understanding. All such as-lived experiences represent knowing, which can be unconscious or conscious. The taxonomy developed by Llewelyn provides for five different types of theories that manifest in uncovering reality for human beings, or are available to researchers as options to craft or contextualize research contributions. These are shown in Table 1.

Table 1. Five Levels of Theorization (from Llewelyn 2003, p. 667)

Level	Theory	Focus
1	Metaphor theories	As a means to ground experience. Examples of metaphors are software development is a game of invention and communication (Cockburn 2002).
2	Differentiation theories	Facilitate "cutting the pie" of experience. Examples of differentiation theories are Maslow's hierarchy of needs or the SDLC cycle.
3	Concept theories	Examples of concept theories are feminism, business process change, etc. These concepts give access to a phenomenal world.
4	Theories which focus on settings	Explaining how contexts for practices are organized. Examples of theorizing settings are challenges in global software development from a South Africa industry perspective.
5	Theorizing structures	Explaining impersonal, large-scale, and enduring aspects of social life. Examples are modernism, post-modernism, and post-colonialism.

3.1 Level 1 Metaphors

Morgan (cited in Llewelyn 2003) argues that a metaphor is a basic structural form of experience by which human beings engage, organize, and understand their world. The organizational metaphor is a well-known way in which organizational experiences are characterized. We have come to understand organizations as machines, organisms, brains, cultures, political systems, psychic prisons, instruments of domination, etc. (Llewelyn 2003). The metaphor is a basic way in which human beings ground their experiences and continue to evolve them by adding new, related concepts that carry aspects of the original metaphor. Later on in this paper, we will argue that the *holon*, or world view, from a systems thinking perspective is a kind of metaphor. The grounding metaphor then plays a role in initiating the conceptual framework. Much as in systems thinking, there is a served system (*holon*) and the serving system, which equates to the human activity system (Checkland 1999; Checkland and Holwell 1998; Checkland and Scholes 1999).

Llewelyn emphasizes the manner in which metaphors allow human beings to understand and experience one kind of thing in terms of another by citing Lakoff and Johnson (1980). The first example given shows that when academic researchers experience arguments as war, some of the expressions of their experiences are given as follows:

- "He attacked every weak point in my argument"
- "I demolished his argument"
- "I've never won an argument with him"
- "He shot down all my arguments"

An important part of Lakoff and Johson's analysis is that the metaphor influences both understanding, and also structures experience. To emphasize the point about metaphors, Llewellyn extends the discussion by showing that if argument is fused with debate instead of war, it was experienced as a give-and-take affair, the exchange of opinions, the realization that other points of view are necessary and everyone has a right to adopt a point of view. Through the discussion provided by Llewellyn it can be concluded that the power of a metaphor is that it provides foundational grounding in understanding of a phenomenon and any subsequent understanding has to either take cognisance of or negotiate the foundational understanding the metaphor has established. Additionally, it can also be inferred that people employ several metaphors to understand, theorize, and experience phenomena (Llewelyn 2003).

Murphy (1996), while acknowledging the pervasive effects metaphors have on imagination, also admits to the difficulty in providing a concise definition. In a structural sense Murphy claims metaphors can be used to represent abstract and complex phenomena using easier to understand domains. Therefore, there is often an attempt to present topics using various vehicles. Obviously the vehicles should not apply to the topics in straightforward or literal ways. Generally the metaphoric domain is carried by the vehicle and the concept is lit up or projected onto this domain. For example, an IS project could be understood as a temporary organization, or a language gamed instead of a life-cycle process.

3.2   Level 2 Theorization: Differentiation

Still ensconced in a world influenced by Cartesian dualism, a seemingly natural way by which human beings have come to understand is to adopt dualisms like in–out, presence–absence, up–down, finite–infinite, mind–body, public–private, objective–subjective, and so on. Many of the dualisms are rooted in spatial and bodily experience. This is perhaps a basic way in which people cut up the pie of experience. As with metaphoric theorization, differentiation theorization can impede and enable new ways of thinking and doing. Differentiation theorization, therefore, aims to create meaning and significance by setting up contrasts and categories that order the world (Llewelyn 2003). In IS project management, there has been a shift from a dichotomous view of project failure and success to differentiating success for the project management process and emergent product.

3.3   Level 3 Theorization: Concept Theories

Concepts are described by Llewelyn as a basic form of theorization that is used to observe and represent the world. Concepts, therefore, give rise to practices. The example given by Llewelyn is that with the introduction of *feminism*, women were able to see their experiences differently. Feminism as a conceptual innovation gave rise to organizations that prioritized the ideals of feminism and challenged established norms. Conceptual innovations often replace, challenge, or change existing concepts. Level 2 differentiation theories can be used to sharpen conceptual categories. For example, feminism can be positioned as two ideals: feminism in developing countries and feminism in developed countries. Such differentiation of the concepts can draw attention to slightly different realities, which call for different sets of actions, which give rise to a phenomenal domain. Concepts, then, are a basic form of theorization that are extended and sharpened using level 1 and 2 categories. In the IS project management area, newer concepts of benefits realization have emerged to draw attention to how benefits accrue over time.

3.4   Level 4 Theorization: Theorizing Settings

Theorizing settings is defined by Llewelyn as the strategy of theorization that defines the contextual influences on specific individual, organizational, or social phenomena. The aim of this theorization is to explain or understand the wider social conditions under which practices are produced. The social settings of practices can exist at a number of levels and are not based directly on observable phenomena, and are therefore not dependent on empiricism. This implies that non-observable structural, social, and institutional phenomena may be included. Theorizing settings or context bound theories offer an understanding of the setting for the experience.

3.5   Level 5 Theorization: Grand Theorizing Structures

According to Llewelyn, grand theorizing is done in the world of ideas rather than the world of practice. In grand theories, practice on the ground is always influenced by structural conditions, and these are not necessarily observable through empirical efforts. Grand theorizing is concerned with understanding relationships of power.

4   How Soft Systems Thinking Treats the Effects of Language

From the works of Weick (1989, 1999), we know that theorizing is very much a process that is dependent on teasing out understanding and striving to make explicit hitherto implicit knowledge. Theorizing is closely linked to learning and sense-making. Soft systems methodology (SSM) is a well-known approach to learning in and about complex IS problems. Surprisingly it has not been used widely in the process of IS theorizing (Sewchurran and Petkov 2006). This may be due to the lack of understanding of the role of language in theorizing and creating reality. Conventional qualitative research methods pay some attention to language but do not give enough attention to the role of language in generating deeper explanations of the *why*, as is prescribed by SSM, through the articulation of *world views* and *root definitions*.

We argue, therefore, that the use of SSM in qualitative research presents an opportunity to deepen theorizing, because it has had success in contributing to understanding situations and concerns in various other interventions.

SSM embraces a number of practices that are grounded in the assumption that language is central to learning, understanding, and behavior. First, SSM emphasizes drawing rich pictures to grasp and express the situation of concern. This emphasis on not using words is an attempt to give structure to the background conditions that give rise to the situation of concern. The value of this process is that it allows for coherent understanding of the background to emerge through symbolism. These symbols represent structural conditions that are difficult to express in words but are manifest in the situation as tacit and embodied assumptions. This first step in the expression of the situation of concern allows for learning to take place. Through discussion and participation in this exercise, stakeholder appreciation and understanding is enhanced because of the orienting effects of conversation. Perhaps the most important reason to pursue the use of SSM in research is that it makes it possible to explore and articulate *world views* and perspectives of why through disciplined and facilitated imagination. These world views are important because they are the analogical basis that gives rise to subsequent attitudes and reactions. Often world views are not adequately investigated or articulated in research and only characteristics of behavior are aggregated in building theories.

Efforts at empirical research often produce theoretical contributions as abstracted models that describe phenomena as concepts with predicate relationships. While these contributions have value, they are often closed off from facilitating conditions and are not connected to representations of why (Smyth and Morris 2007). We argue that these are not forward-looking enough, as they are not developed within an organizing trajectory that is guided by the relevant perspectives. This explanation would also clarify why the research framework given later in this paper provides more forward looking capability than, for example, grounded theory methods. The argument could also be made that contributions developed outside a systemic organizing trajectory will not, by design, be analogical enough to give future related findings coherence. Consequently, research efforts will more likely confound than they will aggregate and emancipate. In this paper we argue that the underlying metaphor or *holons* that gives rise to concepts has not been appreciated enough. There are many reasons for this. The two reasons this paper addresses are, first, there is a general lack of insight into how to structure *holons* as theories, and second, there is not enough emphasis placed on the value such understanding has in generating explanation. Both of these probably emerge from the general lack of appreciation for the value in using the SSM process as a research process to build theory. A suggestion of how this can be done is given in the next section.

5 Prescription on How to Use Soft System Thinking in Research Processes

We have been using the research framework described in this section to study IS projects and this has helped us develop this version of the method. In the context of this paper, we argue that IS project management practitioners and researchers have been constrained by unrealistic notions of projects. Practitioners and researchers are locked into a restricted paradigm of understanding and are having difficulty emerging from it, because narrow metaphors continue to shape experiences of projects in research and practice. From Nelson's (2007) research it is evident how research results are impacted when understanding is restricted to just the observable human activities (*human–activity–system*). The suggestion to use SSM as a research framework puts forward the premise that *world views* and *root definitions* provide more forward-looking explanations than theories modeled at the human activity level, such as Nelson's.

In systems thinking, especially soft systems thinking, a fundamental assumption that is made is that each person is guided by *holons*. An alternative way of expressing this is to say that behavior is, for the most part, perceptually guided and embodied. A *holon* represents the meaningful activity that is worth being pursued. It is accepted in the SSM tradition that *holons* are not normally readily explicable in linguistic terms as they are tacit and embodied. However, SSM promotes that *holons* can be teased out. SSM offers processes and devices to engage in learning to render *holons* explicable. It is, therefore, reasonable to expect that through SSM a linguistic realization of the concepts, analogies, and metaphors that motivate understanding or action in a particular context can be developed.

Figure 1 shows how the core abstractions of *served* and *serving* systems interrelate in the context of an information system. In systems thinking terms, the *holon* represents the *served-system* as the metaphor. This is the basic structural form which defines the essence of purposeful activity or system for a particular stakeholder, or stakeholder group. Research projects that target explanations or descriptions of *served-systems* could make use of SSM.

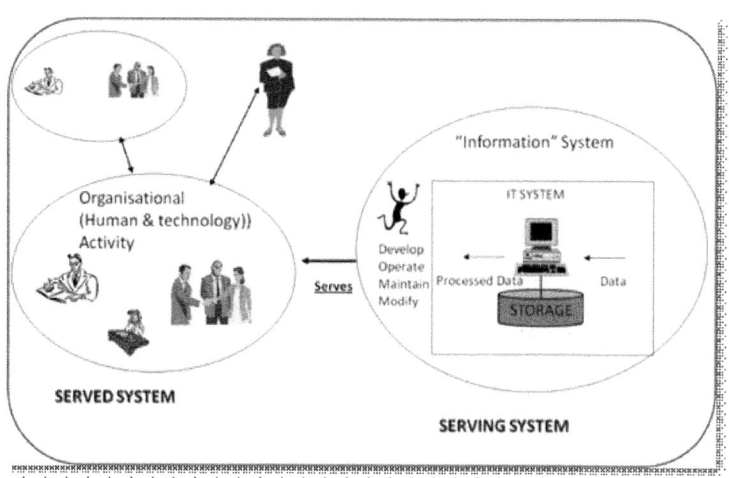

Fig. 1. Information System as Serving and Served Systems (from Checkland and Howell 1998)

Sewchurran and Barron (2008), for example, attempted to do such research to unearth the world views that characterize project experiences among project managers and project sponsors. The aim of their inquiry was to understand the perspectives as well as what influences the perspectives of project managers and project sponsors about how relationships are managed and sustained during the delivery of IT projects, and how the relationships ultimately impact the project outcome. The questioning was thus at the level of the *served-system* rather than *serving-system* (see Figure 1).

The *served* and *serving* systems exist and evolve in an interdependent manner as is highlighted in Figure 1. While SSM's strength has been the definition of the *served-system* the work systems method (WSM) (Alter 2002) which is a relatively new theoretical framework promises to be more rigorous and useful to describe the serving-systems. For our purposes in this paper a serving system is a work system in which human participants and/or machines perform work using IS and other resources to produce products and/or services for internal or external customers. As-lived project experiences can be described using constructs from the WSM. The WSM is both a descriptive theory and an approach (prescriptive theory) on how to think about, model and define the elements of the work systems. The approach can also be used in order to discern how serving systems relate in the context of *served-systems* as is highlighted in Figure 2.

The descriptions of the *served* and *serving* systems are complementary and in a research process should be undertaken together to ensure that the hermeneutic benefits materialize. If an analysis is done using WSM and SSM together, the detail of the serving system will enrich the understanding of the *served systems*. The understanding of the *served-systems* will similarly enrich the understanding of the *serving- system*. This will provide learning from details to abstraction in a complementary way.

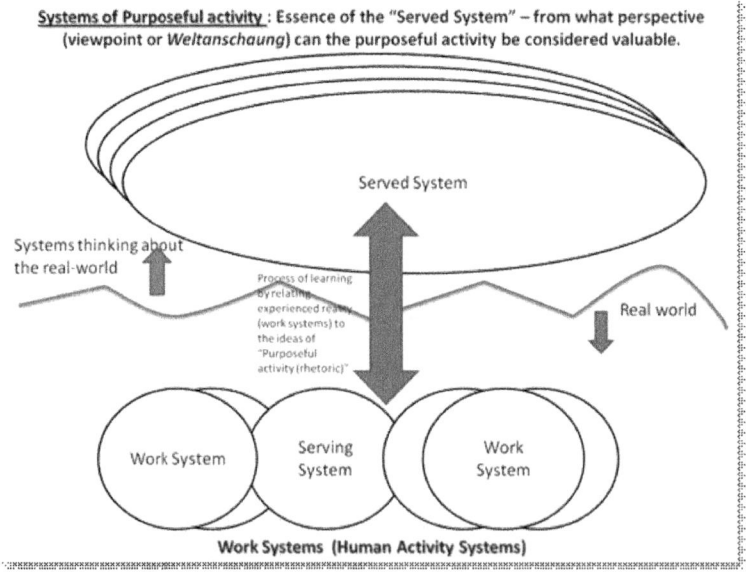

Systems of Purposeful activity : Essence of the "Served System" – from what perspective (viewpoint or *Weltanschaung*) can the purposeful activity be considered valuable.

Served System

Systems thinking about the real-world

Process of learning by relating experienced reality (work systems) to the ideas of "Purposeful activity (rhetoric)"

Real world

Work System

Serving System

Work System

Work Systems (Human Activity Systems)

Fig. 2. The Process of Disciplined Imagination Using SSM and WSM

The use of SSM and WSM presents an opportunity to enhance the abstracted contribution of traditional empirical qualitative research to improve the contributions' analogous value to future problems, as well as to embrace and recognize the embodied role of the researcher and those being studied. Generating forward-looking theories of IS phenomena can then be achieved using system concepts. Figure 2 shows how the two strands of research enquiry guided by the approaches of SSM and WSM can inform a research process by relating experienced reality to ideas of purposeful activity. In this manner, abstract knowledge can be built analogically from more experience-based knowledge.

The SSM technique can be used to learn about a particular situation from a group of stakeholders who have specific experience of the problem area in an instance of the more general problem. The usefulness of the findings will be dependent on careful selection of homogenous instances of the more general problem. Through focus groups or interviews, the researcher can use the SSM sense-making devices of CATWOE (customers, actors, transformation process, world view, owners, environment) analysis, root definitions (definition of systems deemed relevant to the phenomenon under investigation), and WSM concepts to make sense of the participants' ideas of what is going on, or what should go on. As the researcher progresses through interaction with selected groups of stakeholders, he/she has to relate the findings from the study back to the extant literature and feed these connections back to the study on an on-going basis—this we see as the process of disciplined imagination as described by Weick (1989).

The cycle can end arbitrarily or as soon as the findings begin to show saturation. Depending on the findings, the results may need to be categorized or stratified. It may even be necessary for the researcher to present his/her perspective as well if such insight is deemed useful. The emerging results are expected to constitute a systemic account of what is going on and/or what needs to happen from the perspective of those actors working in a common problem space. We argue that such contributions will constitute more holistic and coherent findings and will rival the current approaches of understanding phenomena through factors influencing a phenomenon or critical success factors. Better approximations of what is going on can be achieved. Such findings will also address the need for forward-looking theory as they would be imagined within an organizing trajectory that is analogical. The contributions that emerge from this research process can be structured using Llewelyn's (2003) principles, but will also fall into Gregor's (2006) taxonomy as predictive theory or explanatory-and-predictive theory.

6 Conclusion

In this paper, we presented an approach to using systems concepts in order to generate forward-looking theory that maximally impacts the future. We used our experience of researching IS projects to show how it is sometimes necessary to find new metaphors and analogies to underpin theory development. We first provided insight into the as-lived condition that makes human beings prone to being imprisoned by theories of yesteryear to substantiate the need for forward-looking theories. Heidegger (1962) identified a type of *fore-having* which shapes and affects understanding that sets human existence and becoming along a trajectory. In this paper, we made the case that this fore-having can be estimated using *SSM and WSM concepts*. We presented a research framework that includes SSM and WSM to estimate this fore-having which shapes perspective and behavior. A unique feature of the research framework presented here is the disciplined imagination process that is expected to happen within an organizing trajectory led by relevant world views. We argue that such findings will be more opulent in offering insight that is forward-looking because it is imagined along the trajectory of human becoming. The research framework presented here is being used in current research projects in South Africa. We expect that our ideas of the research framework will evolve with our experiences. While this effort is only a single attempt to imagine how we can generate theory about IS phenomena and ensure that these are forward-looking, we hope we have also contributed by demonstrating the importance language, as-lived reality, and human becoming have on the debate about forward-looking theory.

References

Alter, S.: The Work System Method for Understanding Information Systems and Information Systems Research. CAIS 9, 90–104 (2002)

Banville, C., Landry, M.: Can't the Field of MIS be Disciplined? CACM 32(1), 48–60 (1989)

Benbasat, I., Zmud, R.: The Identity Crisis Within the IS Discipline: Defining and Communicating the Disciplines Core Properties. MIS Quarterly 27(2), 183–194 (2003)

Boroditsky, L., Ramscar, M.: The Role of the Body and Mind in Abstract Thought. Psychological Science 13(2), 185–189 (2002)

Bourdieu, P.: Outline of a Theory of Practice. Cambridge University Press, Cambridge (1977)

Checkland, P.: Systems Thinking, Systems Practice. Wiley, Chichester (1999)

Checkland, P., Holwell, S.: Information, Systems and Information Systems: Making Sense of the Field. Wiley, Chichester (1998)

Checkland, P., Scholes, J.: Soft Systems Methodology in Action. Wiley, Chichester (1999)

Cicmil, S.: Understanding Project Management Practice through Interpretive and Critical Research Perspectives. Project Management Journal 37(2), 27–37 (2006)

Cicmil, S., Williams, T., Thomas, J., Hodgson, D.: Rethinking Project Management: Researching the Actuality of Projects. Intl. J. of Project Management 24(8), 675–686 (2006)

Cockburn, A.: Agile Software Development. Pearson Education, Inc., Boston (2002)

Dalcher, D., Brodie, L.: Successful IT Projects. Thompson, London (2007)

Fuller, M., Valacich, J., George, J.: Information Systems Project Management: A Process Team Approach. Prentice Hall, Upper Saddle River (2008)

Gregor, S.: The Nature of Theory in Information Systems. MIS Quarterly 30(3), 611–642 (2006)

Grover, V., Lyytinen, K., Srinivasan, A., Tan, B.C.-Y.: Contributing to Rigorous and Forward Thinking Explanatory Theory. JAIS 9(2), 40–47 (2008)

Guignon, C.: Heidegger and the Problem of Knowledge. Hackett Publishing Company, Indianapolis (1983)

Heidegger, M.: Letter on Humanism. Cambridge University Press, Cambridge (1947)

Heidegger, M.: Being and Time. Harper & Row, New York (1962)

Hoving, R.: Executive Response: Project Management Process Maturity as a Secret Weapon. MISQ Executive 2(1), 29–30 (2003)

Hughes, B., Cotterell, M.: Software Project Management, 4th edn. McGraw-Hill Companies, London (2006)

Kappelman, L.A., McKeeman, R., Zhang, L.: Early Warning Signs of IT Project Failure: The Dominant Dozen. Information Systems Management 23(4), 31–36 (2006)

Kent, C.: The Project Management Maturity Model. Information Systems Management 23(4), 50–58 (2006)

King, J., Lyytinen, K.: Reach and Grasp. MIS Quarterly 28(4), 539–551 (2004)

Lakoff, G., Johnson, M. (eds.): Metaphors We Live By. The Production of Reality: Essays and Readings on Social Interaction. University of Chicago Press, Chicago (1980)

Latour, B.: On Recalling ANT. In: Law, J., Hassard, J. (eds.) Actor Network Theory and After, pp. 15–25. Blackwell Publishers, Oxford (1999)

Llewelyn, S.: Methodological Issues: What Counts as Theory in Qualitative Management and Accounting Research? Introducing Five Levels of Theorizing. Accounting, Auditing & Accountability J. 16(4), 662–708 (2003)

March, S.T., Story, V.C.: Design Science in the Information Systems Discipline: An Introduction to the Special Issue on Design Science Research. MIS Quarterly 32(4), 725–730 (2008)

Maturana, H.R., Varela, F.J.: Autopoiesis and Cognition: The realization of the Living. Reidel Publishing Company, Dordrecht (1980)

Maturana, H.R., Varela, F.J.: The Tree of Knowledge: The Biological Roots of Human Understanding. Shambhala, London (1998)

Merleau-Ponty, M.: Phenomenology of Perception. Routledge, London (2002)

Morgan, G.: Images of Organizations. Sage Publications, Beverly Hills (1986)

Murphy, G.: On Metaphoric Representation. Cognition 60, 173–204 (1996)

Nelson, R.: IT Project Management: Infamous Failures, Classic Mistakes, and Best Practices. MISQ Executive 6(2), 67–78 (2007)

Niederman, F., Gregor, S., Grover, V., Lyytinen, K., Saunders, C.: ICIS 2008 Panel Report: Is Has Outgrown the Need for Reference Discipline Theories, or Has It? CAIS 24(37), 639–656 (2009)

Raelin, J.A.: Toward and Epistemology of Practice. Academy of Management Learning and Education 6(4), 495–519 (2007)

Reich, B.H., Sauer, C., Wei, S.Y.: Innovative Practices for IT Projects. Information Systems Management 25(3), 266–272 (2008)

Richardson, G., Butler, C.: Readings in Information Technology Project Management. Thompson, Boston (2006)

Schwalbe, K.: Information Technology Project Management. Thompson, Boston (2007)

Sewchurran, M., Barron, M.: An Investigation into Successfully Managing and Sustaining the Project-Sponsor Project-Manager Relationships Using Soft Systems Methodology. Project Management Journal 39, Supplement, S56–S68 (2008)

Sewchurran, M., Petkov, D.: A Systemic Framework for Business Process Modeling Combining Soft Systems Methodology and UML. Information Resources Management 20(3), 46–62 (2006)

Smyth, H.J., Morris, P.W.G.: An Epistemological Evaluation of Research into Projects and Their Management: Methodological Issues. Intl. J. of Project Management 25(4), 423–436 (2007)

Strauss, A., Corbin, J.: Basics of Qualitative Research: Techniques and Procedures for Developing, 2nd edn. Sage Publications, London (1998)

Varela, F.J., Thompson, E., Rosch, E.: The Embodied Mind. MIT Press, Cambridge (1991)
Weick, K.: Theory Construction as Disciplined Imagination. Academy of Management Review 14(4), 516–531 (1989)
Weick, K.: What Theorizing Is Not, Theorizing Is. Administrative Science Quarterly 40, 385–390 (1999)
Winter, M., Szczepanek, T.: Images of Projects. Gower, Farnham (2009)

About the Authors

Kosheek Sewchurran is an associate professor of Information Systems at the University of Cape Town and a research associate with the Centre for IT and National Development in Africa (CITANDA). He currently serves on the editorial boards of *International Journal of Managing Projects in Business* and *International Journal of IT and the Systems Approach* (IJITSA).

Irwin Brown is a professor in the Department of Information Systems at the University of Cape Town where he is also deputy dean of research in the commerce faculty. In addition, he is the director of the Centre for IT and National Development in Africa (CITANDA). He holds positions as the South African national representative of IFIP TC8 (Information Systems) and the IS subeditor of *South African Computer Journal*.

Information Systems Innovation Research:
Between Novel Futures and Durable Presents

Margunn Aanestad

Department of Informatics, University of Oslo, P.O. Box 1080,
Blindern, NO-0316 Oslo, Norway
margunn@ifi.uio.no

Abstract. In this paper, I argue that we should not only orient ourselves to the future by looking forward to the yet unrealized. When researching the future, we should also develop a sensibility to the durability of our past and present creations, and understand how they impact the scope for future innovations. The common emphasis on the visionary and novel components of innovation needs to be complemented with an emphasis on the constants, the slowly changing or non-changing aspects. In the paper, I seek to articulate how we could increase our ability to recognize the durability of the present with respect to empirical study objects, analytic approaches, and theoretical resources.

Keywords: Innovations, infrastructural inversion, maintenance, installed base.

1 Introduction: The Durability of the Present

The call for papers for this conference announced that "it is now time to explore, develop and substantiate the new directions through which our field can shape and influence the future of ICT-based practices. If anticipating and influencing the future is something qualitatively different than immediate research relevance, we must then ask whether and how our approaches to inquiry can affect our ability to do so." In this paper, I will present an argument for researching the future in ways that also pay attention to the role of "durable presents" (Risan 2006).

The dominant way to think about the future in the IS field seems to be to link information and communication technologies (ICT) and innovation. ICTs are often proclaimed to be crucial for the economic growth of nations or regions. This could be directly through the production of innovative ICT solutions for a market, or indirectly in facilitating cost-efficient provision of (public) services through ICT deployment. This coupling between the technology and the wished-for innovation offers an opportunity for IS research to present its research as relevant by contributing to the successful operation of this engine of growth. Such a position entails the risk of sliding into instrumental research, rather than maintaining a questioning and critical position to the legitimacy, purpose, and directions of innovation attempts. A certain pro-innovation bias can be identified both in the IS literature and innovation research

M. Chiasson et al. (Eds.): Future IS 2011, IFIP AICT 356, pp. 27–41, 2011.

(Swanson and Ramiller 2004, p. 554). Mainstream IS research on innovation has mainly sought to produce useful knowledge for managers on topics relevant for increased profitability and market share. If we follow Schumpeter's (1934) distinction between invention (making an idea manifest) and innovation (the practical and commercially viable exploitation of an invention), we can say that the management-oriented literature has focused mainly on innovation at the expense of the process of invention. Becoming "innovative" may thus be limited to only deciding to purchase a novel technology or jumping onto a new bandwagon (Fiol and O'Connor 2003; Swanson and Ramiller 2004;). Typically based on studies of the diffusion of innovations within a population of potential adopters, this research stream has sought to establish either why some organizations are more innovative than others, or what makes certain innovations more adoptable than others (Fichman 2004, p. 317). In more design-oriented research stream the focus has been on the efforts required to bring the invention forth, and researchers study how new ideas become manifest in future workshops, scenario building, and innovation laboratories (Ehn and Sjögren 1991; Kensing and Madsen 1991). Different techniques to facilitate imaginative leaps and study creativity in describing new artifacts, practices, or narratives have been developed. However, within both of these streams the studies tend to emphasize the break with current solutions, expectations, theories and practices.

We tend to assume that the topic for IS innovation research is the activity of creating something new. However, when we look at our world, we see that the "novel futures" that we seek to design are only one part of the story. Continuity with the past has also played a significant role in historical development. Many of our cities consist of buildings belonging to different historical epochs, and the cities may be organized according to street plans laid out several hundred years ago. Our legal and political systems have ancient roots and elements, and historical aspects also feature strongly in the academe's self-perception. As a research field, we should not only look towards novel futures but also develop our ability to examine, assess, and deal with the durable present. The future will consist not only of new stuff; it will also consist of what we have built and what we are building now. Thus the theme of researching the future should also stimulate us to develop a sensitivity to what will remain from what we do today, and how the elements, fragments, and remnants of the past and of the present will form parts of the future's palimpsest.

The motivation for this emphasis is the observation that we, the human race, are capable of (actively) building and (passively) accumulating more complex technological systems that we can hope to fully understand or manage. Our ability to construct complex socio-technical systems may sometimes seem to outrun our capability to govern them. One example of this is our apparent inability to achieve concerted action to avert massive climate changes. In the next section, I will show how challenges stemming from accumulated complexity are also significant within the field of information systems. Thus my motivation is related to the challenges our organizations and societies face when trying to live with the historically accumulated complexity of digital technologies. In the remainder of the paper, I seek to articulate how we can conceptualize these issues and how our research approaches can become sensitive to them.

2 Empirical Motivation: Historical Accumulation of Complexity

In this section, I will argue that the field of information and communication technology has been strongly shaped by a dynamic where self-induced complexity and remedial action are central. In a retrospective view, we see that major innovations and trends have been spurred by efforts to deal with the emergent consequences, both positive and negative, of previous actions or decisions.

For instance, programmers in the 1960s and 1970s attempted to minimize space and capacity requirements for code, since computer memory and storage was expensive. Saving two digits for every date field was considered a sound engineering trade-off that became best practice. At that time, no one expected programs to live very long: "The near immortality of computer software has come as a shock to programmers. Ask anyone who was there: We never expected this stuff to still be around" (Ullman 1999, p. 126). We then learned that code doesn't evolve; it accumulates (Ullman 1999), and the realization of the potential impact of this "best practice" spurred massive activity in preparation for the year 2000, called by some "the largest concerted repair operation in human history" (Graham and Thrift 2007, p. 12). However, while these activities were enormously costly, they also brought about a boom for the industry and widespread renewal of systems portfolios and creation of new backup, redundancy, and maintenance structures.

This intertwined nature of problems and solutions, of success and trouble, is fundamental to the field. When companies today struggle with the "legacy crisis" (Seacord et al. 2003), one of the reasons is the unexpectedly long-lived and still functioning information systems, an aspect captured by the title of Bennett's (1995) seminal paper on legacy systems: "Coping with Success." However, another reason is the concurrent development of novel solutions to deal with the problems. For instance, when mainframe systems started to age, but could not be easily replaced, middleware technologies emerged. These then offered alternatives to full-blown and dramatic migration, by allowing old legacy systems to be wrapped in newer software (Bennet 1995; Bisbal et al. 1999). While this allowed short-term problem solving, it also contributed to the survival of the legacy systems and thus caused today's heterogeneous systems portfolios. In many companies, multiple platforms, operating systems, programming languages, applications, and user interfaces are intertwined into complex assemblages, which are maintained at enormous costs. A widespread claim is that maintenance costs tend to vary between 65 and 80 percent of an IT departments budget (Webster 2008). In the late 1970s it was already apparent that maintenance, improvements, and adjustments were responsible for the larger part of life-cycle costs (Lienz and Swanson 1981; Lienz et al. 1978). More recently, some studies claim that over 90 percent of total software costs were devoted to maintenance and evolution both in 1990 (Moad 1990) and in 2000 (Erlikh 2000). A significant amount of time (around half) is used to understand the old software, which typically has undocumented and unsystematized code, held together by *ad hoc* patches and kludges. Another major challenge is caused by interdependencies, as fixes in one part of the system (or in the hosting environment) can have ripple effects in other parts, with cascading errors (Webster 2008). Security suffers in these complex system assemblages, and the demand for integration and interoperability currently constitute vast markets for consultants and solution vendors.

This accumulated complexity is thus of large practical significance, and currently it strongly shapes the IS practice field. The prime rationale for managerial IT decisions used to be related to arguments about companies' competitive advantage and business agility. However, from practitioners' reports in recent years it may seem that these aspects are overshadowed by the challenges of just coping with IT. IT decisions seem to now be driven by cost considerations and an emphasis on streamlining systems portfolios, reducing complexity and interoperability conflicts, and facilitating manageability. A recent study argued that "software is becoming the limiting factor for progress in all kinds of organizations" (Kalleberg 2007, p. 4). The historically accumulated complexity of information systems has been called "a growing storm on the IT horizon" and a "nightmare of IT staff" that "appears to be approaching the limits of human capability" (Murch 2004).

Historically accumulated complexity also characterizes the situation if we look beyond the organization. Most developed countries struggle with a fragmented digital infrastructure in the public sector. For instance, well-funded, nationally coordinated attempts to standardize information systems and communication in the public health sector have struggled in several countries, including Norway (Hanseth et al. 2006), Denmark (Jensen and Aanestad 2010) and in the United Kingdom, with the NHS's massive National Programme for Information Technology (Currie and Guah 2007; Greenhalgh et al. 2010; Jones 2004). Within e-governance, the preexisting information systems where multiple and incompatible standards are inscribed constitute core obstacles. The complexity associated with this, however, has to do not only with heterogeneous technologies and different organizational structures and cultures. These are also deeply intertwined within an institutionalized "regime" that is upheld by more or less formal regulations of different kinds (Contini and Lanzara 2009). As a result, despite massively funded and nationally coordinated initiatives, widespread interoperability and integration is relatively seldom achieved. Currently, interoperability frameworks and enterprise architectures are the preferred direction of investments (Guijarro 2007; Zachman 1987).

Consequently, it seems that after having digitized the work practice, the organization, and the society, we now have to learn to live with the digital, complex systems assemblages that we have created. This should be a core topic for researchers within the IS field. What are we really doing when we build with information technology? Which futures are we deliberately or inadvertently creating? These are questions that will have great relevance for researching the futures, and the question that I want to develop in the rest of the paper.

3   Resources for Understanding Durability in Innovation

In this section, I seek to identify some relevant resources from the literature on general or ICT-specific innovations.

3.1   Innovation Literature

Research on innovation has, to a small degree, thematized the durability or continuity of preexisting systems, practices, and understandings. Naturally, the preexisting reality is relevant in that it constitutes the basis upon which one builds and from which one simultaneously departs; this is in particular the case for incremental innovations and to a lesser degree for radical innovations. It seems fair to say, however, that in general the preexisting has been conceptualized mainly in the form of barrier and resistance against the new. Since Schumpeter's (1934) emphasis on creative destruction, there seems to have been a stronger interest in the field for radical innovations. For instance, Christensen's (1997) well-known model of disruptive innovations is typical, as it emphasizes how new technologies can surpass the existing, seemingly superior technologies and turn the market landscape upside down.

However, the theme of accumulation, especially of know-how, has been thematized by some researchers. Henderson and Clarke (1990) distinguish between component and architectural innovation, where the latter requires changes (reconfigurations) in the overall scheme of how a solution's components are interrelated. Since the architectural knowledge related to a relatively stable dominant design tends to get embedded into information processes and organizational structures within a firm, established firms may have difficulty reshaping their information processes to fit with architectural innovations. Such conceptualization also has been brought to the study of IT innovations, where significant parts of the innovation process are distributed across heterogeneous networks of actors (Anderson et al. 2008; Boland et al. 2007; Steinmueller 2000; Tuomi 2002).

IT innovations may not follow the traditional manufacturer-oriented and supply-pushed innovation patterns, and research has pointed to the role of open and user-driven innovations (Chesbrough et al. 2006; von Hippel 1988). In these networked innovation processes the technology can be both a target and an engine of the innovation (Boland et al. 2007). A crucial challenge for such distributed innovation processes is whether cumulative innovation is actually facilitated; that is, whether intellectual property rights allow or block competitors building on each others achievements and result in collective innovations (Scotchmer 2006). A core observation made by IS innovation scholars is that these innovations will, to a large extent, incorporate existing technologies and reuse parts from existing solutions in new designs within new architectures. Such is the claim by Yoo et al. (2010), who presents a model of the layered modular architecture. Exemplified by the digitization of the book, they describe how devices, networks, services, and content, conceptualized as different layers, are recombined and how the e-book's product architecture changes over time. Such incorporation and reuse of existing solutions will bring a new organizing logic of innovations, demanding new strategic frameworks and new corporate infrastructures. Their model of the layered modular architecture represents insights that are highly relevant contributions for emphasizing the durability of the present. It mobilizes the notion of architecture and components, and thus allows us to thematize interdependencies between components as well as between layers. Such approaches, which allow us to "dis-entangle" rather than black-box the actual innovations, offer possibilities to better grasp the intricate interplay between the existing and the novel in ICT-related innovations.

3.2 Innovation in the Context of Evolutionary Technological Change

Compared with mainstream innovation research, theories of change developed within an evolutionary paradigm seem to be more oriented toward emphasizing the role that the past and the present play in innovations. For instance, Nelson and Winter's (1982) work on an evolutionary theory of technological change describes the stability and conservative effect of existing routines, technologies, etc. Dosi (1982) emphasized the impact by the dominant technological paradigm on innovation processes. He claimed that market forces (i.e., demand) will have a successful impact only within some boundaries defined by the paradigm. This restrictive view on the role of the past also figured in other discourses, evidenced to the focus on path dependency both in historical sociology (Mahoney 2000) and economic theory (David 1985).

Within science and technology studies (STS), we find several relevant historical analyses of technology development in large technical systems (see Summerton 1994). For instance, Thomas Hughes (1983), in his well-known account of the electrification of America, described the constraints shaping the process of network building. From this and other studies, the notion of "installed base" has spread to the IS field. Specifically, it has been taken up in studies of information infrastructure studies. In a seminal study of the evolution of a distributed collaborative system, Star and Ruhleder (1996) formulated key characteristics of information infrastructures. One of them was that "infrastructure does not grow *de novo*: it wrestles with the inertia of the installed base and inherits strengths and limitations from that base" (Star and Ruhleder 1996, p. 113), a claim that has been further developed and exemplified (Hanseth 2000; Hanseth et al. 1996; Monteiro and Hanseth 1995).

Within the information infrastructure literature, the installed base is seen to offer strengths and opportunities as well as limitations. Its importance is perceived to be so central that "cultivation of the installed base" is proposed as the generic change strategy, replacing traditional planning-oriented and top-down design and development approaches (Ciborra 2000; Hanseth 1996; Hanseth and Lyytinen 2010). Cultivation consists of gradual and incremental extensions, often a long-term process (Hepsø et al. 2009), replacement of elements, utilizing the role of gateways to mitigate conflicts of heterogeneity (David and Bunn 1988; Hanseth, 2001), or to deal with the politicized nature of information infrastructure building (Lyytinen and Damsgaard 2010; Sahay et al. 2009). Thus this stream of research, despite being less innovation-oriented, offers a rich conceptual framework to analyze networked and distributed ICT-related change processes where the existing reality plays a significant role. In particular, the notion of an installed base and the dynamics around it is valuable in this context. Moreover, studies within this stream aim to both encompass the concrete details of their study objects and the larger social and organizational networks of which they are parts, constituting heterogeneous assemblages (Contini and Lanzara 2009), and to explicitly theorize the relations between *small* and *large*.

3.3 Innovation in Practice Studies

If we turn to empirical, practice-oriented studies of inventions and innovation processes, we will see a close engagement with the existing reality. Studies from the STS field as well as the ethnographically inspired work practice studies within organizational studies (e.g., Gherardi and Nicolini 2000) and within streams such as

CSCW and PD, all take part in a move of "relocating innovations" (Suchman and Bishop 1999). The achievement (i.e., the innovation) is here conceptualized as socially constructed (i.e., a result achieved through collective work) in situated material practices occurring within distinctive locations. Several laboratory studies described how scientific facts are established, how a certain understanding and mode of working won through, and how innovation activities are deeply enmeshed into a sociotechnically heterogeneous network (Fujimura 1992; Knorr-Cetina 1991; Latour and Woolgar, 1986; Lynch, 1985). Through such an approach, attention is turned toward, not the outcome of the invention or innovation, but the effort and work that goes into producing it. As such, it describes more explicitly the impact of the preexisting technologies, practices, skills, and resources.

It is important to note that this approach, despite the close empirical contact with concrete cases, does not necessarily imply a "situationism," where one is content with studying local achievements and situated interactions (Kallinikos 2002). Many of these studies explicitly address the theme of how the invention or discovery spreads beyond the local situation, and how stabilization and standardization of large-scale collaborative networks are achieved (Bowker and Star 1999; Fujimura, 1992; Ribes and Bowker 2008; Ribes and Finholt 2007, 2009; Star 2002). In the same vein, Latour (2005) emphasized that account of an action or situation that limits itself to the local is insufficient, as there is a lot more to it than local context or situated interactions. "The word interaction was not badly chosen; only the number and type of 'actions' and the span of their 'inter' relationship has been vastly underestimated" (Latour 2005, p. 212). Any action overflows its context; actors far away in space and time have an impact. Action is dislocated, redispatched, and redistributed, and Latour holds that our theories need to encompass the temporal dislocation of present actions, both into the future and in the past.

Although not stemming from the STS discourse, the study of innovation practices by Spinosa et al. (1997) in a similar manner describe how the past is crucial for innovation. Here they discussed which activities and skills go into innovation (termed *history-making*), and emphasize how the existing is the point of departure that stimulates accumulation, reuse, and recombination. Thus they do not paint a traditional picture of a "heroic innovator" (Sørensen 2008) that identifies a problem or an unmet need and then produces an innovation to solve the problem or fill the need. Rather Spinosa et al. describe practices of working with that which is already present in the situation, and how everyday practices contribute to "historical disclosing" through the practices they name: reconfiguration, cross-appropriation, and articulation. The novelty lies in disclosing, reusing, and interpreting the given and existing in new ways.

These practice studies can contribute to our aim by exemplifying a different take on the empirical object. The practice orientation constitutes a gestalt switch, comparable to what Bowker (1994) called an "infrastructural inversion." To do an infrastructural inversion means that rather than accepting the grand claims about the effects of new technologies, we should "look at the infrastructural changes that preceded or accompanied the effects" (Bowker 1994, p. 235). It is an inquiry driven by uncovering the hidden; we are encouraged to look for the infrastructure this new technology requires, what large hidden system in space and time that has (or will) facilitated its grand, observed (or proclaimed) effects. In the next section, I will argue that, in a similar way, when researching IS innovations, we can perform such an infrastructural inversion and approach our study objects differently, from the bottom up.

4 Studying Durability of the Present

Initially I argued that researching the future should not only emphasize novelty and discontinuity with the past, but should also recognize the continuity with the existing reality. I argued that a core practical problem in the IS field is the ongoing accumulation of complexity that obstructs organizational as well as interorganizational attempts to realize the benefits of information systems. Another, more positive entry point leading to the same argument is the nature of current IS innovation, and to show how recombinations and reuse of existing and new elements make up innovative products and services. In todays highly dynamic product and service ecologies, novel reconfigurations and combinations of existing elements, as well as additions of new elements are central features. Here, the dynamics between the durable presents and the novel futures are playing out before our eyes, and IS researchers should be able to contribute with adequate and relevant understanding of these dynamics. A solid understanding of the evolution dynamics of the technology would allow the IS field to impact the way our society approaches the tasks of design, construction, and governance of ICTs. In this section, I will offer some opinions on how we could pursue such an understanding.

4.1 Empirical Objects: Living with Technologies

Several of our field's constitutive research traditions (such as HCI, CSCW, and ISD) have their roots in design traditions; therefore, the field has developed within a construction or production paradigm. This, I argue, needs to be expanded, and we need to study the reality of living with technologies. When IS researchers during the 1980s started to investigate the phenomena beyond the design and development horizon, such as users' actual usage of systems (Gasser 1986; Kling and Scacchi 1982), or organizational implementation (Keen 1981; Markus 1983), different issues were brought to light and new questions could be asked. *Use* became a domain that offered novel conceptualizations in its own right. Researchers did not just study use and users in order to offer implications for design, which for a long time was a necessary legitimation of a study (Dourish 2006). Today, the thriving field of implementation studies has given us significantly more insight into the interplay between information and communication technologies and organizations, and a better grasp of what characterizes the technologies.

We may need a similar expansion today with respect to innovation studies and future research. We need to complement the design, development, and innovation orientation of our field with empirical studies of how organizations actually live with the innovative technologies we create. Specifically, I argue, we could perform a gestalt switch, or "infrastructural inversion" (Bowker 1994) and address the actual work of usage, maintenance, upgrading, repairing, caring for, and dismantling systems in organizational and interorganizational contexts. Such an orientation toward maintenance and repair is suggested by Graham and Thrift (2007), and some of the same empirical orientation is seen in studies of how technology is made to work (Jewett and Kling 1991), especially in studies of support work (e.g., Orr 1996), thus it is not novel to the field (see also Ciborra 2000).

Such an orientation toward experienced realities can help uncover the way that durability of the present actually plays out. This focus constitutes an infrastructural inversion, a la Bowker, in that it can help us describe the actual work of realization that lies behind the vision, at which cost of maintenance the novel system works, the opportunities it opens, and the ones it closes. Thus we may have a basis from which to estimate the future opportunities, limitations, and costs that we incur in innovative undertakings.

4.2 Analytic Approach: Focus on Relations and Interdependencies

Besides choosing other empirical topics, an appropriate analytic take on the issue is required. Here I suggest we turn to Andrew Barry (2001), who has formulated "a different account of invention; one that does not equate technical novelty with inventiveness" (p. 211). He emphasizes the transformative potential of an invention, the opening up of possibilities as its defining aspect. From this perspective,

> The notion that technology as something like an isolated artefact is prob-lematic. Technology is viewed not so much as an artefact, but as a series of relations and connections between artefacts, physical and mental skills, desires and interests, concepts and information. Seen in these terms, inventiveness should not be equated with the development of novel artefacts, or indeed with novelty and innovation in general. Rather, inventiveness can be viewed as an index of the degree to which an object or practice is associated with *opening up possibilities....What is inventive is not the novelty of artefacts and devices in themselves, but the novelty of the arrangements with other objects and activities within which artefacts and instruments are situated, and might be situated in the future* (Barry 2001, pp. 211-212).

Following Barry, I suggest that the criteria upon which we should assess innovations (or future-generating practices) should consider whether, how, and to what extent they open up possibilities, as well as whether, how, and to what extent they introduce constraints. Our attention should be on the arrangements, the way elements are interrelated. Such an analytic orientation would steer our attention to consider not just the novelty of the specific artifact being designed, but the opportunities and constraints that are introduced when we attempt to reuse, recombine, and accumulate.

This implies that interactions and interdependencies should constitute core targets for our analyses. Which relations are introduced or changed when we recombine elements, or when we add new elements to the existing socio-technical networks? When the set of relations is changed, what implications could it have? Where and for whom will the changes stimulate further innovation; where and for whom will they constitute barriers to growth? In order to investigate such questions, we need theoretical concepts that help us focus on the relationality of socio-technical networks.

4.3 Implications for Theory

We need to go beyond the artifact, device, or system orientation that has been evident in the design-oriented HCI, CSCW, SD, SE, and IS discourses (Tilson et al. 2010). Instead we need to utilize conceptualizations that alert us to relations and connections, to system-level issues related to interactions, couplings, and dependencies. There is a long-standing, but not overly visible, tradition within the IS field that has this orientation. In Orlikowski and Iacono's (2001) literature survey focusing on how the IT artifact was conceptualized, one of their classifications was the "ensemble views," comprising only 12.5 percent of the articles surveyed. An early and prominent example of such an ensemble conceptualization was web models (Kling and Scacchi 1982). The stream of research on information infrastructures (see Hanseth and Lyytinen 2010; Hanseth and Monteiro 1995; Star and Ruhleder 1996; Tilson et al. 2010) has offered significant contributions to understanding large-scale sociotechnical networks. Recent research on digital ecodynamics (El Sawy et al. 2010) and platform-centric eco-systems (Tiwana et al. 2010) approach similar phenomena from different angles. Such theoretical resources would constitute appropriate fundaments for an IS approach that aims to understand and conceptualize the dynamics of technological development.

5 Final Remarks

What do we want to be durable? What do we want to end? How can we distinguish between durability that restricts the envisioned and desired futures from becoming realized, versus durability that allows cumulative innovation? How can we build the future with an orientation toward the consequences of today's action? How can we research today's actions with an orientation toward the future?

I have argued that we need an alternative to the common view on the large-scale, digitally interconnected information systems assemblage that we create. We need other studies and other perspectives in order to complement and emphasize the novel. In her study of innovation, Laura Watts (2009, p. 3) emphasizes that,

> Like the past, the future is made of stuff, of materials, landscapes, and people. Durability and heritage are as much a matter of the future, as a matter of the past. Things endure from past into future. It takes ongoing, unceasing work to conserve, to make things for the world to come.

In her search for a "future archaeology," Watts seeks to create enduring things and bring artifacts into being. Here I wanted to emphasize a related but slightly distinct side of this work to create futures, by arguing that we need to turn our attention to the way our creation has endurance, both in intended and in not intended ways. What we construct today can persist for a long time, either in its original form, or modified and reappropriated in a dynamic digital ecology.

I have suggested that we should perform research investigating the conditions, constraints, and consequences of ICT growth and innovation. In order to do this, studies of the architects and builders (i.e., the designers, developers, managers) should be complemented by studies of repair and maintenance; of the ongoing learning and coping activities of all organizational members and technology users. Based on such studies we can improve our understanding of technology development, our capacity for intervention, and the ensuing implications for action. While the traditional innovation orientation exposes research to the dangers of becoming instrumental and uncritical, an approach that is sensitive to the durability of our creations offers a different critical potential for helping us identify the choices we are facing regarding which futures we will create.

References

Andersson, M., Lindgren, R., Henfridsson, O.: Architectural Knowledge in Inter-Organizational IT Innovation. Journal of Strategic Information Systems 17(1), 19–38 (2008)

Barry, A.: Political Machines: Governing a Technological Society. The Athlone Press, Middlesex (2001)

Bennett, K.: Legacy Systems: Coping with Success. IEEE Software 12(1), 19–23 (1995)

Bisbal, J., Lawless, D., Wu, B., Grimson, J.: Legacy Information Systems: Issues and Directions. IEEE Software 16(5), 103–111 (1999)

Boland, R.J., Lyytinen, K., Yoo, Y.: Wakes of Innovation in Project Networks: The Case of Digital 3-D Representations in Architecture, Engineering, and Construction. Organization Science 18(4), 631–647 (2007)

Bowker, G.C.: Science on the Run: Information Management and Industrial Geophysics at Schlumberger, 1920-1940. MIT Press, Cambridge (1994)

Bowker, G.C., Star, S.L.: Sorting Things Out: Classification and its Consequences. MIT Press, Cambridge (1999)

Chesbrough, H., Vanhaverbeke, W., West, J. (eds.): Open Innovation: Researching a New Paradigm. Oxford University Press, Oxford (2006)

Christensen, C.M.: The Innovator's Dilemma: When New Technologies Cause Great Firms to Fail. Harvard Business Press, Boston (1997)

Ciborra, C.: A Critical Review of the Literature on the Management of Corporate Information Infrastructures. In: Ciborra, C., Braa, K., Cordella, A., Dahlbom, B., Failla, A., Hanseth, O., Hespø, V., Ljungberg, J., Monteiro, E., Simon, K.A. (eds.) From Control to Drift–The Dynamics of Corporate Information Infrastructures. Oxford University Press, Oxford (2000)

Contini, F., Lanzara, G.: ICT and Innovation in the Public Sector. Palgrave Macmillan, London (2009)

Currie, W.L., Guah, M.W.: Conflicting Institutional Logics: A National Programme for IT in the Organisational Field of Healthcare. Journal of Information Technology 22(3), 235–247 (2007)

David, P.A.: Clio and the Economics of QWERTY. American Economic Review 75(2), 332–337 (1985)

David, P.A., Bunn, J.A.: The Economics of Gateway Technologies and Network Evolution: Lessons from Electricity Supply History. Information Economics and Policy 3(2), 165–202 (1988)

Dosi, G.: Technological Paradigms and Technological Trajectories: A Suggested Interpretation of the Determinants and Directions of Technical Change. Research Policy 11(3), 147–162 (1982)

Dourish, P.: Implications for Design. In: Proceedings of the SIGCHI Conference on Human Factors in Computing Systems. Montréal, Québec, Canada, pp. 541–550 (2006)

Ehn, P., Sjögren, P.: From Systems Description to Scripts for Action. In: Greenbaum, J.M., Kyng, M. (eds.) Design at Work: Cooperative Design of Computer Systems, pp. 241–268. Routledge, London (1991)

El Sawy, O.A., Malhotra, A., Park, Y.: Seeking the Configurations of Digital Ecodynamics: It Takes Three to Tango. Information Systems Research 21(4), 835–848 (2010)

Erlikh, L.: Leveraging Legacy System Dollars for E-Business. IEEE IT Pro, May/June 17–23 (2000)

Fichman, R.G.: Going Beyond the Dominant Paradigm for Information Technology Innovation Research: Emerging Concepts and Methods. Journal of the Association for Information Systems 5(8), 314–355 (2004)

Fiol, C.M., O'Connor, E.J.: Waking Up! Mindfulness in the Face of Bandwagons. Academy of Management Review 28(1), 54–70 (2003)

Fujimura, J.: Crafting Science: Standardized Packages, Boundary Objects and "Translations". In: Pickering, A. (ed.) Science as Practice and Culture. University of Chicago Press, Chicago (1992)

Gasser, L.: The Integration of Computing and Routine Work. ACM Transactions on Office Information Systems 4(3), 205–225 (1986)

Gherardi, S., Nicolini, D.: To Transfer is to Transform: The Circulation of Safety Knowledge. Organization 7(3), 329–348 (2000)

Graham, S., Thrift, N.: Out of Order. Understanding Repair and Maintenance. Theory, Culture & Society 24(3), 1–25 (2007)

Greenhalgh, T., Stramer, K., Bratan, T., Byrne, E., Russell, J., Hinder, S., Potts, H.: The Devil's in The Detail: Final Report of the Independent Evaluation of the Summary Care Record and Healthspace Programmes. University College London, London (2010)

Guijarro, L.: Interoperability Frameworks and Enterprise Architectures in Egovernment Initiatives in Europe and the United States. Government Information Quarterly 24, 89–101 (2007)

Hanseth, O.: Information Infrastructure Development: Cultivating the Installed Base. Studies in the Use of Information Technologies, (16), Department of Informatics, Göteborg University (1996)

Hanseth, O.: The Economics of Standards. In: Ciborra, C., Braa, K., Cordella, A., Dahlbom, B., Failla, A., Hanseth, O., Hespø, V., Ljungberg, J., Monteiro, E., Simon, K.A. (eds.) From Control to Drift–The Dynamics of Corporate Information Infrastructures, pp. 56–70. Oxford University Press, Oxford (2000)

Hanseth, O.: Gateways–Just as Important as Standards: How the Internet Won the "Religious War" Over Standards in Scandinavia. Knowledge, Technology & Policy 14(3), 71–89 (2001)

Hanseth, O., Lyytinen, K.: Design Theory for Dynamic Complexity in Information Infrastructures: The Case of Building Internet. Journal of Information Technology 25(1), 1–19 (2010)

Hanseth, O., Monteiro, E.: Social Shaping of Information Infrastructure: On Being Specific About the Technology. In: Orlikowski, W.J., Walsham, G., Jones, M.R., De Gross, J.I. (eds.) Information Technology and Changes in Organizational Work, pp. 325–343. Chapman & Hall, London (1995)

Hanseth, O., Monteiro, E., Hatling, M.: Developing Information Infrastructure: The tension between Standardization and Flexibility. Science, Technology & Human Values 21(4), 407–426 (1996)

Henderson, R.M., Clarke, K.B.: Architectural Innovation: The Reconfiguration of Existing Product Technologies and the Failure of Established Firms. Administrative Science Quarterly 35(1), 9–30 (1990)

Hepsø, V., Monteiro, E., Rolland, K.: Ecologies of eInfrastructures. Journal of the AIS 10(5), 430–446 (2009)

Hughes, T.P.: Networks of Power: Electrification in Western Society, 1880-1930. John Hopkins University Press, Baltimore (1983)

Jensen, T.B., Aanestad, M.: National Initiatives to Build Healthcare Information Infrastructures. In: Proceedings of the MCIS, Paper 43 (2010)

Jewett, T., Kling, R.: The Dynamics of Computerization in a Social Science Research Team: A Case Study of Infrastructures, Strategies and Skills. Social Science Computer Review 9, 246–275 (1991)

Jones, M.: Learning the Lessons of History? Electronic Records in the United Kingdom Acute Hospitals, 1988-2002. Health Informatics Journal 10(4), 253–263 (2004)

Kalleberg, K.T.: Abstractions for Language-Independent Program Transformations. Unpublished Ph.D. thesis, University of Bergen (2007)

Kallinikos, J.: Recalcitrant Technology, Cross-Contextual Systems and Context-Embedded Action. Working Paper Series, (103), London School of Economics (2002)

Keen, P.G.W.: Information Systems and Organizational Change. Communications of the ACM 24(1), 24–33 (1981)

Kensing, F., Madsen, K.H.: Generating Visions: Future Workshops and Metaphorical Design. In: Greenbaum, J.M., Kyng, M. (eds.) Design at Work: Cooperative Design of Computer Systems, pp. 155–168. Routledge, London (1991)

Kling, R., Scacchi, W.: The Web of Computing: Computer Technology as Social Organization. Advances in Computers 21, 1–90 (1982)

Knorr-Cetina, K.: Epistemic Cultures: Forms of Reason in Science. History of Political Economy 23(1), 105–122 (1991)

Latour, B.: Reassembling the Social: An Introduction to Actor-Network Theory. Oxford University Press, New York (2005)

Latour, B., Woolgar, S.: Laboratory Life: The Construction of Scientific Facts. Sage Publications, Beverly Hills (1979)

Lientz, B.P., Swanson, E.B.: Problems in Application Software Maintenance. Communications of the ACM 24(11), 763–769 (1981)

Lientz, B.P., Swanson, E.B., Tompkins, G.E.: Characteristics of Application Software Maintenance. Communications of the ACM 21(6), 466–471 (1978)

Lynch, M.: Art and Artifact in Laboratory Science. Routledge and Kegan Paul, Boston (1985)

Lyytinen, K., Damsgaard, J.: Configuration Analysis of Inter-Organizational Information Systems Adoption. Lecture Notes in Business Information Processing, vol. 60, pp. 127–138 (2010)

Markus, M.L.: Power, Politics, and MIS Implementation. Communications of the ACM 26(6), 430–444 (1983)

Mahoney, J.: Path Dependence in Historical Sociology. Theory and Society 29(4), 507–548 (2000)

Moad, J.: Maintaining the Competitive Edge. Datamation, 61–62 (1990)

Monteiro, E., Hanseth, O.: Social Shaping of Information Infrastructure: On Being Specific About Technology. In: Orlikowski, W.J., Walsham, G., Jones, M.R., DeGross, J.I. (eds.) Information Technology and Changes in Organizational Work, pp. 325–343. Chapman & Hall, London (1995)

Murch, R.: Autonomic Computing. IBM Press, Armonk (2004)

Nelson, R.R., Winter, S.G.: An Evolutionary Theory of Economic Change. Harvard University Press, Boston (1982)

Orlikowski, W.J., Iacono, C.S.: Research Commentary: Desperately Seeking the "IT" in IT Research—A Call to Theorizing the IT Artifact. Information Systems Research 12(2), 121–134 (2001)

Orr, J.E.: About Machines. An Ethnography of a Modern Job. ILR Press, Ithaca (1996)

Ribes, D., Bowker, G.: Organizing for Multidisciplinary Collaboration: The Case of the Geosciences Network. In: Olson, G.M., Zimmerman, A., Bos, N. (eds.) Scientific Collaboration on the Internet. MIT Press, Cambridge (2008)

Ribes, D., Finholt, T.: Tensions Across the Scales: Planning Infrastructure for the Long-Term. In: Proceedings of the 2007 International ACM Conference on Supporting Group Work, pp. 229–238 (2007)

Ribes, D., Finholt, T.: The Long Now of Information Infrastructures. Articulating Tensions in Development. Journal of the AIS 10(5), 375–398 (2009)

Risan, L.: The Duration of the Present and the Risk of Not Telling Large Stories. EASST Review (October 2006), http://www.easst.net/review/oct2006/risan

Sahay, S., Monteiro, E., Aanestad, M.: Configurable Politics and Asymmetric Integration: Health e-Infrastructures in India. Journal of the AIS 10(5), 399–414 (2009)

Schumpter, J.: The Theory of Economic Development. Harvard University Press, Cambridge (1934)

Scotchmer, S.: Innovation and Incentives. MIT Press, Cambridge (2006)

Seacord, R., Plakosh, D., Lewis, G.: Modernizing Legacy Systems: Software Technologies, Engineering Processes, and Business Practices. Addison-Wesley, Reading (2003)

Spinosa, C., Flores, F., Dreyfus, H.: Disclosing New Worlds: Entrepreneurship, Democratic Action and the Cultivation of Solidarity. MIT Press, Cambridge (1997)

Sørensen, B.M.: Behold, I Am Making All Things New: The Entrepreneur as Savior in the Age of Creativity. Scandinavian Journal of Management 24(2), 85–93 (2008)

Star, S.L.: Infrastructure and Ethnographic Practice: Working on the Fringes. Scandinavian Journal of Information Systems 14(2), 107–122 (2002)

Star, S.L., Ruhleder, K.: Steps Toward an Ecology of Infrastructure: Design and Access for Large Information Spaces. Information Systems Research 7(1), 111–134 (1996)

Steinmueller, E.: Does Information and Communication Technology Facilitate Codification of Knowledge? Industrial and Corporate Change 9, 361–476 (2000)

Suchman, L., and Bishop, L.: Problematizing Innovation as a Critical Project. Paper presented in the panel Critical Potential of Innovation Studies, Conference on Critical Management Studies, Manchester, England (1999)

Summerton, J. (ed.): Changing Large Technical Systems. Westview, Boulder (1994)

Swanson, E.B., Ramiller, N.: Innovating Mindfully with Information Technology. MIS Quarterly 28(4), 553–583 (2004)

Tilson, D., Lyytinen, K., Sørensen, C.: Digital Infrastructures: The Missing IS Research Agenda. Information Systems Research 21(4), 748–759 (2010)

Tiwana, A., Konsynski, B., Bush, A.A.: Platform Evolution: Coevolution of Platform Architecture, Governance, and Environmental Dynamics. Information Systems Research 21(4), 675–687 (2010)

Tuomi, I.: Networks of Innovation: Change and Meaning in the Age of the Internet. Oxford University Press, New York (2002)

Ullman, E.: The Myth of Order. WIRED, Issue 7.04 (April 1999)

von Hippel, E.: The Sources of Innovation. Oxford University Press, New York (1988)

Watts, L.: Future Archeologies. Method and Story, Keynote address given at the Society of Museum Archaeologists Conference, Guildhall, Winchester UK (November 5, 2009), http://eprints.lancs.ac.uk/31783/1/watts_futurearchaeologies.pdf

Webster, B.: Surviving Complexity. Baseline Magazine (2008)

Yoo, Y., Henfridsson, O., Lyytinen, K.: The New Organizing Logic of Digital Innovation: An Agenda for Information Systems Research. Information Systems Research 21(4), 724–735 (2010)

Zachman, J.: A Framework for Information Systems Architecture. IBM Systems Journal 26(3), 276 (1987)

About the Author

Margunn Aanestad is an associate professor of Information Systems in the Department of Informatics, University of Oslo, Norway. She is interested in understanding the interaction between technical, social, organizational, and regulatory elements in the development of large-scale information infrastructures, and has studied ICTs in healthcare, both in developed and developing countries. Her research has been published in *Journal of Information Technology*, *MIS Quarterly*, *European Journal of Information Systems*, *Journal of the Association for Information Systems*, and other journals.

The Present as Future: The Problem of Translation in Corporate Science Projects

Eleanor Wynn

eleanorwynn3@gmail.com

Abstract. The paper reviews a set of research projects intended to plan *for the future*. It uses an actor-network construct from Latour's work on science practice, *translation*. The paper contrasts normal science practice with science in a corporate context. Both situations occur in actor networks, require translation and contain arbitrary decisions. The corporate context can be more problematic because of the greater diversity of actors and agendas. The longer the work goes on, the more actors there are. Research *per se* is a sustained effort toward emergent goals; in the context of fluid corporate networks, these goals can become lost in mis-translation from one phase to the next. Results that would otherwise build up science findings miss their mark, are delayed, or are overtaken by other developments. The findings exist, but the outcomes for which they were intended may not materialize.

Keywords: Corporate research, virtual teams, machine learning, desktop information management, 3D user interface, innovation.

> *"Is it our fault if the networks are simultaneously real, like nature, narrated, like discourse, and collective, like society?"* (Latour 1993, p.6)

1 Introduction

Latour emphasizes the role of *translation* from one step of scientific process to another. The results are transportable abstractions that allow the original facts on the ground to be progressively formalized and encoded for dissemination. In *Pandora's Hope*, Latour follows this process through several chapters on the classification of soils from the Brazilian jungle–savannah boundary. The research question was whether the jungle or the savannah was advancing; the answer would be based on soil and plant types. The interdisciplinary team of scientists literally took dirt out of the ground, placed it into a grid of small boxes, and progressively abstracted its form from there, with iterations of process to ensure fidelity: that what came out the other end as "science" actually represented the categories and locations of dirt where it was found. He calls this process translation. At each step the content changes its substance but should be traceable back to the original substance due to fidelity of translation. Therefore, any generalizations made from the abstractions ought to be true of the

M. Chiasson et al. (Eds.): Future IS 2011, IFIP AICT 356, pp. 43–56, 2011.

original material. Latour (1993) includes and even privileges anthropology in the sciences; so this discussion does not engage the quantitative–qualitative distinction.

When science is carried out in a corporation, the translation process easily becomes distorted by other agendas. The context is normally science for the production of some good, either basic processes for products and inventions, or internal uses like manufacturing. More recently, workforce and end users have become subjects for examination. In this engagement, the researcher is likely a well qualified person trained in methods. This person will, therefore, have faithful translation as a basic unstated goal. The difference between corporate and academic science is done with the results. This can change with changing actors. So even though each step of the process may be science, the end-to-end process itself may not. The predilections of actors at a senior level and their long-range views are critical in this fidelity. Since these actors and agendas change, the corporation introduces more variability than our sense of science normally allows.

Actors in the network take the form of human players, management objectives, reward systems, technology capabilities, research methods, and externally sourced solutions, to name a few. The translation lens helps us understand what should happen even in the fragile process of constructing academic science, and what the expectation of a research undertaking is. The violation of this principle explains obstacles in researching the future in a complex situation with a broad range of changing actors.

The present "case" is a series of research projects carried out over 8 years. The purpose of the projects was to guide IT decisions about key features of virtual collaboration tools for the company workforce. Collaboration tools were seen as problematic because the workforce had come to operate in an increasingly distributed fashion based on various policies. Each project led to a new question. A variety of methods came into play depending on the nature of the questions.

It is worth spending a moment to address the question of "problems" and their relationship to researching the future. A problem is a form of breakdown or anticipated breakdown (Dreyfus 1984; Zimmerman 1990). Even though a problem may be "experienced," its causes and details remain unanalyzed until it is reflected upon. The present tends to be taken for granted even when problems are experienced. The process of coping with problems was characterized in Hammer and Champy (2001) as "workarounds"; this characterization still applies. If the present is *ready-to-hand* (Dreyfus 1978) then why analyze it and why think of changes for the future? Workarounds can build up to a point where eventually they cause a breakdown. Then the present is experienced as problematic or *present-at-hand*, and leads to thoughts about a different future. This requires a different perspective on what is actually happening in the present.

The dilemma in an actor network is that what is the future to one actor may be the present to another. Failure to note this difference is part of the problem of translation. These problems are more likely to arise for end user and organizational research than in computer science and engineering because people already have perceptions and opinions about the former, but the latter are not exempt. Many innovations in software development have idled while stakeholders attempt to grasp the science, the usage model, or both. This series of projects contained software innovations that did not translate accurately to higher level actors, or ran into organizational problems like short-term agendas of individual human actors. The people working on a project see the project as fully present and even perhaps behind the current capabilities. Others who lack the same context may see it as so far into the future that it is not yet practical to execute. This becomes self-fulfilling.

Before researching the future, we must locate the future. Latour (1993) claims that it starts in a new understanding of the present. Innovative solutions rely upon insights about present problems or breakdowns and in most cases are paired with new technologies or methods for addressing them. Since the present is mostly ready-to-hand (Dreyfus 1978) and taken for granted, seeing and analyzing those problems is a challenge. Different stakeholders, therefore, see them differently or have different member analyses based on everyday reasoning.

Latour casts the reframing back into the past.

> As soon as we direct our attention simultaneously to the work of purification and the work of hybridization, we immediately stop being wholly modern, and our future begins to change. At the same time we stop having been modern, because we become retrospectively aware that the two sets of practices have always already been at work in the historical period that is ending (Latour 1993, p. 11).

The future and the past are always part of the present. The calendar shows a difference between yesterday and tomorrow but trajectories of events are entangled with concurrent presents, pasts, and futures.

Just as a topic like global warming is concurrently political, scientific, and narrative, yet artificially divided (Latour 1993), the topic also contains within it different time horizons. Past events led to the present, current events affect the future, and, within any given moment, people are acting out different pasts, presents, and possible futures according to their position in a network, a perspective they are committed to, or how they are affected. Escobar (1995) refers to this as hybrid cultures where national and regional cultures include traditional and contemporary stances. Floods in Pakistan and drying mountain lakes in the Andes are the *present* for local people, but to people far away, they represent only a possible and *tentative future*. The researcher is often in a position of having either imagined or seen the possible future as an imminent reality, and then must convey or translate that to others for whom some other scenario occupies the overwhelming present and immediate future. A researcher of informatics in particular is always bridging present and future.

2 Structure

The paper has four major parts: (1) a discussion of researching the future; (2) applicable constructs; (3) thumbnails and rationales for a series of research projects; and (4) a discussion of where things went off track. All the projects together make the case. The case is a process of (1) becoming aware of questions in the environment; (2) efforts to answer those questions with research projects; (3) the sequence of new questions that arose with each project; (4) what happened to those results. The storyline loses momentum at the end because this is what happened to the research series even though the underlying need remains. We use Latour's (1999) *translation* construct in two ways: (1) faithful translation applied in science to get from an untransportable materiality into what counts as science results; (2) varying translations from the work into a corporate context as management changes occur.

The corporation needs the science work in order to move ahead with stated agendas, but can't always use it because of failures in the translation process. The motivation to develop a future ICT normally arises from a problem experienced in the present. The present is, therefore, the starting point for researching the future; however, it turns out that there are many different "presents" in play. Discrepancies in what constitutes the present are part of the problem of translation because of the gap in common perspective on what is futuristic and what is simply the next logical step. Researching the future becomes a sociology of knowledge; so we have also in mind if not in focus the work of Foucault (1972) and of Knorr-Cetina (1999).

3 The Case (A Set of Projects)

Zimmerman (1990) describes Heidegger's concern for the technological mindset where technology is seen as dominating, segmenting, and imposing instead of "uncovering." In this set of studies we adopted the latter, less deterministic process. We *uncovered* new problems in the search for answers to other questions. Unlike a conventional plan of research, we chose new methods opportunistically as questions (how virtual are we?), new facts or factants (most employees work on multiple teams), translation devices (demo), technical elements (an existing software solution), and methods (machine learning) emerged.

The goal of the projects was to provide better tools for collaboration, and to address discovered problems of multiple team memberships, multitasking and cognitive flow. The paper presents a summary of the research efforts and the emergent nature of discovery as each new finding gives rise to a new question. The collection of projects uses different methods over time to discover collaboration obstacles of a globally distributed workforce and potential software tools.

The actor–network construct and the notion of translations helps to explain the divergent outcomes of this research and related development efforts. It shows how research in a corporate environment differs from research in science because the translation mechanisms are damaged or under different pressures. Fidelity of translation is overtaken by other priorities.

The effort came from an IT organization because of IT's role in supplying workforce software tools. At the start of this work, the company had over 80,000 employees worldwide, functionally distributed with substantial proportions collaborating across the globe. This means that a single department had members in different parts of the globe and many of those members were on teams that regularly met periodically. Functional distribution is a strength in terms of creating communication channels and robust social networks across the company, but it poses a technological challenge to support information sharing and productive interaction.

Since we are looking at both the process of discovery and the issues of translation from an actor network perspective, below is an outline of the main actors.

- a core set of human actors interacting over time
- disciplinary backgrounds of the human actors

- agendas arising from the backgrounds
- agendas arising from success criteria for individuals
- software tools for discovery and for development into user interface designs
- other research methods such as survey, interview and machine tracking
- factants or things discovered in the research
- present and future capabilities of software tools
- attraction factors of research findings and software tools
- organizational agendas that supercede the individual human actors and constrain them
- variation over time in all of these

4 The Research Projects

In this section, we review the projects. Each project arose to answer one or more questions and some questions arose from previous results.

The first question was the generalizability of the work practices of a team organized to define the problems and recommend a solution to the virtual collaboration needs of the company. In his writings on theorizing, sociologist Alan Blum (1974) points out that theory arises from everyday experience, but takes this as *present-at-hand* and thus seeks to form an analysis. The group described below engaged in theorizing about the nature of globally distributed teams and their needs. It then became important to test the informal hypotheses that were recurrently expressed as assumptions in the conversation. The expression "we're so virtual" led to a question as to what proportion of employees actually collaborated in ways similar to the team members.

The method for this question was a demographic survey. The second question arose from the challenge of how to represent the implications of the survey results so that more senior management could grasp them. This led to a video mock-up of a proposed design and included a three-dimensional representation of the desktop with interlinked personal and team workspaces. The third question arose from a specific result of the survey, that two-thirds of the workforce were members of many teams (three to five and more). This led to a series of machine learning studies to understand how people managed the information flow from these teams.

The research questions did not come directly from management stakeholders. Senior management created umbrella agendas leading to self-directed work. In most cases, the questions became evident from observed gaps in knowledge. The projects were carried out with normal scholarly process, where the assumed eventual audience would be peers in the academic community. Validity was assumed adequate within the internal audience, and at times the results were widely used by others. At other times, finer points were lost, or the research could not be processed as relevant due to translation gaps.

4.1 The Virtual Collaboration Research Team

A cross-functional team was organized by two senior individual contributors. Members included a workplace anthropologist, a product planner, two engineers, a software trainer, a collaboration product manager, and an engineering manager. Membership was by invitation and voluntary. The topic had a high profile on a vision/mission roadmap for IT. The company had experienced a period of expanded overseas growth and was functionally distributed. This means that all of the *service organizations* (information technology, finance, human resources) were globally distributed; most of the core *product design teams* were organized by geographic specializations around the globe but had to periodically coordinate design sections; *manufacturing* is site-focused but shared best practices and expertise and is highly standardized methodologically; and *software development* is often sourced from offshore; *sales* is highly distributed and typically standalone by region. Each division has different proportions and periodicity of distributed collaboration, but all have it.

4.2 Virtuality Survey

As the VCRT talked about global team collaboration, members periodically exclaimed "we're so virtual!" meaning that the company operates extensively in a "virtual" collaboration mode. But who are "we" and what is "virtual"? What does "we're so virtual" mean? It meant different things to different people. It had many confounded constructs embedded in it. To provide definition, extent, and impact of the different elements of virtual collaboration, we took the starting point of theorizing about our own behavior and undertook a survey to see how much of the workforce had the same experience.

A literature review paper (Watson-Manheim et al. 2002) had identified five factors in common within the IS literature on the use of the term virtual to describe corporations. In consultation with the authors, we defined a survey that would measure a composite index of virtuality along the dimensions of discontinuities in time, geography, culture, business unit, and software tools. We added the discontinuity of multi-teaming because we noted that software products often contained assumptions of single team membership (Chudoba et al. 2005). This demographic survey was conducted using a stratified random sample of all employees in all job types and all geographies (Lu et al. 2003).These results provided a reliable measure of how virtual the company was and which dimensions made a difference. There was a high level of virtuality, with approximately two-thirds of employees being engaged in a virtual team and working across more than one of the discontinuities. The job profiles of people engaged in virtual teaming closely matched the job types within the company. Given these proportions, we could say that virtual teaming was a way of life and obstacles to it would be barriers to everyday productivity. (In a translation not discussed in the paper, the leap from these results to a finance-recognized metric did not materialize).

The survey included a measure of performance that could work across the wide array of job types and regions: the shared company values. These values represented common knowledge that could provide a reliable self-assessment of team performance. This metric held up well over the 7 years the survey was conducted in terms of consistency of response and ability to track a trend. We correlated the virtuality variables with the performance variables to determine the aggravating factors in virtual teaming. These turned out to be consistency of software tools, confirming that this was a problem within the scope of IT. Geography was a factor only when time separation was added, even though geography had been the most visible dimension of virtuality to decision makers. Within the United States, geographic location was neutral to team performance.

The survey thus disconfirmed the supposed negative effects of location along a North-South axis. East-West axis adds the dimension of time separation and a separate study was conducted on that (Cummings et al. 2009). Social variables like trust and friendship were the highest rated performance metrics for teams. This could be because virtual teaming was routine and made use of telephone bridges rather than conference rooms. This places everyone on an equally remote status. Incremental improvements in both internal and vendor supplied software over time smoothed out many hitches in coordination of meeting logistics. One likely organizational effect of virtual teaming was the tendency for people to participate in multiple (three to five) projects as location becomes a neutral factor.

The survey became an actor as the creator of *factants* that established the need for collaboration solutions and identified the types of need. It led to the development of a collaboration scenario that included multi-teaming as a core way of working and added the requirement for both separation of spaces on a display with coordination of content that might be shared across teams. That scenario was expressed in a mock-up that incorporated features of a technically sophisticated user interface that had been abandoned by the company product research labs before the IT collaboration effort began. The existence of this elegant technology became an actor and a pawn in the trajectory of events.

4.3 The Demo

The mock-up was an essential boundary object for translating the intentions the team developed into actions that could be taken by the organization. Many slide presentations were drafted and used for interim presentations; but without a visual display of what the solution would look like and act like, conversations with others elicited comparisons to standalone features of existing software tools. To the team members, those tools were incomplete because they lacked several things: the ability to address multiple team membership, location and cultural references for context, and the *integration* of core design features. Since key problems identified had been "too many tools" and "different tools," the solution of assembling yet another suite of off-the-shelf products was antithetical to providing coordination.

The mock-up performed the role of translation device. At the same time it introduced a new functional element: 3D. This technology had its own history; it became the platform for engaging new actors, securing new funding, and acquiring a higher level of visibility. While these developments at the time seemed highly positive, they eventually led the translation process off track. While the demo communicated well as a simple mock-up, once the more sophisticated technology of the 3D source metaphor became funded, some of its technical virtuosity distracted from the original intent. The narrative of the survey data became a backdrop to why the 3D solution was desirable and together these made a great story and presentation. If they had remained together as rationales, the translation process would have continued along a normal scientific path as Latour describes it.

4.4 3D User Interface for Information Management

Once 3D was introduced as the graphic metaphor for the mock-up, it became obvious that it also contained a solution to one of the key problems encountered in the survey: the fact that two-thirds of employees work on three to five teams at any given point in time. With 3D as the user interface, users could keep all of their teams in mind (termed "all my teams in one place") as they toggled back and forth. This would solve the problem of multiple open and minimized windows that by the 2000s made the virtual desktop no different than a physical desktop with piles of paper on it. The system that inspired the metaphor for the mock-up had the following history and properties.

In the late 1990s, a small group of lab researchers worked on software developments in sense-making. The goal was to break out of file structures to more intuitive ways of organizing and finding information and associated objects. The solution involved the development of a three-dimensional graphical space as the desktop context, whereby documents and other screen objects could be pushed to the "back," retaining their dimensions and appearance but becoming much smaller. The software was intended to incorporate object properties and drag-and-drop links between visual objects (documents, programs, and people) that would then retain their associations. Since it did not depend on file hierarchy, any object could be related to as many other objects as necessary. The purpose was to create a contextual order that was independent of file structure and more naturally followed human associative reasoning. This group was disbanded in 2001 during a reorganization and the software development discontinued. Some of the work that had gone into navigation, zooming, snap-in-place, and 3D rendering and linking was truly pioneering and remains technically impressive (Light and Miller 2002).

This software informed the mock-up that was presented to IT staff at a strategic long range planning meeting. The sponsor who was present at the meeting told the team that the demo had "moved the cause of collaboration ahead by five years in the space of five minutes." There was a great deal of expressed excitement; a lab and group were funded to pursue this and other advanced collaboration solutions including video conferencing. The group had about 10 members, significant for an exploratory group in IT. The group hired one of the original 3D developers and a number of application scenarios were populated to illustrate how this solution would work in different parts of the company. This went along well for a few years until a company-wide reorganization affected the entire department.

4.5 Multi-teaming and Multitasking

Consistent with the thesis that each new discovery leads to another question, we took the opportunity to work with faculty and students in the Department of Electrical Engineering and Computer Science at Oregon State University to try to understand the effects of multi-teaming and multitasking using two software programs developed at the Center for Machine Learning.

What the 3D software lacked at the time it was originally developed was a compelling usage scenario, which we might call another actor in the system. Although it looked good and the developers passionately believed it solved a problem of information management, no such problem had been credibly documented, either for the individual user or for sets of users working on multiple teams. The virtuality survey *uncovered* the structural situation that provided a strong rationale for the use of 3D. Although any given person might be aware of having to work across multiple teams, heretofore nobody had any notion of the extent of this company-wide. Even once it was known it was difficult to say exactly why it was a problem. Eventually the machine learning study revealed the kind of hyperactivity that this widespread and even organizationally functional behavior produced, and uncovered further problems hidden in everyday behavior.

Here several actors/agendas converged: the findings from the survey, the availability of the machine learning project, the ability to fund external research, and the 3D desktop design. The fact that the design was a technical artifact gave it added influence. It helped significantly that it was visually engrossing.

The Oregon State University projects used two different machine learning programs to instrument people's desktops for extended periods. No content was recorded for reasons of information security and end-user privacy. The software tracked a range of activities within the primary office application suite. Between the two programs, the software tracked window and applications switches, interruptions, and operations like cut/paste, file save/save-as, attach, open, etc. (Jensen et al. 2010).

The original pilot with TaskTracer (Stumpf et al. 2009) was meant to create project-based context retention by labeling and then storing together related documents so that they would all be visibly associated and therefore linked together regardless of file structure. This would address one of the issues revealed in the survey: if you are working on multiple teams using various collaboration software programs, how do you track what you are doing with each team? The file hierarchy is not quite adequate since many documents can be used across teams. With a traditional file hierarchy and even with shared storage, a version control problem immediately presents itself.

The first machine learning program, TaskTracer, required human mediation in order to "learn" meaningful associations. Results showed how much window and task-switching was going on, but users quickly tired of trying to train the program. The practical goal of associating content was not realized. There were already so many categories to sort into and so much new information arriving hourly, mostly via e-mail, containing project content (Bellotti et al. 2003) that it became overwhelming to establish the basic sorting framework for the program.

The hyperactivity traced with the program (window switches more than once a minute, 90 percent of file searches repeated in a session, etc.) arises from a scenario like a user participating in a phone bridge, concurrently looking at a document on a shared screen, answering e-mails, looking up information to answer the e-mails, and looking up other information pertinent to the meeting—all in the course of a half-hour. These behaviors are part of the pressures of work and the capability of instant information access and response. It becomes central to a real-time multi-tasking life-world that is efficient in many ways even while it has high cognitive costs.

4.6 Cross-Application Information Flow and Provenance

We funded the research to understand what users were doing on the client. Switching can be a benefit. The windows capability replaced modal computing in the 1980s and was considered an advantage (Tesler 1981). But the amount of switching driven by new models of work without the underlying software model keeping up has become frenetic. A new concept of information management is therefore critical. Because TaskTracer had a high adoption hurdle even as an experiment, we continued with a passive software program, TaskTrail, that solved a different problem, did not require user intervention, and applied pattern-matching after the fact rather than in real time.

TaskTrail tracked operations like opening and closing windows, switching windows, copy/paste, file save/save-as, file attach, and more to find out where information comes from. The work falls into the domain of provenance studies and was the largest such study to date. More than 20 users were tracked over a 2-month period, with initial and halfway interviews to provide the context of practice: "what were you trying to do?" The program, again recording no content, ran in the background. Computer Science/HCI graduate students at Oregon State University performed *post hoc* analysis. These data revealed patterns of information flow on the desktop and highlighted a user focus on *information* as contrasted with a vendor and IT emphasis on *applications*. The results show a long information half-life and heavy reuse patterns as users recontextualize and refine information objects available from various sources.

Significant percentages of information on a given user's desktop were copied from one document and/or application to another. This showed users create original documents by reusing large amounts of information from themselves and from others. They continually recontextualize information they have saved on the client, received in an attachment, or downloaded from a shared file or the Internet. These findings strongly support the *informatization* construct (Zuboff 1984). Each person recreates information relevance in light of a new context. But they are doing this through a maze of operations inconsistent with the model of use. We contend that software tools can make it much easier to coordinate and manage information through the visual interface.

5   Outcomes

The findings of the machine learning studies created more urgency for the use of the 3D environment to manage information, even as the latter motivated the machine learning studies. Supporting external research on hedonic and flow concepts (Reeves and Nass 2002) was brought in to justify 3D. Managers had resisted the notion that work should be like play, but the work on heart rate in first-person shooter videogames and on the effect of visual imagery on neurological flow states (Csikszentmihalyi 1997) were factants that became part of the internal marketing message for the 3D program. Although these findings were consistent with the trajectory of translations, they also led to a divergent path.

The research results could have had an impact on how IT influenced major vendors of office software. But new translation problems arose. The obviousness of the finding that people are focused on information, while vendors focus on applications, was not obvious to the engineering managers who implement new tools. Further, the research findings were overwhelmed by the sudden currency of the hedonic constructs: "work as play" and 3D visualization. Previously rejected in IT, these notions were reintroduced from another quarter at a higher level. The machine learning project ought to have supported an agenda of maximizing cognitive flow, which is the same neurological state for both productive and hedonic purposes. 3D is one way of doing that in the context of multi-teaming and the software was deemed technically first class.

But its technical brilliance and visual appeal gave the 3D piece of the network a life of its own. There had been a circularity of reinforcement. Once the virtuality survey findings justified the 3D user interface, that interface then justified further study of problems on the desktop arising from multi-teaming. This led the research trajectory back in the direction of the original intent of the 3D software effort from the 1990s, even though for a while the software was merely an accessory to illustrate some intentions about collaboration. Having the software and an original developer gave momentum to the 3D effort (along with the lab funding). Then it created a compelling reason to understand more about user behavior than could be provided in the survey or, for that matter, by any other means. This led to the machine learning work and could have led to new information management models.

Instead, shorter-term agendas requiring less faithful translation arose. A senior executive urgently needed materials for a keynote speech on the topic of "play." The 3D UI and its arguments were ready for that. Then the adrenaline of being on a senior management radar narrowed down the scope of participants and voices. Points that distract from the focus of an executive presentation, while essential, may seem like clutter. Once the senior manager was engaged, other managers were encouraged to push the play agenda farther. The 3D UI was now sufficiently developed to launch a joint venture with a company that was creating a virtual collaboration environment in the image of a game.

At this point, translation in Latour's sense became completely lost in other agendas and we switch over to a Foucauldian scenario. Play turned into "game" and game turned into "virtual environment with avatars and realistic rooms." The intellectual underpinnings of the agenda lost out to the shiny parts. In the end, the keynote was short-lived and did not lead to funding; a joint development project with another large company to use this software in an ambitious way fell apart due to decisions at their end; the third-party venture with the small company eventually fizzled (for lack of a compelling usage model). After large-scale organizational changes, the remaining core developer has seen the tide go out on an innovative idea for a second time and is seeking new funding.

It can always come back again once the future catches up to the past. There are organizational data, a usage model based on those data, constructs of cognitive flow, and task switching that have been measured. The research flow still adds up. And the world still needs this solution. All of this, both research and development, and the inspiration that guided them, became enmeshed in other agendas.

6 Analysis: The Translations and Trajectories

A network is both contemporary and historical. There were networks interacting across all of the projects discussed here to greater and lesser degrees. At any point in time, one or another actor had motivations and rewards in carrying the projects forward. Without a historically extended network, there never would have been a cohesive vision since there were temporal gaps in execution. Each person had different skills and levels of investment in the concepts and prototypes. One person was an original developer on the team that created the Labs version. Another focused on collaboration design options, workforce distribution data, and had a spatial (next cube) connection to a different original 3D developer. A third person was contracted to do a visual scheme for a concept presentation and remembered working on the 3D application. Others became persuaded of the 3D option. The availability of the machine learning research agenda led to supporting evidence that no survey or ethnographic method could have captured. The cognitive research on flow supported the general direction and created a back argument against the notion that work and play are two different things. Many translation processes here added up in a reasonable way. The agenda that cross cuts the translation is the need and urge to move the work up to a higher level of visibility and sponsorship. It is a need but it translates differently. The translation became as follows:

Questions about collaboration and the generalizability of team experience led to virtual team demographics. This led to the discovery of approximately two-thirds virtual teaming and the newly identified phenomenon of multi-teaming, which in turn identified shortcomings in software offerings. (Team repositories were created as standalone entities. If a user was on several teams, related documents had to be separately uploaded and version control was lost). This led to the need to translate into a compelling management message to gain funding, which took the form of the demo. The demo borrowed the 3D concept from an earlier abandoned project. The 3D software brought its own question: Just how bad is the information management problem? This gave rise to the machine learning projects. These had two roles, one of them just to understand information management on the desktop and the other to validate a compelling need for 3D as a solution. These things all had a logical sequence, even with the inclusion of the translation for management in the form of the demo.

The departure from translation came from the dynamics of a second round of translation for management. That first translation brought funding but no intervention. The second translation failed to carry along research justifications that went into the forward momentum of the whole effort. It turned 3D into show material and eventually lost its scientific and technological force.

In the rush of opportunity that surrounded the 3D development project as a potential commercial product, the chain of translation that Latour describes as working well in science through the care of human actors broke down. The most compelling representation can easily win out over the most faithful or most useful. The emphasis of the 3D desktop had shifted gradually away from information management: first to the service of a high quality public demo, and then to the allure of a product possibility involving a meeting space with sophisticated graphics. Because at each phase some of the actors and agendas changed, the information management concept dropped out of sight, even as the need for it was further emphasized by the machine learning research. Advocates for the information management usage model either were no longer in the conversation or were kept busy by technical challenges of navigation and visualization in the 3D space.

Instead of visual content management there were visual representations of spatial and physical objects that had game-like realism. Instead of an interface that provides a simplified window into something highly complex, the momentum went into something that was simple but fancy-looking.

7 Summary

This case shows how the future had to be understood by making the present *present-at-hand*. This happened through a series of steps, each informed by the previous one, with new elements coming in opportunely. Research into the implications of the multi-teaming phenomenon revealed in the survey confirmed that this behavior introduces an information management and design challenge. A solution was readily available in the form of an abandoned software project that merited revival. However, due to the lack of translation and the power of certain inscriptions, the whole package of rationales failed to progress together.

The research remains as a finding about a possible future. This could serve as guidance for those who do science for any large institution. It is easy to be caught up in the seemingly intrinsic merits of an approach and findings, and to be unaware of power agendas and the need for two kinds of translation. One is translating not just through stages of science but up through a power hierarchy. Latour's philosophical resources provided the counterpoint of what makes science a method as a human process of faithful translation. The notion of translation, therefore, is precisely that element that can become lost when science is done for other audiences and with other actors. Much credit goes to Latour for his deep vision of anthropology and its capability as the science that pulls together the artificially sundered threads of past–present–future, science–nature–politics, and narrative.

References

Bellotti, V., Ducheneault, N., Howard, M., Smith, I.: Taking Email to Task: The Design and Evaluation of an Email Centered Task Tool. In: Proceedings of the SIGCHI Conference. ACM Press, New York (2003)

Blum, A.F.: Theorizing: On the Beginning of Social Inquiry. Routledge and Kegan Paul, London (1974)

Chudoba, K., Wynn, E., Lu, M., Watson-Manheim, M.B.: How Virtual Are We? Measuring Virtuality in a Global Organization. Information Systems J. 15(4), 279–306 (2005)

Csikszentmihalyi, M.: Flow and the Psychology of Discovery and Invention. Harper Perennial, New York (1997)

Cummings, J.M., Espinosa, J.A., Pickering, C.: Crossing Spatial and Temporal Boundaries in Globally Distributed Projects: A Relational Model of Coordination Delay. Information Systems Research 20(3), 420–439 (2009)

Dreyfus, H.L.: What Computers Can't Do: The Limits of Artificial Intelligence. Harper & Row, New York (1978)

Escobar, A.: Encountering Development: The Making and Unmaking of the Third World. Princeton University Press, Princeton (1995)

Foucault, M.: The Archaeology of Knowledge and the Discourse on Language. Tavistock Publications, London (1972)

Hammer, M., Champy, J.: Reengineering the Corporation. Harper Collins, New York (2001)

Jensen, C., Lonsdale, H., Wynn, E.: The Life and Times of Files and Information: A Study of Desktop Provenance. In: Proceedings of Computer-Human Interaction: 28th ACM Conference on Human Factors in Computing Systems. ACM Press, New York (2010)

Knorr-Cetina, K.: Epistemic Cultures: How the Sciences Make Knowledge. Harvard University Press, Cambridge (1999)

Latour, B.: We Have Never Been Modern. Harvard University Press, Cambridge (1993)

Latour, B.: Pandora's Hope: Essays on the Reality of Science Studies. Harvard University Press, Cambridge (1999)

Light, J., Miller, J.D.: Miramar: A 3D Workplace. In: Proceedings of IPCC, IEEE Professional Communication Conference (2002)

Lu, M., Wynn, E., Chudoba, K., Watson-Manheim, M.B.: Understanding Virtuality in a Global Organization: Toward a Virtuality Index. In: Proceedings of the International Conference on Information Systems (2003)

Reeves, B., Nass, C.: The Media Equation: How People Treat Computers, Television and New Media Like Real People and Places. University of Chicago Press, Chicago (2002)

Stumpf, S., Rajaram, V., Li, L., Burnett, B., Wong, W.-K., Dietterich, T., Sullivan, E., Drummond, R., Herlocker, J.: Interacting Meaningfully with Machine Learning Systems: Three Experiments. International J. of Human-Computer Studies 67(8), 639–662 (2009)

Tesler, L.: The Smalltalk Environment. Byte 6(8), 90–147 (1981)

Watson-Manheim, M.B., Crowston, K., Chudoba, K.M.: A New Perspective on Virtual: Analyzing Discontinuities in Work Environments: In: Proceedings of HICSS (2002)

Zimmerman, M.E.: Heidegger's Confrontation with Modernity: Technology, Politics, and Art. Indiana Series in the Philosophy of Technology, Bloomington (1990)

Zuboff, S.: In the Age of the Smart Machine: The Future of Work and Power. Basic Books, New York (1984)

About the Author

Eleanor Wynn holds a Ph.D. in Linguistic Anthropology from the University of California at Berkeley. Her dissertation research at Xerox Palo Alto Research Center was the first anthropological study of office work in the computer era, using conversation analysis to show cognitive and social processes embedded in group knowledge. She has worked as a researcher senior scientist at Xerox and Bell-Northern and as a Principal Engineer at Intel Corporation, as well as consulting on workforce information system requirements to other large companies. Her academic work includes visiting teaching engagements, scholarly publications, and service as conference chair. Dr. Wynn's current research interest is in organizations as complex systems and the application of complexity modeling methods to enterprise processes at all scales.

Section 2. Critical View of the Future

What Does the Future Hold? A Critical View of Emerging Information and Communication Technologies and Their Social Consequences

Bernd Carsten Stahl

Centre for Computing and Social Responsibility, Department of Informatics,
De Montfort University, Leicester, UK
bstahl@dmu.ac.uk

Abstract. This paper provides an overview of emerging information and communication technologies (ICTs) that can be expected to become socially relevant in the next 10 to 15 years. It describes the results of a dual discourse analysis of publiccations on emerging ICTs. Sources were, on the one hand, government/policy publications and, on the other, publications by research institutions. This discourse analysis led to the identification of 11 emerging ICTs. For each of these ICTs, defining features were collected. In order to gain a larger scale understanding, the defining features were then regrouped to assess which likely effect they might have on the relationship between humans and their environment. These features are then interpreted and investigated with regard to what they betray about the implied assumptions about individuals, society and technology. The paper ends by critically reflecting the chosen approach and asking how this research can help us develop technology in desirable ways.

Keywords: Emerging ICT, methodology, social consequences.

1 Introduction

Narratives of changes in the way we live based on information and communication technologies (ICTs) abound. One can frequently hear references to an information "revolution," which would seem to imply that such technologies fundamentally change the way we live (Floridi 2007). The revolution metaphor is taken up and intensified by commercial interests, which emphasize the significance of changes of consumer products. This view of ICT as revolutionary is linked to a wide-spread perception of an increase in the speed of life. Personal lives become more variable in some respects but also more constrained as more choices are offered and communication is increased.

The present paper takes these perceptions as a backdrop and asks what the future of ICTs may be. Are there ways of gaining a better understanding of emerging ICTs and, if so, can we paint a picture of the future of such technologies that gives an indication of what consequences these emerging technologies have for our lives?

M. Chiasson et al. (Eds.): Future IS 2011, IFIP AICT 356, pp. 59–76, 2011.

This paper justifies, describes, and critically interprets some tentative answers to the question of what information technologies are likely to emerge. Based on the European research project ETICA (Ethical Issues of Emerging ICT Applications), the paper describes one possible way of identifying emerging ICTs and explains the methodology used to implement it. It then outlines the findings and briefly characterizes those technologies that were identified as probable and reasonable candidates to emerge in the next decade or so. The paper constitutes one of the outputs of the ETICA project, which aims to identify emerging ICTs and their ethical aspects in order to develop recommendations on how best to address them. The paper only touches on the initial outcomes of the ETICA project, namely on the identification of ICTs and their implications.

On the basis of this characterization of individual ICTs, the paper then provides a synthesis of the overall technical environment that would arise from these technologies. In the conclusion, the paper will return to the opening paragraph and speculate on societal trends that may arise from the possible future described here.

The main contribution of the paper is that it offers an overview of the ICT landscape that we have reason to expect to emerge in the next 10 to 15 years. The paper goes beyond the more frequent approach of describing and analyzing individual technologies or problem areas. It attempts to draw a larger picture and explore the characteristics of technology-enabled societies in the medium term future. Such an endeavor is by nature and necessity fallible and unlikely to provide an exact prediction of the future. It is nevertheless important because it draws a picture of the way we currently imagine the future, which is important if we now want to make the right decisions, both in terms of technology and policy development, to lead to the society in which we collectively wish to live.

2 Emerging ICTs

It may be too obvious to state, but in order to avoid misunderstandings, it may be necessary to underline that we do not know the future. The future is fundamentally characterized by being unknown and unknowable. But, of course, things do not stop there. Humans' desire to know the future is probably as old as humanity. In addition, there are reasons to believe that some aspects of the future are predictable and, in fact,

Table 1. Research-Related Problems Encountered in Describing Emerging ICTs

Problem	Description
Conceptual Issues	Lack of clarity of all constituent terms, for instance, • Emergence • Information • Technology
Approach and Methodology Scientific justification of the methodology used to identify emerging ICTs	• Uncertainty of the future • Purpose of investigations of futures studies • Sources of knowledge about the future • Justification of chosen sources over others

much of the organization of societies is based on this predictability of the future. Commercial and administrative activities rely on recurrence of activities, usually rightly so. To some degree this predictability extends to technologies.

Research on emerging ICTs has to contend with numerous problems. Table 1 summarizes the core problems that were encountered in this paper.

It is not the purpose of this paper to go into much depth in these problems, which are described in more depth elsewhere (Stahl et al. 2010). It will be necessary, however, to briefly outline how they were addressed in order to render the subsequent description of technologies comprehensible.

2.1 Conceptual Issues

Each of the constituent terms of *emerging information and communication technology* is worthy of detailed analysis in its own right. The term *emergence*, for example, has a long history in philosophy and can be found in a number of other disciplines. Very briefly, it can be understood as a counterpoint to linear and predictable developments. Emergent phenomena are not easily predictable but develop from the interaction of components of a system. Given this position, it is almost a contradiction in terms to do research to determine emerging technologies. They defy easy recognition by definition. There are, however, differences in certainty of knowledge about emerging issues that are related to the temporal horizon in which they are investigated. For the purposes of the present paper, *emerging technologies* are defined as those technologies that have the potential to gain social relevance within the next 10 to 15 years. This means that they are currently at an early stage of their development process. At the same time, they have already moved beyond the purely conceptual stage. This will become obvious later during the introduction of the technologies that were identified, most of which already have social presence, are to some degree already established. Despite this, these emerging technologies are not yet clearly defined. Their exact forms, capabilities, constraints, and uses are still in flux.

A similar conceptual problem is raised by the term *technology*. This paper cannot engage in any depth with the philosophy of technology (Dusek 2006; Olsen et al. 2009). Characteristics of technology that one can typically find include a basis in structured thought, temporal stability, and reproducibility, and a reflection in artefacts which may be (but do not have to be) of a physical nature. Technologies are typically developed for specific ends.

An important issue related to the concept of technology is the question of interpretive flexibility. Interpretive flexibility denotes the property of technology of being constituted by use. It is a position that is opposed to technological determinism, which holds that technology has an observer-independent reality and will have clear and predetermined uses and applications. Proponents of interpretive flexibility argue that technology is not fixed but will develop during perception and use. The tenets of interpretive flexibility are widely recognized in science and technology studies where different positions such as the social study of technology (SST) or the social construction of technology hold such views (Bijker 1997; Grint and Woolgar 1997; Howcroft et al. 2004) and also in related fields such as actor–network theory (Latour 2007; Law and Hassard 1999). Some scholars distinguish between interpretive and interpretative flexibility, with the former referring to the epistemological aspect of the social construction of technology and the latter being a stronger position that sees the construction as ontologically constitutive of technology (Cadili and Whitley 2005).

There is a direct link between emergence and interpretive flexibility. Interpretive flexibility is a function of social interaction and pertains to particular discourses. That means that a technology may emerge in one context even though it may well be established elsewhere. It also means that the same underlying artefact can emerge into different technologies in terms of usage and application. Interpretive flexibility is connected to the social meaning of a technology, which requires researchers to avoid the technical determinist position and to consider the political and social framing of technological meaning.

For the purposes of the present paper, the term *technology* was defined as being on a high and abstract level. A technology in this sense of the word is a high-level system that affects the way humans interact with the world. This means that one technology in most cases can comprise numerous artefacts and be applied in many different situations. It needs to be associated with a vision that embodies specific views of humans and their role in the world.

An example may help explain this. One core technology that has been widely described and researched is that of ambient intelligence (AmI). AmI is characterized by a number of defining features such as embeddedness, interconnectedness, invisibility, adaptivity, and personalization, among others. This technology implies a view of the world in which humans require and desire support, are seamlessly connected, and have an adaptive environment. To realise this vision, numerous artefacts such as sensors, networks, and algorithms can be used. The technology does not depend on any one of these to become reality.

The final conceptual issue to be touched upon is that of the delimitation of information and communication technologies. There is no clear and unambiguous definition of ICT. The terms *information* and *communication* are as complex as *technology*. Concentrating on ICT does rule out a substantial number of potential technologies, but it leaves a large number. In addition, one can observe initiatives to realize the convergence of ICT with other technologies, notably biotechnology, nanotechnology, and cognitive technologies (also called NBIC technologies)[1].

2.2 Approach: Principles of Technology Foresight

Knowing the meaning of emerging ICTs does not imply a particular way of finding out which technologies fall under the concept. This raises the question of whether it is possible to find methodologies that are capable of providing information about emerging ICTs. This, in turn, raises the question of which truth claims are to be associated with research on such technologies.

It was already stated that no absolute truth claims about the future are possible. But what can be the purpose of future-related research? One way of answering this question is to move away from the idea of one determined future to a multiplicity of possible futures. Cuhls (2003) uses the term *foresight* instead of *forecasting* in order to

---

[1] The 2009 conference of the Society for Technology and Philosophy was dedicated to the topic of these converging technologies (see http://www.utwente.nl/ceptes/spt2009/).

underline the difference between one-dimensional and multidimensional views of the future. The present paper can be understood as foresight research in this sense. What is the purpose of foresight research? What can it achieve? A main purpose of this type of research is to explore possible futures with a view to identifying and selecting desirable ones that can then be pursued. This selection is then investigated with regard to its implications for today. As a final step, decisions can be made today that influence the outcome of the future options. The aim of foresight activities is not to describe one true future but some or all of the following (Cuhls 2003):

- To enlarge the choice of opportunities, to set priorities, and to assess impacts and chances
- To prospect for the impacts of current research and technology policy
- To ascertain new needs, new demands, and new possibilities as well as new ideas
- To focus selectively on economic, technological, social, and ecological areas as well as to start monitoring and detailed research in these fields
- To define desirable and undesirable futures
- To start and stimulate continuous discussion processes

These aims underpin the present research. The subsequent outline of the chosen methodology as well as the discussion of findings and extrapolation of emerging ICTs should be interpreted in this light.

2.3 Methodology, Data Collection, and Analysis

In light of the general justification of the approach, the steering committee of the project decided that the most useful way to determine emerging ICTs was to analyze discourses that could claim to have good insight or influence on the way emerging ICTs are being shaped. The steering committee is the main body for making day-today decisions in the project. It consists of the leader of each of the work packages involved in the project. All of the work described in this paper was undertaken by different members of the consortium. Nations involved include Finland, The Netherlands, the United Kingdom, Belgium, Germany, Hungary, Sweden, and Poland. The composition of the consortium was chosen to fairly represent most areas of the European Union. In terms of subject expertise, the individuals working on the project included philosophers, social scientists, and technologists.

In order to gain a comprehensive coverage of the current understanding of emerging ICTs, two discourses were explored: governmental and policy discourses, in particular those discourses relating to funding plans were included because they substantially shape the agenda of researchers by providing incentives. Documents representing such discourses include national research funding strategies, and funding council publications or the EU calls for proposals under the EU's 7th Framework Programme. The other discourse analyzed was constituted by research institutions' publications. The rationale here was that research institutions are closest to the actual research currently going on, and that they have the best insight into the nature of technologies currently under investigation and thus are best placed to estimate the future of these technologies.

In a first step, a pilot exercise was undertaken in which all members of the steering committee attempted to identify the description of emerging technologies in three different documents. A meeting was then held to compare the findings. During this meeting, it became clear that a consistent analysis strategy was needed to ensure the reproducibility of the data.

In order to allow a consistent analysis of these two discourses, an analytical grid (see Figure 1) was developed in a bottom-up way. This structure emerged from the initial attempts to identify emerging ICTs from documents and was shown to be useful in standardizing the collection of data. It is important to understand that the analytical grid is not theory-led but emerged inductively from the data. The rules of analysis were not defined *a priori* but emerged from the engagement with texts and were then collectively inscribed in the analytical grid and its subsequent implementation in a database.

This structure distinguishes between three main types of entities to be identified and categorized:

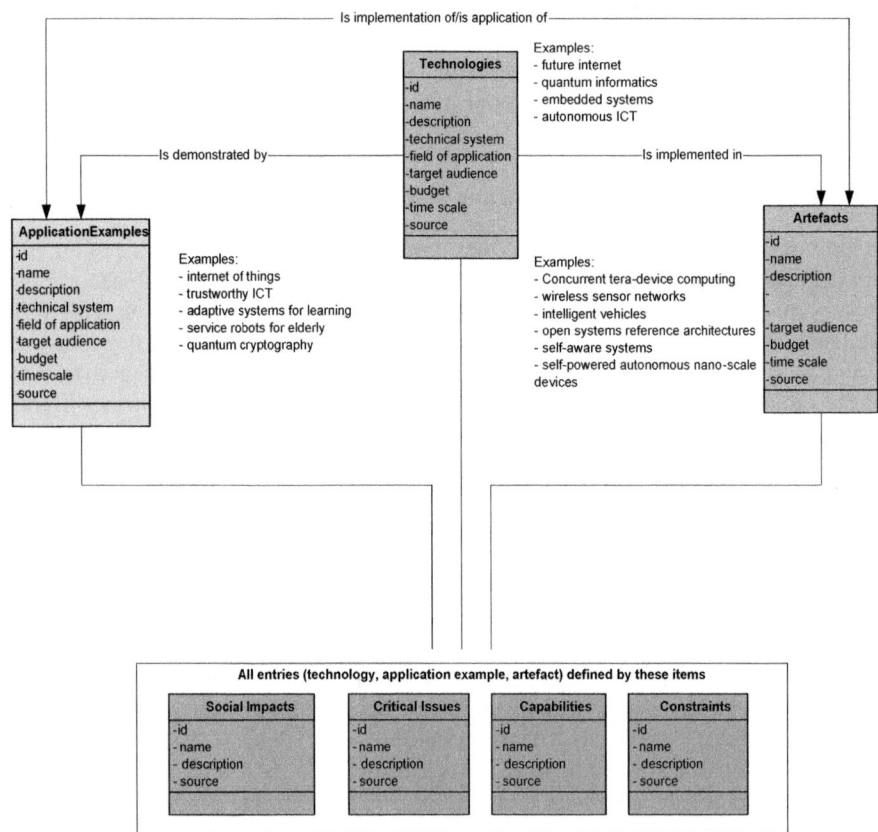

Fig. 1. Analytical Grid for Discourse Analysis

1. Technologies (most general, high-level category)
2. Application examples (the use of technologies in particular contexts)
3. Artefacts (the implementation of the technologies)

The distinction between these three types of entities allowed a concentration on the technologies themselves since these are the main focus of the data analysis. At the same time, it permitted room for the investigation of particular examples, which helped in understanding the nature of the technology, as well as the affordances or issues linked to particular implementations of actual artefacts.

Due to the geographically dispersed nature of the consortium, the steering committee decided to develop a web-based online database to collect data, compare findings, and synthesize the findings. This database was a bespoke database developed on the basis of the analytical grid. It allowed users to input new technologies and categories.

The analyzed documents varied greatly in style, purpose, length, detail, and other aspects. An important problem was, therefore, to ensure consistency and reproducebility of the findings. In order to avoid the injection of bias into the data analysis, it was decided to cross-validate the data analysis. For this purpose, each team member analyzed three different texts. This analysis was then reviewed by and discussed with other team members. The results of these discussions were again captured in a wiki.

It turned out that some of the foreseen problems occurred: there was a lack of agreement on what exactly should count as a technology, application example, or artefact. In addition, analysis by different individuals was done with differing levels of granularity and detail.

Despite these differences in detail, the project team found that the main items and issues were identified in similar ways by different analyzers. Given that it was expected that the data analysis would include a large amount of redundancy (identical technologies being discussed by a number of documents) and that further steps in the project would evaluate and contextualize findings, it was decided that the approach was sufficiently robust to provide the results expected, namely an identification of technologies as viewed by discourses on emerging ICTs.

3 A View of Emerging ICTs

The consortium identified 27 different documents worth analyzing. The criteria for identifying and including documents were that they had to belong to one of the discourses of interest to the research, they had to clearly discuss emerging ICTs, this discussion had to be sufficiently detailed to allow the collection of relevant detail about the technology, and they had to be accessible to the consortium. Data collection was stopped when theoretical saturation was reached (i.e., when no more new items were identified).

The analysis of the texts led to the identification of 107 technologies and 70 applications. A more detailed look at the lists revealed that there was considerable overlap. In addition, there were items on the artefacts list that were not covered elsewhere.

It was, therefore, decided to group the technologies, applications, and artefacts in a way that would correspond with the earlier definition of technology as a high-level and abstract concept that is sensitive to the way humans interact with the world. The aim was to identify those technologies that are at a high level of abstractness and that would cover the applications, artefacts, and contributing technologies.

The initial list of 107 technologies was regrouped, ordered, and categorized to allow the most important high-level technologies to remain, whereas component technologies were subsumed into these high-level technologies. This left a list of about 20 technologies. Several rounds of discussion among project team members and consultation with external experts followed. These external experts were individuals who were knowledgeable in the individual technologies listed in Table 2. They were not members of the consortium and did not receive any remuneration for their involvement. Their main task was to critically review the descriptions of the technologies in order to ensure that these descriptions did not contain factual inaccuracies. During discussions within the consortium and with the external experts, further technologies were eliminated because they were perceived to be applications rather than technologies, did not offer an insight in the underlying vision of the relationship of humans and the world, or because they fell outside the ICT remit of the study. The end result of this process is the list of technologies presented in Table 2.

Table 2. List of Emerging ICTs

Affective Computing
Ambient Intelligence
Artificial Intelligence
Bioelectronics
Cloud Computing
Future Internet
Human–Machine Symbiosis
Neuroelectronics
Quantum Computing
Robotics
Virtual/Augmented Reality

It is important to recapitulate what this list of emerging ICTs represents. It is the result of an analysis of two interlinked discourses on emerging technologies. The claim here is that these are reasonable and robustly determined candidates of ICTs that are likely to have significantly increasing social impact in the next 10 to 15 years. They are thus a good guess of what the future holds in stock and they serve the purpose of reflecting on which futures they will facilitate and which consequences this might represent now.

4 Features and Consequences of Emerging ICTs

Having developed a list of emerging technologies, the next challenge was to understand more clearly what these technologies entailed. The project team, therefore, set out to determine their core features. These are the features that have a potential to influence the relationship between humans and the world, that can change individual lives or social arrangements. In order to find out what these main features are, the project team went back to the database containing the data analysis and extracted the entries pertaining to the respective technologies. This data was used as a starting point to write a short document characterizing each technology. In order to keep an open mind and avoid initial bias coming from particular interests related to the technology, the technology descriptions were developed from a set of application examples. Where these could be found in the database they were used. Other sources were also perused. These application examples were then used to synthesize definitions and defining features. In addition, broader research literature was then used to supplement these descriptions. The descriptions were completed by outlining related technologies and social consequences. After an internal review, these documents were then sent out to external experts in the particular field of technology to ensure that no substantial mistakes or oversights remained.

The structure of each technology description was thus as follows:

- History of the technology and concepts
- Approximately five application examples
- Defining features of the technology
- Critical issues (i.e., ethical/legal questions, capabilities, and constraints)

The individual technology descriptions are available on the project website at www.etica-project.eu. The purpose of this paper is not to discuss individual technologies or engage in the question of whether the list presented in Table 2 is complete (very unlikely) or still contains redundancies (very likely). Instead, the purpose of this paper is to investigate whether there is a larger picture that can be gleaned from the sum of the technologies. For the purpose of the present paper, it was necessary to find a way to render these descriptions accessible. To achieve this, the defining features of all technologies were collected into a single mind map. Each technology was a node with all defining features being assigned a sub-node. The full text descriptions of the defining features were saved in these nodes, so that the researchers could easily access them but so that they did not show in the main mind map.

As an example, the node of affective computing is presented in Figure 2. Clicking on the notepad icon would reveal the full text description of the technology in question. For the first point, for example, this would read

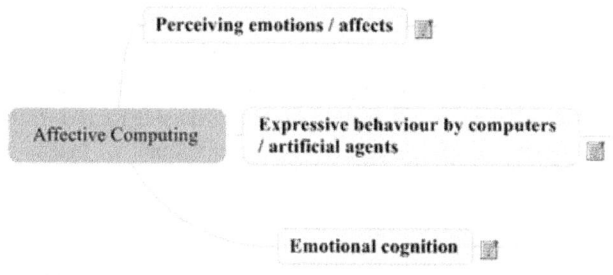

Fig. 2. Mind Map of "Affective Computing"

Perceiving emotions/affects (i.e., sensing of physiological correlates of affect). The principle here is that humans send signals that allow others to infer the agent's emotional state. Such emotional cues may be with the agent's control, such as tone of voice, posture, or facial expression. They may also be outside the agent's control as in the case of facial color (blushing), heart rate, or breathing. Humans are normally aware of such emotional cues and react easily to them. Most current technology does not react to such emotional cues even though they are part of the illocutionary and perlocutionary function of a speech act.

This was done for all technologies, producing the mind map shown in Figure 3.

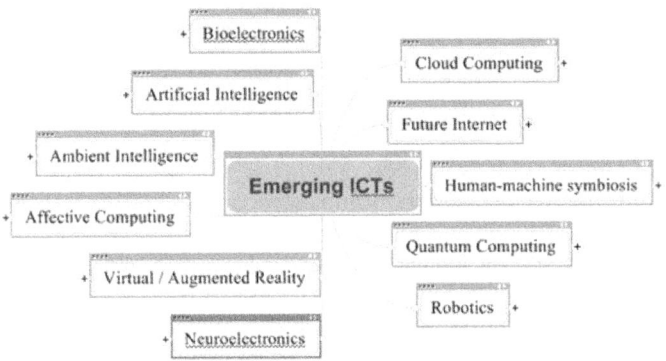

Fig. 3. Mind Map of Emerging ICTs

Expanding to show the defining features of all emerging ICTs results in the map shown in Figure 4.

This overview was then used to regroup the defining features from individual technologies to the more general social consequences or shared assumptions about humans and society they portrayed. The aim of this type of data analysis was to provide an insight into shared, predictable consequences of these different technologies, which would allow for a broader description of how a future society modeled on or involving these technologies would look.

To preempt predictable but unnecessary criticism, we need to state that we are aware of the possible down-sides of this approach. It uncritically accepts descriptions and features of technologies that are still under development. It abstracts from real uses and environments without considering the possible role of human agency, be it in strengthening, changing, or resisting the different technologies and their consequences. Furthermore, it regroups features without deeper regard to the nature of the different technologies, which may lead to combinations of technologies that will never occur.

It is, therefore, important to reiterate what this categorization is meant to represent, namely a view of current discourses on emerging technologies. These discourses are important in that they shape perceptions but also infrastructures and funding that will be used to promote the futures implied in them. Figure 5 should be understood as an attempt to graphically represent dominant discourses. Doing so helps us understand the content of expected technologies as well as their implications, which, in turn, is a condition of engaging in any attempt to change them.

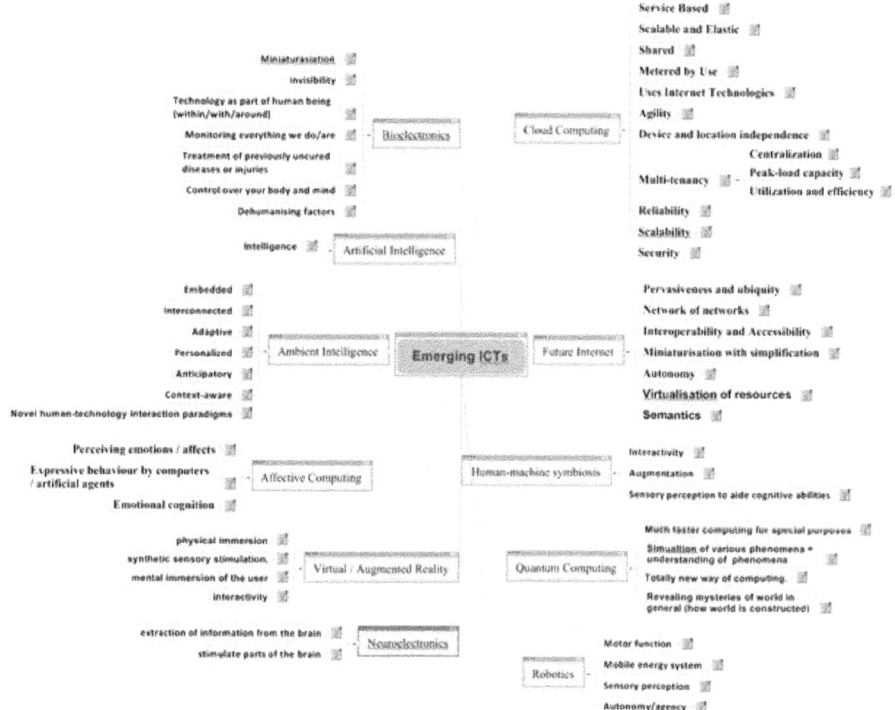

Fig. 4. Defining Features of Emerging ICTs

5 Description of the Social Consequences of Emerging ICTs

Figure 5 deserves a closer look and interpretation. This section will briefly explore each of the main term and spell out its relevance and meaning.

Natural interaction is core to many of the emerging ICTs. The idea behind it is to move away from specialist ways of interacting with technical devices, such as mice, keyboards, or screens, to engaging with them in ways with which users are more familiar. The technologies use a number of ways of gathering information about the user that can be intentionally given information but also contextual information or personal information about which the user may not even be aware (as, for example, emotional states). The user will in many cases not even notice that she or he is interacting with a technology that is deeply embedded in the user's environment.

One recurring aspect of this natural interaction is the **invisibility** of the technology. Technical artefacts recede to the background, making it easy to forget their presence and interacting with users in numerous ways.

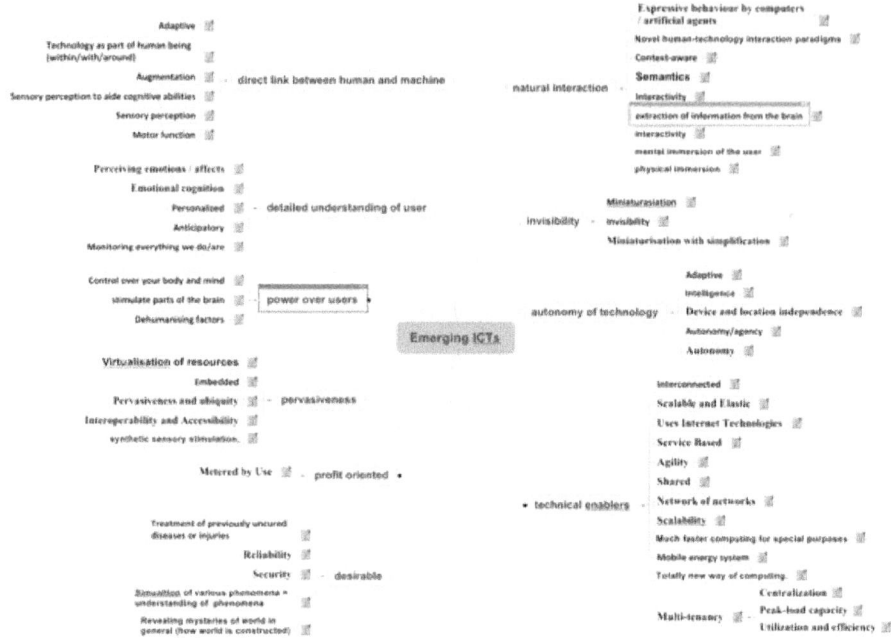

Fig. 5. Social and Socio-Technical Implications of Emerging ICTs

A further aspect of the interaction is the **direct link between humans and technology**. This can either be physically implemented, as in the case of implants, which can be inserted in the user's body and even their brain. In many cases, the direct link is less intrusive, for example, when the technology continuously surveils the user. This direct link is not only an input device of technology but often has the purpose of supporting and strengthening the user and, in particular, those aspect of the user that are viewed as problematic. Technologies are described as adaptive and augmenting, giving users' greater reach of their natural faculties.

This direct link implies that the technology has a **detailed understanding of the user** whose needs, wants, and preferences need to be modeled and interpreted correctly for the augmentation and direct link to be successful. This means that bodily, cognitive, and emotional models of the users need to be embedded, which refers back to the natural and invisible interface between user and technology. In order for this to be possible, the technology needs to be **pervasive** (i.e., embedded in a wide range of environments for the user to be able to profit).

As a consequence, the technology will gain a significant degree of **power over the user** who will need to rely on the technology and embedded models to accomplish the chores with which that technology is meant to help. In extreme cases—for example, in neurocomputing—a direct link between the technology and the human brain can control not only a person's actions but even their thoughts. But even in less intrusive cases, the technology can easily determine and circumscribe avenues of activity.

This power is linked to **autonomy of the technology**, which will be relied upon to make numerous decisions and act proactively in order to achieve its functions. The technology, therefore, needs to be context sensitive, mobile, and intelligent. It correctly interprets the user's situation and acts accordingly.

It is important to note that as a general point the different technologies under investigation are described as positive and **desirable** in their use and consequences. They will allow a better understanding of all sorts of natural and social phenomena. Their aim is to help and support users, in particular in those cases where they find it hard to fend for themselves (e.g., in cases of disability or disease).

In Figure 5, several defining features of different technologies were collected under the heading **technical enablers**. These are aspects of the technologies that are deemed to be necessary to fulfil the functions of the technologies. For space reasons, these are not investigated in more detail here, even though this would doubtlessly be an interesting further task. We will finish this brief attempt to outline the main sociotechnical consequences of the emerging ICTs and move toward a reflection of the assumptions, beliefs, and models that underlie them.

6 Critical Interpretation of the Social Consequences of Emerging ICTs

It may be advisable to start this section with another caveat. Of course the very brief outline of characteristics of emerging technologies in the previous section does not do the technologies justice, nor does it reflect the richness of the descriptions and visions from which they were extracted. Their purpose was to give a basis for the following critical analysis, which will provide a deeper insight into the background and content of the visions of emerging ICTs. These will be split into assumptions about individuals, society, and technology.

6.1 Assumptions about Individuals

The emerging ICTs described above all make explicit or implicit assumptions about the individuals that will use them. Many of these assumptions can easily be deduced from the defining features of the technologies. They are, however, rarely critically reflected and in many cases will find it hard to stand up to scrutiny.

A first assumption about users is that they have particular needs that the technology can fulfil and that they are able and willing to recognize this and make appropriate use of the technology. This may be true of any technology description but it is particularly obvious for these emerging ICTs. It is also empirically questionable given the nature of some of the technologies described.

A further characteristic of the individual users is that they can be described in terms that are conducive to the use of the technology. This implies an objectivist and positivist view of humans. The technologies imply the ability of humans to change but, as a general rule, this change is continuous and logically consistent. Such views of individual stable identities have been questioned by numerous researchers from a range of backgrounds. The objectivist anthropological views underlying much of the technology planning also raises questions of feasibility of the visions behind them.

Such questions include whether human emotions are clearly identifiable, whether human wishes and preferences are consistent and logical, how technology can deal with human inconsistency and self-contradictions, to name just a few.

An important further aspect of the view of humans is related to the question of autonomy. Autonomy is a thorny philosophical concept in its own right, touching on questions of ethics, of freedom of will and of action. With regard to emerging ICTs it is notable that autonomy is an attribute that is increasingly attributed to ICTs. These act autonomously (i.e., without direct input from users). There is an interesting assumption that users are not only comfortable with this but even actively desire it. Such autonomy of ICTs can arguably conflict with the autonomy of users but this issue is not normally explored in descriptions of the technologies.

Summarizing, one can say that the view of humans in relation to the discourses surrounding emerging ICTs explored for this research is rather one-dimensional. Humans are viewed as predictable users with consistent needs and preferences. Rejection or resistance of technologies is generally not expected or foreseen. Based on this simplistic view of humans, a comparable view of society is typically implied.

6.2 Assumptions about Society

Society is rarely explicitly mentioned in discourses on emerging technology, beyond rhetorical references to the importance of the particular technology in meeting societal goals. What can be learned about what the proposers of the technologies think about the society in which it will be used and how it will influence this society tends to be indirect.

An important observation that can be deduced from this is that society is generally not seen as a particularly important aspect of the development and use of emerging ICTs. It is seen as a relatively static background that can allocate resources and regulate but generally has no major role to play. There is an assumption about homogeneity of societies, possibly because technologies tend to be developed for larger markets and across national and cultural boundaries. These boundaries and their implications for technologies are rarely made explicit.

A further background assumption on the societies in which the technologies will be developed and used refers to the socio-economic system. There is typically an implicit belief that the technology will be subject to market forces. Most of the technologies are designed for individual or organizational use and will have to compete with alternative technologies for market share. This view is so pervasive as to become invisible. The fact that there are alternatives to this market-oriented view of society is not reflected. It is worth remembering that, not too long ago, much advanced technology development was state-owned and not related to markets (e.g., nuclear power, military technology).

A final observation on the role of society in emerging ICTs is that the dynamic relationship between these two actors is rarely reflected. A look at the list of technologies and their shared features as developed above indicates that they hold the potential to radically change numerous aspects of society. These range from the nature of work and leisure to notions of ownership and property and political participation. Despite the potentially sweeping changes some of these technologies could induce, the possible consequences for society are rarely discussed.

6.3 Assumptions about Technology

The final set of assumptions worth noting here is about to the nature of technology. As has become clear by now, descriptions of emerging ICTs tend to be simplistic. They display characteristics of technological determinism, where there are assumptions about properties inherent to technology which will lead to predictable use and social outcomes. Individual and social appropriation, redefinition, or resistance are generally not reflected.

Furthermore, there is a general assumption that technology is practically functional, fulfils given needs and desires, and has morally good consequences. A brief look at the technologies mentioned in this paper shows numerous possibilities of undesired effects, side-effects, possibilities of misuse, etc. There are pervasive issues, notably privacy and data protection, but also intellectual property questions that have relevance to all of the candidate technologies. There are, furthermore, less obvious issues that may arise only in particular instances, which nevertheless may shed doubt on the assumption of desirability of the technology.

7 Critical Reflections

This paper states in its title that it aims to give a critical review of emerging ICTs. It is thus fitting to end the paper by critically reflecting whether this has been achieved. This will be done by first considering the approach used in the paper and then asking what this can tell us about the future.

7.1 Critical Reflections on the Approach

There are numerous potential weaknesses of the approach presented here. Most of them are directly related to the topic area—namely, the future of ICT. As pointed out several times, the uncertainty of the future renders it impossible to give a precise account of what will happen. The chosen approach of using a dual discourse analysis provides the paper with academic rigor but even this does not overcome the principal problem of uncertainty.

The paper could also be accused of being too narrow in its choice of sources. By concentrating on governmental/policy publications on the one hand and statements by research institutions on the other hand, the breadth of discourses does not reflect all possible futures. We argue that these two discourses have the advantage of giving a good account of what is being researched at the moment, but one could of course also aim for a broader view, for example by analyzing media discourses or even fictional ones. This would be desirable in a further step of the research.

There are, furthermore, many other ways of addressing the subject area. The approach presented here is only one way of finding access to our understanding of the future. There are numerous other methodologies of future-oriented research (Georghiou et al. 2008). Following any one of these methodologies might have led to different results or different emphases. In the light of what was said earlier about the nature of foresight research, this is not necessarily a problem for this research. As long as the possible futures analyzed here are plausible, interesting, and allow for a discussion of which future we want to achieve, the approach is justified.

The critical interpretation of views of humans, society, and technology in the previous section could be accused of lacking nuance and being, to some degree, self-fulfilling. Given that the technologies under investigation are at a stage of development that prevents empirical accounts, we have to rely on implicit and simplistic assumptions. Technologists must work with views of their users and these views need to be manageable and be conducive to the development work. Similarly, technology developers are normally not experts and often not particularly interested in the relationship to society.

We would concede this point but argue that it is nevertheless important to tease out what these assumptions are and on what basis technologies are being developed. An easy way of understanding why this is important is to conceptualize a different world, for example, one in which intellectual efforts are not subject to legal protection but open to everyone or one where commercial exchange is not the dominant way of allocating access to technology. Such worlds are at least logically conceivable and the interesting question is whether they would lead to the same technologies. If not, then the question is how decisions on future technologies and, by implication, on future societies are made.

7.2 Critical Reflections on the Future

The above description of the social consequences of technology could be criticized as being biased. It is rather dystopian and concentrates on problematic aspects of technologies. This may to some degree reflect the author's prejudices but it is also a consequence of a conscious attempt to counterbalance the typically very positive description of technologies. This is not the only way of categorizing the features of emerging ICTs, but it is one plausible way of doing so. If the reader can agree with this, then it is reasonable to ask whether the vision of the future implied in these technology descriptions is desirable.

The answer to this will be based on personal judgments and not be generalizable. It is not implausible, however, to assume that there are many who do not see these developments as desirable. Do we really want computers and other technologies that recede into the background, become invisible, interact with us in an increasingly human way, and proactively act in ways that we implicitly want them to? To some degree, it might be nice to live in an intelligent environment in which one does not have to remember to turn of the stove and the heating when going out. On the other hand, this may turn into an oppressively comfortable life in which humans become less and less masters of their own present and future as has been described in numerous works of fiction, notably in Huxley's *Brave New World* (1998).

This question of whether the overall development of these technologies lead to a world in which we want to live brings us to the main contribution of the paper. It raises the question how we, as individuals, as societies, or as humankind, can and want to control the development of technology. The core problem seems to be that technology development is currently very much left to market forces. Markets are not bad per se and one could argue that they have democratic properties and allow widely distributed aggregation of choices which allow them to recognize collective preferences. While this argument is valid to some degree, it runs into general problems of markets with regard to lack of information and transparency, which are exacerbated in the case of future technologies, which, by definition, we can know little about.

This paper submits that there should be better ways of democratically controlling the development of technology. And, indeed, there are numerous methods and mechanisms for doing this, such as technology assessment, value-centered design, user-centered design, and many others. The literature in the field of information systems is littered with attempts to integrate more participative methods into technology design.

The value of a study such as this is that it can raise awareness and allow decision makers on different levels to understand which problems may arise. Such awareness can then lead to the employment of a range of methods and approaches to better understand and address them. Or, to put it differently, this paper should be seen as a contribution to a wider discourse with political decision makers as well as technology developers, industry, and users with the aim of better understanding what we currently say about the future, which will hopefully allow us to build a future that we individually and collectively desire.

Acknowledgments

The research leading to these results has received funding from the European Community's Seventh Framework Programme (FP7/2007-2013) under grant agreement no. 230318.

The author acknowledges the contribution of the members of the consortium without whom this paper could not have been written.

References

Bijker, W.E.: Of Bicycles, Bakelites, and Bulbs: Toward a Theory of Sociotechnical Change. MIT Press, Cambridge (1997)

Cadili, S., Whitley, E.A.: On the Interpretative Flexibility of Hosted ERP Systems. J. of Strategic Information Systems 14(2), 165–195 (2005)

Cuhls, K.: From Forecasting to Foresight Processes: New Participative Foresight Activities in Germany. J. of Forecasting 22(2/3), 93–111 (2003)

Dusek, V.: Philosophy of Technology: An Introduction. Wiley, New York (2006)

Floridi, L.: A Look into the Future Impact of ICT on Our Lives. The Information Society 23(1), 59–64 (2007)

Georghiou, L., Harper, J.C., Keenan, M., Miles, I., Popper, R.: The Handbook of Technology Foresight: Concepts and Practice. Edward Elgar Publishing Ltd, Cheltenham (2008)

Grint, K., Woolgar, S.: The Machine at Work: Technology, Work and Organization. Polity Press, Cambridge (1997)

Howcroft, D., Mitev, N., Wilson, M.: What We May Learn from the Social Shaping of Technology Approach. In: Mingers, J., Willcocks, L.P. (eds.) Social Theory and Philosophy for Information Systems, pp. 329–371. Wiley, Chichester (2004)

Huxley, A.: Brave New World. HarperCollins Publishers, New York (1998)

Latour, B.: Reassembling the Social: An Introduction to Actor Network Theory. Oxford University Press, Oxford (2007)

Law, J., Hassard, J.: Actor Network Theory and After. Wiley, Chichester (1999)

Olsen, J.B., Pedersen, S.A., Hendricks, V.F.: A Companion to the Philosophy of Technology. Wiley, Chichester (2009)

Stahl, B.C., Heersmink, R., Goujon, P., Flick, C., van den Hoven, J., Wakunuma, K., Ikonen, V., Rader, M.: Identifying the Ethics of Emerging Information and Communication Technologies: An Essay on Issues, Concepts and Method. International J. of Technoethics 1(4), 20–38 (2010)

About the Author

Bernd Carsten Stahl is Professor of Critical Research in Technology and Director the Centre for Computing and Social Responsibility at De Montfort University, Leicester, UK. His interests cover philosophical issues arising from the intersections of business, technology, and information, including the ethics of computing and critical approaches to information systems. From 2009 to 2011, he served as coordinator of the EU FP7 research project "Ethical Issues of Emerging ICT Applications" (ETICA) (GA 230318, www.etica-project.eu).

Rationality and Foolishness: Alternative Forecasting Systems in a Manufacturing Firm

Charlotte Brown

Lancaster University Management School, Lancaster, UK LA4 4YX
c.brown1@lancaster.ac.uk

Abstract. Forecasters in firms are expected to employ mathematical techniques encoded in information systems in order to predict the future demand for a firm's goods. In practice, many forecasters have eschewed statistical methods of forecasting and depend instead on human expertise. This resistance to the ideals and technologies of forecasting has largely been understood in the literature as a failure of rationality in firms. This paper provides a social and political analysis of forecasting in a case study firm, and examines alternative rationalities present in the firm that legitimate what appears to the forecasting literature as foolish practices. The case study organization, a large manufacturing firm, undertook a process of reform of the forecasting process during the course of the study. This paper explores how resistance to a new forecasting support system was shaped by the local equilibrium that had been reached between rationalities in the firm.

Keywords: Forecasting, organizations, rationality, forecasting support systems.

1 Introduction

Foolishness and rational choice exist side by side in every organization. It is easy to theorize about one while ignoring the other. The challenge is to reconcile them (Freeman 1999, p. 164).

When manufacturing firms think about the future, they do so not only on the grand, sweeping scale of product or market (r)evolution, led by CEOs, strategists or consultants; they also think about the future in a much more pragmatic and short term way. These short-term predictions relate to the demand for their goods and/or services from customers in the immediate future: in the next week, month, or quarter. The employees responsible for this task are often known as forecasters or demand planners, and they typically work within the supply chain department or sales, or in a separate department with links to both functions (Fildes and Hastings 1994). The job of forecasters is to gather information about the past (usually the sales history), about the present (market conditions), and about the future (anticipated promotions or seasonal changes) and synthesize these, often using a specialist information system, into a description of the quantity the firm could sell of each product in the future. This is then put to use by a variety of organizational actors: manufacturing departments use it

M. Chiasson et al. (Eds.): Future IS 2011, IFIP AICT 356, pp. 77–92, 2011.
© IFIP International Federation for Information Processing 2011

to determine what to produce and when; sales departments may use it to set targets; senior managers may use it to make decisions about resource allocation (Makridakis et al. 1998).

Research into forecasting assumes, mostly tacitly, that organizations are rational, profit-maximizing organizations. Better forecasts are expected ultimately to reduce costs and increase revenue by informing decision-making about, for example, optimal production scheduling and inventory management. However, predicting the future, even this relatively near-term and pragmatic aspect of the future, is a notoriously difficult task, made more so by the volume of data that has become available to the forecaster in recent decades. Researchers have, therefore, sought systematic answers to this problem, narrowing attention to the complex but mathematically tractable problem of extrapolating potential futures from trends in historical data (Whitley 1984). They have accordingly developed and elaborated a set of techniques intended to assist the forecaster that are increasingly encoded in specialist forecasting support systems (FSS). Firms are thought to be motivated to purchase and implement these forecasting support systems by the potential for cost savings (Armstrong 2001).

Successful implementation of the technologies of forecasting is thus positioned within the literature on forecasting as a rational choice that precedes good forecasting, and thus good business decisions, and thus profit maximization. However, surveys reveal a rather different picture of forecasting support systems in use (McCarthy et al. 2006; Mentzer and Cox 1984; Mentzer and Kahn 1995). The uptake of forecasting support systems has, it seems, been relatively slow, despite the availability of computing resources in the workplace (Sanders and Manrodt 1994, 2003). Moreover, these surveys suggest that many firms continue to use primarily human–expertise-based approaches to forecasting. They prefer to rely on individuals within the firm, often sales and marketing personnel, to provide opinions about the future that are then used as the basis for forecasts. Even those firms that do use more information technology often seem to do so in ways unintended by the technology developers. They often ignore or misuse the many embedded mathematical techniques that forecasting researchers and experts would consider to be cornerstones of effective practice. This divergence of practice from theory is highly frustrating to forecasting researchers, who are unable to explain this seemingly foolish antagonism of organizations to the proper use of the technologies of forecasting (Mahmoud et al. 1992).

This paper will draw upon a case study of a manufacturing firm in the fast moving consumer goods market to attempt to unpick and reconcile the "rational" and "foolish" choices of a firm that implemented a forecasting system. It will explore how changing ideas of what constituted a successful forecasting practice impacted upon the firm and disrupted forecasting processes.

At the start of the study, the firm maintained two distinct forecasting practices, each very different in approach to the problem of predicting the future. One adhered closely to statistical notions of "good forecasting" while the other was almost wholly deviant from it. We will suggest that forecasters in the case study organization were caught in organizational circumstances that created a very different view on the most rational way to produce forecasts, and their use (or failure to use) quantitative technologies in their forecasting information systems reflected these different rationalities. The paper will then consider how forecasting practices, and thus the balance between rationalities, were then disrupted by the forced introduction of a new forecasting support system by senior managers intent upon imposing a single rational system on the whole firm.

This case study will be laid out in more detail in the third of four further sections below. First, however, this paper will briefly review the literature on forecasting in organizations and relate this to ideas of success and failure within the IS literature. The second section will consist of a short discussion of the methodology used to generate the case study. The third section will introduce and discuss the case study firm, a large alcoholic beverages firm that will be described under the pseudonym of Global Beverages UK. Finally, the paper will reach some conclusions about the problem of the rational in forecasting practice, and consider some future extensions of this research.

2 Literature Review

2.1 The Rational Ideal in the Forecasting Literature

The success or failure of systems is a major theme in the information systems literature. This manifests itself particularly in analyses that locate an IS failure within an organization and then attempt to unravel its origins. This research historically originated in discussions of mechanical deficiencies (Lyytinen 1987), but has increasingly focused on issues not of simple failure to function, but rather of mismanagement, misuse, and abandonment (Wilson and Howcroft 2002).

Epistemologically, two approaches have emerged within this debate, the first of which attempts to isolate the factors that predict and/or permit success. This literature has developed normative descriptions of idealized development and implementtation processes, and proposes multiple tools and techniques to mitigate the risk of failure (DeLone and McLean 1992, 2003). Research of this type suggests that methods can be found to identify, manage, and/or avoid potentially failure-inducing issues related to the organization, human participants, and the organizational culture in which the technology is to operate (Mitev 2000). Much of the existing forecasting literature falls within this category, where success is defined as the implementation and diffusion of the "rational ideal" of the quantitative forecasting system.

Even the most cursory inspection of the academic literature on forecasting reveals a discipline deeply rooted in the science of statistics. The dominant research topic in this field is the development, elaboration, and testing of the technologies of forecasting. This research has produced a set of statistical models and algorithms intended to extrapolate a description of the future from information about the past. The limited capacity of humans for this type of analysis has led to a strong interest in embedding these techniques within forecasting support systems (Hogarth and Makridakis 1981). One of the central concerns of this work is the measurement of statistical accuracy, or the correspondence between the forecast and the actual data for a given period. Much of the forecasting literature assumes straightforwardly that the success of a forecasting process in practice is synonymous with and proportional to the statistical accuracy of the forecast that is produced, with one or two notable exceptions (Lawrence et al. 2000).

A strand of the forecasting literature has explicitly dealt with the problem of forecasting in organizations. This literature is generally highly sympathetic to the outcomes of those studies done in laboratories that suggest that the systematic application of forecasting techniques and technologies, combined with carefully controlled integration of human–expertise, produces the best, which is to say the most statistically accurate, forecasts (Armstrong 2001). Legitimacy is expected to accrue to the forecasting support system and its outputs from the rigor of the underlying mathematics and the integrity of the flow of data to and from the system. The organization itself is broadly understood as a more or less hostile host for this technology. Success, therefore, depends in part on the willingness that the organization evinces to change to accommodate the needs of the new technology and to accord authority to the outputs of the new, more accurate system (Moon et al. 2003).

The neutrality of the forecasting system is never called into question in this literature. Indeed, an unexamined teleology of forecasting practices is tacit in much of this work. These works envisage forecasting practices as moving toward greater accuracy, and thus greater success, through the gradual replacement of the human and judgmental with the systematic and mathematical. As a consequence of this, much of this literature is normative. It seeks to outline the organizational arrangements that best support the successful integration of this machinery of forecasting into the firm. For example, these models of "best practice" call for specific efforts to develop systems of communication and data gathering (Fildes and Hastings 1994); suggest that specialist forecasters be employed to operate forecasting systems and be provided with a position in the organizational hierarchy that provides them with political capital (Moon et al. 2003); and demand the creation of a set of policies and rules in the organization that discourage and stigmatize unnecessary human intervention in forecast outputs (Galbraith and Merrill 1996). More critical viewpoints query whether the particular organizational "improvements" that are proposed have ever been shown empirically proven to improve forecasts, let alone produce the better business decisions that are thought to flow from them (Fildes et al. 2003). However, the notion of a need for improvements of some kind is largely unexamined.

One response to the problem of the inconveniently flawed organization has been to suggest that if organizations are unable or unwilling to mold themselves into good hosts for forecasting systems, the software should be used to impose good policy (Fildes et al. 2006). At a minimum, for example, this ideal of rational forecasting practice requires interested non-forecasters to recognize significant limits to their expertise and to accord authority to the analytical systems that have replaced them. As human judgment "adjustments" are often used to modify statistical forecasts unscientifically and to the detriment of accuracy, it has been suggested that forecasting support systems limit and warn against such adjustments, or even "correct" them as they are made (Davydenko et al. 2010).

This literature, therefore, positions quantitative forecasting methods, and the systems they are embedded within, as the rational choice for resolving the problem of predicting the future. Once implemented in firms, the focus shifts to defending these technologies from the distortions and subversions that arise out of the imperfections of the particular firm. It is assumed that the foolishness these imperfections create can and should be designed away, or at least mitigated, either through direct intervention in organizational design and/or policy or else through the design of the technology itself.

2.2 The Forecaster as Systems Expert

This description of the design and implementation of forecasting technologies is strongly reminiscent of Hirschheim and Klein's (1989) description of "the analyst as systems expert," with the same fundamental assumption that the primary concern of the forecaster is the means of production, rather than the end product itself. Forecasters, like Hirschheim and Klein's information systems developers, are expected to concern themselves first and foremost with the task of choosing and applying techniques and models that produce authoritative, accurate forecasting outputs. The extraction of meaning from these forecasts is assumed to be the province of non-forecasters, usually sales and production employees who take decisions based on their interpretation of the information. Much of the frustration expressed in the forecasting literature concerns the vitiation of the methods of production of forecasts by non-forecasters and/or the reluctance of non-forecasters to cede authority for describing the future to the forecasting system.

Kling (1980) describes analysis of this type as a "traditional management-science approach," imagining how forecasting systems would work in an idealized world. Kling further suggests that it is often followed up by a "human relations" analysis of the same problem which encourages system designers to consider this problem of resistance productively. Kling describes this as a belief that a technical solution can be found that permits the needs of a number of organizational actors to be met, including both the managers requiring information and the various contributors to the system. This manifests itself in the forecasting literature in the various recommend-dations on how to realize the perfect world of forecasting practice by reform of the organization.

2.3 The Analyst as Facilitator

An alternative perspective of the activities of forecasters within the firm, however, is one consistent with Hirschheim and Klein's notion of the "analyst as facilitator." This attempts to understand the forecast not simply as the output of an objective information process that is strictly geared toward producing the forecast, but rather focuses on the method of this production as a meaningful activity in itself. This approach is useful because it allows us to understand differences between theory and practice as more than delinquency. Instead they can be understood as indicative of some meaningful need or desire of participants in the firm. This stance takes the less critical position that forecasting systems develop in an organization in a particular form because this provides the greatest utility to one or more organizational actors. Consequently, we are no longer constrained to treat organizational arrangements as either rational or foolish, but rather to explore and investigate them as the effects of particular organizational attitudes and processes. In this approach we leave it to organizational participants to determine who extracts meaning from forecasts and how they do so, and what measure of success might be applied to these activities. In particular, it suggests that the disinterested, objective measurement of statistical accuracy may be only one measure of success relevant to forecasters and forecast users.

This position is consistent with a second thread of the information systems success/failure debate, which argues that normative and instrumental approaches to understanding the failure of information systems rely on a faulty assumption that technology is inherently neutral (Mitev 2000). The second type of research, by contrast, broadly identifies with constructivist schools of thought. Success or failure of information systems is understood in this view to be socially constituted. It is determined by the dominant narrative that emerges from organizational participants, irrespective of the extent to which the project conforms to checklists of success (Wilson and Howcroft 2002). This type of analysis, therefore, relies on investigating the relationship between value-laden technological change and patterns of interests and power within the firm. Recent examples include Brown and Jones (1998), who consider narratives of doom that emerged in a failed IS project at a UK hospital; Fincham (2002), who considers the emergence of different dominant success/failure narratives within two financial services firms; and Bartis and Mitev (2008), who discussed the impact of managers "disguising" a failure as a success in order to save face or secure power in a case study firm.

In this paper, the intention is to apply these ideas to a single case study as an example of this approach. It aims to examine how rationality, so clear cut in the mathematical approaches to forecasting, is in fact contingent upon the firm and the socio-political processes that surround the initiation, processing, outcome, and inter- pretation of forecasts. In this view, behaviors and outcomes from a forecasting system, which might appear foolish under functionalist viewpoints, can be construed alternatively as rational. We are also able to explore how an established practice was recast from successful to failing by means of the interpolation of a technology con- trolled and promoted by a group with particular organizational power. Before describing this case in detail, however, the next section will briefly outline the methodology used to generate data about the firm in question.

3 Methodology

This investigation into the problem of forecasting practice sought to explore the experiences and behavior of forecasters within an organizational context. This study, therefore, took an interpretive case study approach (Walsham 1995). The firm chosen for this case study was a large multinational manufacturing firm that produces alcoholic beverages. The firm was considered to be a useful example of forecasting practice as it has a relatively stable and well-documented forecasting process. Data was generated from 2008 to 2010 through a set of 15 semi-structured interviews with two forecast managers and two senior forecasters at the UK headquarters of the firm, as well as two non-forecasters: a supply manager and an inventory manager. Inter- views were conducted primarily with a single interviewee, with one extended inter- view involving both forecasting managers, and typically lasted between one and one and a half hours. The interview guide consisted of a set of queries intended to elicit details about the day to day creation, revision, dissemination, and review of forecasts in the firm. Forecasters, for example, were asked to describe their routine interacttions with forecast inputs and outputs, forecast users and other data related to forecasts, as well as their use of the forecasting support system. Forecast managers were asked questions that related to these issues, and to issues surrounding the measurement and perception of forecasts and forecasters in the firm. All but one of the interviews was recorded, transcribed, and the transcripts, or notes in the case of the one unrecorded interview, were shared with the interviewees for further clarification and checking. Additionally, the organization supplied internal documents related to forecasting outcomes, processes, and hierarchies within the firm.

It is also useful to consider the role of the researcher in conducting this research. This case study forms part of ongoing research undertaken as part of my doctoral studies. Prior to undertaking this research I worked in a firm in a different industry that was nevertheless experiencing some similar challenges in terms of the implementation and use of forecasting techniques. In the course of interviews at the case study firm, I disclosed my previous work experience, and this revelation of my own history may have affected their description of practice in particular ways unknown to me, or to have influenced their choice of terminology or the topics, within the bounds of the semi-structured nature of the interviews, that they chose to discuss. As with all interpretive cases, I must note the contingent nature of this description, which is necessarily constructed in ways consistent with my understanding of the world, both tacit and explicit.

With these caveats, in the next section the forecasting practices of the case study firm, which will be called Global Beverages UK, will be described in detail, followed by analysis and discussion of the case in order to explore the issues raised in earlier sections of this paper.

4 Case Study

4.1 An Introduction to Global Beverages UK[1]

Global Beverages UK is the British subsidiary of a global alcoholic beverage manufacturer and distributor. The parent organization, Global Beverages Worldwide, operates in most parts of the world where alcoholic beverages are consumed. At the time of the study, the Global Beverages Worldwide parent company was divided for managerial purposes into several geographic groups known internally as business units, each of which had a regional headquarters site and employed a number of employees dedicated to certain centralized functions as well as senior managers responsible for the entire region. Global Beverages UK was part of the European Business Unit (EBU), which had physical headquarters in mainland Europe and was responsible for operations throughout the European Union and Scandinavia, although the UK, France, and Germany were the largest markets. The UK market for Global Beverages' goods was fiercely competitive, made more so by a long-term decline in sales volumes and a gradual erosion of profit margins. In response to these trends, Global Beverages UK was focused on reducing costs to maintain profitability in shrinking sectors.

---

[1] Names and some minor identifying details have been changed to preserve the anonymity of participants.

Historically, the managerial oversight provided by the EBU in national markets was fairly limited, with major markets like the UK permitted considerable control over their own operations. Over the period from about 2005 to 2010, however, a series of cost saving programs were initiated by supply chain managers at the EBU with the aim of eliminating or at least reducing duplication of activities between the various national organizations. These functions were in some cases consolidated into a multinational team based in the EBU headquarters or else, most recently, to a new service center based in a lower labor cost country in Eastern Europe. Although several related supply chain functions were affected by these changes, responsibility for demand planning had, for the time being, remained with the local Global Beverages organization. However, EBU supply chain managers were increasingly interested in forecasting outcomes and intervened regularly in processes, metrics, and systems related to forecasting. This included an EBU-initiated project to review and streamline forecasting in the UK under the aegis of a well-known management consultancy firm. A particularly critical element of these interventions was a series of redefinitions within the firm of the meaning of "success" as it related to both forecasting practice and forecasting outcomes.

4.2 Forecasting at Global Beverages UK

At the time of the study, forecasters in Global Beverages were split into two teams, each serving a distinct customer group which represented approximately half the total revenue of the firm. Each team consisted of a number of forecasters and a forecasting manager with overall responsibility for the forecasts and the team. The two customer segments were known as (1) the licensed trade and (2) the at-home or retail trade. These segments differed very significantly in both customer profile and their treatment by the firm for forecasting purposes.

4.2.1 The Licensed Trade

The licensed trade consisted of sales to business premises where customers consumed beverages on site. In the UK, this sector included a large pub, bar, and club trade, as well as licenses held by, for example, the operators of large sporting stadia. While there were some large accounts in the licensed trade, no single customer was felt to be critical to the on-going success of this side of the business.

The licensed trade was seasonal, with spikes and troughs in demand related to major sporting events (such as the football World Cup) and calendar events. However, there was little significant promotional activity in this segment, and much of the seasonal variation could be foreseen months ahead based on historical sales patterns. Moreover, a relatively small number of stock-keeping units (SKUs), at most two dozen, accounted for the vast majority of sales to all licensed trade customers nationwide, including promotional sales. These factors together produced a relatively stable and predictable demand pattern. From a forecasting perspective, this was seen as an ideal situation in which to use statistical forecasting techniques and the forecasters, therefore, employed a software package to produce forecasts. These were reviewed only by exception or when specific information was provided to them (for example, about a forthcoming promotion). Forecasters in this department consistently produced the most accurate forecasts of any in the EBU countries throughout the period of the study, and were considered to be the "best practice" forecasting department in the EBU and beyond.

4.2.2 The At-Home Trade

The at-home trade consisted of sales to premises where customers purchased beverages to consume at home. This was further divided, organizationally, into (1) wholesale accounts that purchased in bulk and then resold goods to smaller retail outlets and (2) multi-store retailers, notably three to four large and fiercely competitive national supermarket chains. This latter group was by far the most significant set of customers in the at-home trade side of the business. One retailer in particular, a very large multi-store grocer, was identified as business critical. Meeting the demand from this customer was, therefore, an organizational priority, even if doing so resulted in disappointing other customers.

At the total volume level (i.e., the total number of liters of product, however packaged), sales of most brands were reasonably predictable in this channel, with seasonal and event driven spikes and troughs that were not dissimilar to those observed in the licensed trade. However, at the level of the physical product, demand in the at-home trade was chaotic, with multiple packaging types producing hundreds of different SKUs, some of them customer and/or promotion specific. In addition, forecasters had to factor in several SKU-specific promotions every month, both major and minor, many agreed with retailers in the same month or even week that they occurred. The dynamics of the competitive multi-store grocer market made the outcome of these promotions particularly difficult to predict. At the SKU level, therefore, historical data was thought to provide little clue to future demand for particular package types and sizes. The department had consequently come to rely heavily on judgmental, which is to say human–expertise-based, methods of forecasting. The basis of forecasts for these products was a set of views collected from sales and marketing personnel about their sales and promotion expectations for the next several months.

The Global Beverages UK at-home team had the worst forecasting accuracy in the EBU throughout the period of the study, much worse than comparably sized at-home markets in France and Germany. This produced additional costs for manufacturing and supply planning departments, and occasionally led to difficult customer service situations when demand could not be met from Global Beverages' inventory. Historically, however, the at-home team were also understood to be highly successful. Despite their relatively poor forecasting accuracy, market conditions were such that tolerance for error was much greater, and the ability of forecasters to negotiate between the needs of the production departments and sales teams at the mercy of demanding retail customers was held in high esteem.

However, during the course of this study, the definition of what it meant to be a successful at-home forecaster at Global Beverages UK changed. Senior EBU supply chain managers were keen to improve forecasting accuracy to something closer to that achieved in France and Germany, if not to the level of the UK licensed trade segment. Additionally, the means of production of forecasts became more important. Part of a review of the UK forecasting process in 2010 was intended to determine how to implement the statistical forecasting techniques in the at-home trade, despite previous failures at this task and the opposition of both the forecasting managers and UK sales managers.

4.3   Change at Global Beverages

During the course of the study at Global Beverages, the EBU stepped up the pace of a long-standing project of integration and harmonization of supply chain processes across the member countries. The forecasting function was affected by multiple rounds of reform over the course of the study. In 2008, the FSS that the licensed trade team had used for many years was abandoned in favor of a single software platform, SAP APO. This was to be used by all forecasters in EBU countries and integrated with the enterprise resource planning software already in use in production departments, although by 2010 only the UK had completed the transition. In 2010, a major consulting project undertaken at the behest of supply chain managers at the EBU examined forecasting processes in several of the major markets. This project determined that too few products were forecast using statistical techniques in the UK. This latter project coincided with the departure from the firm of the at-home forecasting manager and one further forecaster, who were made redundant in a related cost-saving program. This removed a major obstacle to statistical forecasting in the at-home division. The forecasting manager had been vehement in his rejection of these methods for his department and had previously worked with the licensed premises forecasting manager and senior sales managers in the UK to preserve the status quo.

These reforms produced little change for forecasters in the licensed premises team. However, forecasters in the at-home market side of the business were told that henceforth a majority of forecasts were to be completed first in the FSS, which used statistical models, and then adjusted for managerial information such as promotions. The aim was, therefore, to move away from a situation in which human experts forecast half the revenue and more than 80 percent of all SKUs qualitatively, to a new regime in which no more than 20 to 25 percent of SKUs would be forecast manually and the remainder would be produced statistically. The level of accuracy that was acceptable was also reset at a significantly higher level.

Forecasters were skeptical about the change in methods and reluctant to abandon previous ways of working in the at-home segment. It was argued that because of the volatility created by promotional activities, most SKUs could not be forecast with any more success using statistical methods than they had been using human judgment, and in many cases these forecasts were actually worse than the forecasts produced using judgment. However, as new measures introduced by the EBU now reviewed not only the accuracy of forecasts, but also the way in which they were produced, forecasters had no option but to acquiesce. In the short-term, forecasters were committed to a course of action that involved producing both judgmental and system forecasts and choosing whichever seemed more plausible given sales histories. Although forecasters were, as required, now disseminating forecasts from within the mandated software, a line in the forecasting software had been enabled that allowed forecasters to overwrite the "system forecast" with a "manual" alternative, which they produced judgmentally in the same manner they had always done.

5 Discussion

The striking thing about the Global Beverages UK example was that there were two forecasting practices operational within the same firm that used diametrically opposed forecasting techniques, and which experienced wildly different accuracy outcomes. It is even more remarkable that despite the disparity in the accuracy of outputs, managers in these teams saw no contradiction in the coexistence of these practices. It was not until new narratives, backed by the organizational power of the regional headquarters, began to emerge about what constituted successful, legitimate forecasting processes that this status quo was called into question.

5.1 The Functionalist Perspective on Global Beverages

Forecasters throughout the organization described themselves as being squeezed between cost-minimizing supply chain managers and revenue-maximizing sales directors, their role one of go-between, translator, and whipping boy all at once. Forecasters in both departments thought of their role as providing a neutral middle ground between these two sets of interests, with one forecasting manager remarking that he thought only forecasters had any sense of the organization's over-arching desire for profit maximization, rather than one or another of the components of this goal. This is consistent with many of the descriptions in the functionalist literature that emphasizes the importance of objectivity. This functionalist position appeared to triumph in Global Beverages, as EBU managers mandated the harmonization of forecasting practices, arguing that the reasons provided by the at-home forecasters for their deviation from these methods were no longer sufficient to explain the failure to use statistical techniques. From the forecasting research perspective, this change at Global Beverages represents a natural, rational evolution of forecasting practice toward a desirable end. The decision of forecasters to circumvent the system in the early stages of deployment appears both baffling and foolish.

5.2 A Facilitative Interpretation of Global Beverages

Examining this situation from a different perspective, however, it is useful to consider how information technologies in use in the two forecasting practices reflect a perception of rational choice within the department, irrespective of the dysfunction this may have created in outputs.

In the licensed premises segment, demand was relatively stable, predictable, and involved a relatively small number of products. There were many low-volume customers, and a combination of the market strategy these customers pursued and national regulations on the sale of alcohol inhibited promotions. There were additionally some barriers for customers who wanted to switch between vendors in the licensed premises trade that further discouraged volatility. Relationships with customers were consequently relatively long-term and slow to change. Although the sector was still competitive, forecasting in this segment of the market was relatively undemanding. Forecasters described the data sets as regular and predictable, and the decision to use quantitative techniques was described as has having followed the determination that the data set supported their use.

Even in this department, with a pattern of respectable, technical forecasting, forecasters were passionate about the development of credible forecasts, and about the importance of personal relationships with contributors to forecasts, forecast users, and even with the data itself in producing credible forecasts. Despite their emphasis on the importance of their role as the neutral information broker between supply chain and sales, in this department, forecasters viewed their role as more strongly oriented toward the needs of the production department, and therefore closely aligned with the cost-minimizing inventory, efficiency, and planning goals of manufacturing managers.

In the at-home trade, by contrast, the scenario with regard to customer relationships was much more complex. A small number of customers exerted enormous influence over the visibility and availability of Global Beverages' products to end consumers. Switching costs for the retailer were relatively low, particularly since there were two or three highly competitive firms offering similar and, it was felt, increasingly commoditized products in most categories. The retailers, moreover, were themselves thought to be positioning their resources to be highly responsive to the end-consumers they served. They demanded a supply relationship that would permit rapid responses to small changes in demand arising from weather changes, competitive dynamics, and the like.

Against this background of an extremely dynamic customer base who perceived their needs to change on a weekly, if not daily, basis, sales people working in Global Beverages were equally active and responsive. The comfortable certainty of business in the licensed trade sector was absent, and instead sales people were described as under constant pressure to maintain and increase sales to a small number of demanding and capricious customers. There was a sense among forecasters that failure to meet those demands would result in not only the loss of that volume to a competitor, but also a damaging black mark against the business that would result in the loss of future sales. Forecasters, therefore, understood their role as sales focused and revenue-maximizing, rather than cost-minimizing. The perceived chaotic nature of the historical data had resulted in disinclination toward quantitative techniques. Perhaps more importantly, however, the sense that individual sales people, or at least the customers they represented, could make or break the revenue expectations of the division resulted in a significant reliance on their qualitative expertise. The appeal of the objective measure of accuracy was much lower than more subjective measurements of customer satisfaction and willingness to purchase.

In this customer-led environment, therefore, formal statistical methods were understood as an intrusion upon the agency and importance of the salesperson and his or her people skills. Consequently, the forecaster had become a collector rather than a producer of information, a historian of sales information. The authority of the forecast derived from the ability of the forecaster to render many narratives about the future into a single, credible narrative consistent with the past.

5.3 The Impact of Disruptions to Practice

The position taken by the forecasters, therefore, that the separation of their function into two distinct pieces was adapted to the needs of the organization was then disrupted by the change in the definition of successful forecasting that occurred. The investigations of the consultancy firm into forecasting at Global Beverages UK produced, without any particular investigation of the data set, the recommendation that the firm should achieve cost savings by forecasting more SKUs using quantitative methods within an FSS. It was too early at the conclusion of the research project to determine the accuracy of this statement, although forecasters at the firm initially claimed that it was not the case. However, it is interesting to consider the motivation of EBU managers in mandating this change.

It seems unlikely that an ideological commitment to statistical forecasting was strongly felt among supply chain managers at the EBU. A forecasting manager noted instead that the drive toward quantitative forecasting appeared to arise at least partly from a desire for systems integration among member countries. More cynically, the forecasting manager also expressed a belief that that a revolution in forecasting practice that forced the at-home practice onto the same technical footing as other groups would permit further cost savings in future. In particular, the manager pointed to the changes in other supply chain functions, where activities were first rationalized, then moved on to a common platform, and then finally moved to a service center in a lower labor cost country in Eastern Europe as an example of how these cost savings might be achieved in later years.

EBU supply chain managers, therefore, seem to have taken the position that expertise in forecasting ought primarily to be of a technical nature, de-emphasizing the idea of the forecaster as a neutral go-between. This position assumed also that the forecast would have a claim to authority and validity as a result of the system from which it originated, a system that EBU managers now controlled. This was in sharp contrast to the expressed belief of all the forecasters that the credibility of their forecasts depended in part upon the long-term relationships they had built with users and the data. The forecasting literature would regard this change in practice as neutral, part of the natural evolution of forecasting processes. However, in Global Beverages, this change was far from neutral; it represented a significant shift in the relative power of the forecasters and the EBU supply chain managers at regional headquarters.

A further demonstration of this issue was observed when EBU managers began to question the role promotions played in the department, challenging the perception that the UK had special market conditions that resulted in the use of promotions. Instead, UK managers were asked whether the use of promotions had created the market conditions they faced. It was suggested that customers could be "retrained" to expect fewer promotions and a more favorable trading environment for Global Beverages. The revenue-maximizing rationale of the sales department is entirely absent from this discourse: EBU managers were in effect asking Global Beverages UK sales people to conduct business in a way that made forecasting easier, and therefore reduced costs.

If forecasters under the original regime felt themselves to be squeezed between the complementary rationales of revenue-maximization and cost-minimization before, these reforms imposed upon them by EBU substantially increased the pressure. In the early stages of the implementation, it is hard to say what equilibrium will eventually be reached. However, even as a classic rational, technical forecasting package was apparently implemented in the at-home trade department, there were unintended consequences: qualitative forecasts were now written into a line in the technical forecast, taken from an unregulated set of spreadsheets put together by forecasters;

and sales managers had taken steps to shelter forecasters within their own departments, with unknown consequences.

Reflecting back on the forecasting literature, it is easy to understand the frustration of rationalist expert forecasters confronted with this determined delinquency from the rational course of action. Here, the firm has taken one of the necessary steps to reform forecasting practices only to experience resistance and subversion of the new system. The perspective of the forecaster-as-facilitator, however, makes sense of some of these apparently foolish behaviors. What has been rendered in the forecasting literature as resistance to the technology occasioning from ignorance, self-interest, or stubbornness can be understood from this perspective as arising instead from the disruption of a finely balanced equilibrium of interests. The forecasting support system intrudes upon the forecaster's position as mediator between the cost minimizers and revenue maximizers, and upon the salesperson's agency and expertise. It attempts to establish the credibility of forecasts as being obtained through the means of their production, rather than from the process of collecting, sharing, and making sense of this information. Although neither practice is entirely functional, it is clear that at least within the organization what forecasting experts might code as folly appears rational.

6 Conclusions and Future Research

The problem of practice in the forecasting literature has typically been presented as a failure by firms to diffuse the technologies of forecasting in a way forecasting experts have deemed adequate. This paper examined forecasting practice from a more social and political perspective, using the example of Global Beverages UK in order to explore how the practices dismissed as foolish by the rationalist approach persist in firms. This discussion of two different forecasting practices within the same firm found that, in each case, forecasters had developed a practice that most effectively mediated between pressures to minimize cost and to maximize revenue in markets of different levels of uncertainty. When a top–down process of reform, intended to diffuse forecasting technologies more widely, was implemented, it produced a conflict between the forecaster's sense of the role salespeople and forecasters played in forecasting processes, and the paradigm of the uninvolved technical forecaster. These conflicts play out in the organization as resistance to and subversion of the rational forecasting support system, but are indicative of the balance that has been struck between rational interests that participants see no alternative but to preserve.

A paper of this length provides little scope to explore further some of the questions raised by this case study. This description of forecasting in a firm raises further questions about the role of information systems in creating and legitimating a view of the future. In Global Beverages, different levels of uncertainty produced various degrees of reliance on human judgment, and the question of how uncertainty affects the use of forecasting support systems bears further investigation. Finally, this is just one case study, and while useful as a description of the conditions that can affect firms, further exploration of this notion of alternative rationalities as they affect forecasting practice in other firms would no doubt be enlightening.

References

Armstrong, J.S.: Principles of Forecasting: A Handbook for Researchers and Practitioners. Kluwer Academic, Boston (2001)

Bartis, E., Mitev, N.: A Multiple Narrative Approach to Information Systems Failure: A Successful System That Failed. European Journal of Information Systems 17, 112–124 (2008)

Brown, A.D., Jones, M.R.: Doomed to Failure: Narratives of Inevitability and Conspiracy in a Failed IS Project. Organization Studies 19, 73–88 (1998)

Davydenko, A., Fildes, R., Trapero Arenas, J.: Judgemental Adjustments to Demand Foremcasts: Accuracy Evaluation and Bias Corrrection. Lancaster University Management School Working Paper (2010)

DeLone, W.H., McLean, E.R.: Information Systems Success: The Quest for the Dependent Variable. Information Systems Research 3, 60–95 (1992)

DeLone, W.H., McLean, E.R.: The DeLone and McLean Model of Information Systems Success: A Ten-Year Update. Journal of Management Information Systems 19, 9–30 (2003)

Fildes, R., Bretschneider, S., Collopy, F., Lawrence, M., Stewart, D., Winklhofer, H., Mentzer, J.T., Moon, M.A.: Researching Sales Forecasting Practice: Commentaries and Authors' Response on "Conducting a Sales Forecasting Audit" by M. A. Moon, J. T. Mentzer and C. D. Smith. International Journal of Forecasting 19, 27–42 (2003)

Fildes, R., Goodwin, P., Lawrence, M.: The Design Features of Forecasting Support Systems and Their Effectiveness. Decision Support Systems 42, 351–361 (2006)

Fildes, R., Hastings, R.: The Organization and Improvement of Market Forecasting. The Journal of the Operational Research Society 45, 1–16 (1994)

Fincham, R.: Narratives of Success and Failure in Systems Development. British Journal of Management 13, 1–14 (2002)

Freeman, J.: Efficiency and Rationality in Organizations. Administrative Science Quarterly 44, 163–175 (1999)

Galbraith, C.S., Merrill, G.B.: The Politics of Forecasting: Managing the Truth. California Management Review 38, 29 (1996)

Hirschheim, R., Klein, H.K.: Four Paradigms of Information Systems Development. Communications of the ACM 32, 1199–1216 (1989)

Hogarth, R.M., Makridakis, S.: Forecasting and Planning: An Evaluation. Management Science 27, 115–138 (1981)

Kling, R.: Social Analyses of Computing: Theoretical Perspectives in Recent Empirical Research. Computing Surveys 12, 61–110 (1980)

Lawrence, M., O'Connor, M., Edmundson, B.: A Field Study of Sales Forecasting Accuracy and Processes. European Journal of Operational Research 122, 151–160 (2000)

Lyytinen, K.: Different Perspectives on Computer Systems: Problems and Solutions. ACM Computing Surveys 19, 5–46 (1987)

Mahmoud, E., DeRoeck, R., Brown, R., Rice, G.: Bridging the Gap between Theory and Practice in Forecasting. International Journal of Forecasting 8, 251–267 (1992)

Makridakis, S., Wheelwright, S.C., Hyndman, R.J.: Forecasting: Methods and Applications. Wiley, New York (1998)

McCarthy, T.M., Davis, D.F., Golicic, S.L., Mentzer, J.T.: The Evolution of Sales Forecasting Management: A 20-Year Longitudinal Study of Forecasting Practices. Journal of Forecasting 25, 303–324 (2006)

Mentzer, J.T., Cox, J.E.: Familiarity, Application, and Performance of Sales Forecasting Techniques. Journal of Forecasting 3, 27–36 (1984)

Mentzer, J.T., Kahn, K.B.: Forecasting Technique Familiarity, Satisfaction, Usage, and Application. Journal of Forecasting 14, 465–476 (1995)

Mitev, N.: Towards Social Constructivist Understandings of IS Success and Failure: Introducing a New Computerized Reservation System. In: Proceedings of the 21st International Conference on Information Systems, Brisbane, Australia, pp. 84–93 (2000)

Moon, M.A., Mentzer, J.T., Smith, C.D.: Conducting a Sales Forecasting Audit. International Journal of Forecasting 19, 5–25 (2003)

Sanders, N.R., Manrodt, K.B.: Forecasting Practices in US Corporations: Survey Results. Interfaces 24, 92–100 (1994)

Sanders, N.R., Manrodt, K.B.: Forecasting Software in Practice: Use, Satisfaction, and Performance. Interfaces 33, 90–93 (2003)

Walsham, G.: Interpretive Case Studies in IS: Nature and Method. European Journal of Information Systems 4, 74–81 (1995)

Whitley, R.: The Fragmented State of Management Studies: Reasons and Consequences. Journal of Management Studies 21, 331–348 (1984)

Wilson, M., Howcroft, D.: Re-conceptualising Failure: Social Shaping Meets IS Research. European Journal of Information Systems 11, 236–250 (2002)

About the Author

Charlotte Brown is a Ph.D. student in the Department of Management Science at Lancaster University in the UK. Prior to undertaking her Ph.D. studies, Charlotte spent a decade in a variety of roles in blue chip firms, including Johnson & Johnson and Sun Microsystems. Most recently she worked as a business intelligence analyst reporting at board level on sales and market forecasting. She has a BA (Hons) from Oxford University, an MBA from Cornell University, and an MRes from Lancaster University.

Section 3. Technological Futures

What Future? Which Technology? On the Problem of Describing Relevant Futures

Bernd Carsten Stahl

Centre for Computing and Social Responsibility, Department of Informatics,
De Montford University, Leicester, LE1 9BH, UK
bstahl@dmu.ac.uk

Abstract. Doing research on future and emerging technologies raises a number of significant ontological and epistemological challenges. The fundamental uncertainty of the future, combined with problems of appropriate descriptions of technology in general, render it difficult to come to an appropriate account of the likely shape and use of future technologies. This paper discusses several streams of research that address this issue, including the question of relevant description and context, interpretive flexibility, affordances of technology, and multi-stability of technological trajectories. The paper proposes that some of these problems may be addressed by using a democratic and participative approach to technology research and development. Participative technology assessment is then discussed as an example of an established way of democratically engaging with technology stakeholders during research and development. The paper concludes by discussing the promises and limitations of such a participative approach with regard to the question of understanding and researching future technologies.

Keywords: Emerging ICT, epistemology, ontology, participative technology assessment.

1 Introduction

The core problem of researching the is that the future is, by definition, unknown. While it would doubtlessly be desirable to have certainty about the future, this can never be the case, simply because of the epistemic uncertainty of the future. The initial response to the IFIP WG8.2 conference theme "Researching the Future" is, therefore, what future? Given the rapid development of technology, the technologies that may shape the (unknown) future are unlikely to be the same we have now. This increases the uncertainty: we are now looking at unknown information technology for an unknown future. Briefly, we can know neither future information technologies nor any of the other aspects of the future. At the same time, however, we need to make decisions based on assessments of the future that will then, in turn, influence the way the future will turn out in practice. This raises a number of practical problems on an individual, organizational, and political level. These practical problems cannot be solved without due attention to the underlying philosophical issues that cause them.

M. Chiasson et al. (Eds.): Future IS 2011, IFIP AICT 356, pp. 95–108, 2011.

This paper addresses these core philosophical questions. It starts out with a discussion of several theoretical positions that aim to describe the theoretical uncertainty of the future, and in particular of future technologies. The paper proposes that while individuals face a number of ontological and epistemological problems when assessing the future, collectively they may be in a better position to do so. In addition, such collective perceptions of the future have the potential to provide a sound and legitimate basis for policy decisions. Drawing on the literature in participatory technology assessment (pTA), different methods are discussed that can be used to address the problem. This leads to the conclusion, which discusses the limitations of this approach and underlines its importance and implications for information systems research.

The paper's main contribution to the body of work on future technologies is its discussion of the different fundamental philosophical problems that are encountered when trying to identify emerging ICTs and provide descriptions of them. An awareness of these problems is important to understand the limitations and validity claims of about the future. In addition, the paper develops the argument that these fundamental ontological and epistemological issues can be addressed by participative methods. These methods, some of which have been discussed and used in the area of information systems for considerable time, offer what may be our best bet to come to a reasonable understanding of the future and the role ICTs can play in shaping it.

2 Descriptions of Future Technologies

The fact that the future is not known is not particularly surprising by itself. Aristotle's study of temporal logic was caused by the observation that statements about the future have different properties from a-temporal statements. Briefly, a statement concerning the future is, at the present moment, neither true nor false. For example, the proposition "it will rain tomorrow" may or may not be true. We can only know with certainty tomorrow. The purpose of this paper is not to explore temporal logic or the general philosophical assessment of the future but to concentrate on future technologies. This section discusses several alternative theories of why exact knowledge of future technologies is impossible. This means that general issues of uncertainty of the future, such as the fact that we don't know how a particular technology will be used in 10 years because by then the world may have come to an end, will not be discussed here. But even disregarding such general issues, there are still a number of reasons why we cannot know future technologies with certainty.

An initial conceptual clarification required here concerns the concept of technology. It is not the purpose of this paper to engage in the general philosophy of technology (Dusek 2006; Olsen et al. 2009). Characteristics of technology that one can typically find include a basis in structured thought, temporal stability and reproducibility, and a reflection in artifacts which may (but do not have to be) of a physical nature. Technologies are typically developed for specific ends. This raises the question of the relationship between technologies and their application. It is easily conceivable that a particular technological artefact can raise different questions depending on context and application of use but also on the technology's conception and representation.

Technologies are not fixed and objectively given. The position that posits such an objectivity of technology, which would allow for a straightforward prediction of uses and consequences on the basis of the description of the technology, is often called technological determinism. Adam (2001, p. 239) defines technological determinism as

> the perspective that views developments in technology as driving society; "impacts" is the term often used. Such impacts are seen as inevitable, the relationship of technology and society is regarded as linear and mono-directional, i.e., from technology toward society.

Technological determinism is generally agreed to be conceptually misleading and empirically untenable. However, choosing a description of technology that is not determinist can lead to a number of problems. The problems with which this paper is concerned are a combination of ontological and epistemological ones. They are caused by the nature of technology (ontological) and the related issue of how we can know about it (epistemology). Some of these issues are caused by the fact that the phenomenon in question is a future one; others are equally pertinent for present technology. The paper will touch on the question of how one can know that an appropriate description of the technology in question was made. This leads to a discussion of the problem of interpretive flexibility of technology, followed by the related issue of multi-stability of technology.

All of these questions are highly theoretical and require abstract conceptualizations. In order to make it easier for the reader to follow the argument, the paper will employ one ongoing example of an emerging technology, namely ambient intelligence (AmI). AmI can be seen as an emerging technology because a significant percentage of current ICT development is invested in areas that are directly related to it. As a vision of technological developments, it has been around for several decades. The principle behind AmI is that computing technologies are removed from the perceptual foreground and blend into the background. Intelligent applications surround human agents and provide them with customized services. Wellknown examples of these ideas are the refrigerator that automatically orders missing stock from the supermarket or the intelligent house that regulates heating and lighting autonomously according to the occupiers' preferences. AmI is a technology—or maybe better, a socio-technical system—which comprises a large number of potential applications and artefacts. It is a high-level technology that has the potential to significantly affect the way humans interact with their human and nonhuman environment. For this reason it is of high social and ethical relevance. Given that it is not truly in existence at present, it can serve to exemplify the problems of description and democratic governance of technology.

2.1 Relevant Description and Context

Whenever researchers (or anybody else, for that matter) describe a phenomenon, they need to draw a boundary around the phenomenon in question. In this context, it is important to point out that phenomena are always human constructs. This recognition goes back to Kant (1995), who pointed out the important distinction between the thing as in itself (*Noumenon*) and its appearance (*Phaenomenon*). This distinction has been criticized by philosophers for a variety of reasons. This paper does not engage in that particular discourse but needs to make clear that it concentrates on phenomena. These are seen as the object of cognition and they are clearly humanmade. This is not to deny the existence of the thing in itself. Indeed, much of the following subsections are concerned with the question of how to conceptualize the relationship between thing in itself and phenomenon.

The initial question arising from the desire to describe a technology is how one can know whether the description is appropriate. The choice of the boundaries of the description of the phenomenon determines the conclusion that can be drawn from it. If, for example, one wants to conduct an analysis of a particular technology or its use or if one wants to regulate design and use, the findings will depend on the content of the description. This "problem of relevant description" (van der Hoven 2010) is not a new one in philosophy. Anscombe (1958), for example, critiqued Kant's categorical imperative as useless without stipulations concerning relevant description.

This problem of relevant description applies to any description of technical phenomena. How can an observer know whether a phenomenon under observation is appropriately described? This is a broad problem that relates to epistemology and theories of truth. This question is clearly pertinent for emerging technologies but it is similarly important for well-established technologies. The example of AmI demonstrates the problem. The earlier introduction of AmI is limited. Individuals knowledgeable in the area might focus on technical infrastructure, user interfaces, or novel devices. At the same time, one could argue that the important aspect of AmI is the way in which it models human beings or the novel types of data AmI will require and bring into existence. One could look at technical artifacts (e.g., particular sensors), subsystems (e.g., wireless sensor systems, wearable computers), socio-technical systems (e.g., the sales process of the refrigerator to order missing milk), etc. An added problem is that there will be a range of equally valid descriptions. Some positions on AmI are clearly colored, for example, the sales pitches of companies aiming to sell AmI products. They emphasize the potential strengths and tend to ignore potential weaknesses. It is clearly too simple, however, to attribute bias to vendors without acknowledging bias emanating from others. In fact, the whole issue of bias comes back to the question of what would be a correct (or true) description of the technology, which is at the core of this paper. Finally, AmI is an emerging technology, which means that it is currently not mature or widely used. AmI is surrounded by uncertainty as to possible and likely uses. This adds to the complexity and ambiguity because a description of an emerging technology cannot draw on applications and examples for evaluation.

If asked to describe the technology AmI, which of these (or additional) perspectives should be taken? And even if this question could be answered, then the immediate follow-on question would be: How do we know that the particular perspective has been described appropriately and in the level of detail and depth that is required?

The literature offers a number of conceptualizations and theories that provide conceptual tools for capturing this uncertainty of emerging technologies. Some of the more prominent ones are discussed in the following sections.

2.2 Interpretive Flexibility

In the field of information systems, one well-developed approach to the problem of appropriative descriptions of technology is connected with the idea of interpretive flexibility. Interpretive flexibility denotes the property of technology of being constituted by use. Proponents of interpretive flexibility argue that technology is not fixed but will develop during perception and use. The tenets of interpretive flexibility are widely recognized in science and technology studies where different positions such as social study of technology (SST) or the social construction of technology hold such views (Bijker 1997; Grint and Woolgar 1997; Howcroft et al. 2004) and also in related fields such as actor–network theory (Latour 2007; Law and Hassard 1999). Some scholars distinguish between interpretive and interpretative flexibility with the former referring to the epistemological aspect of the social construction of technology and the latter being a stronger position that sees the construction as ontologically constitutive of technology (Cadili and Whitley 2005).

The concept of interpretive flexibility tends to be invoked to describe variable uses of extant technologies. It is often brought to bear against the assumption that a particular technology or IS will have specific and predictable results and uses. Technologies can be interpreted depending on context, culture, organizational environment, and many other variables. Interpretive flexibility can explain why a successful technology used in one organization does not have the same consequences in another one that looks similar in many respects.

What is less well explored, at least in the field of IS, is the question of the relationship of interpretive flexibility with future and emerging technologies. There is a direct link between emergence and interpretive flexibility. Interpretive flexibility is a function of social interaction and pertains to particular discourses. That means that a technology may emerge in one context even though it may be well established elsewhere. It also means that the same underlying artefact can emerge into different technologies in terms of usage and application.

2.3 Affordances of Technology

The preceding discussion of interpretive flexibility is deeply rooted in social constructivism or constructionism (Gergen 1999). Social constructivism pervades much of science and technology studies and has been a strong answer to determinist positions (Grint and Woolgar 1997). One strong opposing argument against social constructivism is that it is too open, that it allows socially constructing technologies in ways that would not happen in reality. To put it differently, the question is what are the limitations of social construction? In the case of most extant and widely used technologies, there are a number of widely shared possible interpretations. A car, for example, can be used as a means of transport, a status symbol, or an investment. There are other, less frequent, uses such as the automobile as a place to sleep, as a weapon, or a means to block roads. At the same time, there are numerous interpretations of cars that one does not come across. Cars are not conceptualized as blankets, as educational toys, or as a means to get to the moon (even though in fiction all of these might be conceivable). For the case of AmI, one can conceive of interpretations of the technology as surveillance mechanism or an alleviator of chores. The question is whether one can exclude possible interpretations *a priori* (i.e., before the technology has been used).

One answer to this question is contained in the theory of affordances (Hutchby 2001). The theory of affordances was prominently put forward by James Gibson (1977). It is worth noting that for Gibson, affordances played a role in biology and the animal kingdom. His main interest in affordances relates to the psychology of perception. He suggests the definition that "affordance of anything is a specific combination of the properties of its substance and its surfaces taken with reference to an animal" (p. 67). This definition shows that Gibson's primary interest is in animal perception, but of course it applies to humans as well. An example he discusses in some depth is the affordance of sitting-on. In order for an object to have this affordance, the object has to display several properties. These include that it has to be sufficiently rigid, level, flat, extended, and—for humans—approximately of knee-height. An object displaying these properties allows humans to sit on them, independent of other properties, such as color, material, smell, etc.

The interesting characteristic of affordance is that it is a combination of subjective and objective properties that are not random. An object that does not have the properties does not afford sitting-on, but at the same time, a chair for humans would not afford sitting-on to giants. Gibson believes that affordances are real in the ontological sense (i.e., not subject to social construction). The problem here is that this would suggest that a specific combination of subject and object would have a clearly defined set of affordances. From a philosophical perspective this raises the question how we can know what the affordances are. And if we have no way of knowing whether we have identified a complete set of affordances, it furthermore raises the question whether there is a point of speaking of real and objective affordances if we cannot answer the previous question.

The theory of affordances has become popular among technologists, in particular among those who create and build systems such as specialists in human computer interaction (Gaver 2010). It is sometimes described as a way to develop new research avenues in established fields of technology research (Suthers 2006). Such research has to contend with the question whether affordances are real or whether they are socially constructed. In order to sidestep this philosophically difficult problem, the distinction between real and perceived affordances was introduced (Norman 1999). The point of this distinction is to explain the fact that individuals may not notice the presence of affordances of technologies, which for all intents and purposes renders these affordances irrelevant.

The problem of perceived affordances is that it reintroduces uncertainty into the description of technology that the theory of affordances was meant to overcome. If we are only interested in perceived affordances, then we have no objective measure that will allow us to determine whether a description of technology is complete. Affordances then become individual and reliant upon a number of accidental properties of the user, such as education, experience, age, etc. The affordance of a particular piece of software, for example, then changes between users and over time. In the case of technologies such as AmI, this raises additional problems given that one of the core features of AmI is its invisibility. It is thus possible to not notice it at all, which may imply that it has no affordances. In order to evade this trap, some sort of awareness raising or education will be required, which means that the affordances of the technology will depend not only on the technology itself and its users but also on the process of introducing the technology and the motivations of those who introduce it.

2.4 Multi-stability of Technology

Don Ihde (1999) has developed a different terminology that is meant to address the same problem as that of technological affordances. Ihde argues that technology is multi-stable. His argument refers to the issue of technology prognosis and the role that philosophy can play in it. Retrospective evaluation of technology and its conesquences may be possible, but prospective work encounters the problem of multistability. By multi-stability he means that technology cannot take on any social role and use, thus addressing the problem of indefinite possibilities that arises from social constructivism and interpretive flexibility. But while the possibilities that exist are not infinite, they are still greater than one. Technology, once it develops, will become stable but which of a number of possible trajectories it takes is not foreseeable. This multi-stability refers to uses but also effects, side effects, and other outcomes.

The idea of trajectories within multi-stable technologies is the key to addressing the problem of prognosis. Ihde contends that full prognosis may be impossible, but that the trajectories are at least partially determined which can allow a limited prediction of possible futures.

2.5 The Description and Prognosis of Emerging Technologies

This position seems to suggest that it is possible to get some sort of acceptable handle on dealing with emerging ICTs. This section has discussed the problems of describing technologies. Using arguments from several backgrounds, it was argued that it is difficult to give a correct account of any technology, including the most widely spread ones. This difficulty is exacerbated when the object of investigation is no longer an existing technology but shifts to future technologies. The further the temporal horizon of investigation, the less clear the description becomes (Collingridge 1981).

With regards to our problem of AmI, we can now distinguish several aspects of the uncertainty of the concept. The uncertainty of AmI is partly explained by the interpretive flexibility, which means that the individual's view of the technology is not determined by his or her perceptions. This is all the more the case because AmI exists more as a concept than a present socio-technical reality. Because of this uncertainty, it is unclear what the affordances of AmI are. We have seen that there is disagreement about the ontological status of affordances (i.e., whether affordances are real properties of technologies or whether they are observer-dependent). Even if one were to concede that affordances are objective, the next problem would remain: that the developing nature of AmI make them difficult if not impossible to determine. This corresponds with Ihde's point about the multi-stability of technology. At present it is not possible to predict which trajectory AmI will take. While there is significant marketing activity which supports particular paths, it is unclear whether these will materialize.

The contribution of this section is to show that there are at least four different positions that seek to explain the same phenomenon, namely the impossibility of comprehensively describing technology and especially of finding a description of relevant futures. The paper does not claim that these are the only ways of framing the problem. It aims to underline, however, that all of these positions have some influence on the debate in information systems, but even collectively they have not sufficed to convince the field of the importance of addressing the problem. If we have no way of knowing whether a particular description of technology is the right one, then how can we do research on the technology and how can we make policy decisions that provide the basis of a desirable future?

3 Participative Technology Assessment: A Way Forward?

The problem of uncertainty of emerging technology cannot be solved in the same way a technical problem may be solved. The different perspectives outlined above all point to the inevitability of uncertainty. However, we still have to make decisions about the future, despite this uncertainty. There are numerous ways of doing this, all of which have different advantages and disadvantages. This paper suggests that there are established ways of dealing with technologies that can compensate for some of the uncertainties of emerging technologies. Specifically, the paper suggests that participatory technology assessment (pTA) can overcome some of the problems. As will be argued in more detail below, pTA can overcome the epistemological problem by broadening the knowledge base of new technologies. At the same time, it is based on democratic principles and therefore can contribute to the legitimacy of decisions based on the descriptions of technology, even where these may be contested.

pTA is a branch of technology assessment (TA) that uses participatory methodologies and approaches. TA has a long history, going back to the 1960s, as an institutionalized attempt to understand issues of science and technology. Much early TA work was inspired by the U.S. Office of Technology Assessment with many countries creating similar institutions at the parliamentary or governmental level with the specific remit of providing policy advice (Joss 2002). Much early TA work was expert-centered but, as the limitations of this expert-centered approach became obvious, participatory methods were increasingly employed. There are several competing concepts that cover the same area, such as constructive TA (Joss and Belucci 2002; Schot 2001; Schot and Rip 1996). For the purposes of this paper, the differences between these concepts are of secondary importance and we will, therefore, use the term pTA following Joss and Belucci's (2002, p. 5) definition that "the term 'participatory technology assessment' (pTA) refers to the class of methods and procedures of assessing socio-technological issues that actively involve various kinds of social actors as assessors and discussants." pTA has been established as a useful and legitimate way of undertaking TA. The cognitive, normative, and pragmatic benefits outlined above have given rise to significant experimentation with pTA to the point that there now is wide acceptance of its importance and contribution (Joss 2002).

Methodologies of pTA are not necessarily simple and clear-cut. They depend on a number of factors including the research question, intended outcomes, type of respondents, experience of facilitators, cultural background, and political embedding to name but a few. Methodologies need to be carefully tuned and customized for any specific project (Hennen 2002).

Having proposed pTA as the response to the problem of this paper, namely the appropriate description of emerging ICTs, it is worthwhile reviewing the pTA literature in order to cross-check whether the expected benefits have been identified by pTA practitioners and to assess whether work in the area has led to the identification of problems that can jeopardise the success of the approach.

3.1 Benefits of pTA

Belucci et al. (2002) distinguish two main arguments in favor of participative work: pragmatic arguments that underline the function of participation as a means to improve decision making and normative arguments that underline the democratic aspect. These lines of arguments are linked to two main underlying problem areas: uncertainty and inequality. These lines of argument, while analytically different, are practically closely intertwined. A further dimension in addition to the pragmatic and the normative one is the cognitive.

The cognitive dimension has to do with knowledge of the problem area in question. Participation involves the individuals who are affected by the problem area and who have the most advanced local knowledge. By being able to tap into this often unused pool of local knowledge, a better understanding of the problem is developed. Genus and Cole (2005) hold that epistemological advantages of participation include an anticipation of impacts of technology, thus exhibits a move from reaction to proactive involvement. The "deep learning" that they associate with participation covers not only facts but also associated values. There is furthermore an aspect of reflexivity which ensures that the actors in participative projects develop a better understanding of their mutual roles and interests. The importance of this cognitive role of participation is caused by the often problematic role of the subject area. Political, social, or ethical implications of technology do not result from their design but from a combination of design features, meanings associated with them, and social and material structures and practices of implementation (Brey 2002).

An important aspect of the cognitive dimension is related to risk or dangers posed by the technology. The intensive discussion of technical risks during the last two decades (Beck 1986) indicates quite clearly that risks emanating from technologies are not objective and easily measurable entities but are intrinsically related to stakeholders' perceptions and beliefs. Identifying such risks, dangers, and uncertainties is therefore something that requires the involvement of stakeholders beyond the technical experts (Callon et al. 2009). At the same time it is beyond doubt that early addressing of risks would be desirable and in many cases would open more possibilities than attempting to fix problems after they arise. This requires a better understanding of problems as provided by the cognitive function of participation.

Participative engagement in science and technology can overcome cognitive closures by forcing different participants to take each others' views seriously. This helps overcome expert bias in that expert opinions are taken seriously as an important contribution to socially constructed knowledge but are recognized as one among several such sources (Klüver 2002). Participation requires mutual respect and effects mutual learning between different actors. This mutual learning is an important aspect and outcome of participative work, which may render it worthwhile even in those cases where manifest pragmatic outcomes such as measurable influence on policy making do not materialize (Hansen 2006).

This means that participation needs to play a central role not only in determining policy choices with regard to ICT, but also that it needs to start earlier, at the problem definition and framing stage. Emerging ICTs are by their nature uncertain and not clearly defined. Local knowledge and stakeholder engagement, the input of "hybrid forums" (Callon et al. 2009) are necessary to ascertain that the problems are appropriately understood and expressed before governance or policy can be considered.

This question of appropriate framing refers back to the earlier discussion of the nature of technology, to interpretive flexibility and multi-stability. The value of such a participative approach is therefore not only confined to research and policyoriented activity but has also been recognized by businesses that increasingly leverage user knowledge in product innovation (von Hippel 2006), thereby making use of the same underlying phenomenon.

In addition to the cognitive and epistemological advantages of participation, there are also political and normative advantages which lead to an increase in the legitimacy of policy. As Bütschi and Nentwich (2002) point out, despite the increased knowledge base, participative engagement in science and technology rarely leads to unforeseen or unforeseeable results. It can still provide important inputs by giving new ways of understanding the problem and bestowing legitimacy on decisions. This is based on the increasingly obvious political nature of science and technology (Callon et al. 2009) which requires decisions to gain political legitimacy. This legitimacy is achieved by giving a voice to those who are affected (Genus and Coles 2005), which ensures higher levels of acceptability of outcomes than purely expert-drive procedures (Hennen 2002).

One of the mechanisms that bestow higher levels of legitimacy on participatively arrived-at outcomes is that participation can be interpreted as a type of democratization. Democracy, along with freedom and justice, is a primary virtue of a good society, and it implies that citizens have an equal say in decisions (Brey 2008). Representative democracy as the main implementation of the democratic principle in modern democratic states runs into a number of problems, notably with regard to the representation of minorities (Callon et al. 2009). Other, more direct forms of democracy, as emulated in some methods of participation, can overcome this problem and thereby strengthen the legitimacy of outcomes.

At this point political mechanisms such as direct democracy and technical developments converge on the concept of empowerment. Technology has become a primary means of empowerment but at the same time leads to potential differences in empowerment (Brey 2008). Recognizing such issues is a task of participation.

In addition to the cognitive, normative, and pragmatic advantages, there seems to be another attraction of participation, which is its theoretical background. Participation is based on discursive exchanges and it can therefore build on the rich background of discourse theories. The range of discourse theories, including the notable examples of Habermas's and Foucault's views on discourse (Ashenden and Owen1999; Kelly 1994), provide scholars with a rich background from which to draw descriptions and conceptualizations. It points to a rich body of knowledge concerning empirical interventions and interpretations of discourses.

3.2 Problems of Participative Technology Assessment

The link to discourse theory can also serve to highlight some of the disadvantages and limitations of participative interventions in science and technology. The much-discussed differences between Habermas and Foucault, for example, can be used to identify problems of participative methods (Genus and Coles 2005). The nature of the discursive relationship among participants can determine the success of the overall intervention. The arguments in favor of participation are based on deliberative ideals which are rarely realized in practice (Hansen 2006). This lack of fulfilment of theoretical conditions can have a direct effect on the outcomes.

There are a number of problems that can arise in the course of participation. Discourses may take place in an environment where preconceived notions dominate all possible outcomes, thereby leading to an infinite regress of identical arguments. There can be skewed discourses based on differing levels of discursive abilities of participants or because of strategic interests of particular participants. Particular interests may attempt to highjack the discourse for their purposes.

But even if none of these situated and particular problems arise, it may still be the case that participation does not lead to the desired outcomes. This may be because some stakeholders are not available to participate and cannot be represented in an appropriate way. It may also be the case that no shared view of the problem emerges and not even an agreement on central disagreements is possible. The legitimacy of participation may be jeopardized when it is perceived to be in conflict with representative democracy. And finally, even in the positive case that the process fulfils the hopes invested in it, it is entirely possible that the outcomes are not clear-cut, recommendations are ambiguous, and answers remain vague.

Returning to the ongoing example of Ami, this discussion of pTA could be translated into an approach to participatively understand and shape AmI. This would require an appropriate mechanism of stakeholder involvement, which pTA can provide. On the basis of a representative and legitimate process, stakeholders could contribute their understanding of the technology as well as collectively develop a clearer picture of real and desired or undesired properties of the technology. Such a view would to some degree address the epistemological uncertainty surrounding AmI. More importantly, a participative approach might define roadmaps for a technology future that is deemed to be desirable and acceptable by the stakeholders. Such a roadmap could then provide the basis for democratic policy development. This scenario at the same time also shows the limitations of the approach. While collective action may claim a higher degree of knowledge, it is just as fallible as individual. The legitimacy of participative engagement can conflict with the legitimacy of representative democratic processes. There is thus no perfect solution. However, the example of AmI should have shown that we have a better chance of coming to technologies that are conducive to individual and social aims when we employ participative methods than if we continue to leave them purely in the hands of unsupervised market forces.

4 Conclusion

This paper was motivated by the apparent ease with which terms such as "future IT" or "emerging ICT" are used in public discourses, including the theme of this IFIP conference. It set out to explore the problems of this usage of terms. Drawing on several streams of the philosophy of technology and other theoretical arguments, it demonstrated that a correct, appropriate, or even true description of technologies is difficult to achieve. This is true in the case of existing and widely spread technologies, but even more so for technologies that are not yet fully developed and in some stage of emergence.

The epistemological uncertainty of emerging technologies can be explained using concepts such as interpretive flexibility, affordances, or multi-stability. While such concepts are theoretically helpful in understanding the limitations of research on these technologies, they offer little practical recourse to overcome these problems. This is a significant problem because it renders obsolete any attempts to steer the development of technology in desired paths. This is true for high-level policy makers on a national or international level, but it raises similar issues for decision makers on a sectoral or organizational level. If we don't know what future technologies to expect, then how can we plan for them?

Drawing on the literature surrounding pTA, it was argued that the epistemological as well as the ethical issues raised by emerging ICTs can be addressed by means of pTA. This does not promise perfect solutions but it provides a way forward where otherwise the only solutions might have been to ignore the problem of emerging ICTs or to simply extrapolate past developments into the future.

The paper makes a significant contribution to the theoretical discourse on emerging ICTs and thereby to the field of IS. It brings together the main strands of debate: the epistemology of technology (i.e., interpretive flexibility, affordances, multi-stability), and the discourse surrounding pTA. This allows a better understanding of theoretical and conceptual issues that an evaluation of technology in general, and of emerging technology in particular, raise. It provides ways of crosspollination between these strands of discourse that improves our understanding of technology. It also points the way toward approaches and methodologies that will allow us to give answers to the difficult questions surrounding future technologies.

While the main contribution of the paper is of a theoretical nature, it has interesting implications for practice. If the argument of the paper holds, then this implies that improving our understanding of emerging ICTs will require engaging in participative methods of assessment. There are numerous such methods that have been explored, ranging from focus groups to consensus conferences or citizens' panels. What is less well explored is how these can be used for a range of problems to which they have not been applied. This refers in particular to the question of participation being organized on a local or company level.

The present paper thus points the way toward a rich and complex area of empirical research. Which participative methods are suitable and conducive for which type of technology? This is a question that should be of interest to decision makers in charge of technology policy on a range of levels. A further question is how this participative idea relates to other approaches. There are numerous ways of designing ICT that actively seek to include user and stakeholder views and positions. These include approaches such as human-centered and value-sensitive design, but also many of the more established methodologies that evolved from soft systems and related approaches. The theoretical and practical compatibility of these approaches are in need of investigation.

When technology assessment was in its infancy, much technology development was directly steered or undertaken by the state. This is no longer the case and certainly not in the area of ICTs. This raises the question whether participative interventions, such as the ones suggested here, can actually have a place and a practical outcome in the current socio-economic climate.

All of these questions are theoretically interesting and practically important. Together they can inform us whether we are still in control of technology development and how this control can be implemented in a transparent and democratic manner.

Acknowledgments

The research leading to these results has received funding from the European Community's Seventh Framework Programme (FP7/2007-2013) under grant agreement no. [230318].

References

Adam, A.: Computer Ethics in a Different Voice. Information and Organization 11(4), 235–261 (2001)

Anscombe, G.E.M.: Modern Moral Philosophy. Philosophy 33(124), 1–19 (1958)

Ashenden, D.S., Owen, D.D.: Foucault Contra Habermas: Recasting the Dialogue between Genealogy and Critical Theory. Sage Publications Ltd, London (1999)

Beck, U.: Risikogesellschaft. Auf dem Weg in eine andere Moderne. Suhrkamp, Frankfurt (1986)

Belucci, S., Bütschi, D., Gloede, F., Hennen, L., Joss, S., Klüver, L., Nentwich, M., Peissl, W., Torgersen, H., van Eijndhoven, J., van Est, R.: Research Framework: Theoretical Perspectives, Analytical Framework, Research Protocol. In: Joss, S., Belluci, S. (eds.) Participatory Technology Assessment: European Perspectives, pp. 13–58. Centre for the Study of Democracy, University of Westminster, London (2002)

Bijker, W.E.: Of Bicycles, Bakelites, and Bulbs: Toward a Theory of Sociotechnical Change (Rev. Ed.). MIT Press, Cambridge (1997)

Brey, P.: The Technological Construction of Social Power. Social Epistemology 22(1), 71–95 (2008)

Bütschi, D., Nentwich, M.: The Role of Participatory Technology Assessment in the Policy-Making Process. In: Joss, S., Belluci, S. (eds.) Participatory Technology Assessment: European Perspectives, pp. 235–256. Centre for the Study of Democracy, University of Westminster, London (2002)

Cadili, S., Whitley, E.A.: On the Interpretative Flexibility of Hosted ERP Systems. Journal of Strategic Information Systems 14(2), 167–195 (2005)

Callon, M., Lascoumes, P., Barthe, Y.: Acting in an Uncertain World: An Essay on Technical Democracy. MIT Press, Cambridge (2009)

Collingridge, D.: The Social Control of Technology. Palgrave Macmillan, London (1981)

Dusek, V.: Philosophy of Technology: An Introduction. Wiley Blackwell, Chichester (2006)

Gaver, W. W.: Technology Affordances [Internet]. In: Proceedings of the SIGCHI Conference on Human Factors in Computing Systems: Reaching through Technology, New Orleans, LA, pp. 79–84 (1991)

Genus, A., Coles, A.: On Constructive Technology Assessment and Limitations on Public Participation in Technology Assessment. Technology Analysis & Strategic Management 17(4), 433–443 (2005)

Hutchby, I.: Technologies, Texts and Affordances. Sociology 35(2), 441–456 (2001)

Gibson, J.J.: The Theory of Affordances. In: Shaw, R.E., Bransford, J.D. (eds.) Perceiving, Acting and Knowing, pp. 67–82. Lawrence Erlbaum Associates, Hillsdale (1977)

Grint, K., Woolgar, S.: The Machine at Work: Technology, Work and Organization. Polity Press, Cambridge (1997)

Hansen, J.: Operationalizing the Public in Participatory Technology Assessment: A Framework for Comparison Applied to Three Cases. Science and Public Policy 1(33), 571–584 (2006)

Hennen, L.: Impacts of Participatory Technology Assessment on its Societal Environment. In: Joss, S., Belluci, S. (eds.) Participatory Technology Assessment: European Perspectives, pp. 257–275. Centre for the Study of Democracy, University of Westminster, London (2002)

Howcroft, D., Mitev, N., Wilson, M.: What We May Learn from the Social Shaping of Technology Approach. In: Mingers, J., Willcocks, L.P. (eds.) Social Theory and Philosophy for Information Systems, pp. 329–371. Wiley, Chichester (2004)

Ihde, D.: Technology and Prognostic Sredicaments. AI & Society 1(13), 44–51 (1999)

Joss, S.: Toward the Public Sphere–Reflections on the Development of Participatory Technology Assessment. Bulletin of Science Technology Society 1(22), 220–231 (2002)

Joss, S., Belucci, S.: Participatory Technology Assessment in Europe: Introducing the EUROPTA Research Project. In: Joss, S., Belluci, S. (eds.) Participatory Technology Assessment: European Perspectives, pp. 3–11. Centre for the Study of Democracy, University of Westminster, London (2002)

Kant, I.: Kritik der reinen Vernunft. Neuauflage, Studienausgabe, Suhrkamp (1995)

Kelly, M.: Critique and Power: Recasting the Foucault/Habermas Debate. MIT Press, Cambridge (1994)

Klüver, L.: Project Management: A Matter of Ethics and Robust Decisions. In: Joss, S., Belluci, S. (eds.) Participatory Technology Assessment: European Perspectives, pp. 179–208. Centre for the Study of Democracy, University of Westminster, London (2002)

Latour, B.: Reassembling the Social: An Introduction to ActorBNetwork Theory (Rev. Ed.). Oxford University Press, Oxford (2007)

Law, J., Hassard, J.: Actor Network Theory and After. Wiley Blackwell, Chichester (1999)

Norman, D.A.: Affordance, Conventions, and Design. Interactions 6(3), 38–43 (1999)

Olsen, J.B., Pedersen, S.A., Hendricks, V.F.: A Companion to the Philosophy of Technology. Wiley Blackwell, Chichester (2009)

Schot, J.: Towards New Forms of Participatory Technology Development. Technology Analysis & Strategic Management 13(1), 39–52 (2001)

Schot, J., Rip, A.: The Past and Future of Constructive Technology Assessment. Technological Forecasting and Social Change 54(2/3), 252–268 (1996)

Suthers, D.: Technology Affordances for Intersubjective Meaning Making: A Research Agenda for CSCL. International Journal of Computer-Supported Collaborative Learning 1(3), 315–337 (2006)

van den Hoven, J.: The Use of Normative Theories in Computer Ethics. In: Floridi, E.B.L. (ed.) The Cambridge Handbook of Information and Computer Ethics. Cambridge University Press, New York (2010)

von Hippel, E.: Democratizing Innovation. MIT Press, Cambridge (2006)

About the Author

Bernd Carsten Stahl is Professor of Critical Research in Technology and Director the Centre for Computing and Social Responsibility at De Montfort University, Leicester, UK. His interests cover philosophical issues arising from the intersections of business, technology, and information, including the ethics of computing and critical approaches to information systems. From 2009 to 2011, he served as coordinator of the EU FP7 research project "Ethical Issues of Emerging ICT Applications" (ETICA) (GA 230318, www.etica-project.eu).

Conceptualizing Consumer Perceptions of Making M-Payments Using Smart Phones in Ireland[*]

Pavel Andreev[1], Aidan Duane[2], and Philip O'Reilly[3]

[1] Sagy Center for Internet Research & the Study of the Information Society,
The Graduate School of Management,
University of Haifa, Israel
andreevil@gmail.com

[2] The School of Business, Department of Accounting and Economics, Waterford Institute of Technology (WIT), Waterford, Ireland
ADuane@wit.ie

[3] Department of Accounting, Finance & Information Systems, University College Cork, Cork, Ireland Philip
OReilly@ucc.ie

Abstract. Consumer adoption of smart phones is growing globally at an exponential rate presenting significant commercial opportunities for all organizations. The percentage of the population using mobile phones in Ireland is the largest in Europe, with market revenue of €2 billion in 2009, and 117.3 percent penetration. However, the commercial growth potential of smart phones is being hindered by an industry failure to adopt an accepted m-payment model to facilitate the widespread adoption of m-payments. Furthermore, previous research has shown there is a lack of a willingness among consumers to make m-payments. However, little is known about consumers' perceptions of m-payments using a smart phone or what factors impact upon these perceptions. In response, this paper develops a theoretical smart phone m-payment model, and applies it using an online survey, to explore Irish consumers' perceptions of making an m-payments for products/ services using their smart phones. The empirical findings of the developed PLS model, illustrate that respondents display a strong willingness to transact using m-commerce but trust is the key factor in explaining consumer's willingness to make an m-payment for products/ services using their smart phones. Another significant finding for m-payment companies is that respondents considered using a secure and trusted third-party payment company as the preferred method of making an m-payment for products/ services. Significant levels of concern regarding perceived privacy control, together with the authority and independence of regulatory bodies and the robustness of the legislative frameworks governing m-commerce, were also very evident from the empirical findings.

Keywords: Smart phones, pm-payment adoption, trust, consumer percep tions.

---

[*] All authors contributed equally to this paper.

M. Chiasson et al. (Eds.): Future IS 2011, IFIP AICT 356, pp. 109–129, 2011.
© IFIP International Federation for Information Processing 2011

1 Introduction

Smart phones have developed and evolved to incorporate multiple applications and wide ranging functionality, including SMS, MMS, mobile web, GPS navigation, photo, and video camera. Such functionality is an enabler of a wide range of commercial products and services. Indeed, the notion that smart phones could become valuable and critical business tools for the delivery of electronic products and services has long been touted by academics, professionals, and the media (Bauer et al. 2005; Gao and Küpper 2006; Hsu and Kulviwat 2006; Leppäniemi and Karjaluoto 2005; Varshney and Vetter 2002). From a commercial perspective, smart phone strategies are being adopted by major global organizations, and these organizations are eager to explore the personal, interactive, and ubiquitous features of smart phones to increase the effectiveness of their service provision and product commercialization beyond the use of traditional media channels. Furthermore, the growth of smart phones is phenomenal with global shipments of smart phones growing 50 percent each year, reaching 54 million units in the first quarter of 2010 (Evans 2010). The percentage of the population using mobile phones in Ireland is the largest in Europe, with market revenue of €2 billion in 2009, and 117.3 percent penetration based on a population of 4,459,300 people (ComReg 2009). In 2010, one out of every two mobile phones sold in Ireland were smart phones (Vodafone Ireland 2010).

However, the realization of the remarkable commercial potential of smart phones is contingent on consumer willingness to employ these devices for transactional tasks, such as bookings, ticketing tasks, accessing GPS services, and gathering information on and purchasing products/services. Inherently, these tasks require a secure, efficient and reliable m-payment system. An m-payment may be defined, in the context of this paper, as any electronic payment where a smart phone is used to initiate, authorize, and confirm exchange of financial value in return for products and services.

While growth forecasts for m-payment services have been very positive, the reality is quite different with a study by the Gartner Group illustrating that in 2008, only 1 percent of all mobile phone users had used m-payment services. This observation leads to the question of why consumers have not adopted m-payments. Mallat (2007) notes that there is considerable evidence that users perceive significant risks and uncertainty in transacting with Internet vendors through computers, an issue yet to be explored in relation to smart phones. McKnight et al. (2003) argue this issue is compounded by extensive media coverage about privacy, security, and fraud on the Internet. While such research issues have been examined in the realm of computers, they are yet to be explored for smart phones.

The absence of standardized, interconnected, and widely accepted payment procedures, crucial for the successful diffusion of m-payments, is also a significant growth inhibitor of the commercialization of smart phones (Zhong 2009). This may be a consequence of the significant number of potential stakeholders and vested interests in the area of m-payments including banks, mobile network operators, credit card companies, and third-party payment companies, which all have proposed various models aimed at streamlining the m-payment market. Essentially, these proposed m-payment models center on (1) mobile network operator led, (2) bank and financial institution led, and (3) third-party led models, or numerous variations/combinations of these (Turner 2009). Despite these efforts, an accepted m-payment model to facilitate the widespread adoption of m-payments has not been adopted. Consumers will play a key role in determining the "winning" model as without consumer buy-in, any proposed m-payment model will not succeed.

While extant research (Matthews et al. 2009) illustrates that most users utilize the phone, SMS, MMS, and Internet services of the mobile phone, little is known about consumers' perceptions of m-payment using a smart phone or what factors impact their perceptions. Therefore, gaining insight into consumers' perceptions of m-payments using a smart phone is crucial as, within the extant literature, there remains a lack of insight into consumers' perceptions of m-payments. It is the objective of this paper to begin to bridge this gap in understanding by developing and applying a theoretical smart phone m-payment model to explore Irish consumers' perceptions of making a m-payments for products/services using their smart phones. The smart phone m-payment model is applied using an online survey hosted on www.SurveyMonkey.com, an online subscription based surveying tool. The target population of Irish mobile phone users were informed of this survey by email and through a private Irish mobile phone users' discussion group on www.Boards.ie. This paper also answers the call for research by Dahlberg et al. (2008, p. 178), who state

> Yet, we believe that more theory based empirical research is needed to enhance the current understanding of the m-payment services markets....to improve the quality and relevance of m-payment research, we also recommend that researchers collect more empirical data backed by guiding theories.

2 Conceptualization of Consumers Perceptions of M-Payment

Consumers' lack of willingness to make an m-payment is a significant barrier to m-payment adoption, and it is very much influenced by their assessment of the risk involved (Mallat 2007). Viehland and Leong (2007) state that in order for m-payments to succeed, they must be secure (consumer perception), convenient, and easy to use. Therefore, perceived payment reliability—a consumer's perception of the reliability of making an m-payment using a smart phone—and ease of use are important issues if smart phones are to realize their true commercial potential. Thus far, m-payment services have failed to entice consumers and several m-payment companies and initiatives in the EU have failed or have been abandoned (Mallat 2007; Dahlberg and Oorni 2007). With many and varied payment models proposed (Turner 2009), gaining an understanding of consumers' perceptions of making m-payments using smart phones is thus required in order to develop m-payment services successfully (Dahlberg and Oorni 2007).

In order to develop a model to explain consumers' willingness to make m-payments using smart phones, literature in the areas of trust and consumer behavior (including the theory of planned behavior, decision theory, and the theory of reasoned action) were reviewed. Several studies (Chen and Barnes 2007; Gefen et al. 2003; Jarvenpaa et al. 2000; Vewrhagen et al. 2006) have found that trust is a significant determinant influencing consumers' willingness to conduct e-commerce transactions and a key obstacle to vendors succeeding on the Internet, as a lack of trust discourages consumers making an e-commerce transaction. Similar studies (Mallat 2007; Siau et al. 2004; Xu and Gutierrez 2006) indicate that trust is also a significant determinant of consumers' willingness to make m-commerce transactions and m-payment. Trust is a significant factor for m-commerce transactions because of the spatial and temporal separation between buyers and sellers when buyers are required to provide personal and payment data to suppliers (Grabner-Kräuter and Kaluscha 2003).

In the context of e-commerce, as illustrated in Table 1, Cheung and Lee (2000) captured a significant set of trust antecedents by synthesizing the literature on consumer trust including perceived security control, perceived privacy control, and perceived integrity.

Table 1. Trust Antecedents for E-Commerce (adapted from Cheung and Lee 2000)

Trust Antecedents	Description
Perceived Security Control	User's perception of Internet vendor's ability in fulfilling security requirements, such as authentication, integrity, encryption, and non-repudiation.
Perceived Privacy Control	User's perception on the ability of Internet vendor's in protecting consumers' personal information collected from electronic transactions, from unauthorized use or disclosure.
Perceived Integrity	Refers to the perception of Internet users on the honesty of Internet vendors. For instance, whether it has consistent actions, whether its' actions are congruent with its own words and whether its transactions are fair.

Similar trust antecedents emerge from the literature on m-commerce. Shortcomings in security and privacy controls reduce people's trust in m-payment systems and hinder the emergence of these systems (Chou et al. 2004). Consumers' concerns about the privacy and security of m-payments as they relate to authentication and confidentiality, and privacy and ethical issues relating to concerns about third-party use and unauthorized access to payments and user data (Dewan and Chen 2005), are notable in previous research. Thus, consumer trust in legal frameworks and independent regulatory bodies to protect and regulate their transactions and data, are also essential to reduce consumers perceived risks of m-commerce and making an m-payment (Cleff 2007). Regulation of data protection often clashes with commercial practices to maximize m-commerce activities via mobile technologies (Cleff 2007). Critically, Mallat (2007) found that trust in merchants and in m-payment and mobile network service providers was essential to encourage consumers to engage in m-commerce transactions and to reduce consumers perceived risks of m-payments. Trust has a positive impact on consumer loyalty and satisfaction towards m-commerce (Lin and Wang 2006) and it is, therefore, a critical component of any model seeking to explain consumers' willingness to transact in an m-commerce environment and to make an m-payment.

Reviewing these trust antecedents as they relate to consumers' willingness to engage in electronic commercial transactions and willingness to perform an m-payment, results in the identification of several trust measures, presented in Table 2, and the generation of two specific hypotheses:

Hypothesis 1a: Consumer trust in the ethical, privacy, and data protection controls of service providers, and perception that the legal and regulatory frameworks are sufficiently robust and independent, positively impact consumers' willingness to engage in m-commerce transactions using a smart phone.

Hypothesis 1b: Consumer trust in the ethical, privacy, and data protection controls of service providers, and perception that the legal and regulatory frameworks are sufficiently robust and independent, positively impacts upon consumers' willingness to make m-payments using a smart phone.

Table 2. Trust Measures Utilized for this Study

Element	*Literature*
Legal Frameworks: The perception by consumers that the legal frameworks governing transactions and payments using smart phones are sufficiently robust to protect consumers.	Cleff 2007; Johanssen 2003
Ethical Commitment: Consumers perception that service providers act ethically when capturing, retaining, processing, and managing my personal data.	Mallet 2007; McKnight et al. 2003; Chou et al. 2004; Dewan and Chen 2005; Johanssen 2003
Providers Perspectives on Consumer Privacy: Consumers perceptions that service providers are concerned with consumers' privacy.	Mallet 2007; McKnight et al. 2003; Chou et al. 2004; Dewan and Chen 2005; Johanssen 2003
Privacy Controls of Service Providers: Consumers confidence in the privacy controls of Service Providers.	Mallet 2007; McKnight et al. 2003; Chou et al. 2004; Dewan and Chen 2005; Johanssen 2003
Transfer of Consumer Data to Third Parties: Consumers beliefs that service providers will not divulge consumers' personal data to third parties.	Mallet 2007; McKnight et al. 2003; Johanssen 2003
Power of Regulatory Bodies: Consumers perceptions that regulatory bodies for service provision are sufficiently authoritative to regulate smart phone Service Providers.	Clef 2007; Johanssen 2003
Independence of Regulatory Bodies: Consumers perceptions that the regulatory bodies for service provision are sufficiently independent to regulate smart phone service providers.	Clef 2007; Johanssen 2003

Kim and Zhang (2009) state that an individual's rationale for adopting smart phone services is under-investigated in the extant literature. Indeed, Kim and Zhang note that there can be numerous factors influencing people's adoption of smart phone services. The technology acceptance model (TAM) proposed by Davis (1989) has been a widely cited model for predicting and explaining user behavior and IT usage through focusing on perceived usefulness and perceived ease of use. Perceived usefulness refers to one's tendency of using or not using an application to the extent that the person believes it will help them perform their tasks better (Davis 1989) Perceived ease of use is defined "as the degree to which a prospective user expects the target system to be free of effort" (Davis 1989, p. 321). Extant research has illustrated that perceived ease of use has a direct effect on perceived usefulness, and that both determine the consumer's attitude toward use (Viehland and Leong 2007).

TAM has previously been utilized to explore m-payments. Viehland and Leong (2007) examined perceived usefulness and perceived ease of use on consumers' willingness to use m-payment services for retail point-of-sale payments. Given the technical limitations of mobile devices, ease of use becomes an imminent acceptance driver of mobile applications. Schierz et al. (2010) note that this is especially true for m-payment services, which compete with established payment solutions and thus need to provide benefits when it comes to ease of use. Therefore, one of the main reasons for the slow diffusion of m-payments, in particular, could be a failure in understanding the perception among consumers of the ease of use of m-payments using smart phones.

Utilizing the logic inherent in extant research on TAM (Davis 1989; Venkatesh and Davis 1996), a system must be both easy to learn and easy to use. Applying this logic to smart phones, we hypothesize that the perceived ease of use of smart phones in relation to (1) transaction-based services and (2) m-payments will impact upon utilization of both of these categories of services on smart phones. These concepts can be incorporated into our model in order to determine the relationships between the perceived ease of use/usefulness of smart phones and their association with consumers' willingness to transact using a smart phone and consumers' willingness to make an m-payment for products/services using a smart phone. The supporting literature upon which these are based is outlined in Table 3. This leads to the generation of two additional hypotheses:

Hypothesis 2a: The perceived ease of use of services available through smart phones positively impact consumers' willingness to engage in m-commerce transactions using smart phones.

Hypothesis 2b: The perceived ease of use of services available through smart phones positively impact consumers' willingness to make an m-payment for products/services using a smart phone.

Table 3. Perceived Ease of Use Measures

Element	*Literature*
Ease of Use: Consumers' perceptions of the overall ease of use of smart phones for transactional and payment purposes .	Viehland and Leong 2007; Kim and Zhang 2009; Davis 1989
Knowledge: Consumers' perceptions that the use of smart phones does not require a lot of knowledge.	Viehland and Leong 2007; Davis 1989; Kim et al. 2010
Technical Skills: Consumers' perceptions that the use of smart phones does not require a lot of technical skills.	Viehland and Leong 2007; Davis 1989

Kim et al. (2010) note that there is a certain amount of empirical evidence in the mobile technology literature regarding users' intention to use mobile technology, with users using m-payment systems when they find the system to be useful for their transaction needs. From a commercial perspective, it would be beneficial to understand if there is an association between consumers' willingness to use smart phones for m-commerce transactions and consumers' willingness to make an m-payment for products/ services using a smart phone. This enables the generation of one final hypothesis:

Hypothesis 3: A consumer's willingness to engage in m-commerce trans-actions through their smart phone will positively impact their perceptions of making smart phone m-payments.

By combining these hypotheses, we can present a smart phone m-payment model (Figure 1).

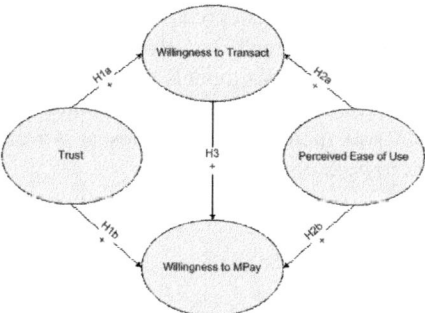

Fig. 1. A Smart Phone M-Payment Model

In operationalizing the constructs in this study, indicators from the literature were adopted enabling questions to be developed for the data collection aspect of the study. These indicators and their associated questions are outlined in Appendix A, Table A1.

3   Method

3.1   Data Collection

In operationalizing the model (Figure 1), a survey instrument was developed. A number of previous studies (e.g., Verhagen et al. 2006; Davis 1989) have utilized a number of the constructs documented in this study. We adopted these reflective constructs to smart phones to generate candidate items for each construct. Manifest variables representing these constructs were measured using a seven-point Likert scale. Once an initial iteration of the instrument documented in Appendix A was generated, as per Hair et al. (2006), we pre-tested the instrument with targeted smart phones "experts" (people who all possessed and actively utilized smart phones as part of their daily lives) in order to assess the semantic content of the items. Those items that best fit and reflect the definitions of the constructs were retained, a process that facilitated the refinement and streamlining of the items included in this survey. The next phase of this research involved posting the survey live on the web using www.SurveyMonkey.com, a subscription-based online surveying tool. The survey was posted live for a one month period in June 2010 with Irish mobile phone users specifically being targeted in order to eliminate environmental and cultural issues. Irish consumers were informed of the survey by email and through a private online mobile phone users' discussion group on www.boards.ie.

3.2 Data Analyses

Structural equation modeling, a second generation[1] model testing tool, was used for the data analysis and hypotheses testing. Choosing the partial least squares (PLS) approach, which uses component-based estimation, is appropriate since it allows simultaneous exploration of both the measurement and the structural models. In addition, the PLS approach, compared to covariance-based SEM, allows testing the relationships in the model with less restrictive requirements. Another reason of choosing PLS is that this tool is considered to be appropriate for testing theories at earlier stages of development (Fornell and Bookstein 1982). PLS model might be described from the perspective of two models (Chatelin et al. 2002; Diamantopoulos 2006; Tenenhaus et al. 2005), the measurement (outer) model, relating the measurement variables (MV) to their latent variables (LV), and the structural (inner) model, relating the LVs to each other.

4 Results

4.1 Data Statistics

A total of 82 valid responses to the survey were received. Respondents originated from 12 of Ireland's 26 counties, including the 3 most densely populated cities of Dublin, Cork, and Waterford which, when combined, accounted for 68 percent of respondents. Of the respondents, 57 percent were in the 30–50 years age bracket, while 23 percent were between 18 and 30 years of age. In all, 85 percent of respondents were employed, with student respondents only accounting for 13 percent; 68 percent of respondents were educated to third (i.e., graduate diploma, master's) and fourth level post-graduate level (i.e., post-doctorate, Ph.D.) including 11 percent at post-doctorate and Ph.D. level, while 32 percent were educated to undergraduate third level (i.e., degree, diploma, certificate). Income levels of respondents included 46 percent with an annual salary between 40,000 and 80,000 Euros, while 17 percent earned more than 80,000 Euros per year. A total of 85 percent of respondents already owned a store loyalty smart card and 76 percent had registered for electronic or paperless billing/statements.

---

[1] The term second generation refers to the differentiation of classes of data analyses techniques rather than to a discrete point of time. This term has been used in IS research (and in other disciplines). For example, according to Gefen et al. (2000, p. 55), "Second generation data analysis techniques: Techniques enabling researchers to answer a set of interrelated research questions in a single, systematic, and comprehensive analysis by modeling the relationships among multiple independent and dependent constructs simultaneously."

This would indicate that the demographic attributes of a typical respondent to this survey is a person

- between the ages of 30-50 years,
- living in a large Irish city,
- educated to a post-graduate level,
- in full-time employment earning between 40,000 and 80,000 Euros per year, and
- already using smart cards and electronic billing/statements.

A total of 62 percent of respondents use the Internet for more than 2 hours per day, but 83 percent of respondents access the Internet using their mobile phone for less than 1 hour a day. In all, 90 percent of respondents talk on their phone for less than an hour per day, while 40 percent send more than 10 SMS messages per day. However, 78 percent of respondents never send an MMS from their mobile phone while 56 percent never send an email from their mobile phone. Of the respondents, 27 percent spend between 1 and 5 Euros per month on mobile phone services/applications, while 15 percent spend between 5 and 50 Euros per month.

This would indicate that the mobile technology profile of a typical respondent to this survey is a person who

- accesses the Internet via their mobile phone for less than an hour per day,
- talks on their mobile phone for less than an hour per day,
- regularly uses their mobile phone for SMS but rarely for MMS or email, and
- is currently using their mobile phone to purchase mobile services/applications.

On average, respondents indicated that they perceived smart phone services to be easy to use, and not requiring a lot of knowledge or technical skills to use. Respondents also displayed a strong willingness to transact, particularly to use smart phones for pulling information, ticketing, bookings/reservations, and using GPS functionality. Interestingly, respondents considered using a secure and trusted third-party payment company as the most preferred method of payment for products/services using their smart phone, while using their existing mobile network operator (MNO) to pay for products/services was also rated highly. Respondents displayed significant levels of concern regarding perceived privacy control and the authority and independence of regulatory bodies, and in the robustness of the legislative frameworks governing m-commerce.

4.2 Model Evaluation

Chin (1998) proposed the list of criteria to assess PLS models with reflective constructs. These criteria are highly accepted and adopted by researchers from different research fields (e.g., Gefen et al. 2000; Henseler et al. 2009; Tenenhaus et al. 2005). The evaluation process of the PLS path model results involves two steps. Step 1 necessitates the testing of the quality of the measurement (outer) models. As Step 1 was successful and latent constructs were found reliable and valid, Step 2, which necessitates the assessment of the structural (inner) model, was conducted (Henseler 2009). SmartPLS 2.0 M3 was employed for the PLS model assessment.

4.2.1 Assessment of Measurement Models

Reliability. The first criterion of assessment of measurement models is reliability, which is traditionally tested by internal consistency reliability and indicator reliability. Internal consistency reliability might be tested either by Cronbach's α, which indicates an estimation for the reliability assuming that all items are equally reliable, or by composite reliability, where different item loadings are taken into account. Although these two reliability measures differ, either of them may be used. As can be seen in Table 4, both parameters have high values (all values are above 0.91), while the requirement value should be above 0.7 at the earlier stage of the research and above 0.8–0.9 in the advanced stages (Henseler et al. 2005).

Table 4. Internal Consistency Reliability Test

Construct	Composite	Cronbach's
Per Ease of Use	0.9451	0.9127
Trust	0.9558	0.9461
Willingness to MPay	0.9665	0.9535
Willingness to Transact	0.9528	0.9341

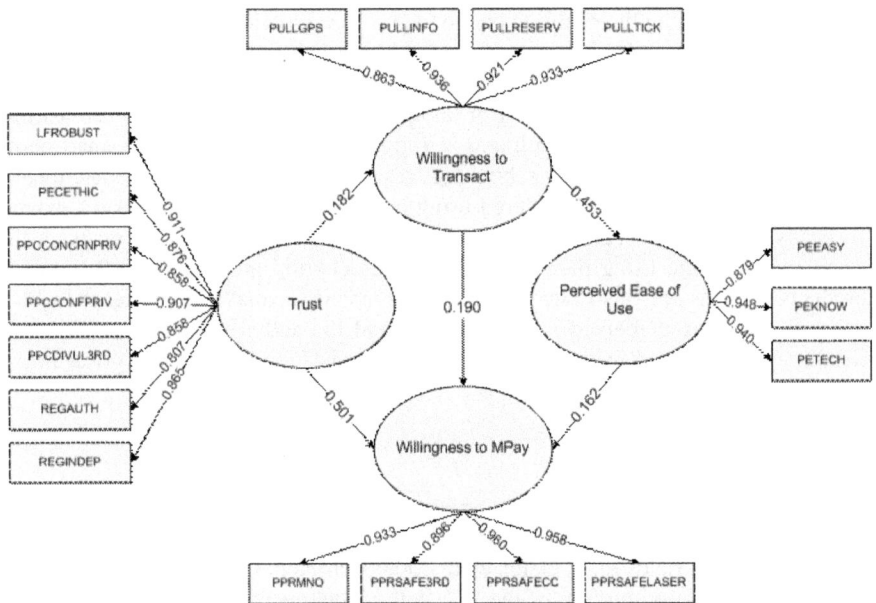

Fig. 2. PLS Results of Measurement and Structural Models

Individual reliability of the indicators relies on the expectation that latent variable variance should explain at least 50 percent of the indicator. In other words, loadings of manifest variables should be not less than 0.707 (Chin 1998; Gefen et al. 2000; Henseler et al. 2009).

Figure 2 demonstrates that magnitude of all indicators is higher than required the 0.707, with the lowest value of 0.807. Based on the two tests, we can conclude that all indicators are reliable.

Table 5. Construct Cross-Correlation Matrix and AVE Analyses

AVE	Construct	Per Ease	Trust	Wil to	Wil to
0.8517	Perceived Ease of Use	**0.9229**			
0.7558	Trust	0.3324	**0.8694**		
0.8782	Willingness to MPay	0.4261	0.6183	**0.9371**	
0.8348	Willingness to Transact	0.5138	0.3323	0.4398	**0.9137**

Table 6. Cross Loadings

Construct	Items	Per Ease	Trust	Wil to	Wil to
Perceived Ease of Use	PEEASY	**0.8793**	0.285	0.4119	0.526
	PEKNOW	**0.9483**	0.302	0.394	0.4378
	PETECH	**0.9395**	0.334	0.3676	0.4475
Trust	LFROBUST	0.2838	**0.9109**	0.5394	0.2823
	PECETHIC	0.3189	**0.876**	0.5498	0.2636
	PPCCONCRNPRIV	0.2924	**0.858**	0.6147	0.2985
	PPCCONFPRIV	0.3241	**0.907**	0.6264	0.3461
	PPCDIVUL3RD	0.3549	**0.8576**	0.5137	0.2067
	REGAUTH	0.2079	**0.8072**	0.3921	0.2705
	REGINDEP	0.2246	**0.8646**	0.4741	0.3395
Willingness to MPay	PPRMNO	0.414	0.6083	**0.9332**	0.3931
	PPRSAFE3RD	0.3431	0.5043	**0.8958**	0.4294
	PPRSAFECC	0.4564	0.5969	**0.9602**	0.4312
	PPRSAFELASER	0.3766	0.6013	**0.9578**	0.3981
Willingness to Transact	PULLGPS	0.4215	0.2262	0.258	**0.8628**
	PULLINFO	0.5481	0.3255	0.4232	**0.936**
	PULLRESERV	0.4779	0.2846	0.4085	**0.9214**
	PULLTICK	0.4203	0.36	0.4843	**0.9326**

Validity. The convergent validity and the discriminant validity are employed to examine the validity of four reflective constructs. The first column in Table 5 shows that the average variance extracted (AVE) for all constructs is higher than 0.5, which indicates sufficient convergent validity and means that each latent variable explains more than 50 percent of their indicator variance on average. Discriminant validity refers to the appropriate patterns of inter indicators of a construct and other constructs. First, variance of a construct should be assigned more with their own indicators than with other constructs. For this purpose, construct cross-correlation and the square root of each construct's AVE were compared. As can be seen in Table 5, all constructs have sufficient discriminant validity since the square root of each latent construct's AVE (values on the diagonal) is much larger than the correlation of the specific construct with any other reflective constructs in our research model. We also tested discriminant validity with cross-loading test. Results of the test presented in Table 6 demonstrate that an indicator of any specific construct has higher loading on its own construct than on any other constructs. The results of the tests show that manifest variables (indicators) presented in the research model are reliable and valid.

4.2.2 Assessment of the Structural Model

In assessing the explanatory and predictive power of the structural model, we employed a number of recommendations (Andreev et al. 2009; Chatelin et al. 2002; Chin 1998; Gefen et al. 2000; Henseler et al. 2005).

Explanatory Power. An overview of the structural model evaluation results is presented in Figure 3. The complete evaluation, containing both structural and measurement models, can be seen in Figure 2.

The central criterion for evaluating the structural model is the level of explained variance of the dependent construct *Willingness to MPay*, for which the R-square was 0.463. Thus, the model explained 46.3 percent of the construct's variance. The variance of the construct was explained at the moderate level according to Chin's (1998) criteria. R^2 values of 0.67, 0.33, or 0.19 for endogenous latent variables are described as substantial, moderate, or weak (Chin 1988, p. 323). The *Willingness to Transact* was explained at 29.3 percent by *Trust* and *Perceived Ease of Use*.

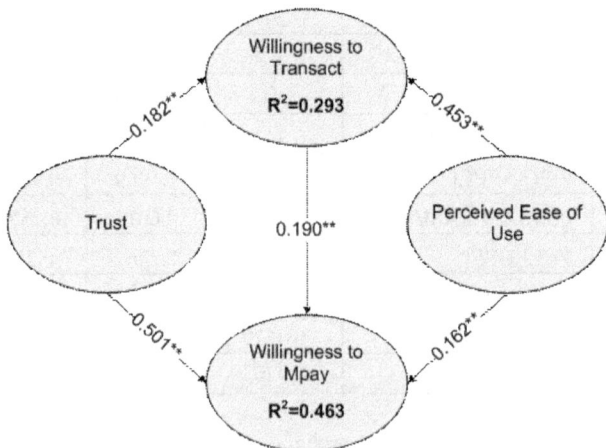

Fig. 3. Evaluation of Structural Model

Changes in R-square were explored to investigate the substantive impact of each independent construct on the dependent constructs, carrying out the effect size technique by rerunning three PLS estimations, excluding in each run one of the explaining latent constructs. PLS estimations of each model can be found in Appendix B.

Chin (1998) proposed using the effect size f^2 of PLS constructs, which is similar to Cohen's implementation for multiple regression and might be small ($f^2 = 0.02$), medium ($f^2 = 0.15$), or large ($f^2 = 0.35$).

Table 7. Effect Size Test

Construct	$R^2 excl$	$R^2 incl$	f^2	Effect
Perceived Ease of Use	0.446	0.463	0.03	small
Trust	0.248	0.463	0.40	large
Willingness to Transact	0.439	0.463	0.04	small

The results of the effect size test presented in Table 7 show that while *Perceived Ease of Use* and *Willingness to Transact* have small effects (with f^2's equal to 0.03 and 0.04, respectively), *Trust* has a large effect with magnitude of $f^2 = 0.4$.

Predictive power. The statistical significance of the path coefficients was tested by employing the bootstrapping re-sampling technique, using the SmartPLS software, with the graphical output for the structural model evaluation presented in in Appendix A, Figure A1. All path coefficients were found to be highly significant.

Willingness to MPay, as expected, was found to be positively affected by *Trust* (H1b supported with $\beta = -0.637$ and $p < 0.001$), *Willingness to Transact* (H3 supported with and $p < 0.001$), and *Perceived Ease of Use* (H2b supported with $\beta = -0.193$ and $p < 0.001$).

Willingness to Transact was found to be positively affected by *Trust* (H1a supported with $\beta = -0.637$ and $p < 0.001$), and *Perceived Ease of Use* (H2a supported with $\beta = -0.193$ and $p < 0.001$).

Our analysis revealed that all hypotheses were supported. For the evaluation of the *predictive relevance* of the structural model, the Stone and Geisser Q^2 test was performed using the blindfolding procedure, for which Chin (1998) stated that Q^2 reflects an index of goodness of reconstruction by model and parameter estimations. A positive Q^2 provides evidence that the omitted observations were well-reconstructed and that predictive relevance is achieved, while a negative Q^2 reflects absence of predictive relevance. As can be seen in Table 8, all values of Q^2 were greater than zero, indicating predictive relevance for the endogenous constructs of the research model.

Table 8. Blindfolding Test for Predictive Relevance

Construct	ΣSO	ΣSE	Q^2
Willingness to MPay	324	43.7389	0.865
Willingness to Transact	324	63.1417	0.8051

5 Discussion and Conclusions

Consumers' perceptions of using smart phones for m-transactions and m-payments is of scientific and practical interest. Smart phones present organizations with a vast potential for commercial opportunities. For commercial organizations, an understanding of consumer's perceptions of smart phones is of paramount importance. Yet, in an academic context, the extant literature is still immature. This paper, by exploring consumer's willingness to m-pay using smart phones, makes a number of contributions, which are of value to researchers and practitioners alike. A smart phone m-payment model is developed from a thorough analysis of the literature from a variety of fields including trust, consumer behavior (incorporating the theory of planned behavior, decision theory, and the theory of reasoned action).

Extant literature (Malat 2007; Viehland and Leong 2007) illustrates that users perceive significant risks associated with m-payment. Indeed, Mallat (2007) noted that consumer's unwillingness to make (conduct) m-payments is the greatest barrier to further adoption of this phenomenon. Extant literature (e.g., Viehland and Leong 2007) states that consumer's willingness to make an m-payment using a smart phone is an issue impacted by perceived ease of use and trust. However, both factors are treated the same in the extant literature with no differentiation being made between these factors in relation to their impact upon consumer's willingness to use m-payment. In explaining consumer's willingness to use smart phones for m-payment, this study presents a conceptual framework and provides empirical evidence that trust, willingness to transact, and perceived ease of use are key factors in explaining consumer's willingness to make an m-payment, with trust having the largest explanatory power.

Perceived ease of use has widely been documented in the literature (Venkatesh and Davis 1996) as having a key influence on the adoption and use of new technologies. However, the findings of this study, illustrate that while causation exists between perceived ease of use and willingness to make an m-payment, the association is relatively weak. This illustrates that perceived ease of use of the technology is not a key determinant of consumers' willingness to make an m-payment using a smart phone. Therefore, this study contradicts the findings of Schierz et al. (2010) and illustrates that although perceived ease of use is important, it is not actually a key factor in explaining the slow diffusion of m-payments using smart phones. However, respondents did have a high level of education, which may also be a factor in determining their perceptions of the ease of use of smart phone services. However, perceived ease of use is a key determinant in explaining a consumer's willingness to utilize smart phones for transactional tasks, such as bookings, ticketing, accessing GPS services, and pulling information on products/services. In interpreting these findings and trying to understand why perceived ease of use is a key determinant of a consumer's willingness to transact but yet has much less of an influence on consumer's willingness to make an m-payment, a possible explanation may be the current state of diffusion of the respective services, with consumers being much more familiar with, and having greater access to, transaction-based services. Furthermore, the findings illustrate that willingness to transact via a smart phone is a limited predictor of willingness to make an m-payment.

The findings of this study present conclusive evidence of the association between trust and consumer's willingness to make an m-payment using a smart phone. By exploring trust in detail, our analysis illustrates that consumer's perceptions of legal frameworks and the regulation of these frameworks are integral parts of trust. Analysis also revealed that consumer's perceptions of the privacy controls employed by smart phone service providers is a critical element of trust. This analysis would be of interest to practice.

In order to increase consumer's willingness to make an m-payment using smart phones, commercial entities need to communicate to consumers that they implement policies and utilize the latest technologies to protect the privacy and data of consumers. For government and commercial entities who wish to develop an m-payment culture, the implications of our findings are that a key step in getting consumers to utilize m-payment is to ensure that adequate legal frameworks are in place. Furthermore, the belief among consumers that regulatory bodies have sufficient powers to take actions against service providers who do not adhere to such frameworks is a key issue in building trust among consumers in order to get them to make m-payments using smart phones. Presently, among Irish consumers at least, this is not the case, with our findings illustrating that consumers perceive that regulatory bodies are not sufficiently authoritative or independent to regulate smart phone service providers. We are currently conducting a comparative study in an international context which will examine this further.

This paper is a response to calls for a better understanding of the emerging phenomenon of consumer utilization of smart phone m-payments and it represents a suitable response to the call for research by Dahlberg et al. (2008) and Kim and Zhang (2009). Nevertheless, there are a number of limitations to this study. The study is limited by its sample size with findings based on 82 respondents participating in the study. Therefore, further research needs to be conducted to reexamine the model with a larger sample size. This model also needs to be tested on a younger population as the majority of respondents to this survey were between 30 and 50 years of age. The authors are currently engaged in an international study, specifically examining the perceptions of a younger population of mobile phone users.

In testing this smart phone m-payment model, we examined all possible products/ services without differentiation. Further research is in progress to investigate the explanatory power of the model for different socio-demographic groups and for specific products/services. Such research may provide further insight on the impact of ease of use of m-payments. As Mallet (2007) states, trust is a multi-object construct. Therefore, we call for further scientific investigation of trust as it pertains to m-payment using smart phones.

References

Andreev, P., Heart, T., Maoz, H., Pliskin, N.: Validating Formative Partial Least Squares (PLS) Models: Methodological Review and Empirical Illustration. In: Proceedings of ICIS 2009, p. 193 (2009)

Bauer, H.H., Barnes, S.J., Reichardt, T., Neumann, M.M.: Driving Consumer Acceptance of Mobile Marketing: A Theoretical Framework and Empirical Study. Journal of Electronic Commerce Research 6(3), 181–192 (2005)

Chatelin, Y.M., Vinzi, V.E., Tenenhaus, M.: State-of-Art on PLS Path Modeling through the Available Software. Les Cahiers de Recherche, 764, Groupe HEC (2002)

Chen, Y.H., Barnes, S.: Initial Trust and Online Buyer Behaviour. Industrial Management and Data Systems 107(1), 21–36 (2007)

Cheung, C., Lee, M. K.O.: Trust in Internet Shopping: A Proposed Model and Measurement Instrument. In: AMCIS, pp. 681–689 (2000)

Chin, W.W.: The Partial Least Squares Approach to Structural Equation Modeling. In: Marakas, G.E. (ed.) Modern Methods for Business Research, pp. 295–336. Lawrence Erlbaum Associates, Mahwah (1998)

Chou, Y., Lee, C., Chung, J.: Understanding M-Commerce Payment Systems through the Analytic Hierarchy Process. Journal of Business Research 57(12), 1423–1430 (2004)

Cleff, E.B.: Implementing the Legal Criteria of Meaningful Consent in the Concept of Mobile Advertising. Computer Law and Security Report 23(3), 262–269 (2007)

ComReg: Quarterly Key Data Report Q4 2009 (2009), http://www.comreg.ie/publications/quarterly_key_data_report_q 4_2009.583.103581.p.html (retrieved February 17, 2011)

Dahlberg, T., Mallat, N., Ondrus, J., Zmijewska, A.: Past, Present and Future of Mobile Payments Research: A Literature Review. Electronic Commerce Research and Applications 7(2), 165–181 (2008)

Dahlberg, T., Oorni, A.: Understanding Changes in Consumer Payment Habits: Do Mobile Payments and Electronic Invoices Attract Consumers? In: Proceedings of HICSS, p. 50 (2007)

Davis, F.D.: Perceived Usefulness, Perceived Ease of Use, and User Acceptance of Information Technology. MIS Quarterly 13(3), 319–340 (1989)

Dewan, S.G., Chen, L.: Mobile Payment Adoption in the USA: A Crossindustry, Cross-Platform Solution. J. of Information Privacy & Security 1(2), 4–28 (2005)

Diamantopoulos, A.: The Error Term in Formative Measurement Models: Interpretation and Modeling Implications. J. Model Management 11, 7–17 (2006)

Evans, J.: Apple Beats Moto in USA as Global IPhone Sales Explode (2010), http://www.9to5mac.com/iphone_sales_explosive (retrieved May 11, 2010)

Fornell, C., Bookstein, F.L.: Two Structural Equation Models: LISREL and PLS Applied to Consumer Exit-Voice Theory. J. of Marketing Research 19(4), 440–452 (1982)

Gao, J., Küpper, A.: Emerging Technologies for Mobile Commerce. J. of Theoretical and Applied Electronic Commerce Research 1(2) (2006)

Gefen, D., Karahanna, E., Straub, D.W.: Trust and TAM in Online Shopping: An Integrated Model. MIS Quarterly 27(1), 51–90 (2003)

Gefen, D., Straub, D.W., Boudreau, M.-C.: Structural Equation Modeling and Regression: Guidelines for Research and Practice. CAIS 4(7), 1–70 (2000)

Grabner-Kräuter, S., Kaluscha, E.A.: Empirical Research in Online Trust: A Review and Critical Assessment. International Journal of Human-Computer Studies 58(6), 783–812 (2003)

Hair Jr., J.F., Black, W.C., Babin, B.J., Anderson, R.E., Tatham, R.L.: Multivariate Data Analysis. Prentice Hall, Upper Saddle River (2006)

Henseler, J., Ringle, C.M., Sinkovics, R.R.: The Use of Partial Least Squares Path Modeling in International Marketing. Advances in International Marketing 20, 277–319 (2009)

Hsu, H.Y.S., Kulviwat, S.: An Integrative Framework of Technology Acceptance Model and Personalisation in Mobile Commerce. International J. of Technology Marketing 1(4), 393–410 (2006)

Jarvenpaa, S.L., Tractinsky, N., Vitale, M.: Consumer Trust in an Internet Store. Information Technology and Management 1(1), 45–71 (2000)

Johannsen, K.S.: Regulatory Independence in Theory and Practice: A Survey of Independent Energy Regulators in Eight European Countries. Institute of Local Government Studies. AKF Forlaget, Denmark (2003)

Kim, Y., Zhang, P.: Individual Users' Adoption of Smart Phone Services. In: Proceedings of SIGHCI 2009, p. 19 (2009)

Kim, C., Mirusmonov, M., Lee, I.: An Empirical Examination of Factors Influencing the Intention to Use Mobile Payment. Computers in Human Behavior 26(3), 310–322 (2010)

Leppäniemi, M., Karjaluoto, H.: Factors Influencing Consumers' Willingness to Accept Mobile Advertising: A Conceptual Model. International Journal of Mobile Communications 3(3), 197–213 (2005)

Lin, H.H., Wang, Y.S.: An Examination of the Determinants of Customer Loyalty in Mobile Commerce Contexts. Information & Management 43(3), 271–282 (2006)

Mallat, N.: Exploring Consumer Adoption of Mobile Payments–A Qualitative Study. J. of Strategic Information Systems 16(4), 413–432 (2007)

Matthews, T., Pierce, J., Tang, J.: No Smart Phone is an Island: The Impact of Places, Situations, and Other Devices on Smart Phone Use. Research Report RJ10452, IBM (2009)

McKnight, D.H., Choudhury, V., Kacmar, C.: Developing and Validating Trust Measures for E-Commerce: An Integrative Typology. Information Systems Research 13(3), 334–359 (2003)

Schierz, P.G., Schilke, O., Wirtz, B.W.: Understanding Consumer Acceptance of Mobile Payment Services: An Empirical Analysis. Electronic Commerce Research and Applications 9(3), 209–216 (2010)

Siau, K., Sheng, H., Nah, F., Davis, S.: A Qualitative Investigation on Consumer Trust in Mobile Commerce. International J. of Electronic Business 2(3), 283–300 (2004)

Tenenhaus, M., Vinzi, V.E., Chatelin, Y.-M., Lauro, C.: PLS Path Modeling. Computational Statistics & Data Analysis 48(1), 159–205 (2005)

Turner, A.: M-Payment Models: Starting to Look Good, Payments Cards and Mobile (May/June 2009), http://www.paymentscardsandmobile.com

Varshney, U., Vetter, R.: Mobile Commerce: Framework, Applications and Networking Support. Mobile Networks and Applications 7(3), 185–198 (2002)

Venkatesh, V., Davis, F.D.: A Model of the Antecedents of Perceived Ease of Use: Development and Test. Decision Sciences 27(3), 451–481 (1996)

Verhagen, T., Meents, S., Tan, Y.H.: Perceived Risk and Trust Associated with Purchasing at Electronic Marketplaces. European J. of Information Systems 15(6), 542–555 (2006)

Viehland, D., Leong, R.: Acceptance and Use of Mobile Payments. In: Proceedings of the 18th Australasian Conference on Information Systems, 5 (2007)

Vodafone Ireland: Vodafone Ireland Preliminary Results Announcement for the Quarter Ended December 31st 2010 (2011),
http://www.vodafone.ie/aboutus/media/press/show/BAU012194.shtml
(retrieved February 17, 2011)

Xu, G., Gutierrez, J.A.: An Exploratory Study of Killer Applications and Critical Success Factors in M-Commerce. J. of Electronic Commerce in Organizations 4(3), 63–79 (2006)

Zhong, J.: A Comparison of Mobile Payment Procedures in Finnish and Chinese Markets. In: Proceedings of Bled 2009, 37 (2009)

About the Authors

Pavel Andreev is a postdoctoral research fellow at Sagy Center for Internet Research and the Study of the Information Society, Graduate School of Management, University of Haifa, where his research focus is organizational aspects of electronic activities, including e-government, e-health, e-learning, and e-commerce. During 2009–2010, he was a postdoctoral research fellow in Business Information Systems, University College Cork, Ireland, where he was engaged in the open code, content and commerce (O3C) project. He earned his Ph.D. in the Department of Industrial Engineering and Management at Ben-Gurion University of the Negev, Israel.

Aidan Duane is a lecturer of Business Information Systems at Waterford Institute of Technology (WIT) in Ireland. Aidan holds a Ph.D. in Business Information Systems from University College Cork, Ireland. He has acted as both a rincipal investigator and research team member in securing research funding for WIT since 2005. Aidan's research interests include m-commerce, m-learning, telecommunications, electronic monitoring and surveillance, information technology control, security and ethics, project management, database programming, and web development. Aidan will cochair a stream in ECIS 2011 and also coauthor a special edition of the *International Journal of E-Business Research* in 2012 on "Smart Mobile Media Services." His work has also been published in a number of international journals including *Information Systems Journal, International Journal of E-Business Research,* and *Information Resources Management Journal*, and he has presented at conferences including the International Conference on Information Systems and the International Conference on Electronic Commerce (ICEC).

Philip O'Reilly is a tenured lecturer in Business Information Systems at the University College Cork, Ireland. He has been a leading member of research teams that have been successful in securing in excess of €1 million in research funding since 2007. His research interests are in the area of e-commerce, specifically electronic marketplaces, mobile technologies, and green IT. Philip's work has been published in leading international journals including *European Journal of Information Systems* and *Information Technology and People*, and he has presented at leading conferences including, the International Conference on Information Systems and the European Conference on Information Systems. An analysis of his research reveals that Philip belongs to the central node of leading academics at ECIS.

Appendix A. Re-sampling Test of Coefficient Significance

Table A1. Indicators Description

Construct	Item	Survey Statement
Perceived Ease of Use	PEEASY	Overall, I find SMMS easy to use.
	PEKNOW	Use of SMMS does not require a lot of knowledge.
	PETECH	Use of SMMS does not require a lot of technical skills.
Trust	LFROBUST	Legal frameworks for SMMS provision are sufficiently robust to protect consumers.
	PECETHIC	I believe that SMMS providers will act ethically when capturing, retaining, processing, and managing my personal data.
	PCCONCRNPRIV	I believe that SMMS providers are concerned with consumers' privacy.
	PPCCONFPRIV	I am confident in the privacy controls of SMMS providers.
	PPCDIVUL3RD	I believe that SMMS providers will not divulge consumers' personal data to 3rd parties.
	REGAUTH	Regulatory bodies for SMMS provision are sufficiently authoritative to regulate SMMS providers.
	REGINDEP	Regulatory bodies for SMMS provision are sufficiently independent to regulate SMMS providers.
Willing-ness to MPay	PPRMNO	I consider it safe to make an m-payment through my mobile network operator when using SMMS.
	PPRSAFE3RD	I consider it safe to make an m-payment through a third party payment company when using SMMS.
	PPRSAFECC	I consider it safe to make an m-payment with my credit card when using SMMS.
	PPRSAFELASER	I consider it safe to make an m-payment with my laser card when using SMMS.
Willing-ness to Transact	PULLGPS	I intend to use SMMS to access GPS services
	PULLINFO	I intend to use SMMS to find information on products/services.
	PULLRESERV	I intend to use SMMS for booking or reservation tasks
	PULLTICK	I intend to use SMMS for ticketing tasks

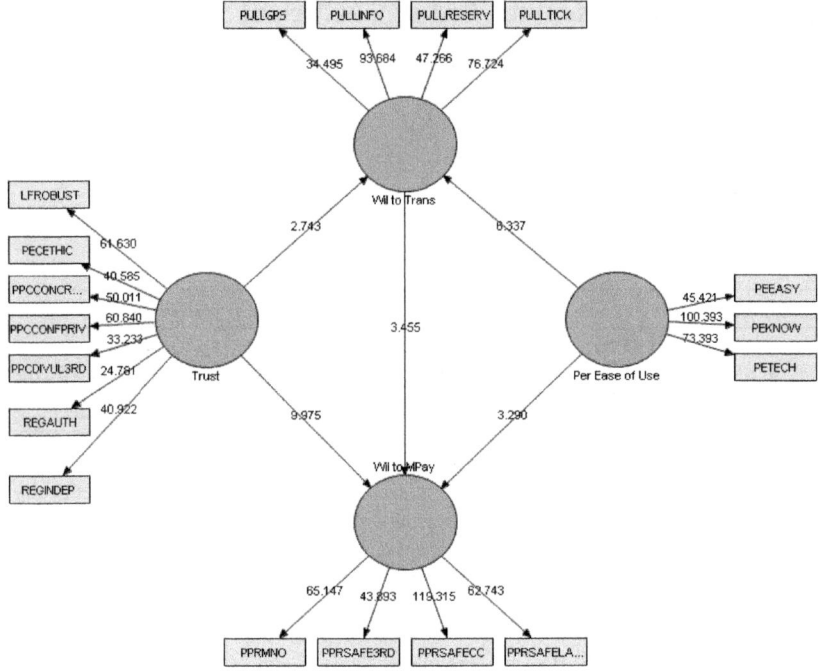

Fig. A1. Bootstrapping

Appendix B. Effect Size Test

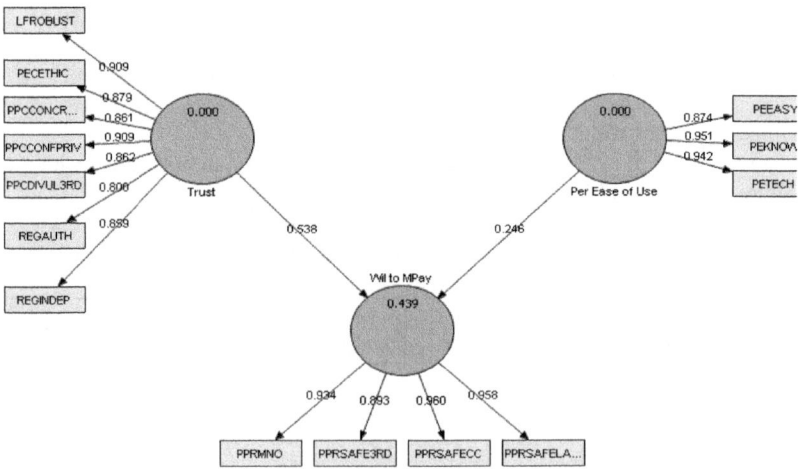

Fig. B1. Effect Size Test: Willingness to Transact Is Excluded

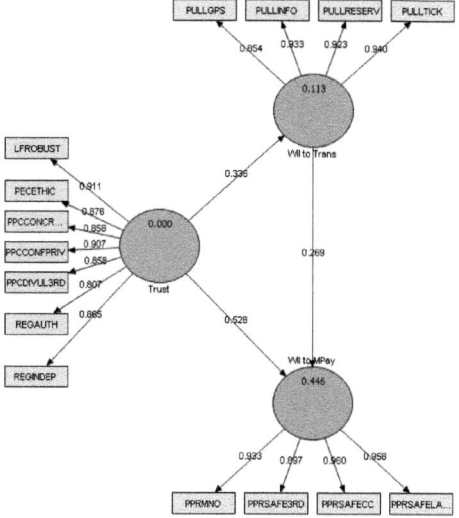

Fig. B2. Effect Size Test: Perceived Ease of Use Is Excluded

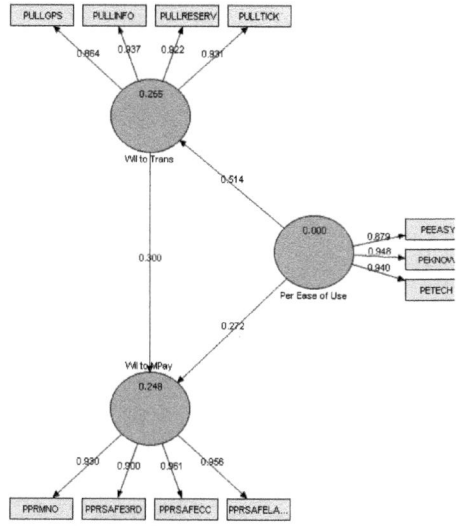

Fig. B3. Effect Size Test: Trust Is Excluded

The Impact of Instant Messaging Tools on Knowledge Management and Team Performance

Carol X.J. Ou[1], Darren W.L. Leung[2], and Robert M. Davison[3]

[1] Department of Information Management, Tilburg University, The Netherlands
carol.ou@uvt.nl
[2] Department of Computing, Hong Kong Polytechnic University, Hong Kong
06245602D@polyu.edu.hk
[3] Department of Information Systems, City University of Hong Kong, Hong Kong
isrobert@cityu.edu.hk

Abstract. Instant messaging (IM) has become increasingly popular as a form of social communication. However, the adoption of IM in the workplace remains controversial due to the challenges associated with quantifying organizational benefits. In this study, we evaluate the effects of using IM tools on facilitating knowledge transfer and knowledge generation at work, and their subsequent influence on work performance. The proposed model is validated by a survey of work professionals at a small company with the support of a social networking diagram. Implications and conclusions are discussed.

Keywords: Instant messaging (IM), computer-mediated communication (CMC), knowledge transfer, knowledge generation, work performance.

1 Introduction

Advances in information technology have resulted in the development of various computer-mediated communication (CMC) tools of which the instant messenger (IM) is one of the most prevalent. An IM tool has the capability to overcome geographical distance and facilitate "instant" interaction among interlocutors. Researchers have demonstrated IM's potential in promoting multi-tasking, as well as improving working efficiency (Cho et al. 2005; Quan-Haase et al. 2005). For example, managers and employees often communicate with each other in multiple social networks: they are not embedded in a single workgroup (Teigland 2000). Given the flexibility provided by IM, organizations increasingly allow employees to use IM as a substitute for email as they engage on collaborative tasks.

On the other hand, many researchers and practitioners have pointed out that the interruptive nature of IM can negatively affect work efficiency and reduce productivity (Isaacs et al. 2002; Nardi et al. 2000). Consistent with academic research, Deloitte's (2010) recent survey revealed that only 41 percent of 750 participating companies allow using social networking tools such as IM in the workplace. The under-employment of IM at work may be largely due to IM's controversial impacts.

M. Chiasson et al. (Eds.): Future IS 2011, IFIP AICT 356, pp. 131–148, 2011.

Given the above dilemma, in this study we investigate the impact of IM on knowledge management (KM) in the workplace. KM is a key business process responsible for shaping organizational competitive advantage (Nonaka 1994). Prior research on KM has often focused on formal, enterprise-wide KM systems (KMS) (Bock et al. 2005). The impact of informal CMC tools, such as IM, on KM has been overlooked. We argue that by connecting working professionals in multiple social networks, IM has the potential to contribute to knowledge transfer and generation in the workplace, subsequently enhancing team performance.

In addition to investigating the contribution of CMC tools to KM, we also use the social network analysis (SNA) technique to develop social network diagrams in order to visualize employees' or team members' email- and IM-based interactions. Furthermore, SNA results enable an examination of the correlation between the elements of social networks (including degree centrality, closeness centrality, betweenness centrality, density, and tie strength) and KM at work. These analyses and diagrams have the potential to render both theoretical and practical explanations with respect to KM, where the network literature has previously provided few insights into the specific elements that facilitate knowledge transfer and generation.

In the following section, we propose a theoretical model, grounded on social network theories, to describe the impacts of IM and social networks on KM in the workplace. After describing how we conducted a survey in a small-sized company in Hong Kong, we then present a combined analysis of the research model and the social networks that we discovered. We conclude the paper with key findings, implications, contributions, and directions for future research.

2   Theoretical Development

We rely on social network theories (Granovetter 1973; Krackhardt 1992; Wellman et al. 1996) to develop the theoretical model about IM's impacts on KM and subsequent work performance. Specifically, Wellman et al. (1996) coined the term *computer supported social networks* because computer networks connect people. In networks such as those facilitated by the Internet, individuals can seek information and collaborate online when they leverage these new modes of synchronous and asynchronous communication. Granovetter's (1973) theory on the strength of weak

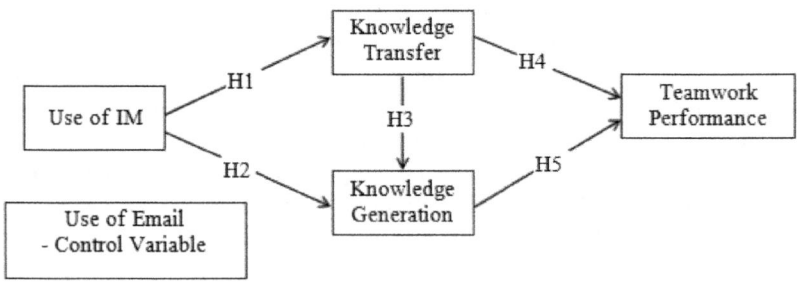

Fig. 1. The Proposed Research Model

ties suggests that individual members of social networks obtain novel information from other members with whom they have weaker ties. However, while weak ties may be more useful for obtaining or soliciting new knowledge, strong ties play a role in facilitating the knowledge transfer process (Krackhardt 1992).

In this article, we draw on these social network theories to study the impacts of IM, as a social CMC tool, on facilitating KM and explore its downstream effects on work performance. Figure 1 outlines the research model. The definitions of constructs used are summarized in Table 1. We provide the detailed arguments on the proposed research model in the following sections.

Table 1. Definitions of Constructs and Source

Principal Constructs	Definitions	Source
Use of IM	The use of IM tools as work-related contact and communication tools to raise questions and perform work-related socialization	Cho et al. (2005); Quan-Hasse et al. (2005)
Knowledge Transfer	The extent to which the employee can explain their key ideas, concepts and theories in their area of expertise	Reagans and McEvily (2003)
Knowledge Generation	The extent to which the employee is able to generate new solutions, ideas and ways of working as well as facilitate organizational learning	Soo et al. (2002)
Teamwork Performance	The employees' perceptions of outcome satisfaction, outcome quality and team satisfaction.	Fuller et al. (2006)

2.1 The Impact of IM on Knowledge Transfer

KM has been defined as the process of capturing, storing, sharing and using knowledge (Davenport et al. 1998). In these four processes, knowledge transfer occurs whenever knowledge is diffused from one individual to others (Roberts 2000). This diffusion can be effected through processes of socialization, education and learning (Roberts 2000). More specifically, both conceptual (e.g., Granvetter 1973; Krackhardt 1992) and empirical (e.g., Levin and Cross 2004) studies have suggested that weak ties within social networks foster information search activities, while strong ties facilitate knowledge transfer among individuals.

We argue that, IM, as a social CMC tool, connects work professionals in a network (see Wellman et al. 1996). IM can stimulate an instant interaction via the pop-up message dialogue feature. The bilateral, near-synchronous form of communication then enabled closely resembles the openness and transparency associated with face-to-face communication. Unlike traditional social networks, IM-enabled social networks are able to overcome the constraints imposed by temporal and spatial communication barriers which people often encounter in face-to-face social networks. With such rapid IM interaction, the development of strong ties between distributed team members no longer needs to rely on physical contacts.

By connecting people, IM tools provide work professionals with a valuable channel for sharing, transferring and documenting knowledge. During the interaction process, team members can clearly negotiate work expectations, explore social contexts and collaborate on team work (Cho et al. 2005). Indeed, the characteristics of tools used to transfer knowledge have been found to affect the success of knowledge transfer (Argote and Ingram 2000). IM's informal and casual characteristics make it easier for team members to transfer knowledge. IM, therefore, constitutes an effective CMC tool that can be used both for complex work collaboration and for simple task coordination. We thus propose that

> **Hypothesis 1**: *The use of IM enhances the ease of knowledge transfer in the workplace.*

2.2 The Impact of IM on Knowledge Generation

Knowledge generation activities at work can occur in many different ways (Simon 1991). In addition to information processing, organizations often generate new knowledge through action and interaction (Levinthal and Myatt 1994). Scholars have suggested that knowledge generation requires intensive communication (Nonaka 1994). Indeed, smooth knowledge generation often requires a robust yet informal communication network (Soo et al. 2002), because interlocutors need tools such as images and other visual aids to help them to present their ideas to others.

We argue that IM is a very suitable tool to support the transmission of rich content. With such additional functions as file transfer and video conferencing, IM can serve as a functionally rich CMC tool that facilitates the knowledge generation process. Knowledge workers can leverage IM as a flexible and informal means to engage in intensive communication with their colleagues. Such information exchange allows new and innovative ideas to flow through and into the company.

As suggested by the theory of weak ties (Granovetter 1973), individuals often obtain more new information or ideas from weak ties than from strong ties within a social network. This is because weak ties play the role of an information "bridge" to connect different clusters of people who can then bring in new information. We argue that IM, in addition to facilitating intensive communication between strongly tied members of social networks, offers a valuable means to loosely connect people. The list of contacts maintained in an IM tool are not restricted only to close friends or colleagues, but also include less frequently contacted individuals. In this sense, the contact records in an IM tool can be leveraged for searching information and identifying new knowledge. IM provides a bridge for different clusters of people to get in touch when necessary and possibly to acquire new knowledge within a loosely connected social network. Putting the above arguments together, we therefore propose that

> **Hypothesis 2**: *The use of IM facilities knowledge generation in the workplace.*

2.3 Generating Knowledge via Knowledge Transfer

Knowledge generation is often related closely to the expansion of the existing knowledge pool (Tracey et al. 2002). Knowledge itself is thus an important source for further knowledge creation. According to Nonaka (1994), the process of knowledge creation involves interactions between explicit and tacit knowledge. In the process of knowledge generation, individuals may find it relatively easier to access and integrate knowledge with colleagues located in other offices (Teigland and Wasko 2009), consistent with the theory of weak ties (Granovetter 1973).

We argue that facilitating knowledge generation by knowledge transfer can be enhanced by the IM-enabled work environment. The attributes of IM facilitate the conduct of searches for solutions or information across departments or even across national boundaries. By shaping the network structure, IM creates communication patterns that can affect knowledge structures, in terms of knowledge transfer and generation in organizations, and thus helps to spread knowledge widely within an organization. With the aid of IM tools in sharing visual, task-related information, mutual understanding and new knowledge is more likely to be generated. We therefore propose that

> **Hypothesis 3**: *Knowledge transfer contributes positively to knowledge generation.*

2.4 Enhancing Work Performance with Knowledge Transfer and Knowledge Generation

In a highly competitive and turbulent environment, organizations need to modify their structures continually. Strategic knowledge generation is viewed as fundamental to an organization's development and to successfully building competitive advantage, especially in SMEs (Cantú et al. 2009). Increased frequency of interaction and knowledge sharing can enable more comprehensive consideration and comparison of alternative problem solutions. Such a knowledge sharing and transfer process can thus lead to improved decision making, which will ultimately improve work performance (Stasser and Titus 1985). Consistently, research (e.g., Srivastava et al. 2006) has provided empirical evidence for the positive relationship between knowledge sharing and teamwork performance.

The problems faced by companies have become more sophisticated in the current knowledge era. This situation often pushes companies to acquire or generate ever more innovative ideas in order to survive. This is especially true for SMEs, where there is little organizational slack. With new and innovative ideas flowing into work teams, SMEs may solve sophisticated problems more effectively, even with resource constraints. The greater the amount of knowledge that flows in to the organization, the greater the capability to solve problems in a more effective way (Soo et al. 2002). Meanwhile, the knowledge creation process will result in a stock of new knowledge and subsequently have a positive impact on the employees' performance in the workplace. As a result, team performance will be influenced by those individuals who are able and willing to apply new knowledge in making decisions. Taking the above arguments together, we hence propose that

> **Hypothesis 4**: *Knowledge transfer has a positive relationship with teamwork performance.*

> **Hypothesis 5**: *Knowledge generation has a positive relationship with team-work performance.*

2.5   Analytical Elements of Social Networks, IM and KM

From the SNA perspective, a social network refers to the social structure connecting individuals called nodes (Wasserman and Faust 1994). The structure itself is tied by one or more relationships which, in the workplace, may include friendship, common interest, knowledge exchange, collaboration, and collegiality (see Cho et al. 2005).

In this study, we focus on the interrelationships among IM, KM, and the analytical elements of a social network, including centrality, density, and tie strength. The literature on KM has provided rich insights into the contribution of interpersonal relationships on knowledge sharing (e.g., Bock et al. 2005; Chow and Chan 2008). However, the influence of the characteristics of interpersonal relationships and social networks (such as centrality, density, and tie strength) on effective KM is yet to be identified.

Wasserman and Faust (1994) provide clear definitions of the analytical elements (i.e., measures) of social networks for the purpose of SNA. Specifically, centrality refers to how well the nodes connect to the network, which can be measured by betweenness (the extent to which a node lies between other nodes in the network), closeness (the degree to which an individual is near other individuals in a network), and degree (the count of the number of ties to other actors in the network). Density represents the proportion of ties in a network relative to the total number possible. Tie strength refers to emotional closeness between individuals (Granovetter 1973), which can be quantitatively but vicariously measured by frequency of interaction, closeness and time known with other actors in a social network (Marsden 1990; Marsden and Campbell 1984).

We argue that the use of IM can strengthen these characteristics of social networks, given that it is widely used to connect people and maintain interpersonal relationships socially (Li et al. 2005) as well as in the workplace (Cho et al. 2005). IM provides an effective communication channel to facilitate the collaboration among team mates or other organizational members at work, thus enhancing the connectivity of the interlocutors in social works in the workplace (i.e., centrality). It is easy to search for and add friends in the buddy list, facilitating the creation of "unforgettable" online contact lists and a well connected online network, and thus contributing to enhancing the density of social networks in the workplace. As explained in the previous sections, the instant interaction via IM can enable team members to clearly negotiate work expectations and explore social contexts (Cho et al. 2005), and thus help strengthen the strong work-related and interpersonal relationships among team members. We therefore hypothesize

Hypothesis 6: *The use of IM is positively associated with centrality (H6a), density (H6b), and tie strength (H6c) of a social network.*

The literature on KM has suggested that a strong interpersonal relationship encourages knowledge sharing and transfer (Bock et al. 2005; Szulanski 1996). From an SNA perspective, a dense and centralized network means individuals are well connected and individuals in the network know each other. We argue that density is positively associated with knowledge transfer. This is because a well connected network embeds some levels of cooperative relationship where everybody has the responsibility to cooperate and share knowledge. If the network members do not cooperate, non-cooperation behavior will spread quickly to other network members and restrict their future interaction (Reagans and McEvily 2003). However, we argue that a network characterized by an extremely high density and centrality (meaning nearly everybody connects with each other) may not be effective for generating new knowledge, since information is already available to everyone in the same social circle and little new knowledge may emerge. Such an argument is consistent with Granovetter's (1973) theory of the strength of weak ties. Specifically, Granovetter argues that weak ties facilitate the creation of new knowledge, while strong ties contribute to comprehensive knowledge transfer. This is because "weak ties provide people with access to information and resources beyond those available in their own social circle; but strong ties have greater motivation to be of assistance and are typically more easily available" (Granovetter 1983, p. 209). We therefore hypothesize

Hypothesis 7: Knowledge transfer is positively associated with centrality (H7a), density (H7b), and tie strength (H7c) of a social network.

Hypothesis 8: Knowledge generation is negatively associated with centrality (H8a), density (H8b), and tie strength (H8c) of a social network.

2.6 Control Variables

In addition to IM, email is commonly encountered in organizations as a means to facilitate social networking and knowledge management. We thus account for the effect of email in the research model by incorporating this construct in data analysis.

3 Methodology

We targeted a small-sized company in Hong Kong as our research focus. We used a survey to collect empirical data that was used to test the research model. We also undertook a social network analysis (SNA) of the survey data.

3.1 The Research Context

The company, which we refer to by the pseudonym of Version Limited, had 75 employees at the time of our study. The company is composed of six departments: sales, marketing, customer service, logistics, accounting, and IT. Version Limited conducts its business around the Asia Pacific area, including Hong Kong, Taiwan, China, and Singapore. Its main business is to develop and distribute communication systems, Internet software, security, network, and media products. The company is headquartered in Hong Kong, where there are two offices. It is a norm of Version Limited that every staff member, even the CEO, has an IM tool installed in their computer, enabling them to communicate with other colleagues as they wish.

3.2 The Measures

We relied on existing measures to develop the survey questions. The independent variable, IM use at work, is measured by adapting scales from Kankanhalli et al. (2005) and Cho et al. (2005). Knowledge transfer is measured with the scale developed by Reagans and McEvily (2003). Knowledge generation is measured by adapting questions from Soo et al. (2002). Work performance is measured with scales developed and validated in Fuller et al. (2006). Teamwork performance is measured with three sub-constructs, viz., group satisfaction, outcome satisfaction, and outcome quality. Teamwork performance is operationalized in this study as a subjective measure at the individual level, rather than as an objective measure at the group level.

In addition to the above seven-point Likert-scale questions, the survey also includes the relational data collected for the SNA diagram for Version Limited. Specifically, the survey participants were asked to provide information on their interlocutors with respect to the frequency of contacting them using an IM tool and email, the length of time they had known each person, and perceived closeness. These data can be used to measure the "tie strength" of interlocutors in a social network (Granovetter 1973). A summary of all the measures used in the survey is available from the authors.

3.3 Social Network Analysis (SNA) Technique

Common SNA includes the calculation of several characteristics of a social network, viz., centrality, density, and tie strength where centrality is decomposed into degree centrality, closeness centrality, and betweenness centrality (Borgatti et al. 2002; Freeman 1978). The method used to calculate the relative degree centrality of an individual is to divide the number of direct connections (degree) by the network size:

$$\text{Centrality(Degree)} = \frac{Degree}{Network\ Size} \tag{1}$$

The typical way to measure the "closeness" of a point is that calculated from the sum distance, the sum of the geodesic distances to all other points in the graph (Sabidussi 1966). If the matrix of distances between points in an undirected graph is calculated, the sum *distance* of a point is its column or row sum in this matrix. In this research, we use the sum distance as the indicator of closeness that a point with a low sum distance is close to a large number of other points. We list the calculation of closeness centrality in formula (2).

$$\text{Centrality(Closeness)} = \sum_{i=1}^{n} d(Pi - Pk) \tag{2}$$

where n = number of vertices in the graph and d = geodesic distance from point i to point k.

The calculation of betweenness centrality is based upon "the frequency with which a point falls between pairs of other points on the shortest or geodesic paths connecting them" (Freeman 1978, p. 221). In this sense, the betweenness of a point suggests "the extent to which an agent can play the pan of a 'broker' or 'gatekeeper' with a potential for control over others" (Scott 1988, p. 86). The centrality of Point k^1 in terms of betweenness can be calculated with formula (3).

$$CB(Pk) = \sum_i^n \sum_{<j}^n bij(Pk) \qquad (3)$$

where n is the number of points in the graph.

Density is a measure of network cohesiveness and is the ratio of the existing number ties to the maximum ties possible. The number of lines in a graph is directly reflected in its inclusiveness and the degrees of its points (Scott 1988). We adopt the following (4) to calculate the density of the social network at Version Limited.

$$D = \frac{t}{n(n-1)/2} \qquad (4)$$

where t = number of direct connections with other actors. This measure can vary from 0 to 1; for an actor who has connections to all other individuals within the network, the result will be 1.

In social network studies, emotional closeness is a commonly used indicator of tie strength resulting from extending Granovetter's (1973) theoretical notion on tie strength (e.g., Borgatti et al. 2002). Other indicators of tie strength include frequency of contact and time known (Marsden 1990; Marsden and Campbell 1984). The calculation of tie strength of an actor is measured as the average of all tie strengths in terms of frequency of interaction, closeness, and time known with all other actors within the network (as shown in Table 2).

Table 2. Item Use for Measuring Tie Strength

Items	Scale used
Frequency of interaction	Five point likert scale (from daily to less often)
Degree of closeness	Five point likert scale (from especially close to distant)
Time known	Five point likert scale (from over 3 years to less than 6 months)

3.4 Sample

In this research, data were collected from employees of Version Limited on a voluntary basis. The employees were provided with both hard and soft copies of the survey questionnaire. Over a period of three weeks, we collected 43 responses, a

---

[1] According to such a measure, the larger the data related to centrality closeness between two individuals shown by the data actually suggests that they are more distant in reality. This means that a reverse scale has been used to measure the actual centrality closeness.

response rate of 57 percent. Due to questions not answered, two responses were removed from the data analysis. Therefore, a total of 41 valid responses were available for analysis. Table 3 summarizes the demographic data of the respondents.

Table 3. Demographic Data of Respondents (n = 41)

Items	Indicators	Percent	Items	Indicators	Percent
Gender	Male	52.5%	Education level	Senior High School or Technical School	2.5%
	Female	47.5%		Diploma/Associate Degree	32.5%
Age range	18 – 22	40%		Bachelor Degree	65.0%
	23 – 25	25%	Working experience in current company	6 Months - 2 Years	50.0%
	26 – 30	27.5%		2 - 5 Years	37.5%
	31 – 40	7.5%		More than 5 Years	12.5%
Department	Sales and Marketing	37.5%	Number of IMs used for work	1.00	72.5%
	Customer Service	32.5%		2.00	17.5%
	Accounting	10.0%		3.00	5.0%
	Logistics	10.0%		4.00	2.5%
	IT	7.5%		5.00	2.5%
	Other	2.5%			
Office location	Mong Kok	72.5%	Years of using IM at work	1 - 5 Years	22.5%
	Science Park	27.5%		More than 5 Years	77.5%

4   Data Analysis

We used the statistical package for the social sciences (SPSS) and partial least squares (PLS) to calculate the validity and reliability of the constructs and the robustness of the research model.

4.1   Validating the Measurements

First, the validity is confirmed by the factor analysis (omitted for brevity). All the eigenvalues of the constructs are larger than the suggested value of 1.0. The communality scores are higher than the suggested value (0.50). These results indicate adequate reliability of measures (Hair et al. 1995). Second, the reliability is validated by using Cronbach's alpha and composite reliability scores. Cronbach's alphas of all constructs range from 0.87 to 0.95 and all composite reliability are above 90 percent, which suggest acceptable internal consistency (Hair et al. 1995). The square roots of the average variance extracted (AVE) are greater than 0.8 (see Table 4), which are greater than all other cross correlations, implying that all of the constructs capture more construct-related variance than error variance (Pavlou and Gefen 2004).

Table 4. Descriptive Statistics, Correlation Matrix, and AVE of Principal Constructs

Principal Constructs	Composite Reliability	Mean (STD)	UIM	KT	KG	WP
Usage of IM (UIM)	0.91	5.58 (1.06)	**0.85**			
Knowledge Transfer (KT)	0.92	4.91(1.01)	0.55**	**0.89**		
Knowledge Generation (KG)	0.96	4.6(1.26)	0.37*	0.54**	**0.92**	
Work Performance (WP)	0.95	5.18(0.91)	0.34*	0.62**	0.39*	**0.83**

*Significant at $p < 0.05$; **Significant at $p < 0.01$

4.2 Testing the Research Model

The structural model in this study was examined with PLS. As shown in Figure 2, the results indicate that all hypotheses, except H2 and H5, are supported by the data. IM use at work has a significant positive effect (b = 0.48, $p < 0.01$) on knowledge transfer, supporting H1. Together with the usage of email at the workplace, the usage of IM at work explains 41 percent of the variance of knowledge transfer. The direct influence of the usage of IM on facilitating knowledge generation is moderate (b = -0.02, $p > 0.01$), rejecting H2. Regarding the impact of knowledge transfer on knowledge generation, the results provide support for H3 (b = 0.31, $p < 0.01$). Knowledge transfer also has a significant effect on performance at the workplace (b = 0.66, $p < 0.01$), validating H4. However, the path from knowledge generation to work performance is not significant (b = 0.12, $p > 0.01$), rejecting H5. Knowledge transfer and generation explain 54 percent of the variance of work performance. In sum, the R^2 scores for all dependent variables and the high factor loadings yield an adequate goodness-of-fit for the overall research model (Chin 1998).

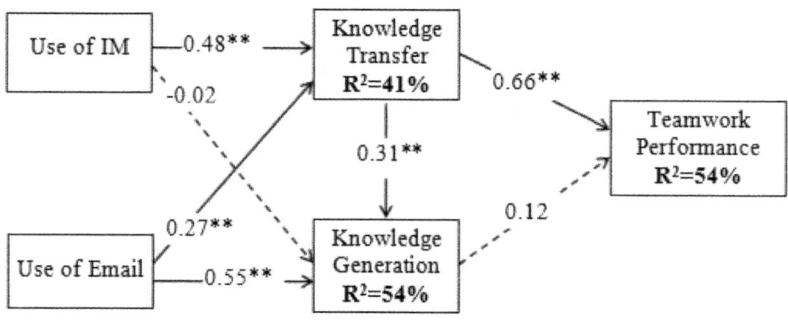

*Significant at $p < 0.05$, **Significant at $p < 0.01$

Fig. 2. PLS Results of Structural Model

4.3 Social Network Analysis (SNA)

With the collected data from the name generation process, a social network diagram for Version Limited is drawn using UCINET 7, relying on the calculations explained in the methodology (Figure 3). A total of 41 respondents participated in the name generation process with a total of 69 unique names produced as a result. To protect the participants' privacy, we use a symbol, instead of the participant's real name, in the diagram to present an individual employee at Version Limited. We discuss the corresponding insights drawn from the SNA diagram in the next section.

In addition to the SNA, we also use SPSS to perform a correlation analysis among IM usage and the attributes of the social network at Version Limited. The results of the correlation analysis indicate that the use of IM has a significant effect on some of the components of SNA (see Table 5).

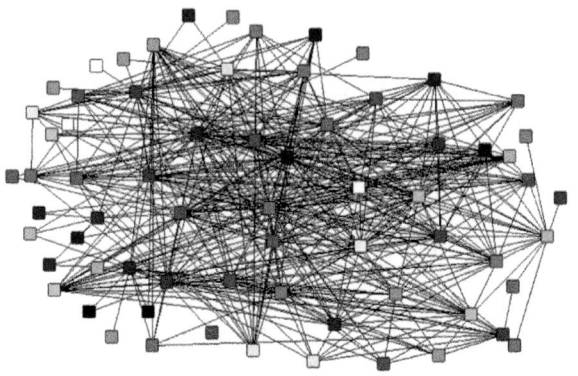

Fig. 3. Social Network Diagram

Table 5. Correlation Table of Usage of IM and Social Network Components

	Use of IM	DC	CC	BC	Density	TS
Degree Centrality (DC)	0.37**					
Closeness Centrality (CC) [2]	-0.37**	0.13				
Betweenness Centrality (BC)	0.21	0.61***	0.41***			
Density	-0.42***	-0.56***	-0.19	-0.72***		
Tie Strength [3]	0.29*	0.71***	0.08	0.23	-0.36**	
Knowledge Generation (KG)	0.37**	0.32**	-0.35**	0.09	-0.19	0.29*
Knowledge Transfer (KT)	0.56***	0.17	-0.18	-0.05	-0.21	0.33**
Work Performance (WP)	0.34**	-0.04	-0.08	-0.05	-0.10	0.23

*Significant at $0.05 < p < 0.10$; **Significant at $0.01 < p < 0.05$; ***Significant at $p < 0.01$

The correlation analysis results shown in Table 5 indicate that the data supports H6a (b = 0.37, p < 0.01 for IM with degree centrality and close centrality) and H6c (b = .029, 0.05 < p < 0.10), but rejects H6b (b = -0.42, p < 0.01). Knowledge transfer is found to be positively associated with tie strength (b = 0.33, p < 0.01), thus validating H7c. We found significance neither in the correlation between knowledge transfer and centrality, nor in the correlation between knowledge transfer and density, thus rejecting H7a and H7b. Opposite to the hypotheses of H8a, H8b, and H8c, data suggest knowledge generation is more effective in a social network characterized by high centrality, density, and tie strength. We discuss these key findings and corresponding implications in the next section.

5 Key Findings, Implications and Future Research

5.1 Findings Related to the Research Model

This research has a number of key findings. IM tools are well accepted as a social networking technology. This study provides empirical evidence that using IM tools at work can exert a positive effect on work performance via effective technology transfer. Although IM's direct effect on knowledge generation is not significant, the analytical result indicates that IM use is highly correlated with knowledge generation (b = 0.37, p < 0.05). Our *post hoc* analysis indicates that knowledge transfer fully mediates the direct relationship between use of IM and knowledge generation. This full mediation effect suggests knowledge transfer is the building block of knowledge generation in the workplace. In other words, the easier it is for individuals to share knowledge with other colleagues, the more likely it is that new knowledge will be generated; however, the mere existence of IM is not sufficient for knowledge generation.

Surprisingly, our data did not support the hypothesis that knowledge generation at work will improve teamwork performance. This unexpected outcome can be explained as follows. In KM, one of the factors affecting knowledge sharing activities within an organization is the willingness of individuals to share the knowledge acquired or created by them (Bock et al. 2005). If the individual obtains new knowledge to solve a problem but decides not to share it, the overall performance of the team or the firm may not be enhanced (Gibbert and Krause 2002). Version Limited does not reward individuals who contribute new knowledge to the company. Thus, even if the employees have new knowledge or new ways of solving problems, the new knowledge may not necessarily be brought to the team or organization level. Therefore, knowledge generation at the individual level has much less influence on the overall improvement of the team or organization work performance.

5.2 Findings Related to the Social Network Analysis (SNA)

Figure 3 visualizes the major social network at Version Limited. According to this SNA, we include the means and standard deviations (STD) of the five critical characteristics of the social network, viz., tie strength, degree centrality, betweenness centrality, closeness, and density. Our *post hoc* analysis of the social network at Version Limited suggests the social network enabled by IM is averagely dense (with a mean density of 0.48 out of 1). The average network size is 20. The betweenness of the social relationships varies considerably (with a mean of 61 and STD of 85). Five survey participants serve as "gate keepers" of the social network, with a betweenness value higher than 200. The average centrality degree is low at 0.30 (maximum of 1). This data suggests that there is still room for developing an efficient and well connected social network at Version Limited.

Table 5 suggests the significance of IM in building the social network at Version Limited. The use of IM is significantly correlated with all characteristics of the social network including degree centrality, closeness centrality, betweenness centrality, density, and tie strength. Specifically, the correlation between IM use and degree centrality ($b = 0.37$, $p < 0.05$) implies that IM has enabled a quick and simple communication channel for users that will probably increase the ease of communicating and encourage people to have more interactions with their colleagues even if they are located in different offices. Closeness centrality is measured by the distance among individual network members. The significantly negative correlation between IM and closeness centrality ($b = 0.27$, $p < 0.05$) implies that the distance of an individual from other people should be reduced when they use IM tools more frequently. Notably, the use of IM is negatively related to density of the network. Such a finding suggests the use of IM can create a sparse network. This is indeed consistent with the above social network diagram, which suggests that Version Limited only has a moderately dense network. IM tools can be used as a valuable means to maintain occasional contacts (i.e., people with weak ties) that are accessed only when necessary. IM tools thus help to spread the social network around. The data also implies the use of IM helps strengthen the ties between social actors ($b = 0.29$, $0.05 < p < 0.10$). Taking all of these results together, the use of IM appears to strengthen the whole social network at Version Limited.

Tie strength, as proposed by Granovetter (1973), is expected to be positively correlated with knowledge transfer, but negatively correlated with knowledge generation activities. Our data provided strong support for the correlation between tie strength and knowledge transfer ($b = 0.33$, $p < 0.05$). However, our analysis also indicated that tie strength contributes to knowledge generation ($b = 0.29$, $0.05 < p < 0.10$). We suspect that in this IT-focused, knowledge-intensive company, employees are linked to different knowledge pools through different network links. When knowledge-intensive work is involved, strong ties foster complex knowledge transfer where complexity of knowledge is directly associated with the tacitness of knowledge (Hansen 1999). Meanwhile, the generation of new knowledge relies on the interaction of tacit and explicit knowledge (Nonaka 1994). Accordingly, strong ties facilitate faster and more complex knowledge transfer including highly tacit knowledge which is required for new knowledge generation during the process of tacit and explicit knowledge interaction. Therefore, the importance of strong ties for work professionals in a company's social network cannot be discounted for the individuals in knowledge-intensive work to perform.

5.3 Theoretical and Practical Implications

Prior research (e.g., Cho et al. 2005; Quan-Haase et al. 2005) has provided a foundation to investigate the significance of IM in enhancing social networks and work performance. The current study conceptualizes IM's contribution to knowledge management, considering its valuable capability in enabling work professionals to instantly share and transfer specific knowledge to each other in real time. The utilization of the constructs of knowledge transfer and knowledge generation in IM-enabled communication provides social network studies a theoretical angle to investigate the effects of social networking tools in knowledge management as well as the subsequent impacts on teamwork or the organization as a whole.

At the same time, IS-related social networking has received increased attention from both academics and practitioners. Most research has examined the social network as a whole and investigated its characteristics. Relying on the SNA technique, in this study we explored more specific components of a social network (including centrality, density, and tie strength) and the relationship between the social networking tool (i.e., IM) with those components. This research provides a springboard for further research on the effectiveness of other social network tools in shaping the social network.

Practically speaking, with the advancement of information and communication technologies, applications of information technologies have been found both useful and effective for individuals, groups, organizations, and society at large. This research provides compelling reasons for organizations to utilize effective communication technologies such as IM at work to improve performance. The flexibility and informality of IM allow employees to retain control of communication in the workplace, task activities, and team work. IM tools can be used to record and codify knowledge in the online interaction process. The online conversation transcripts can be easily made available for other work professionals looking for similar ideas or knowledge. In this sense, IM can effectively function as a productivity tool that facilitates real-time exchange of knowledge.

5.4 Future Research

The current study provided empirical evidence on the positive contribution for the adoption of IM tools in the workplace by facilitating the process of knowledge management. Future research can usefully evaluate the negative values that are associated with the use of IM tools (e.g., interruption to operations, security issues, etc.). By including the negative impacts of IM used at work, we can achieve a more complete overview for the adoption of IM tools in the workplace.

In terms of analysis, this study measured perceived teamwork performance at the individual level. Future research can aggregate teamwork performance at the individual level to a group level for a more comprehensive analysis. Analytical rigor can be further enhanced by collecting both subjective and objective measures for all constructs used in the research.

Due to the constraints associated with the company studied, we only investigated one social networking tool (i.e., IM) in this research. However, IM is not the only social networking tool that can be used in organizations. Other Web 2.0 tools, such as Facebook and Twitter, can also be applied to knowledge management activities, as well as marketing and product design (Deloitte 2010). Research into both theoretical and empirical aspects of the utilization of social networking tools in the organizational context will enrich our understanding of the relationships among social networks, IT, and the SNA technique, as well as how social networking tools can render a competitive advantage for organizations.

6 Conclusion

A well-connected social network in the workplace can augment the organization's collective knowledge and sharpen its capability to act on what people know in time.

By connecting people with various social networking tools, such as IM, blogs, Facebook, and Twitter, the organization can become an effective web of interaction. This study provides a compelling rationale to embed social network tools into the organizational context. The technology related to social networking tools is evolving. We believe more theoretical and practical research will emerge in this field.

References

Argote, L., Ingram, P.: Knowledge Transfer: A Basis for Competitive Advantage in Firms. Organizational Behavior and Human Decision Processes 82(1), 150–169 (2000)

Bock, G.W., Zmud, R.W., Kim, Y.-G., Lee, J.N.: Behavioral Intention Formation in Knowledge Sharing: Examining the Roles of Extrinsic Motivators, Social-Psychological Forces, and Organizational Climate. MIS Quarterly 29(1), 87–111 (2005)

Borgatti, S.P., Everett, M.G., Freeman, L.C.: UCINet for Windows: Software for Social Network Analysis. Analytic Technologies, Harvard (2002)

Cantú, L.Z., Criado, J.R., Criado, A.R.: Generation and Transfer of Knowledge in IT-Related SMEs. Journal of Knowledge 13(5), 243–256 (2009)

Chin, W.W.: Issues and Opinion on Structural Equation Modeling. MIS Quarterly 22(1), vii–xvi (1998)

Cho, H.-K., Trier, M., Kim, E.: The Use of Instant Messaging in Working Relationship Development: A Case Study. Journal of Computer-Mediated Communication 10(4) (2005)

Chow, W.S., Chan, L.S.: Social Network, Social Trust and Shared Goals in Organizational Knowledge Sharing. Information and Management 45, 458–465 (2008)

Davenport, T.H., Prusak, L.: Working Knowledge. Harvard Business School Press, Boston (1998)

Deloitte: Resistance to Change, Budget Constraints and Cost-Cutting Delay New Technologies into the Workplace. Deloitte Poll (2010)

Freeman, L.C.: Centrality in Social Networks: Conceptual Clarification. Social Networks 1(3), 215–239 (1978)

Fuller, M.A., Hardin, A.M., Davidson, R.M.: Efficacy in Technology-Mediated Teams. J. of Management Information Systems 23(3), 209–235 (2006)

Gibbert, M., Krause, H.: Practice Exchange in a Best Practice Marketplace. In: Davenport, T.H., Probst, G.J.B. (eds.) Knowledge Management Case Book: Siemens Best Practices. Publicis Corporate Publishing, Erlangen (2002)

Granovetter, M.S.: The Strength of Weak Ties. The American Journal of Sociology 78(6), 1360–1380 (1973)

Granovetter, M.S.: The Strength of Weak Ties: A Network Theory Revisited. Sociological Theory 1, 201–233 (1983)

Hair, J.F., Anderson, R.E., Tatham, R.L., Black, W.C.: Multivariate Data Analysis with Readings, 4th edn. Prentice Hall, Englewood Cliffs (1995)

Hammer, M.: Explorations into the Meaning of Social Network Interview Data. Social Networks 6, 341–371 (1984)

Hansen, M.T.: The Search-Transfer Problem: The Role of Weak Ties in Sharing Knowledge Across Organization Subunits. Administrative Science Quarterly 44(1), 82–111 (1999)

Isaacs, E., Walendowski, A., Whittaker, S., Schiano, D., Kamm, C.: The Character, Functions, and Styles of Instant Messaging in the Workplace. In: Proceedings of the 2002 ACM Conference on Computer Supported Cooperative Work, New Orleans, LA, pp. 11–20 (2002)

Kankanhalli, A., Tan, B.C.Y., Wei, K.K.: Contributing Knowledge to Electronic Knowledge Repositories: An Empirical Investigation. MIS Quarterly 29(1), 113–143 (2005)

Krackhardt, D.: The Strength of Strong Ties: The Importance of Philos In Organizations. In: Nohria, N., Eccles, R. (eds.) Networks and Organizations: Structures, Form and Action, pp. 216–239. Harvard Business School Press, Boston (1992)

Levin, D.Z., Cross, R.: The Strength of Weak Ties You Can Trust: The Mediating Role of Trust in Effective Knowledge Transfer. Management Science 50(11), 1477–1494 (2004)

Levinthal, D., Myatt, J.: Co-Evolution of Capabilities and Industry: A Study of Mutual Fund Processing. Strategic Management Journal 15, 45–62 (1994)

Li, D., Chau, P.Y.K., Lou, H.: Understanding Individual Adoption of Instant Messaging: An Empirical Investigation. The Journal of the Association for Information Systems 6(4), 102–129 (2005)

Marsden, P.: Network Data Measurement. Annual Review of Sociology 16, 435–463 (1990)

Marsden, P., Campbell, K.E.: Measuring Tie Strength. Social Forces 63, 482–501 (1984)

Nardi, B., Whittaker, S., Bradner, E.: Interaction and Outeraction: Instant Messaging in Action. In: Proceedings of the 2000 ACM Conference on Computer Supported Cooperative Work, Philadelphia, PA, pp. 79–88 (2000)

Nonaka, I.: A Dynamic Theory of Organizational Knowledge Creation. Organization Science 5(1), 14–37 (1994)

Pavlou, P.A., Gefen, D.: Building Effective Online Marketplaces with Institution-Based Trust. Information Systems Research 15(1), 37–60 (2004)

Quan-Haase, A., Cothrel, J., Wellman, B.: Instant Messaging for Collaboration: A Case Study of a High-Tech Firm. Journal of Computer-Mediated Communication 10(4) (2005)

Reagans, R., McEvily, B.: Network Structure and Knowledge Transfer: The Effects of Cohesion and Range. Administrative Science Quarterly 48, 240–267 (2003)

Roberts, J.: From Know-How to Show-How: Questioning the Role of Information and Communication Technologies in Knowledge Transfer. Technology Analysis & Strategic Management 12(4), 429–443 (2000)

Sabidussi, G.: The Centrality Index of a Graph. Psychometrika 31, 581–603 (1966)

Scott, J.: Social Network Analysis: A Handbook. SAGE Publications, London (1988)

Simon, H.A.: Bounded Rationality and Organizational Learning. Organization Science 2(1), 125–134 (1991)

Soo, C., Devinney, T., Midgley, D., Deering, A.: Knowledge Management: Philosophy, Processes, and Pitfalls. California Management Review 44, 129–150 (2002)

Srivastava, A., Bartol, K.M., Locke, E.A.: Empowering Leadership in Management Teams: Effects on Knowledge Sharing, Efficacy, and Performance. Academy of Management Journal 49(6), 1239–1251 (2006)

Stasser, G., Titus, W.: Pooling of Unshared Information in Group Decision Making: Biased Information Sampling during Discussion. Journal of Personality and Social Psychology 48, 1467–1478 (1985)

Szulanski, G.: Exploring Internal Stickiness: Impediments to the Transfer of Best Practices Within the Firm. Strategic Management Journal 17, 27–43 (1996)

Teigland, R.: Communities of Practice at an Internet Firm: Netovation vs. On-Time Performance. In: Lesser, E.L., Fontaine, M.A., Slusher, J.A. (eds.) Knowledge and Communities: Resources for the Knowledge-Based Economy, pp. 151–178. Butterworth-Heinemann, Woburn (2000)

Teigland, R., Wasko, M.: Knowledge Transfer in MNCs: Examining How Intrinsic Motivations and Knowledge Sourcing Impact Individual Centrality and Performance. Journal of International Management 15(1), 15–31 (2009)

Tracey, P., Clark, G.L., Lawton Smith, H.: Cognition, Learning and European Regional Growth: An Agent-Centred Perspective on the "New" Economy. Economics of Innovation and New Technology 13(1), 1–18 (2004)
Wasserman, S., Faust, K.: Social Network Analysis: Methods and Applications. Cambridge University Press, Cambridge (1994)
Wellman, B., Salaff, J., Dimitrova, D., Garton, L., Gulia, M., Haythornthwaite, C.: Computer Networks as Social Networks: Collaborative Work, Telework, and Virtual Community. Annual Review of Sociology 22, 213–238 (1996)

About the Authors

Carol X. J. Ou is an assistant professor of Information Management at Tilburg University. Her research interests include social networks, computer-mediated communication, electronic commerce, website design, and knowledge management in organizations. Her publications have appeared in in such journals as *Communications of the ACM, Journal of AIS, International Journal of Human–Computer Studies, Information Technology & People, Journal of IT Management*, and *Chinese Management Studies*. Carol is also serving as a senior editor for *Information Technology & People, Electronic Journal of Information Systems in Developing Countries*, and *International Journal of E-Adoption*. She is a Certified IS Auditor, an Academic Advocate of IS Audit and Control Association, as well as a committee member of various conferences on information systems and technologies.

Darren W. L. Leung is a Bachelor of Computing student at the Hong Kong Polytechnic University. His research focuses on social networks and knowledge management in organizations.

Robert M. Davison is an associate professor of Information Systems at the City University of Hong Kong. His current research focuses on virtual knowledge management and collaboration in Chinese SMEs. He has published over 50 articles in a variety of journals such as *Information Systems Journal, Information Technology & People, IEEE Transactions on Engineering Management, Decision Support Systems, Journal of the AIS, Communications of the AIS, Communications of the ACM*, and *MIS Quarterly*. Robert is the editor-in-chief of *Electronic Journal of Information Systems in Developing Countries*, a senior editor for *Information Systems Journal*, coeditor of *Information Technology & People*, and an associate editor for *MIS Quarterly*.

Section 4. The Future of Information Technology and Work-Related Practices in Health Care

Journey to DOR: A Retro Science-Fiction Story on Researching ePrescribing

Valentina Lichtner and Will Venters

Information Systems and Innovation Group, Department of Management London School
of Economics and Political Science, Houghton Street, WC2A 2AE London, UK
{V.Lichtner,W.Venters}@lse.ac.uk

Abstract. The core of this paper is a science fiction short story. We are on
planet DOR. A group of scientists are working on an experiment, changing
underlying mechanisms of transmissions of a colossus machine—a complex
system of gears and levers, wires and pipes. Some of its mechanisms are also
known as *D* for doctors, *F* for pharmacists, *P* for patients. Observers travel from
Earth to study the experiment. Their dilemmas are unaided by their advanced
research tools. The story is inspired by research carried out for the evaluation of
the forthcoming electronic prescription service in England. Our story is fiction,
but it is also a methodological means, a reflexive lever to elaborate and explore
our research texts and to question the feasibility, meaning, and impact of
researching future technology.

Keywords: Future, technology, fiction, systems for electronic transmission of
prescriptions, reflexivity, research methods.

1 Preface

> *"I had missed the precious moment when the planet first came into view.*
> *Now it was spread out before my eyes; flat, and already immense"*
>
> Stanislaw Lem, *Solaris*, 2003

The core of this paper is a science fiction story. This preface provides the rationale for
writing the story, which is then followed by reflections. Some readers may wish to
begin by reading the story first (Section 2), then read this preface.

As researchers adopting a social constructionist perspective (Crotty 1998), we seek
to produce coherent accounts of our research context through interpretation. We are
involved in a project to evaluate the introduction of an electronic prescription service
(EPS) in primary care and thus EPS is our research context. Our research project is
evaluating EPS at the same time EPS is being developed. EPS compliant software
applications are being piloted by a few prescriber (e.g., local doctors surgery) and
dispenser (e.g., local pharmacy) sites in England. The challenges of evaluating a
national IT project in development are perhaps self-evident: the lack of a definite set
of IT systems in place and in use, changing requirements and specifications, and,
more generally, shifting ground. The very existence of EPS has been under scrutiny.

M. Chiasson et al. (Eds.): Future IS 2011, IFIP AICT 356, pp. 151–161, 2011.
© IFIP International Federation for Information Processing 2011

This is made more complex by major changes in the UK National Health Service (NHS) brought about by a newly elected government. Evaluating EPS in the present is thus researching its future, with all its uncertainties, and with very limited space for contributing to steering its course.

Our evaluation project is undertaking detailed observations of, and interviews with, general practitioners, pharmacists, technologists, and various other stakeholders. Such observations and interviews are recorded, transcribed, and entered into our evidence base as research texts. Our epistemology is that of interpretivism—we seek not an objective truth but interpretations of the world of EPS. Yet as researchers we seem to face the gravitational pull of an enlightenment straightjacket, taught since our birth and embedded within our research culture; in our observations we naturally seek objective data, evidence, theory, and conclusions in order to produce research papers. Such papers rely heavily on research texts[1] produced from literature, project documents, transcripts, conversations, etc. Our papers are open to scrutiny and must be produced in this way; speculation and conjecture can have no place in an evaluation of such a politically charged context.

But what if we were to say that this is important but not sufficient? That as researchers we are always ethnographic, physically embedded within a research context we do not (and cannot) fully grasp? We constantly seek our own interpretations of this context in order to move forward to a future of modest understanding. We visit EPS sites, attend meetings, talk with people, read, reflect, and discuss, and in this we assimilate personal understanding which we struggle to record or express. Further, our interpretations of the EPS implementation include non-verbal clues, tacit perceptions, feelings, moods, incoherent contradictory ideas, and conspiracy theories—all emerging from our experience of the field, but "invalid" for traditional research purposes.

Seeking to find a way to express this kind of "unscientific" understanding of EPS, we welcome the invitation to write a non-traditional paper.[2] We are thus challenging ourselves by seeking to use fiction and storytelling to reflexively elaborate our tacit knowledge so as to better understand the EPS research context in which we are undertaking research, and through this to improve our traditional research practices.

Fiction and storytelling have an important role in knowledge sharing and reflexive analysis (Denning 2000; Snowden 2000) providing a fluid structure in which knowledge can be expressed and "infusing events with meaning...through the magic of plot" (Gabriel 2000, p. 180). This allows concepts to be remembered, altered, and shared, and allows meaning to diffuse. Similarly, the use of metaphor can help in sharing tacit knowledge (Nonaka 1991). Engagement with stories and the "emotional mind" has been promoted to teach software quality (McBride 2008) and used effectively to communicate information systems leadership ideas (Austin et al. 2009).

---

[1] By texts, we mean the broad set of evidential material produced in research: transcripts, videos, audio-recordings, written observations, etc.

[2] This paper was written in response to the call for papers for the IFIP WG 8.2 conference "Researching the Future" (https://www.wg82.abo.fi/callforpapers.php). The call invited non-traditional approaches and formats, such as science-fiction.

Most vitally, writing allows for a self-reflexive analysis of our understanding, turning the lens inward on the researcher.

While we could further discuss fiction as a research method, we wish to leave center-stage to the fiction itself. We leave to the reader the interpretations of its meanings, in terms of technology for the electronic transmission of medical prescriptions and, more generally, in relation to more-or-less utopian IT systems in healthcare and other sectors, and the role researchers play in their implementation. In concluding this paper, we include some of the comments and reflections to our fiction and provide a set of questions as a starting point to the wider debate on researching the future.

The reader remains free to like or dislike the fiction, agree or disagree with the questions, although we hope this exercise will inspire others to consider writing fiction as part of their methodological arsenal, as a reflective "mode of thought to question and imagine change" (Higgins 2001, p. 5). We should be humble of our inevitable limitations as researchers—and "such humility is essential in creating an environment in which we can learn about the complex systems in which we are embedded and work effectively to create the world we truly desire" (Sterman 2002, p. 527).

2 Journey to DOR[3]

The colossal machine was built on a tall thin grid that enabled scientists and observers to work on both sides. Dials, buttons, knobs, and levers were connected by a partially visible intricacy of pipes and wires—a giant radio-like structure without its case. A constant luminous flow was running through the pipes, cylinders and drums moving regularly up and down, while interconnected gears turned one another at various speeds similar to the hour, minute, and second arms of a clock. A scaffold was erected around the machine, so that only the very upper part was accessible. This scaffold gave a bottomless view of the machine below, and its hazy boundaries on the eastern and western sides. It left a vague awareness that other scaffolds might exist at the edges.

A readoscope device connected amongst the pipes produced constant monitoring of inputs and outputs, rates of flows and volumes of stock—state of health, volume of medicines, monetary value. Tiny fluorescent labels identified some of the main controls: D for doctors, F for pharmacists, M for the manufacturers of medicines, L for money, P for the patients and those caring for them.

Since the start of the new equinox, scientists had been working on an experiment to introduce a new layer into the apparatus, a new messaging system E, based not on pipes of liquid but on electrical impulses. The aim of this transition was to improve the quality of the readoscope results, and the flow and gearings. They had invited the observers to study the experiment and report back to the home planet on its outcome.

---

[3] This text is loosely based on Stanislaw Lem's book Solaris (2003, first published in 1961, translated to English in 1970). Words taken literally from Solaris are highlighted in italics (with page numbers referenced in superscript); Lem's words have been taken out of their original context and placed in this new, completely different story.

The observers were expected to land at any time, their expedition having been delayed by an interstellar ethical storm. E was already in place, all wired-up, and the scientists were anxious to begin.

***

From the portholes of the spaceship they could see the stars, but this portion of *the sky was unfamiliar to*[2] them. Some of them had heard of it, but none of them had visited DOR before. As they got closer to the station, they realized they were landing on a shifting ground, moving at variable speed. They left their cabin at a point of temporary still, but as soon as their feet touched ground they *had to take a step forward in order to keep* their *balance*[5]. The expected welcoming party had been cancelled, and the observers were ushered through empty corridors and piles of papers, directly to the machine room. Were the scientists happy to see them?

The observers took a position behind the grid, providing them with a parallel view of all the mechanisms. The scientists were on the other side, with access to the controls. The machine was running its flows and glows, more or less smoothly. A roll of printed paper was spinning out of the readoscope, although little was made of it by those in the room; it simply fell through an opening in the scaffolding. Introductions were made, and the observers were given information materials on the experiment. It was explained to them that E had already been put in place, to save time, and that the countdown was ready to start. Did they have any questions?

The observers tried to pay attention but their eyes were distracted by the rhythmic move of this glowing apparatus with a life of its own, while their bodies were struggling to stay still on the shifting foot-base. They tried to decipher the mechanisms and their movements—make a map of them in their mind—but they struggled to understand the roles and relationships in the little time available. They decided to focus on E, ask for further details on its inner working and expected benefits.

A transparent thin glass was layered in front of the machine and a projection of E was superimposed on its mechanisms. The scientists had used this method before quite successfully to illustrate their vision. The starting point was the doctors. E was expected to reduce the load on D; the corresponding gear would run more easily and transmit the effect on F; a temporary increased load on F would be transformed by its inner circuits in tighter controls on P, which at the same time would reduce volumes in M and pressure on L. The result was expected to be a smoother, more efficient, productive, effective, safer apparatus. The nonlinear equations in the underlying mathematical model had shown that E would also save energy and generally improve the health status of the planet. Minor glitches were expected in the transmission mechanisms, due to inertia–resistance forces, but the scientists were confident that they could be greased and recast as and when necessary.

As the thin glass projection screen retracted, the countdown began – *two-hundred and fifty, two-hundred and forty-nine, two-hundred and forty-eight*[3]...

Keep a hold on thyself. *Be open to* see *anything*. That was *the only advice* they had been given before boarding. The observers could *not think of anything better*[11]. During the presentation the scaffold had temporarily paused its shifting, making *ground* for sound *mathematical certitude*[20]. But the rolling had slowly started again as soon as the countdown button had been pushed. And the strong starlight coming through the portholes cast *double shadows*[27] that were hindering the observations. The closer they tried to position themselves to the machine, the more defined were the double contours of their own shadows.

...five, four, three, two point nine, two point eight, two point seven nine, two point seven eight...roll-out. The start button pushed to its full length, the E gear began to slowly turn, steering D to a skewed angle. The transmissions led to a shaking of the whole machine, gear by gear, pipe by pipe, with jolts and scratches. The scientists were reading the readoscope prints, while tightening bolts, loosening belts, oiling pins—mechanics tuning the engine. Speed began to increase, the shuffling of M more rapid. The scientists kept an eye on the observers, as if to read their minds and share enthusiasm for the new venture. The observers glanced back through the grid, almost hypnotized by the rhythmic movement of the machine but unsure what to read in the scientists' faces. The load on D initially increased, as expected, but it was now slowly diminishing; F was taking on the work and modifying its internal circuits to cope with the pressure, a groaning could be heard from that part of the machine, although P was running as usual, something only the scientists initially noticed. The gear did not seem to modify its behavior the way it should have. The scientists hoped the lack of change in P would be unnoticeable to the observers. Absence is more difficult to notice than presence, usually, isn't it? That would give them time to fix the malfunction without the need to account for it. They turned to the readoscope. They knew the high volume of data it was producing was of great value.

***

The observers had prepared for this machine by reading books and papers, but the reality was far more complicated. It was made of more gears and control devices than those explained in the presentation: G.overnment, M.edia, M.ass and P.ersonalized M.edicine, I.T, G.enomics, to name but a few. Changes were appearing on these mechanisms too, but the observers couldn't say if the changing was related to E. How were they going to report in simple terms such an immense, constantly moving, interconnected frenzy of relationships and differences, wires and gears? Each gear in itself was a rich, intricate lace. Their notebooks were filling up with data, text, numbers, sketches as they tried to capture the flow of events and changes in progress. It seemed it was not possible to observe the makeup of the flow itself but clearly it was vital to the operation of the machine. They struggled to see the simplicity the scientists had presented, so enthralled were they by the system's complexity. Perhaps they could have interpreted the machine low-pitched murmuring—the very voice of the machine itself—but *they lacked the ears to hear it*[126]. What were they missing, the whole for the gears? Were they focusing on the right layers? Where were the outcomes? More observation work was necessary.

The observers split into groups. The youngest gave themselves more precise tasks, capturing with stopwatches accurate timings of the flow and speed of dials. The most senior took a mimal out of their toolbox, the handheld micromagnetolens that had been applied in many successful projects before to produce real time picotgraphic representations of the combined smaller-and-bigger picture. Gears, pipes, and wires were coming in and out of focus. They tried positioning themselves at a different angle on the shifting platform. If only the ground would stop moving, their work would be much easier.

As the scientists attempted to repair the reaction mechanisms in P, they saw that M was having an increased effect on the whole system. They knew there was a risk but they didn't think it would reveal itself so soon. Critical mass—and time—is usually needed before such transformations take place. M's power was increasingly influencing P's behavior now that E had freed P from D's control. P was freely turning to F, generating an exponential growth of M and corresponding value of L. The scientists tried to intervene on F by pulling a few levers, but with limited effect. Humming and glowing, the machine had found a new equilibrium, leading to a steady and more fluid growth of M and a more rapid turning of P, but no signs yet of dramatic change in the health of the nation, nor energy saving. The readoscope printouts were now showing alarming figures of L and risks for P, but no alarm bells were ringing. The scientists stood back to discuss the variables in the mathematical model. *So much for the mathematicians*[22]...

The observers were still at work and had not realized the experiment had ended. It seemed changes were still in progress, the machine was still moving. They did notice, though, that the scientists had stopped working on the machine, and they took the opportunity to ask for a few clarifications. Why was E implemented? An easy, straightforward question.

The scientists looked at each other. Apparently the reasons kept changing as the years passed and the project developed, and nobody could recall why it had begun. But they were sure it could be done; it was technically feasible and therefore desirable, a certain technical improvement to the system. In fact, the experiment had demonstrated its success, with the machine moving more fluidly, smoothly—more efficiently.

***

The observers were on their capsule back to Earth. *The night stared* them *in the face, amorphous, blind, infinite, without frontiers*[26]. Traveling gave them a quiet time to write their report. Unfortunately *the assiduous efforts of so many years had not resulted in a single indisputable conclusion*[23]. They were concerned, but they were back down to Earth. Looking back, they could see that they had flown to DOR not so much to observe the experiment but to acquaint themselves with the machine. *With a muffled sigh of resignation, the* spaceship *expelled its* hot *air*. They were *free*[5].

3 Reflections

Postmodernist critical theory suggests reflexivity as one way in which researchers can come to terms with their own research circumstances (Gouldner 1970; Calás and Smircich1999). Reflexivity "aims at interpretation, open, language sensitive, identity-conscious, historical, political, non-authoritative and textually aware understanding of the subject matter" (Alvesson and Deetz 2000, p. 115). It concerns recognizing the ambivalent relationship of the research texts and evidence to the realities studied (Ashmore 1989) and focuses on the researchers themselves and their experience. Yet a significant constraint to such research practices is the act of writing academic papers. The traditional academic paper defines some limits of our writing (Calás and Smircich 1999) and reflexive research should seek alternative writing styles in order to explore the social, historical, and political context of their research (Ashmore 19899), in particular to explore the tacit dimension (Polanyi 1967) of research knowledge which researchers develop in their experience of the field. Perhaps it is the duty of all researchers to come to terms with their own circumstances "before allowing [themselves] the arrogant luxury of disengaged pronouncements on the circumstances of others" (Gouldner 1970, cited in Ashmore 1989, p. 78).

For this reason, we here explore the writing of explicit fiction as a means to elaborate our research "reality" and come to terms with our own research circumstances, drawing on our reflexive understanding, but expressly avoiding "facts" and factual text. As "every reality depends upon the ceaseless reflexive use of a body of knowledge in interaction" (Mehan and Wood 1975, p. 21), so the authoring of this fictional account provided an opportunity to reify and discuss dissatisfaction, concern, and self-critique within EPS and within our EPS evaluation project. Ensuring a focus away from the specifics of the current research project and creating projections and extrapolations—fiction—and especially the sci-fi genre based in the future (McHugh 2001) avoids or reifies ethical and moral concerns so allowing them to be expanded upon but in a less threatening manner (although interestingly we were asked to highlight the disclaimer on the fictional nature of the piece).

Our fictional account is an exercise in futureology; it is inspired by the novel *Solaris*, by a socio-technical view of the world (Petrakaki and Cornford 2010), and by Peter Checkland's (1981) soft systems thinking. The text is clearly and explicitly not of this world, of this time, of this reality, and thus cannot be seen as a direct representation of our research project. Writing science fiction provided us with the freedom from our own inner academic self-censor. Our story is retro: "a sci-fi vision from the 1950s about a social and political reality now," as one reader described it. The story is about our now, and in particular our problems today in identifying outcomes. It is science fiction, but like all science fiction it is based on the social reality of the present, for why else would it be possible to have retro-sci-fi?

Similarly to writing about the future, researching the future is also always based on the present, or rather the "remembered past" (Lukacs 1994). In a dialectical perspective, "whether studying the past or the future, it is chiefly a matter of looking back, deriving presuppositions from the forms that contain them" (Ollman 2003, p. 122). Just as the hindsight bias skews any research of the past, so the past skews any projection of the future. Look in either direction and the researcher can only see the present.

Solaris was chosen as the basis for our story for its literary strengths and conceptual rather than narrative or plot based structure, and yet this novel can offer us an additional layer for reflection. The book recounts the story of four men in a space station, on a planet, Solaris, a live ocean-like creature with whom Man has been striving to establish contact for centuries. Human theories and models of the ocean fill the space station's library. The ocean resounds like an amorphous, threatening, marvelous, incomprehensible being. It is a psychological story, as the ocean communicates with the four men by presenting them embodiments of their own remorse, hidden in their subconscious. We read it as an epistemological tale: humans are unable to communicate with an entity that they can only know and describe through the humans' own theories and nomenclature (our hermeneutic bind, that we are limited by our socially constructed language); the positivism of the Solarian scientists is replaced by the skepticism over their possible achievements and the limitations of the human minds. The ocean is a multiple metaphor—in this case, one of our attempts to research the present/future of EPS, or the observers' attempt to draw outcomes out of the E experiment on the machine of DOR.

When facing the E, the observers found themselves in a struggle to know and judge its effect on the system. Technology is embedded in complex socio-technical systems; it is not neutral (Winner 1999); it affects/is affected by the relations that surround it and the expressed intentions for its coming to be, the expressed goals might easily turn into unexpected/unwanted ones (Lem calls this effect the "bifurcation of goals"[4]). The view of the whole is complex, and made more complex, and both more and less knowable, by an interpretative perspective.

In contrast the scientists in our story had a clearer purpose and a narrower perspective; a pragmatic approach to get the job done. Perhaps we should have called them engineers, as engineers design and build, while in science fiction, especially movies, scientists "being a clearly labeled species of intellectual...are always liable to crack up or go off the deep end" (Sontag 1966, p. 45).

As researchers we find ourselves in dilemmas that leave behind an inability to act. The question is how to overcome them and contribute shaping the technology of our present and future. The difficulty is that what is required is often an answer to trans-scientific questions, ethical questions not answerable with science (Weinberg 1972), a matter of choice, trade-offs, power, values, accountability. Often we are under considerable pressure to provide simple rational answers—and to be servants of the powerful sponsors of research (Baritz 1960). We must at least attempt to resist.

4 Postscript

This fictional piece was inspired by research undertaken to evaluate the electronic prescription service, a Connecting for Health project, part of the NHS National Programme for IT. This paper is a creative reflexive account of researching the future, inspired by the work carried out for the Evaluation of the Electronic Prescription Service in Primary Care. We must explicitly state that this account is not, and cannot be interpreted as, a direct representation of the NHS Electronic Prescription Service or preempt the outcomes of the independent evaluation still in progress.

EPS builds on a set of electronic messaging functionalities newly implemented in existing prescribers' and dispensers' software applications already available on the market (i.e., electronic patient records systems currently used in GP surgeries and pharmacies). The program is being developed in a series of releases: the purpose of EPS-Release 1 was mainly to introduce and test the infrastructure; at the time of writing, EPS-Release 2 compliant systems/functionalities are in the testing phase and getting ready for wider roll-out. Release 2 will introduce electronic signatures and

---

[4] See Stanislaw Lem, "The Official Site," at
http://english.lem.pl/works/essays/summatechnologiae/
108-a-look-inside-summa-technologiae

potentially replace paper prescriptions. More information on EPS can be found on the NHS website.[5]

The evaluation of EPS focuses on Release 2. It is an independent research project structured in four different work packages, aimed at assessing different aspects of EPS, including safety of dispensing, changes of work practices in doctors' surgeries and pharmacies, views of patients, and effects on the wider context (e.g., market structures). The different themes are investigated with a mix of qualitative and quantitative research methods, including observations, interviews, participants' self-reported activities, task analysis, stakeholder mapping, etc. The wider EPS context has been the subject of semi-structured face-to-face interviews with representatives of prescribers, dispensers, software suppliers, and other stakeholders. Thirty interviews/meetings were conducted between June 2009 and July 2010. The process of identifying and mapping stakeholders has been described and discussed in Lichtner et al. 2010. Research is still in progress at the time of writing.

Acknowledgments

The EPS evaluation project is lead by the School of Pharmacy/University of London, in collaboration with the University of Nottingham and the London School of Economics and Political Sciences. More information on CfHEP004 is available on the project website: http://project.epsevaluation.org.uk/.

Investigations on the micro and macro scenarios of EPS have been shared with and supported by the CfHEP004 team, especially (in alphabetical order) Tony Cornford and Dimitra Petrakaki (London School of Economics); Nick Barber, James Davies, and Ralph Hibberd (School of Pharmacy/University of London); and Anthony Avery, Matthew Boyd, Jasmine Harvey, and Justin Waring (Nottingham University). Our thanks to Nick Barber and Tony Cornford for the useful comments on an earlier version of this paper. Special thanks also to the anonymous reviewers, especially for a suggestion on the title. We are indebted to Stanislaw Lem's fictional masterpiece *Solaris*. Our thanks to Lou Alba for recommending *Solaris*.

References

Alvesson, M., Sköldberg, K.: Reflexive Methodology: New Vistas for Qualitative Research. Sage, London (2000)

Alvesson, M., Deetz, S.: Doing Critical Management Research. Sage Publications, Thousand Oaks (2000)

Ashmore, M.: The Reflexive Thesis. University of Chicago Press, Chicago (1989)

Austin, R.D., Nolan, R.L., O'Donnell, S.: The Adventures of an IT Leader. Harvard Business School Press, Boston (2009)

Baritz, L.: Servants of Power. Wesleyan University Press, Middletown (1960)

Calás, M.B., Smircich, L.: Past Postmodernism? Reflections and Tentative Directions. The Academy of Management Review 24, 649–671 (1999)

---

[5] http://www.connectingforhealth.nhs.uk/systemsandservices/eps

Checkland, P.: Systems Thinking, Systems Practice. John Wiley and Sons, Chichester (1981)

Crotty, M.: The Foundations of Social Research. Sage, London (1998)

Denning, S.: The Springboard: How Storytelling Ignites Action in Knowledge-Era Organizations. Butterworth-Heinemann, New York (2000)

Gabriel, Y.: Storytelling in Organizations: Facts, Fictions, and Fantasies. Oxford University Press, Oxford (2000)

Gouldner, A.W.: The Coming Crisis of Western Sociology. Basic Books, New York (1970)

Higgins, M.: Introduction: More Amazing Tales. In: Smith, W., Higgins, M., Parker, M., Lightfoot, G. (eds.) Science Fiction and Organization, pp. 1–12. Routledge, London (2001)

Lem, S.: Solaris. Faber and Faber, London (2003)

Lichtner, V., Petrakaki, D., Hibberd, R., Venters, W., Cornford, A., Barber, N.: Mapping Stakeholders for System Evaluation: The Case of the Electronic Prescription Service in England. In: Safran, C., Reti, S., Marin, H. (eds.) Medinfo 2010—Proceedings of the 13th World Congress on Medical Informatics, Cape Town, South Africa, pp. 1221–1225 (2010)

Lukacs, J.: Historical Consciousness: The Remembered Past. Transaction Publishers, Piscataway (1994)

McBride, N.: Using Performance Ethnography to Explore the Human Aspects of Software quality. Information Technology & People 21, 91–111 (2008)

McHugh, D.: Give Me Your Mirrorshades: Science Fiction "Methodology" Meets the Social and Organizational Sciences. In: Smith, W., Higgins, M., Parker, M., Lightfoot, G. (eds.) Science Fiction and Organization, pp. 15–30. Routledge, London (2001)

Mehan, H., Wood, H.: The Reality of Eethnomethodology. John Wiley & Sons, New York (1975)

Nonaka, I.: The Knowledge-Creating Company. Harvard Business Review 69, 96–104 (1991)

Ollman, B.: Dance of the Dialectic: Steps in Marx Method. University of Illinois Press, Urbana (2003)

Petrakaki, D., Cornford, T., Klecun, E.: Sociotechnical Changing in Healthcare. In: Aarts, J., Nohr, C. (eds.) Information Technology in Health Care (ITHC). IOS Press, Aarhus (2010)

Polanyi, M.: The Tacit Dimension. Doubleday, New York (1967)

Snowden, D.: New Wine in Old Wineskins: From Organic to Complex Knowledge Management through the Use of Story. Emergence 2, 50–64 (2000)

Sontag, S.: The Imagination of Disaster. In: Against Interpretation and Other Essays, pp. 209–225. Farrar, Straus and Giroux, New York (1966)

Sterman, J.: All Models Are Wrong: Reflections on Becoming a Systems Scientist. System Dynamics Review 18, 501–531 (2002)

Weinberg, A.M.: Science and Trans-Science. Minerva 10(2), 209–222 (1972)

Winner, L.: Do Artifacts Have Politics? In: McKenzie, D., Wajcman, J. (eds.) The Social Shaping of Technology, pp. 28–40. Open University Press, London (1999)

About the Authors

Valentina Lichtner is a postdoctoral research officer at the London School of Economics and Political Sciences. She is interested in adoption and adaptation of IT in healthcare, evaluation of systems, identity and identification technology, human–computer interaction, and patient safety. She is currently conducting research into the introduction of electronic health records and electronic transfer of prescriptions in the English NHS.

Will Venters is a lecturer in the Department of Management at the London School of Economics and Political Sciences. His research focuses on distributed work practice, and in particular the development of distributed systems to support distributed work. He is currently conducting research on socio-material understanding of information systems, and agile systems development practices within contexts including Particle Physics at the LHC, UK electronic prescribing, and general practices.

The Standardized Nurse: Mission Impossible?

Rune Pedersen[1], Gunnar Ellingsen[1], and Eric Monteiro[2]

[1] University of Tromsø Telemedicine Laboratory
rune.pedersen@uit.no gunnar.ellingsen@hn-ikt.no
[2] Department of Computer and Information Science,
Norwegian University of Science and Technology
eric.monteiro@idi.ntnu.no

Abstract. Socio-technical approaches, with their over-emphasis on situated and contextual differences, find it difficult if not impossible to account for ICT-supported standardization of healthcare work. Empirically, not all efforts of standardization fail. How can that be theoretically conceptualized, even when key tenets of a situated perspective are maintained? We discuss an interpretative case study where standardization of nursing work—to an interesting degree—has been achieved. We analyze the process of co-construction of the standards (i.e., standards in practice). Standards are partly imposed from the top, and partly enacted through the active involvement and ingenuity of users.

Keywords: Standardization, nursing work, quality, dependency and efficiency.

1 Introduction

Perspectives on standardization of work tend to be polarized: either standardization is perceived as a typically top-down effort promoting "best practices" or, as often argued in socio-technical approaches to ICT in health care(Ellingsen et al. 2007; Timmermans and Berg 1997), standardization is considered futile, as health work is inherently situated and thus unique. Such a position is unsatisfactory for practitioners (they will find it hard to accept that any form of standardization is impossible) as well as inadequate from a research point of view. There is thus a sense in which standardized work in hospitals does not work in theory (i.e., the academic literature), but works in practice.

We wish to emphasize the importance of a theoretical perspective for the standardization of Information System embedded service work. The key questions this paper addresses are

(1) How can processes for standardization of healthcare work be described socio-technically?
(2) How can one identify practical key implications of heterogeneous work practices to promote IT-based standardization?

Empirically, we draw on the broad efforts of standardization of healthcare work at Akershus University Hospital (AHUS), one of the largest hospitals in Norway. Since

M. Chiasson et al. (Eds.): Future IS 2011, IFIP AICT 356, pp. 163–178, 2011.

2005, the hospital has embarked on an ambitious effort aimed at a level of standardization of healthcare work unprecedented in Norway. Certainly, the boldest ambitions regarding standardization have not been achieved. However, significantly more standardization than the literature suggests has been achieved. Our empirical focus is on the standardization of nursing work, an IT-based system focusing on electronic patient records (EPR), and IT-based standardization of nursing plans and associated procedures for nursing. The standardization efforts also included efforts to associate standardized "pools" of patient beds and wards together with a generic pool of nurses.

2 Conceptualizing Standardization in Healthcare

Historically, IS research has a deeply embedded role in the ongoing transformation of modern organizations (Ellingsen et al. 2007). Standardization in information systems has a long history, from programming language, to communication protocols, to exchange formats (Schmidt and Werle 1998). There is an even stronger tradition of *de facto* standards for applications, operating systems, and file formats (Hanseth et al. 1996). However, an issue that has received considerably less attention in IS research is IS-based initiatives for the standardization of work and routines (Ellingsen et al. 2007; Timmermans and Berg 1997). Given the increasingly importance of the service sector in IS research, it is vital to extend the focus from standardization of artefacts and products to include standardized, IS-embedded service work—such as work processes in hospitals (Ellingsen et al. 2007). In addition, the maturing of technology alongside significant practical experiences substantiates current visions of a working e-infrastructure (Hepsø and Monteiro 2009).

In relation to the historical context, which entailed a technocratic top-down approach to standardization (Ure and Proctor 2009), the field has matured. We now see increasing consideration of a broader conceptualization in which standards form the backbone of socio-technical networks. Standardizing the work of nurses, physiccians, and other health workers has proven remarkably difficult to achieve, and is interwoven with efforts to improve efficiency and quality in health care (Bowker and Star 1999; Ellingsen et al. 2007; Timmermans and Berg 1997). Modern nursing is embedded in a highly politicized and institutionalized arena where governmental and managerial rules, regulations, and politics are negotiated against local concerns and priorities (Timmermans and Berg 2003). A fundamental characteristic of this work is its pragmatic, fluid character. Despite the obvious potential for improvements in efficiency, safety, and quality, standardization efforts seldom meet their objectives (IOM 2001). One reason for this is that health care in general and hospitals in particular are characterized by highly specialized—and thus unique—routines and procedures that differ across wards, areas, and geography. Like other complex work activities, health care is characterized by the constant emergence of contingencies that require *ad hoc* and pragmatic responses. Although much work follows routinized paths, the complexity of health care organizations and the never fully predictable nature of patients' reactions to interventions result in an ongoing stream of sudden events (Berg 1999). In her book on the process of developing from a novice to an expert, Patricia Benner (1984) has described how beginners and experts do things differently, and how a nurse's competence changes as her clinical career develops. This approach is described as underpinning the role of core personnel in the organization. Brenner's theory builds on the Dreyfus model, which illustrates the situational, experience-based premises that differentiate the levels of skilled performance. Learning from theory and from context-dependent judgement and skills are vital to this. In addition, health care work is typified by ongoing negotiations about the nature of the tasks and the relationships between those who execute the tasks (Button and Harper 1993). For example, Hughes (1988) has documented how experienced nurses often help inexperienced residents by suggesting the way to a diagnosis, or by hinting at the necessary treatment. Even though our interpretations do not compare nurses and physicians, the nurse versus nurse relation could be inherently situated.

However, the ever-increasing level of change in health care is problematic. Economic and qualitative requirements for treatment and care constantly challenge health care authorities to make increasingly strained efforts to maintain their budgets. Hence, the need to curb large and seemingly ever-increasing health care expenditures is an explicit feature of managerial agendas for the increased standardization of health care work (IOM 2001). In this regard, IS in general and nursing care plans (Berg 1999; Voutilainen et al. 2004) in particular are considered key means for standardizing nursing work to obtain increased efficiency as well as improved quality of care (Ellingsen et al. 2007).

While a great deal of the medical informatics literature, such as Kalra (2006), promotes a top-down approach to standardization, the STS and CSCW literature (Hanseth and Lundberg 2001; Pollock et al. 2007) promotes a more careful approach. Along these lines, Hanseth and Lundberg (2001) maintained that in organizations with particularly complex work practices, such as hospitals, only the users themselves would know the practice well enough to be able to design a system for the organization, resulting in a bottom-up approach to standardization.

Our aim is not to engage in a debate between the two extremes, but to position ourselves somewhere in the middle. The contexts of the use of EPR nursing plans are always individually different and characterized by highly idiosyncratic practices, whereas technologies are singular and monolithic; localization is the means by which the standard and the unique are brought together. One strand of research highlights the diversity of specific organizational contexts while others recognize that the apparently similar systems are being used across the same settings(Pollock et al. 2007). Several researchers believe that systems can merge across different practices equally; adjustments thus always need to be made. For instance, Pollock et al. (2007) have pointed out how large-scale systems can be successfully transferred across organizational boundaries. One example is a student administration system, the campus management model (GM) developed by the German software house SAP, which in the end was launched in the wider market as a "global university solution" (Pollock et al. 2007). Our position is to flag bottom-up approaches for health care institutions while at the same time recognizing the importance of top-down initiatives. Our intention is to develop an understanding of information systems embedded in the standardization of hospital work. From a co-constructive perspective on standardization, in which standardization and practice mutually shape and constitute each other, standardized work always involves "local universalities." Global standards both shape and are shaped by local work practice (Berg 1997).

3 Method

The focus of our field work has been on the challenges constructed by the heterogeneity of hospital work, with the focus on IT, information systems standards such as the electronic patient record (EPR) based nursing plans, and interconnected work process standards such as generic pools for beds and personnel.

The importance of social issues related to computer-based information systems has been increasingly recognized over the last decade, and this has led IS researchers to adopt empirical approaches that focus particularly on human interpretation and meanings(Walsham 1995). In practice, the flow of health care work activities is often much less linear than it is in other arenas, as it has flexibly defined roles. Interpretive methods of research in IS are aimed at producing the information system, and the process whereby the information system influences and is influenced by the context. Interpretive research can help the IS researcher to understand human thought and action in social and organizational contexts (Klein and Myers 1999). Further, Orlikowski and Baroudi (1991) define interpretive research as follows: interpretive studies assume that people create and associate their own subjective and intersubjective meanings as they interact with the world around them. The interpretive researcher thus attempts to understand through accessing the meanings participants assign to them. Our study adheres to an interpretive research tradition of this nature. Interviews, observations, and document analysis have focussed on key actors, mostly nurses, physicians, and project managers, as well as architecture and artefacts. In general, qualitative research methods like interviews and observations are optimally suited to understand a phenomenon from the participants' point of view, and in particular the social and institutional context. Qualitative research techniques can provide deep insight, identify problems, and answer the *why* and the *how* questions that quantitative studies cannot answer (Ash et al. 2004).

> Ethnography produces in- depth understanding of real-world social processes. Properly done, it provides detailed insight into the concepts and premises that underlie what people do—but that they are often unaware of (Forsythe 1999, p. 129)

3.1 Data Collection

We have employed four modes of data collection during a period from September 2009 to March 2010: observations, semi-structured interviews, document analysis, and analysis of central logs with general numbers on the use of nursing care plans.

In total, the first author conducted 170 hours of observations and 10 semistructured interviews averaging 80 minutes at the Cardiology department of AHUS in the period 2009–2010. The third author conducted six interviews at the Department of Pulmonary Medicine as a supplement to the standardization of work processes in the same period. The first author further conducted eight semi-structured interviews of personnel who had practical importance for the recommendation of a classification system for nursing, an initiative that in the future will secure a nationally embraced, consistent use of terminology in Norway. The interviews lasted between 60 and 140 minutes, with an average of 100 minutes.

The length of the observations varied from between one and eight hours, and included tracing patient trajectories through the hospital to understanding the adoption and use of IT: based information carried out by nurses and physicians in different circumstances, such as between people, between people and technology, and between people and artefacts.

3.2 Data Analysis

The overall process of collecting data has been open-ended and iterative, with a gradually evolving focus on specific situations from work practice. Crucial to the evolving questioning has been interviews both among experienced nurses and novices. The analytical categories emerged from internal discussions and reading of field notes.

Essential to the case, and taking an interpretive position, is the subjective and intersubjective meanings taken by experienced nurses and novices. Handwritten field notes were transcribed shortly after the data was gathered. All transcriptions of the interviews were done immediately after the interviews themselves, as, according to Malterud (2003), early transcription is crucial in order to clarify uncertainties and the meaning of unclear sentences. The interviews were done using a tape recorder, and we posed only a few open-ended questions that were semi-structured and shaped according to how the interviews evolved.

Our findings have been discussed among fellow students, as well as discussions the first author with the second and third authors of this article, both of whom have a thorough understanding of and experience in working with IS studies and, specifically, with nursing plans, handovers, and classifications.

3.3 Context of Study

The research was conducted at the Akershus University Hospital (AHUS), which has about 4,700 employees and a total of 820 beds. Our study took place at the Division of Cardiology, specifically, the general Department of Cardiology, which consists of 28 beds.

The hospital is built on a model from Johns Hopkins Hospital in Baltimore, Maryland, globally acclaimed for its exceptional services and a program striving for standardization and efficiency in health care.

The reallocation of AHUS to new premises during 2008 brought additional initiatives to standardize nursing work, particularly to avoid bottlenecks caused by overly specialized services. One measure was to establish standardized beds and nurses for patients (i.e., the capacity to allocate patients to beds outside "their" wards and having nurses work in wards other than their "own"). To allocate patient beds, a new unit for patient logistics was established, which would book the beds for patients. As a rule, this unit would try to assign patients where they normally belonged. In cases of overbookings, the patient logistics unit prioritizes the serious incidents and moves less serious cases out of the "home" wards and into any of two generic bed wards. Here, nurses have special training in caring for patients with a wide variety of conditions, but no serious illnesses. As one nurse noted, *"the biggest change was for the physicians, as they now also have to visit the generic bed wards."* Key mechanisms for volunteering nurses to circulate in other wards have been the incentives offered: salary and flexibility. Salaries are increased by an extra 5 percent for those who choose to circulate. Equally important, especially for family-oriented nurses, is that signing up for circulation gives nurses greater control over *when* they are to work.

From 2007, the responsibility for collecting blood specimens was, on the whole, decentralized to a departmental level and to the hospital's nurses. The potential effects of this were related to efficiency. Previously, technologists from the medical biochemistry laboratory collected blood specimens on fixed rounds three times a day, which resulted in delays and rigidity in the routines. In particular, blood specimens collected on an *ad hoc* basis or in emergencies had to be handled manually.

However, collecting blood specimens is a resource-demanding procedure that, one nurse complains, *"has resulted in much more work for us, and is not time-saving."* Still, the time from requesting a laboratory analysis until the result is available was greatly decreased throughout the first year. In addition, there were positive side effects. The nurses spend more time with the patients, and the patients no longer have to interact with so many different personnel.

4   Standardization of Nursing Work

4.1   History of Standardized Nurse Work

The EPR used at AHUS since 2005 includes a module for nursing (see Figure 1 for explanation). Along the lines of standardization, the nursing care plan, including the classification systems NIC and NANDA, was viewed as a means for making nursing work more effective and offering both quality assurance and future research capabilities. The classification systems are ICT-based standards integrated with the care plan. The diagnoses are represented by the international classification system of the North American Nursing Diagnosis Association (NANDA), consisting of 206 nursing diagnoses (NANDA 2007). The interventions are represented by the Nursing Intervention Classification (NIC) system, consisting of 486 interventions (Bulechek et al. 2008). Further, PPS is a decision support system for nursing, developed in collaboration with the authorities and distributed to educational institutions, municipalities, and hospitals nationwide.

The foundation of an independent nursing division was introduced in 2007 with its own spokesman on the hospital staff, established to sharpen the focus on nursing activities, such as utilization of resources, research, and development of expertise.

More recently, a national initiative stressed establishing a national incentive for recommending an all-encompassing classification system. The agenda of the initiative was first to get the National Directory of Health interested in nursing classifications and thereby included in their portfolio of classification systems, which first and foremost means financial support for further development. This process has detained the use of NIC and NANDA on a national level, and is a typical topic discussed and solved in the collaborating groups.

Several hospitals in Norway have used NIC and NANDA for a decade, and the vendor has estimated that, on a national level, they have more than 25,000 users of the nursing module.

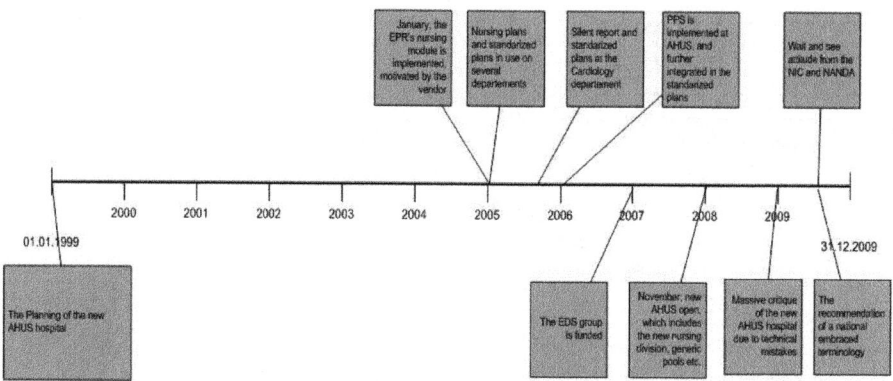

Fig. 1. Time line, from early planning of the new AHUS hospital and up to today

4.2 The Care Plan

Care plans are increasingly made to replace the use of free text in the documentation, foremost to establish a common, formalized language based on best practice. Freetext documentation is whatever information the nurses share about the patient in the EPR in addition to or without writing formalized care plans. However, the implementation of the EPR led to a systematic use of standardized care plans. Too much time was spent documenting unessential information (free-text) such as "eaten two slices of bread with jam and cheese" and "been for a walk."

The care plan has been organized such that each diagnosis, dimension, and action is firmly attached to the plan with a start and a stop date. When standardizing these plans, the nurse can easily choose several actions from a predefined list for the applicable diagnosis. By doing this, the nurse saves time, and at the same time the standardized sentences work as a quality indicator. Figure 2 illustrates the ordinary and the standardized plans respectively. Basically, the nursing plan is an overview of nurse-related diagnoses for a particular patient group combined with relevant interventions (NIC interventions, following the NANDA diagnosis).

4.3 Standardized Plans and Silent Handover at the Cardiology Department

Standardized plans and a silent handover were introduced as a "package" late in 2005 at the Cardiology department. Equal for all of the IT-based standards described in our case—the care plan, standardized plan, and PPS—is that they were adopted and used before the reallocation process started. The standardized plan represents a care-fully selected combination of NANDA diagnoses and NIC interventions for a given medical diagnosis or clinical speciality. A number of plans were made by and for each speciality, with 17 for cardiology, and 406 plans in total. Some plans are also generic, covering diagnosis and interventions for patients with composite diagnoses. The standardized plans have been added to a shared list (Figure 2 on the right). The list has further been synthesized into one continuous list with a common search engine where you search for specialities like medicine (MED) and surgery (KIR), and an applicable diagnosis like nausea.

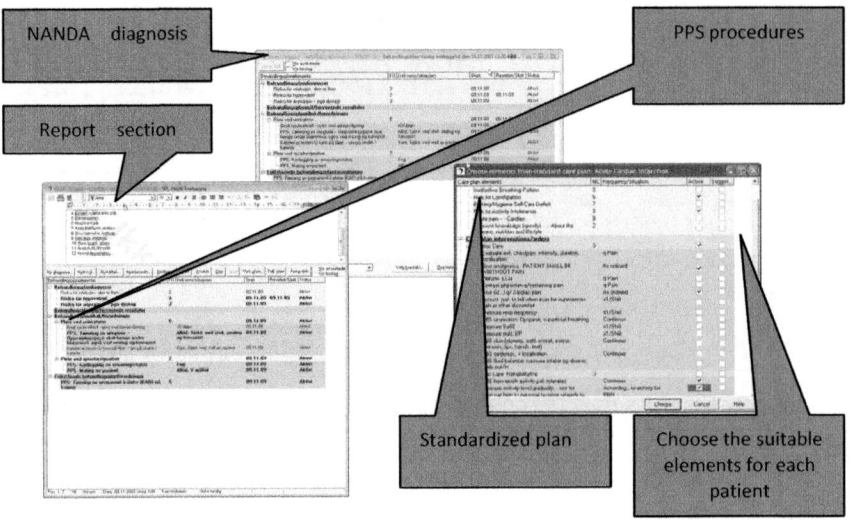

Fig. 2. The nursing plan in different views. The ordinary care plan to the left and the standardized plan to the right.

The well known oral handover was challenged as being ineffective and it was relevant to scrutinize efforts which aimed to replace the oral handover with a written handover, such as a silent handover. *"We wished to pursue a silent handover for several reasons. Our goals were to use less time compared to the oral report, hence there would be more time with our patients and improved quality of the documentation"* (experienced nurse). Nursing handover has a pivotal role in standardized documentation, both in order to increase efficiency by replacing long, time-consuming oral handovers, and by focusing on the quality of the written documentation. The nurses in Cardiology spoke unanimously in favor of silent handover, as several nurses stated, *"We spend much less time on the handovers now than before using oral handovers. We spent too much time on 'small talk.' The socialisation aspect is important, but we always find time to socialize during the shift or during the lunch break."*

Consequently, the implementation of the EPR has, with AHUS as with other hospitals, been organized from the vendor's perspective, which has presented the content, the possibilities, and the outcome of using the classification systems. Further, it has been up to local management and user groups to decide which content to apply. At AHUS, several departments grasped and used the standard plans early in the implementation process at the beginning of 2005. The Cardiology department was not the first user, although it was one of the first departments that used several standards systematically alongside using the silent report and, gradually, PPS.

Standard plans were introduced in order to simplify the way problem descriptions should be written. With this as a backbone, the first goal was to increase the number of standardized plans used. Management used a two-step model: first, they focused on the quantity, the number of created standardized plans, without looking at the content, and second, they focussed on quality by scrutinizing the content of the existing plans. Further, 5 to 10 minutes were used each morning to discuss progress and developments. In the next phase, they used ten minutes on each of the nurses discussing the content of the plans they had created, focusing on quality. In this way, the users were put center-stage, securing the implementation with the ingenuity of users, and a visible bottom-up approach. A central implication to this is that the effort invested at the time of implementation, the bottom-up approach, has not been continuously repeated given the constant turnover of personnel.

The search engine for the development of standardized plans has received some negative attention for being less than appropriate or accurate, and too time-consuming. When the nurses were trying to find the appropriate standardized plan, it was obvious that there were not enough search compositions for each standard plan. The right words and numerical orders were needed to find the applicable diagnosis. This procedure was easy when screening for the 17 plans made especially for Cardiology, and also because they consist of the same search words. The problem occurred when they searched for other diagnoses applicable for the patient, but created for another speciality. *"If the number of search combinations for each diagnosis were much more numerous, we could find the diagnosis easier by using words that, in using common sense would lead us in the right direction"* (inexperienced nurse).

Further, the standardized care plans for cardiology and some of the more generally constructed ones were frequently used by the experienced nurses. In comparison, the standardized plans for other specialities were less frequently used, as *"I...always end up with free-text interventions. There is no logical explanation on how to find the diagnosis you are searching for, therefore, I always end up with writing free text"* (experienced nurse).

This may not be a big issue when "other specialities" are less relevant to the ward. However, most wards deal with heterogeneous diagnoses where more general standardized plans are developed and definitely should be used. As an example, one of the nurses tried to find a standardized plan for nausea, which is one of the generally developed plans. She searched using different terms such as med-nausea, surgical-nausea, gastric, and nausea without finding the right diagnosis and gave up, went back to the care plan and made nausea a free-text diagnosis. Free-text diagnoses are often used, hence it is better to make free-text plans than no plans at all.

4.4 The Nurses' Working Routine with the Standardized Care Plan

Care plans were almost always written by experienced nurses during the first day after hospitalization, usually in the morning. Any updates on other patients were done simultaneously. The experienced nurses' participation in the project period, which included the bottom-up focus of users, has increased their knowledge about the significance and advantages that standardized plans bring to their profession. Hence, they wrote thorough care plans, but the maintenance of already-written plans became insufficient due to the heterogeneity of work practice. If the care plan was used thoroughly on each shift, using free-text, standardized sentences, or both, it is of such a high quality that it could replace all free-text documentation in the EPR. Since the standardized plans also contain PPS procedures, they could give the nurses a complete overview of the patient trajectory. In addition to the improved quality brought forth by using standardized procedures, and standardized sentences, there is a significant efficiency benefit since the plans are very easy to maintain.

In contrast, the novices that attend the work practice don't get the magnitude of knowledge about standard plans necessary to understand its importance for efficiency and quality of care. Inexperienced nurses typically wrote their reports in the free-text area as *"I write my report mostly using free text in the report section....I haven't learned how to make standardized plans so I try to do updates on the plans written by the more experienced nurses."* In general, a follow-up on this quotation shows that the nurses with less than two years in this particular work practice did not have any education on how or why to use the care plan. The experienced nurses support this, and pinpoint the importance of a new bottom-up initiative in the near future to overcome this problem.

According to the staff of the Cardiology ward, the use of standard plans has decreased after the reallocation process. Hence, general numbers derived from the local IT department covering all clinical departments at AHUS gives a clear indication of the relatively stable use of standardized plans, meaning that the drop was a direct consequence of the reallocation, changes in personnel, and new standards. The longitudinal statistics from a period of six months indicates an overall use close to 20 percent, with slight variations among departments. These numbers fit well with the numbers from the Cardiology department. A cross-section of numbers divided from the Cardiology department indicates that approximately 17 percent of the patients in the ward have standardized plans, measured in the third quarter of 2009. Basing our observation on four consecutive weeks, we see that 40 percent of the patients have a care plan, and that 42 percent of them have a standardized plan.

4.5 The PPS Integration Process

The second part of the two-fold project was to integrate a fully operational and automatically updated nursing procedure system: first, with locally adopted procedures and quality documentation, and second, to integrate them with the standardized plans. In contrast to the standardized care plans, the PPS implementation was a top-down decision. The only task performed by local management was to organize the internal education which included two hours of in-house training.

In 2006, AHUS started the PPS project as a decision support system in nursing, and for gaining ISO certification. In addition, the PPS is linked to electronic quality systems (EQS). The PPS database contains 267 detailed procedures for nursing practice, developed by carefully selected professionals around the country, applying to evidence based guidelines for nursing practice.

The existing procedures were evaluated and compared to the PPS procedures with the intention of potentially replacing them with PPS-based procedures. Of the 267 PPS procedures, 191 have replaced existing local ones, 47 have been adjusted to local practices, 26 were not recommended for use at AHUS, and 31 received recommendations for additional procedures. The procedures are further upgraded once a year. Since 2007, PPS has been integrated with the standardized care plan, providing a link between NIC and relevant PPS procedures. The direct integration with the standardized care plan confirmed the hospital's general intention to increase the quality of nursing work with a focus on efficiency. PPS could be accessed on four different levels: from the AHUS intranet, from the main page of the EPR, from the care plan, and from the standardized plans. For entry of a NANDA diagnosis, the standard provides the opportunity to choose from a number of predefined interventions appropriate to the patient's condition. Linked to some of the interventions in the standardized plan are short cuts to PPS procedures (see Figure 3). When one specific intervention is selected in the continuous list and the OK button is pressed, the procedure is Web-based with all descriptions attached.

Further, the departments use small handwritten manuals containing summaries of the most frequently used PPS and EQS procedures especially developed for new personnel as a substitute for PPS. Newcomers do not have to chase down the other nurses to access the procedures, and the procedures are followed as prescribed in the PPS. The problem with this method is the possibility of neglecting new or updated procedures.

One problem with the PPS procedures attached to the standardized plans is that there is nothing visual that explains whether a procedure has been updated or not; therefore, the system now demands that the user access PPS occasionally to catch any recent updates. There is also red light telling you to check out any of the attached procedures. All PPS procedures are also integrated in EQS and can be accessed from there.

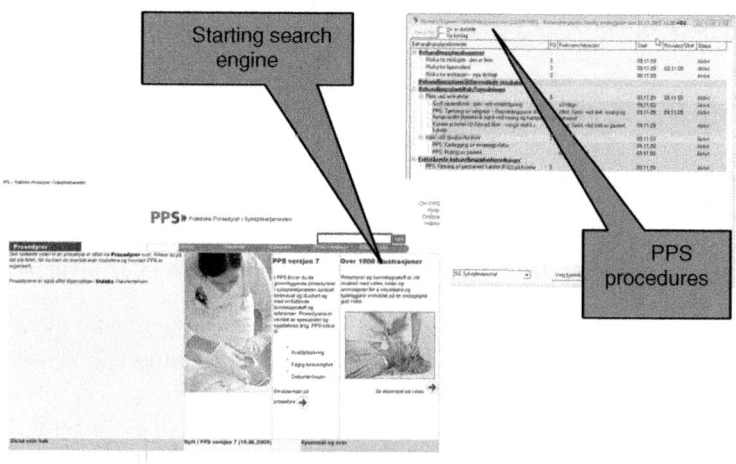

Fig. 3. The PPS front-page with access to the search engine. AHUS employees have access from the intranet and several possibilities in the EPR. This further illustrates standard care plans including direct access to PPS through the selected intervention.

One potential advantage of PPS is that the novices are very skilled in using it. PPS training has been a significant part of their training to become a nurse through the education program. Unfortunately, the experienced nurses and assistants in this department do not use PPS very often. One reason for this is that it is difficult to find the correct procedure, as one nurse explains, *"Finding the right procedure in the PPS search engine is not based on intuition. It becomes too time consuming, It is often better to use the handwritten manual or ask the more skilled nurses."*

Another challenge is the way the PPS is tightly connected to the standardized plans. The top-down initiative PPS, which has been a part of the education of nurses on a national level for several years, and further top-down because of the tight anchorage to hospital management's need for standardized procedures as quality indicators, doesn't fit the use of the bottom-up initiative that exists among the experienced nurses in using standard plans. For instance, given the different level of education and knowledge among the two groups of nurses, and thereby the adoption of the different standards, there will be transversal use. Direct access to PPS through standard plans could have reduced all nurses' difficulties in finding the applicable procedures in the database despite in-house training. The problem is that novices use the care plan mostly as an extension of what the experienced nurses have produced. As one nurse states, *"I don't use PPS much in my daily routines, and I don't have the knowledge required to make standardized care plans. I see the opportunities that lie in standardized plans and the direct access to PPS procedures as extremely valuable for us novices. The instructions are very easily accessible."* The novices use the PPS procedures linked to the standard plan created by the experts. The experienced nurses used the standardized plans frequently, but they seldom used the associated PPS procedures, for two reasons. First, the procedures were connected to NIC interventions that were frequently used, meaning that the nurses were comfortable with the content of the procedures. Second, when they did not find the correct NANDA diagnosis, they did not find the PPS procedures attached to the predefined interventions.

5   Discussion and Conclusion

Perspectives on standardization of work tend to be polarized: either standardization is perceived as a typically top-down effort promoting best practices or, as often argued in socio-technical approaches to ICT in health care (Ellingsen et al. 2007; Timmermans and Berg 1997), standardization is futile, as health work is inherently situated and thus unique.

The perspective emerging from our work provides a theoretically more appealing and empirically more compelling middle position. Standardized work—we focus on nursing practices—is neither straightforward nor uncontroversial. Yet it is not impossible. Essential to standardization with the use of IT in practice, as suggested by our case, is the co-constructing of the standards, in part imposed from the top, in part provided by the active involvement and ingenuity of users.

Throughout our case, we have described scenarios where the focus has been centered on the EPR in use, the IT-based nursing module: two cases, the standard plan, and the PPS.

5.1   The Co-construction of Standardization

As claimed, it is vital in IS research to move the focus from the standardization of artefacts and products to include standardized IS-embedded work in the service sector (Ellingsen et al. 2007). Theoretically, we move from the typical top-down perspective to a co-constructive perspective in which standardization and work practice mutually shape and constitute each other. With the introduction of electronic nursing documentation, the information work has shifted from a chronological status note to process-oriented, structured documentation where the EPR care plan, especially the standardized plan, is positioned at center stage. First, the reallocation process introduced several new standards. As a result, management wished to invest more effort in the silent handover, finding it crucial to uphold the quality of this part of the documentation process to avoid total collapse in the ongoing work with other standards such as the standard plan. The strategy chosen by the management in the Cardiology ward was built on the established success factors of the silent handover, the accuracy of the documentation, the structure of care plans, and the categorization of standardized plans.

Pursuing the silent handover system was important to enable reliance on written information, since the long-standing oral transformation processes no longer existed. The silent handover is considered a success, and all clinical personnel support its benefits as providing a powerful tool to improve efficiency as well as quality of documentation, which in turn depends on a well-functioning EPR system.

Crucial to the success of this long-term process has been a bottom-up perspective on the implementation of care plans, which has constituted an enhancement of performance among experienced nurses. At the time of integration, the introduction of standard plans was achieved appropriately, with a bottom-up approach that included the ingenuity of the users. Nurses who experienced this period and who have continued working at the ward have become the best ambassadors for future development.

5.2   The Potential in the Novice–Expert Relationship

According to the Dreyfus model, nursing practice is shaped and developed by expert nurses, and nurses in general pass through four steps of education before becoming an expert. The five layers of competence are novice, advanced beginner, competent, proficient, and expert (Orlikowski and Baroudi 1991). Hence, in all work practices including hospital departments, there is a differentiation in skills among personnel. For instance, in this case, novices enter the work practice with skill in the use of PPS. We, therefore, find the integrated standard PPS interesting to our case. Up until now, the effect of the PPS integration has failed to materialize, at least in clinical terms and according to the logs, local evaluation of PPS, and interpretations from the user. The top-down perspective utilized in the implementation of PPS has not contributed to the use of procedures, which at this point, and after more than three years, is limited. For PPS to become a success, the interdependency between the PPS procedures integrated with the EPR nursing plans is crucial. We find this interesting, as the novices in the department have skills from which the experts could benefit in the long term depending on the future integration of standard plans with the PPS. The conceptuallization in Benner's (1984) book on the Dreyfus model from novices to experts is interesting with regard to our case in the discussion of further development, expectations for the future of integrated care plans, and PPS. The Dreyfus model does not consider the possibility that the novices could be experts in certain areas such as the use of PPS, and because of recent integration in education. In this way, the expert versus novice relation becomes a bidirectional synergic process, were novices enter the work practice as skilled PPS users, with additional knowledge that the experts could learn from, which again could balance the novice—expert relation. Hopefully, this restructuring will prove fruitful in the future, building on the novices' skills in using IT-based tools for standardization of nursing plans, and the way interdependency gradually makes them become equals.

5.3   The Effect of an Array of Coordinated Standardization Efforts

A new perspective has been the efforts made to overcome heterogeneity in work practice, which seemingly could contribute to the co-construction of standardization (Ellingsen et al. 2007). Exploration of the effects of these standards made it clear that the achieved effect, in relation to increasing both efficiency and quality of work processes, could end up being inherently positive. These standards show the interdependent effect on the IT-based standards installed because of a positive contribution to an easier work practice for nurses. For instance, the generic pool for personnel has secured a continuous flow of substitute nurses who know the environment, routines, and permanent staff. The way these nurses are reused in the departments ensures continuity of care while at the same time allowing the permanent personnel to concentrate on their work process instead of apprenticeship training. Further, the generic wards decrease the number of patients with short-term trajectories of less than 24 hours, which makes the continuity of documentation more transparent. In the long term, these efforts could be a strong contribution to an increased focus on documentation as the nurses' work trajectory becomes more visible. In terms of efficiency, these efforts make work practice more transparent, both for the permanent staff and for others.

The standardization of blood specimen collection has a similar character, even if the decentralization process has failed to compensate for the blood specimen collection. Hence, it has become more transparent and to a different degree organized into the daily routines of the nurses, giving them more time with the patients. Further, the patient does not need to relate so much to continuously alternating personnel. Along this line of standardization, both the transparency and the fixed routines contribute to less work pressure and predictability that positively influence other standards.

The entanglement of different standards, technological and work-process oriented, increases the potential long-term profit when the goal is highly standardized, efficient, and high quality work trajectories, under which conditions the nurses could easily plan and execute the work. The different standards operating in the same working environment contribute to the success of the other standards and underscore the importance of co-constructed standards.

References

Ash, J.S., Berg, M., Coiera, E.: Some Unintended Consequences of Information Technology in Health Care: The Nature of Patient Care Information System-Related Errors. J. Am. Med. Inform. Assoc. 11, 104–112 (2004)

Benner, P.: From Novice to Expert. Addison-Wesley Publishing Company Inc., Boston (1984)

Berg, M.: Rationalizing Medical Work: Decision Support Techniques and Medical Practices. MIT Press, Cambridge (1997)

Berg, M.: Patient Care Information Systems and Health Care Qork: A Sociotechnical Approach. Int. Journal of Medical Informatics 55, 87–101 (1999)

Bowker, G.C., Star, S.L.: Sorting Things Out. The MIT Press, Cambridge (1999)

Bulechek, G.M., Butcher, H.K., Dochterman, J.M.: NIC: Nursing Interventions Classification, 5th edn. Elsevier, New York (2008)

Button, G., Harper, R.H.R.: Taking the Organization into Accounts. In: Button, G. (ed.) Technology in Working Order. Studies of Work, Interaction, and Technology, pp. 98–107. Routledge, London (1993)

Ellingsen, G., Monteiro, E., Munkvold, G.: Standardization of Work: Co-constructed Practice. The Information Society 23(5), 309–326 (2007)

Forsythe, D.E.: It's Just a Matter of Common Sense: Ethnography as Invisible Work. Computer Supported Cooperative Work, 127–145 (1999)

Hanseth, O., Lundberg, N.: DesigningWork Oriented Infrastructures. Computer Supported Cooperative Work 10(3/4), 347–372 (2001)

Hanseth, O., Monteiro, E., Hatling, M.: Developing Information Infrastructure Standards: The Tension between Standardization and Flexibility. Science Technology & Human Values 21(4), 407–426 (1996)

Hepsø, V., Monteiro, E.: Ecologies of E-Infrastructure. JAIS 10(5), 430–446 (2009)

Hughes, D.: When Nurse Knows Best: Some Aspects of Nurse/Doctor Interaction in a Casualty Department. Soc. Hea. Illn. 10, 1–22 (1988)

IOM: Crossing the Quality Chasm: A New Health System for the 21st Century. Institute of Medicine. National Academy Press, Washington (2001)

Kalra, D.: Electronic Health Record Standards. IMIA Yearbook of Medical Informatics, 136–144 (2006)

Klein, H., Myers, M.: A Set of Principles for Conducting and Evaluating Interpretive Field Studies in Information Systems. MIS Quarterly 23(1), 67–94 (1999)

Malterud, K.: Kvalitativ metode I medisinsk forskning: 2. utgave. Universitetsforlaget (2003)

NANDA-1: Nursing Diagnosis: Definitions and Classification 2007-2008. NANDA International, Kaukauna (2007)

Orlikowski, W., Baroudi, J.: Studying Information Technology in Organizations: Research Approaches and Assumptions. Information Systems Research 2(1), 1–28 (1991)

Pollock, N., Williams, R., D'Adderio, L.: Global Software and its Provenance: Generification Work in the Production of Organizational Software Packages. STS 37(2), 254–280 (2007)

Schmidt, S.K., Werle, R.: Coordinating Technology. Studies in the International Standardization of. MIT Press, Telecommunication. Cambridge (1998)

Timmermans, S., Berg, M.: The Gold Standard: The Challenge of Evidence-Based Medicine and Standardization in Health Care. Temple University Press, Philadelphia (2003)

Timmermans, S., Berg, M.: Standardization in Action: Achieving Universalism and Localization through Medical Protocols. Social Studies of Science 27, 111–134 (1997)

Ure, J., Proctor, R.: The Development of Data Infrastructure for E-Health: A SocioTechncal Perspective. JAIS 10(5) (2009)

Voutilainen, P., Isola, A., Muurinen, S.: Nursing Documentation in Nursing Homes: State-of-the-Art and Implications for Quality Improvement. Scand. Journal Caring Sci. 18, 72–81 (2004)

Walsham, G.: Interpretive Case Studies in IS Research: Nature and Method. Eu. J. Inf. Systs. 4, 74–81 (1995)

About the Authors

Rune Pedersen is a Ph.D. student in the program on E-health and Telemedicine at the University of Tromsoe, Norway. He is in his fourth year of studies and is writing his thesis, which he expects to complete by March 2012. Before starting his Ph.D., he worked as a research associate at the University Hospital of North Norway, educated as a nurse with a Master's degree in Public health. His research interests center on the use of electronic patient records and, in particular, nursing work, IT and work process standards, and IT-based classification systems. He has published in several conferences, including the Information Systems Research Seminar in Scandinavia, the International Conference on Information Technology in Health Care, and the European Conference on Information Systems.

Gunnar Ellingsen is a post-doctoral student in the program on E-health and Telemedicine at the University of Tromsoe, Norway. Before completing his Ph.D. in 2003, he worked for several years as an IT consultant at the University Hospital of North Norway. His research interests center on the design and use of electronic patient records in hospitals. He has published articles in *Information and Organization, Journal of Computer Supported Cooperative Work, Methods of Information in Medicine, Scandinavian Journal of Information Systems, International Journal of IT Standards & Standardization Research*, and *British Medical Journal*.

Eric Monteiro is a professor at the Department of Computer and Information Systems at the Norwegian University of Science and Technology. He is broadly interested in organizational transformations and ICT in general, and issues of standardization and globalization in particular. His publication outlets include *MIS Quarterly, Journal of CSCW, Science, Technology & Human Values, Information and Organization, Methods of Information in Medicine, The Information Society*, and *Scandinavian Journal of Information Systems*.

The Role of Technology in Shaping the Professional Future of Community Pharmacists: The Case of the Electronic Prescription Service in the English National Health Service

Dimitra Petrakaki[1], Tony Cornford[1], Ralph Hibberd[2],
Valentina Lichtner[1], and Nick Barber[1]

[1] Information Systems and Innovation Group, Department of Management,
London School of Economics and Political Science
[2] Department of Practice and Policy, The School of Pharmacy, University of London

Abstract. Information and communication technology (ICT) has been extensively proposed in the last decade as a means to reform, modernize, and reshape national health systems around the globe. In so doing, it inevitably changes work practices, and may have longer term consequences for health care professions. This paper considers how ICT may shape the professional future of community pharmacists by drawing on ongoing research into a national project in England to establish the electronic transmission of prescriptions between doctors and pharmacies. The project illustrates how technology opens up various possibilities that may influence pharmacists' professional standing in the future by shaping their work practices, jurisdictions, roles, values, power, and boundaries. Our aim is not to evaluate these subtle and contradictory changes but to develop an appropriate analytical framework, and to contribute to the debate concerning the role of technology in shaping professional futures.

Keywords: Professionals, technology, community pharmacy, electronic prescriptions.

1 Introduction

> *The future is already here—it is just unevenly distributed.*
> (attributed to William Gibson)

Information and communication technology (ICT) has in the last decade been extensively proposed as a means to reform, modernize, and even reshape national health systems. Introduction of ICT based systems is expected to achieve cost effectiveness, support clinical decision making, improve patients' privacy and safety, speed-up delivery, and improve the quality of healthcare (Bates and Gawade 2003; Berg 1997; Chiasson and Davidson 2004). Introducing ICT systems is not without consequences; they challenge health professionals' work practices and roles, the types of knowledge they use, and the modes of collaboration they employ (Aarts et al. 2007). The focus of this paper is on the possibilities that ICT opens up for reshaping

M. Chiasson et al. (Eds.): Future IS 2011, IFIP AICT 356, pp. 179–195, 2011.

the work and profession of community pharmacists. Community pharmacists serve the public in high street shops, supermarkets, and some medical centers. They constitute the largest subgroup within the overall pharmacy profession, which includes hospital pharmacists who provide clinical advice to hospitals and healthcare professionals and those who work in pharmaceutical research. From now on reference, to pharmacy(-ists) will imply community pharmacy(-ists).

Our account here is a possible projection of professionalism in the future that is created from research interviews and by an amalgamation of people's recollections of the past, experiences from the present, and expectations for the future. The motivation for the paper is found in the introduction of the electronic prescription service (EPS) into primary care in the English National Health Service. This is a national program to allow doctors to send electronic prescriptions to community pharmacists, and for pharmacists subsequently to send them on for reimbursement by the NHS[1]. This requires a sound infrastructure, networks, software, databases, and new operating procedures, indicating the increased role of ICT in mediating for the generation, transmission, and receipt of prescriptions between doctors and community pharmacists, as well as in serving the processes of reimbursement. We are interested here in exploring the role of this new technical intervention in shaping pharmacists' work practices and profession. To do so, we draw upon a part of our current research evaluating EPS.[2] We develop two arguments in this paper. First, we propose that EPS can shape six aspects of pharmacists' work: work practices, values, roles, jurisdictions, power, and professional boundaries. Second, we see the consequences of this technology for the pharmacy profession are multiple and often contradictory; on some occasions, technology strengthens and expands pharmacists' professional standing by fostering their values and expanding their jurisdictions, opening up opportunities for re-professionalization. On other occasions, technology challenges pharmacists' role, power, and professional boundaries by allowing new business models and logic to emerge, conditioning in that way possible deprofessionalization. We propose a framework that depicts how and in what ways ICT might shape professional futures.

The paper is structured as follows. Section 2 presents our theoretical framework, drawing upon the sociology of professionals, critical studies on technology, and secondary studies on pharmacists' profession. Section 3 describes our research methodology. Section 4 provides an account of our research into EPS, which is followed by a discussion. The paper ends with some concluding remarks.

2 Theoretical Framework

2.1 Conceptualizing Professionalism

Professions constitute a "homogeneous group of occupations sharing a unique character and destiny" (Johnson 1993). Professionals are typically organized into associations, which are established in order to promote and protect their interests and rights (Abbott 1988). Professional associations define the skills needed in order to

---

[1] See http://www.connectingforhealth.nhs.uk/systemsandservices/eps.

[2] See http://www.epsevaluation.org.uk/.

become a legitimate member, establish career patterns, and set up mechanisms that regulate entrance and operation in their profession (Abbott 1988; Clarke and Newman 1997; Perkin 2002; Timmermans and Berg 2003). Implicit in this is the establishment of norms, values, and standards of occupational behavior, what is understood as professional conduct (Adamcik et al. 1986). The process of establishing a profession (professionalization) is, therefore, a boundary-making process that binds professionals under a specific regime of work (Adamcik et al. 1986; Kirkpatrick and Ackroyd 2003). Professionalization is both a process of enactment, in as far as it depends on individuals acting their assigned roles as professionals, and a process of subjectification during which individuals are "made-up" as professionals (Hodgson 2005).

For Abbott (1988), the most distinctive characteristic of professionals is the "abstractification" of their knowledge which distinguishes professionals' claims from those of ordinary technical work (Adamcik et al. 1986). This differentiation serves to create a relationship of dependence between professionals and laymen (Johnson 1993) and is thought to (re-)produce professionals' power and authority (Kerr 1997). Abstract knowledge legitimizes professionals' status and prestige because it is typically associated with science, logic, and future practical value. Of course, professionals also undertake mundane tasks, rendering their work a hybrid of conceptual and manual activities (Causer and Exworthy 1998).

Professional groups are expected to exercise high degrees of power and authority (Flynn 1998). Their power is their ability to retain jurisdiction (Abbott 1988), for example, to make decisions based upon 'internalised norms and expert knowledge' (Flynn 2002; Timmermans and Berg 2003), to influence policy, and to decide on their remuneration (Edmunds and Calnan 2001). Professional power is largely dependent upon the state's support by, for instance, defining the type and mode of services they alone can offer (Johnson 1972).

Further, professionals' power is influenced by institutional standards, codes of ethics, and behavioral norms drawn from the profession but also, to degrees, from their employing organizations (Benson et al. 2009; Johnson 1972). It can be further limited by clients' ability to organize themselves into powerful groups that set requirements, pursue their rights, and demand certain types of service (Johnson 1993).

2.2 (Re-)Constructing Professionals through Information Technology

The introduction of ICT in any work setting conditions changes to work practices, roles, and identities. Typically, ICT is used to gather, maintain, process, and disseminate data and information across temporal and spatial boundaries. ICT can achieve a parallel centralization and decentralization of data and information as it renders it available to anyone, anywhere (Bellamy and Taylor 1998; Bloomfield and Coombs 1992; Zuboff 1989). Further, such data can be statistically processed, ranked, compared, accumulated, and inscribed into reports, generating in that way new types of information with new uses and users (Clarke and Newman 1997; Doolin 2003; Latour 1988; Zuboff 1989). One significant way in which ICT influences professionals' work is by rendering their outputs visible (Bush et al. 2009), for example, concerning work aspects such as performance, outputs, time and date of work, and history of activities. This then renders professionals *legible*, in particular to managers (Lyon 2009). This transparency that technology provides enables constant surveillance and control, which in turn may influence reward structures and the way in which professionals do their work. For instance, Aarts et al. (2007) describe how the introduction of a computerized physician order entry (CPOE) system depersonalized healthcare professionals' collaboration and made nurses lose visibility of, and thus power over, aspects of their work.

ICT is also used to automate processes and practices (Bellamy and Taylor 1998), with implications of simplification, rule following, and tasks undertaken without human knowledge, judgment, or discretion. This promotes predictability, quantification, and centrally controlled rule-based decision making (Garson 1988). Automation is often associated with attempts to de-skill professionals and undermine their claims to professional status (Bush et al. 2009).

ICT is not always perceived as a machine that automates but may be seen as an intervention that *informates* work (Zuboff 1989). It does so by eliminating unnecessary activities, undertaking mundane tasks and then providing back to professionals processed information upon which they can act. In this way, ICT serves professionals in decision making and may encourage them to develop new capacities as they exploit the value of this new information (Abbott 1988). This then conditions possibilities for re-skilling by expanding the breadth and depth of their responsibilities (Zuboff 1989). In a study of a health information system in a cardiology department, Cho et al. (2008) found that ICT provided opportunities for re-skilling nurses by allowing them to download patients' images and discuss them with doctors during ward rounds.

2.3 Pharmacists as Health Professionals

Unlike other clinical professions, pharmacists do not specialize in specific parts of the body and do not directly intervene in the body (Barber 2005). Their work is fundamentally technological[3] (Adamcik et al. 1986) in that it deals at the primary level with material objects, namely chemical components and models, delivery devices, medications, prescriptions, tokens. What distinguishes pharmacists from other healthcare professionals involved with medicines is their knowledge (abstracttion) about the ingredients of medicines, the way in which they work in the body, and their effects on it. This knowledge constitutes for Barber (2005) the "pharmaceutical gaze." Another critical feature of community pharmacists working in the high street is their hybrid role as both healthcare professionals with clinical expertise, jurisdictions, and social-service orientation, and as business owners who look for the future viability of their business (Bush et al. 2009; Edmunds and Calnan 2001; Hibbert et al. 2002; Hughes and McCann 2003). The intrusion of the business orientation into pharmacists' profession is thought by some to condition de-skilling and standardization, leading to the rise of what Bush et al. (2009) described as the "McPharmacist."

Nonetheless, pharmacists tend to follow a scientific and rational model of thinking and acting that draws largely upon the law, and their own codes, rules, and standard operating procedures and policy guidelines (Benson et al. 2009; McDonald et al. 2010; Timmermans and Berg 2003). The profession is driven by two major values.

---

[3] *Technological* is defined here as the ability to use expertise and techniques in order to achieve particular objectives.

The first is the value of managing medicines in a safe and reliable way (Benson et al. 2009); the second is treating the patient as a person with particular needs, values, culture, and beliefs.

In practice, however, pharmacists' work is not as rational and normative as it may look from the outside. Benson et al. (2009) present a number of examples which illustrate that pharmacists work in a non-prescriptive way in their attempt to deal professionally with complex situations. For instance, pharmacists often need to bend the rules in order to treat a patient in a "better" way or they may ration services by prioritizing some patients over others (Benson et al. 2009).

Traditionally skills and expertise of pharmacists are founded on combining the right ingredients in order to compound medicines (Adamcik et al. 1986; Eastoe 2010; Edmunds and Calnan 2001). Industrialization and increasing regulation of medicines reduced some medical risks, automated the production of many medicines, thereby increasing it, and led to the creation of new drugs with new adverse effects (Barber 2005; Bush et al. 2009; Edmunds and Calnan 2001). These changes limited the involvement of pharmacists in the production of drugs, which was now the responsibility of drug manufacturers (Bush et al. 2009), and reduced pharmacists' work to labeling and record keeping (Adamcik et al. 1986) and their role to "mere dispensers" (McDonald et al. 2010). However, in the last few years, the role of pharmacists has been reconsidered and some have argued for it to be transformed from a product-focused (Wilson et al. 2010) profession into a more clinical profession with new responsibilities for the management of prescriptions, common ailments, and long-term illness, and for the provision of medical advice on healthy lifestyles (Adamcik et al. 1986; Benson et al. 2009).

Since the 1980s, the English NHS has undertaken a number of initiatives in an attempt to re-professionalize pharmacists such as campaigns that prompt patients to turn to pharmacists for medical advice and initiatives to use their skills in order to assess patients' use and experience from medicines (McDonald et al. 2010). These initiatives, however, have not been successful in substantially strengthening the pharmacists' profession. It has been suggested that this is because pharmacists often have insufficient skills to undertake clinical responsibilities, the risk of potential conflicts with doctors, and their general weak professional power to shape public policy (Adamcik et al. 1986; Bush et al. 2009; Edmunds and Calnan 2001). In contrast to such concerns, a recent official report on hospital doctor prescribing errors[4] acknowledged that almost all errors are detected and corrected by pharmacists, illustrating the high level of clinical expertise hospital pharmacists have.

3 Research Methodology

This research drew upon the qualitative paradigm (Creswell 1994; Maykut and Morehouse 1994) and specifically interpretivism (Klein and Myers 1999; Orlikowski and Baroudi 1991). In following an interpretivist methodology, we intended to understand through participants' oral and written accounts the meaning they attributed to

---

[4] See
http://www.gmc-uk.org/FINAL_Report_prevalence_and_causes_of_prescribing_errors.pdf._28935150.pdf.

EPS and how they projected its consequences on pharmacists' work and profession (Klein and Myers 1999).

This paper draws upon data gathered through interviews and documents. A total of 19 interviews were conducted with a number of different organizations and their representatives involved in EPS such as software suppliers for dispensing systems, community pharmacists, clinical and local EPS leads, representatives of pharmacists' associations, and representatives of Connecting for Health, the agency commissioned by the Department of Health to manage EPS. Interviews took place from June 2009 until March 2010. They were semi-structured, recorded, and when this was not possible, notes were kept. Interviews lasted 60 minutes on average and were transcribed (when possible) verbatim.

We also drew upon government documents and reports concerning the future of pharmacies, contractual arrangements, and business and workflow models. Documents and secondary studies on the profession of pharmacists, outlined above, were important in contextualizing our research and enabling us to discuss our findings in a dialogical manner that confirmed or disconfirmed our arguments (Klein and Myers 1999).

Data were analyzed by following a thematic analysis. Themes and sub-themes emerged by both our theoretical underpinnings (e.g., automation, visibility, jurisdictions, professional roles, jurisdictions) and our data (e.g., clinical orientation, temporal flexibility, patient orientation). Themes were then compared and contrasted and during this process some were merged, eliminated, further developed, and refined (Creswell 1994). Through our analysis, we constructed an analytical framework (Table 1 in Section 5) which, we hope, contributes to the more general debate about the implications of technology for professions.

4 The Case of the Electronic Prescription Service (EPS)

4.1 The Introduction of EPS in English Community Pharmacy

In England, community pharmacies are contracted by the NHS to provide pharmaceutical services in the local community (McDonald et al. 2010). Their function is influenced by a number of other organizations responsible for working with them and protecting pharmacists' interests at a national and local level (National Pharmacy Association, local pharmaceutical committees), negotiating their contractual obligetions (Pharmaceutical Services Negotiating Committee), and reimbursing them (Prescription Pricing Authority). Community pharmacies are paid to deliver NHS services and have a contract to do so, just like family doctors who work in their own businesses. Yet, their relation to the NHS is at times a contested area; one of our respondents described community pharmacists as being "in name only part of the NHS family," reflecting a view of them as independent enterprises or parts of multiple retailers rather than essentially of the health care system (Hibbert et al. 2002). However, in most cases, the majority of their income derives from fulfilling prescriptions for the NHS and their very existence is largely dependent upon NHS policy decisions which often open up critical business issues for them.

The EPS was initiated in 2003. It is a part of the National Programme for IT (NPfIT) for the NHS in England, which is delivered by the Department of Health agency Connecting for Health (CfH). EPS refers to the electronic generation, transmission, and receipt of prescriptions from a prescribing authority (e.g., doctor or nurse) to a dispensing authority (e.g., community pharmacist). EPS is being rolled-out in two releases. The first (EPS1) aimed to set up and test the central infrastructure and the second (EPS2) to achieve a paperless and fully electronic transmission of prescriptions[5]. EPS2 also introduced new electronic functionalities: electronic cancellation, repeat dispensing of prescriptions, and pharmacy nomination. We explore the last two functions and their potential consequences for pharmacists' professional work in the following subsections.

With EPS, electronic prescriptions are sent via a central server, the Spine, which is linked to community pharmacies and general practices via the NHS's own network, N3. The Spine holds some patient demographic information and it is planned one day to hold a summary care record of each patient (Greenhalgh et al. 2010). The Spine is supported by a message handler and a broker whose role is to integrate and ensure consistency between the messages being exchanged. Prerequisite for accessing the Spine are EPS-compliant local systems and role-based access through personal user smartcards. A number of prescribing and dispensing software suppliers have been modifying their systems in line with centrally set specifications to enable the creation and exchange of electronic prescriptions. EPS has been envisioned as a project that will bring considerable benefits to pharmacists' work such as cost reduction, legible prescriptions, faster dispensing process, faster access to information, and time savings[6]. Most importantly for this paper, EPS opens up opportunities for (re-)shaping pharmacists' work and profession. This is discussed below.

4.2 Changing Pharmacists' Work Practices through EPS

Ideally, the introduction of EPS will automate aspects of the dispensing process (for example, labeling) and reduce the amount of paper that is generated. In theory, electronic prescription messages can be downloaded from the Spine and accessed and dispensed by any EPS-enabled community pharmacy across the country. Electronic prescriptions are more legible, and thus safer, and are devoid of costs associated with paper prescriptions. A paperless/paper-light process implies that pharmacists will dispense from information presented onscreen.

In the non-EPS world, the time of dispensing is defined by the patient at the point of his or her request. Under EPS, dispensing becomes temporally dispersed; it can start as soon as the prescription message is forwarded to a pharmacy. EPS2 facilitates repeat dispensing, the issuing of multiple instances of the same prescripttion for a patient to collect at the pharmacy as and when medication runs out, without the patient having to request a new prescription from the doctor each time. Through

---

[5] EPS Release 2 Business Guidance for Initial implementers, April 2009 (http://www.connectingforhealth.nhs.uk/systemsandservices/eps/staff/guidance/release2guide.pdf).

[6] "Pharmacy in England: Building on Strengths—Delivering the Future," White Paper, 2008 (Department of Health,
http://www.dh.gov.uk/en/Publicationsandstatistics/Publications/
PublicationsPolicyAndGuidance/DH_083815).

repeat dispensing, pharmacists may be able to pre-dispense and so manage better their stock and time, reduce patient waiting time, and potentially keep a patient as a repeat customer.

The prescription message populates the local computer record with patients' demographic details and the prescribed items reducing the need for manual data entry while ensuring data consistency. At the same time, it may make a pharmacy's daily functions more dependent upon complex technology and infrastructure (N3, Spine, prescribing software, etc.). In case of a technological breakdown, the pharmacy's function is likely to be brought to a halt with patients redirected to other dispensers (with possibly significant business implications).

4.3 Changing the Values of Pharmacy Work

Some interviewees described EPS as a means to render the relationship between doctors and pharmacists less dependent on personal acquaintance and familiarization. A representative of a pharmacists' association argued that in the pre-EPS model, the pharmacist who encountered a prescription error would, after a discussion with the doctor, perhaps by phone, dispense the correct medication and wait for the correct prescription to arrive in retrospect. This process leaves the pharmacist in a limbo both legally and financially and renders professional trust essential. In the EPS world, however, when an error is detected and changes agreed with the doctor, the pharmacist can expect the doctor to send in real time a new prescription—and indeed may not feel able to proceed until it is done. This manifests the role of technology in rendering familiarization and trust a secondary issue in computer mediated interprofessional communication. As a community pharmacist told us,

> At the moment I receive a prescription which clearly has an error I attach a note to that prescription, possibly write a note on it and send it back to the surgery telling the error and the reasons for the error. If you just cancel a prescription—which is effectively what you are doing by sending it back to the spine, then...they become disconnected, which actually adds another weakness to the system possibly.

In contrast to this view, other interviewees argued that EPS could be a mechanism that fosters trust between doctors and pharmacists through the functionality of repeat dispensing. In this case, as described above, doctors rely on pharmacists to dispense the correct medication, advise on the correct dosages, pick up patient queries, and continue dispensing for the prescribed period of time. Further, a dispensing software supplier argued that the possibilities for electronic monitoring that EPS enables could potentially allow doctors to monitor whether (or not) their prescriptions have been dispensed, facilitating trust, although this functionality is not a part of EPS2.

Some participants highlighted the risks that may emerge as a prescription message gets "translated" while being transferred from a prescribing to a dispensing EPS-enabled system. This may happen because different prescribing and dispensing software systems are embedded with different dictionaries—especially in relation to how medicines and their dosages are coded. As a dispensing software supplier explained,

You don't have the proof of a piece of paper and the GP sees on his screen that he's typing out Gaviscon for instance, but what is actually sent in the message, he doesn't see that.

Some participants suggested that pharmacists will be rendered liable for undertaking these risks by using their professional judgment in order to dispense without often having complete or correct information. Professional judgment is also required with the current paper-based system, but the feeling expressed was that EPS could increase the volume of such cases.

The other new functionality that EPS2 provides is *nomination*, which refers to a patient's choice as to which pharmacy to use. Patients are given the opportunity to nominate any EPS2-enabled pharmacy across England from which to collect their medication. In the patient interest, and in the interest of maintaining flexibility and competition among pharmacist, nominations are expected to be easily changed. Assuming the patient does not change her nomination too frequently, nomination may allow pharmacists to accumulate data concerning patients' treatment and thus to provide more customized advice, monitor patients' health, and intervene when necessary. To a degree, such data is already held by pharmacies, but the nomination process may enable more complete information. As a representative of a dispensing software supplier said,

It's sort of like a loyalty card in the sense that, I'll always come back to you and I'll always come and get my prescriptions from you. You're tied to the patient. Therefore, you get to know who Mr Smith is.

Pharmacists, however, worry that nomination depersonalizes their relationship with patients because it makes choice less reliant on personal acquaintance and more dependent on convenience of location. Thus nomination is expected to influence the geographical distribution of pharmacies and the business potential of pharmacies in residential areas. The representatives of a pharmacy chain argued that the empowerment of patients to nominate prioritizes speedy collection of medicines over the provision of pharmacists' clinical advice. Also, some interviewees expressed concerns about the potential for "script direction," suggesting that nomination opens up the possibility for a style of competition that improves the position of large pharmacies in the market and excludes smaller pharmacies. As an interviewee said,

Pharmacies...are scared of EPS, because they think that they are going to lose control and they are going to lose business. So what pharmacists are going to do, as soon as they become EPS-enabled, is they are going to start collecting nominations from every patient that walks in their door.

Policy makers have attempted to address this risk by imposing new norms that guide prescribers and dispensers' behavior. "EPS Release 2 Business Guidance for Initial Implementers" articulates how prescribers and dispensers should behave in relation to nomination:

[Dispensing staff] shall not give or offer any gift or reward to encourage a patient to nominate them; this also includes the offering of share dividends of points, discounts and loyalty points....NHS Pharmaceutical Service Regulations 2005, prohibit pharmacists or their staff from offering inducements to encourage patients to nominate them (p. 41).

4.4 Changing Pharmacy Business

EPS2 constitutes a business critical issue for most pharmacies, clearly linked to their future viability. Its potential to electronically connect pharmacists with the NHS renders pharmacists an identifiable part of it. As an official from CfH said,

> *You put in the technology, so you are making them part of the NHS family technically. They are all connected to N3 either directly or indirectly. They are all having smart cards, so that they can be uniquely identified.*

Connection to the Spine requires a large financial investment in purchasing new software and a commitment for its future maintenance. This, according to a representative of a dispensing software supplier, will squeeze pharmacies' profit margins in the future. But this can be seen as part of a wider shift in the ecology; access to the Spine may potentially give pharmacists access to a summary of patients' electronic health record (the Summary Care Record) if and when this becomes widely available. The director of an independent pharmacy saw this as very important because it can inform pharmacists about patient conditions under which medicines are prescribed and allows them to judge the appropriateness of the prescription, as happens in a hospital pharmacy. Visibility of patients' records may empower pharmacists and give them more control over their work and allow them to be more patient-oriented. Apart from just viewing this information, the opportunity for feeding information into a patient record was also highlighted by some participants as an important potential advantage for pharmacists of broader EPS-enabled systems. A representative from a software supplier argued that, unlike doctors, pharmacists know the type of deregulated and over-the-counter medicines that patients take beyond what is prescribed. Feeding this information back could give a more thorough view of the patient to the doctor and lead to better consultations.

Access to patients' records may thus render the pharmacist's profession more clinically oriented. The dispensing process, we may hypothesise, would become more a back-office operation undertaken by non-professional pharmacy staff, such as accredited checking technicians, as pharmacists make better use of their skills focusing on the provision of clinical care. Indeed, as a CfH official said, the inclusion of more clinical services into pharmacists' work seems to be one vision for pharmacies in the futurex[7]:

> *A first port of call for minor illnesses...and also as an additional service... for long term condition management.*

Further, EPS could potentially give rise to new business models. Web-based pharmacies, existing and new stakeholders, such as Amazon, wholesalers or central supermarket online stores may enter into the pharmacy business in the future. These new models, which are less likely to get into the provision of clinical services, may in the future challenge pharmacists' professional identities.

---

[7] "Pharmacy in the Future—Implementing the NHS Plan: A Programme for Pharmacy in the National Health Service," September 2000 (Department of Health, http://www.dh.gov.uk/en/Publicationsandstatistics/Publications/PublicationsPolicyAndGuidance/DH_4005917).

Finally, the Spine has the potential to provide the Department of Health with real-time information concerning prescribing and dispensing activity. This information, which was up until now obscured and estimated, may enable a more effecttive governing of pharmacies in the future. This is despite the fact that EPS, as a CfH official argued. has not been intentionally designed for such a purpose:

> *There [are] funny goings on in pharmacies and in prescribing that we don't know about. We do know about, but we've got no evidence. It's not the job of EPS to deal with that, but...there will be better quality information, quality data which people, at some point can take action and look at in detail, should they wish.*

5   Analysis

This section discusses the possibilities that technology opens up to transform pharmacists' work and profession. Table 1 illustrates the core analytical remarks we make below.

5.1   Screen-Level Pharmacists: Challenging the Temporal and Material Nature of Pharmacists' Work

The case of the EPS can be seen as a manifestation of the way in which professionals can be influenced by technological advancements (Abbott 1988; McDonald et al. 2010). In summary, EPS can influence pharmacists' work in three ways. To begin with, the parallel centralization and decentralization (Bloomfield and Coombs 1992) of electronic prescriptions intends to eliminate paper and in doing so to dissociate the dispensing process from its material aspects. The strength of paper prescriptions is that they are mobile and combinable (Latour 1988); pharmacists hold a paper prescription throughout the dispensing process and check against it the medications they dispense. The mediation of technology, however, transforms them into "screen-level" pharmacists, to borrow Bovens and Zouridis' (2002) term, who continuously need to consult a computer interface in order to conduct their daily activities.

Also, EPS might bring temporal flexibility to the dispensing process, which has been typically a temporally and spatially bound process that starts with the receipt of a paper prescription and ends with the dispensing of medications. EPS, however, transgresses temporal boundaries by allowing pharmacists to decide when they dispense (Giddens 1991; Walsham 2001). Further, EPS affords far more automation of the dispensing process by feeding complete data into pharmacists' systems, eliminating manual data entry (Bellamy and Taylor 1998).

5.2   Clinical (Dis)orientation and Responsibilization

EPS has the potential to generate data that informates pharmacists work (Zuboff 1989). Through the functionality of nomination, pharmacists may be able to acquire large amounts of data concerning patients' treatment and develop a better understanding of them (Benson et al. 2009). At the same time, the focus of nomination on patients' convenience may, in the long run, transform pharmacists from professionals into mere providers of pre-packed medications. This is likely to weaken their distinctive "pharmaceutical gaze" (Barber 2005), threaten their professional status and condition de-professionalization (Abbott 1988).

Our initial findings suggest that EPS may expand pharmacists' jurisdictions by adding further responsibilities (Abbott 1988). Electronic prescription messages may be modified while being exchanged between doctors and pharmacists. This can happen, for instance, due to possible mismatches in mapping data dictionaries. Pharmacists are then rendered responsible for interpreting the messages they receive and exercising their professional discretion, as they did in the past with handwritten and sometimes illegible prescriptions. With a high level of use of repeat dispensing, one of the main benefits claimed for EPS, pharmacists will become the primary health professional monitoring chronic diseases for periods of up to 12 months. This will often require making decisions when pharmacists have limited knowledge about the detail of a patient's case. Despite the risks that such a scenario may entail, it is likely to raise the status of the pharmacists' profession by prompting their further re-skilling (Abbott 1988).

Further, a number of participants in this research argued that EPS may provide pharmacists access to an electronic summary of a patient record. This would condition two possibilities. First, pharmacists are informed not only about what has been prescribed but also the reasons for its prescription. By knowing patients' diagnosis and treatments they also know when they should (and should not) provide specific over-the- counter medications based on possible adverse effects. They are thus able to make professional judgments and provide more clinically oriented services. One could, therefore, interpret pharmacists' possible access to a summary patient record as another government attempt to re-professionalize pharmacists by fostering the use of their clinical skills and professional judgment (Edmunds and Calnan 2001; McDonald et al. 2010). Second, and perhaps more important, pharmacists may be able to provide feedback to a patient's record. For instance, by providing information concerning over- the-counter medications patients buy (information that prescribing authorities can hardly know) pharmacists may generate information that assists clinical decision making across the prescribing and dispensing process (Doolin 2003; Latour 1988; Zuboff 1989).

5.3 System and Interprofessional Trust through Control

Another consequence of EPS for the pharmacy profession concerns interprofessional trust. As our research indicated, EPS has the potential to weaken personal trust by mediating between doctors and pharmacists, thus making them less interdependent. Specifically, personal and often intuitive ways of communicating are overtaken by electronic exchanges of messages between geographically distant recipients often unknown to each other. In this, EPS brings impersonality, devalues interpersonal ties, and fosters system trust (Giddens 1991).

Perhaps some interprofessional trust could be ensured through the (unintended) possibility that EPS provides for electronic monitoring. Specifically, provided that pharmacists and patients are compliant with what is prescribed, doctors may be able to monitor whether (or not) and when their prescriptions have been dispensed independently of personal acquaintance with either the patient or the pharmacist. By making pharmacists' outputs visible and legible (Lyon 2009), interprofessional trust is strengthened, which confirms the argument by Knights et al. (2001) that electronic monitoring technologies can substitute for the lack of trust in virtual environments.

5.4 Professional Control, Boundaries, and Inclusion: Pharmacists as Entrepreneurs; Entrepreneurs as Pharmacists?

Finally, Similarly, there are under-explored possibilities that EPS may provide to the government for electronic monitoring of pharmacists' outputs (Bush et al. 2009). The provision of real-time data will shed light on previously obscure aspects of the pharmacy business such as mismatches between prescribed and dispensed items. This may in turn enable auditing and decisions concerning future health budgets and pave the way to more government intervention in and thus control over pharmacists' work (Abbott 1988; Johnson 1972). Being connected to the Spine is also likely to bring about two consequences for pharmacists' professionalization. By allowing pharmacists' access to NHS-related information, such as patients' demographic information and diagnoses and treatments, and by making them identifiable to and tractable by the NHS, it also renders them, to use a participant's words, a part of the NHS family. This indicates one role that technology—as a boundary creating mechanism—might play in professionalizing pharmacists through deeper inclusion into the NHS (Adamcik et al. 1986). Access to patient data may also create more business opportunities for pharmacists by allowing them to target patient groups effectively and provide customized services.

At the same time, the possibilities for inclusion that EPS provides may shift the boundaries of pharmacists' profession in other ways, for example, by enabling new business models to emerge such as Internet-based pharmacies using the Internet,

Table 1. The Implication of ICT in Pharmacists' Profession

ICT possibilities	Aspects of Profession	Features of Change
Centralization/Decentralization of information	Work practices	Immaterial aspects
		Temporal flexibility
		Elimination of manual tasks
Automation	Roles	Screen-level pharmacists
Generation of information	Values	Informatization and patient orientation
	Roles	Delivery orientation
	Jurisdictions	Responsibilization
Transformation	Jurisdictions	Clinical orientation
Computer Mediated Communication	Values	System trust and impersonality
Visibility	Control and Power	Governing
		Interprofessional trust/control
Connectivity	Professional boundaries	Inclusion
		New business models

telephone, and post. Interviewees underlined the risks that new business models may bring for pharmacists. They mentioned the potential for illicit competition and patient direction and the diffusion of a business logic that would corrode pharmacists' professionalism by redirecting it toward a profit-driven delivery model. This aligns with a number of studies that emphasize the entrepreneurial character of many public service professionals (Clarke and Newman 1997; Du Gay 2000) and suggests that EPS could be perceived as an intensification of entrepreneurialism in healthcare—a feature of the recently elected government's health policy. Such risks are historically counter-balanced by governmental interventions that protect and maintain pharmacists' professional status (Johnson 1972), but should we count on it?

6 Conclusion

The paper discusses the possibilities that technology opens up to transform the pharmacist profession in the future. We have argued that technology has the potential to centralize and decentralize, automate and informate practices and processes, generate new information, mediate communication, and render outputs visible. The six aspects of pharmacists' work we consider, work practices, values, roles, jurisdictions, power, and boundaries, are all open to adjustment. By accommodating multiple interpretations, we present different and often opposing narratives of the future of the pharmacist profession (Klein and Myers 1999). One possible interpretation is that pharmacists' work will become an immaterial, temporally dispersed computerized process, and that pharmacists will be transformed into screen-level professionals as providers of accurately specified medicines. But EPS could potentially bring about more fundamental changes that run counter. For example, pharmacists' values may change to become more patient-oriented as they develop more clinical roles. And system trust may be a powerful substitute for interpersonal trust as EPS strengthens their profession by expanding their responsibilities, and thus their jurisdictions. Further, EPS could provide nuanced forms of electronic control that can enable better monitoring and management of dispensing outputs and foster interprofessional trust.

These changes, presented in Table 1, constitute the framework we have developed to project and analyze the implications of technology for professionals. We provided a critical analysis of these implications but did not make a prediction about how these will shape professionals in the future. This is not just because EPS has not been nationally rolled-out but primarily because changes in professions and the way that professionalization is enacted are long-term, multidimensional— evolving in parallel with political, technological, and financial changes—and thus open to interpretation. They can hardly be known in advance.

Acknowledgments

The authors would like to thank the interviewees that participated in this study, James Davies, Ph.D. candidate at the School of Pharmacy, University of London, and the research team for their comments in an early draft of the paper.

The Evaluation of the Electronic Prescription Service in Primary Care is a collaboration between The School of Pharmacy, University of London, The London School of Economics and Political Science, and The University of Nottingham, under the leadership of Professors N. Barber, A. Avery, and R. Elliott, and Dr. T. Cornford. It is funded by the Connecting for Health Evaluation Programme.

This report is independent research commissioned by the National Institute for Health Research. The views expressed in this publication are those of the author(s) and not necessarily those of the NHS, the National Institute for Health Research, or the Department of Health.

References

Aarts, J., Ash, J., Berg, M.: Extending the Understanding of Computerized Physician Order Entry: Implications for Professional Collaboration, Workflow and Quality of Care. I. J. of Medical Informatics 76, S4–S13 (2007)

Abbott, A.: The System of Professions: An Essay on the Division of Expert Labor, 1st edn. University of Chicago Press, Chicago (1988)

Adamcik, B.A., Ransford, H.E., Oppenheimer, P.R., Brown, J.F., Eagan, P.A., Weissman, F.G.: New Clinical Roles for Pharmacists: A Study of Role Expansion. Social Science & Medicine 33(11), 1187–1200 (1986)

Barber, N.: The Pharmaceutical Gaze—The Defining Feature of Pharmacy. The Pharmaceutical Journal 275, 78 (2005)

Bates, D.W., Gawande, A.A.: Improving Safety with Information Technology. The New England J. of Medicine 348(25), 2526–2534 (2003)

Bellamy, C., Taylor, J.: Governing in the Information Age. Open University Press, New York (1998)

Benson, A., Cribb, A., Barber, N.: Understanding Pharmacists' Values: A Qualitative Study of Ideals and Dilemmas in UK Pharmacy Practice. Social Science & Medicine 68(12), 2223–2230 (2009)

Berg, M.: Rationalizing Medical Work: Decision-Support Techniques and Medical Practices. MIT Press, Cambridge (1997)

Bloomfeld, B.P., Coombs, R.: Information Technology, Control and Power: The Centralization and Decentralization Debate Revisited. J. of Management Studies 29(4), 459 (1992)

Bovens, M., Zouridis, S.: From Street-Level to System-Level Bureaucracies: How Information and Communication Technology is Transforming Administrative Discretion and Constitutional Control. PAR 62(2), 174–184 (2002)

Bush, J., Langley, C., Wilson, K.: The Corporatization of Community Pharmacy: Implications for Service Provision, the Public Health Function, and Pharmacy's Claims to Professional Status in the United Kingdom. Research in Social and Administrative Pharmacy 5(4), 305–318 (2009)

Causer, G., Exworthy, M.: Professionals as Managers across the Public Sector. In: Professionals and the New Managerialism in the Public Sector. Open University Press, Stony Stratford (1998)

Chiasson, M., Davidson, E.: Pushing the Contextual Envelope: Developing and Diffusing IS Theory for Health Information Systems Research. Information and Organization 14(3), 155–188 (2004)

Cho, S., Mathiassen, L., Nilsson, A.: Contextual Dynamics During Health Information Systems Implementation: An Event-Based Actor-Network Approach. European J. of Information Systems 17, 614–630 (2008)

Clarke, J., Newman, P.J.E.: The Managerial State: Power, Politics and Ideology in the Remaking of Social Welfare. Sage Publications Ltd., London (1997)

Creswell, D.J.W.: Research Design: Qualitative and Quantitative Approaches, annotated edition. Sage Publications, Inc., Thousand Oaks (1994)

Doolin, B.: Narratives of Change: Discourse, Technology and Organization. Organization 10(4), 751–770 (2003)

Du Gay, P.: Enterprise and its Futures: A Response to Fournier and Grey. Organization 7(1), 165–183 (2000)

Eastoe, J.: Victorian Pharmacy Remedies and Recipes. Pavilion, Philadelphia (2010)

Edmunds, J., Calnan, M.: The Re-professionalization of Community Pharmacy? An Exploration of Attitudes to Extended Roles for Community Pharmacists Amongst Pharmacists and General Practitioners in the United Kingdom. Social Science and Medicine 53, 943–955 (2001)

Flynn, R.: Managerialism, Professionalism and Quasi-Markets. In: Professionals and the New Managerialism in the Public Sector. Open University Press, New York (1998)

Flynn, R.: Clinical Governance and Governmentality. Health, Risk & Society 4(2), 155 (2002)

Garson, B.: The Electronic Sweatshop: How Computers Are Turning the Office of the Future into the Factory of the Past. Simon & Schuster, New York (1988)

Giddens, A.: The Consequences of Modernity. Stanford University Press, Stanford (1991)

Greenhalgh, T., Stramer, K., Bratan, T., Byrne, E., Russell, J., Hinder, S., Potts, H.: The Devil's in the Detail: Final Report of the Independent Evaluation of the Summary Care Record and Health Space Programmes. University College London, London (2010)

Hibbert, D., Bissell, P., Ward, P.R.: Consumerism and Professional Work in the Community Pharmacy. Sociology of Health & Illness 24(1), 46–65 (2002)

Hodgson, D.: Putting on a Professional Performance: Performativity, Subversion and Project Management. Organization 12(1), 51–68 (2005)

Hughes, C., McCann, S.: Perceived Interprofessional Barriers between Community Pharmacists and General Practitioners: A Qualitative Assessment. British J. of General Practice 53(493), 600–606 (2003)

Johnson, T.: Expertise and the State. In: Foucault's New Domains, Routledge, London (1993)

Johnson, T.: Professions and Power, 1st edn. Palgrave Macmillan, Basingstoke (1972)

Kerr, A., Cunningham-Burley, S., Amos, A.: The New Genetics: Professionals' Discursive Boundaries. Sociological Review 45(2), 279–303 (1997)

Kirkpatrick, I., Ackroyd, S.: Archetype Theory and the Changing Professional Organization: A Critique and Alternative. Organization 10(4), 731–750 (2003)

Klein, H.K., Myers, M.D.: A Set of Principles for Conducting and Evaluating Interpretive Field Studies in Information Systems. MIS Quarterly 23(1), 67–93 (1999)

Knights, D., Noble, F., Vurdubakis, T., Willmott, H.: Chasing Shadows: Control, Virtuality and the Production of Trust. Organization Studies 22(2), 311–336 (2001)

Latour, B.: Science in Action: How to Follow Scientists and Engineers Through Society. Harvard University Press, Cambridge (1988)

Lyon, D.: Identifying Citizens: ID Cards as Surveillance. Polity Press, Cambridge (2009)

Maykut, P., Morehouse, R.: Beginning Qualitative Research: A Philosophical and Practical Guide, 1st edn. Routledge, London (1994)

McDonald, R., Cheraghi-Sohi, S., Sanders, C., Ashcroft, D.: Professional Status in a Changing World: The Case of Medicines Use Reviews in English Community Pharmacy. Social Science & Medicine 71(3), 451–458 (2010)

Orlikowski, W.J., Baroudi, J.J.: Studying Information Technology in Organizations: Research Approaches and Assumptions. Information Systems Research 2(1), 1–28 (1991)

Perkin, H.: The Rise of Professional Society: England Since 1880, 2nd edn. Routledge, London (2002)

Timmermans, S., Berg, M.: The Gold Standard: The Challenges of Evidence-Based Medicine and Standardization in Health Care. Temple University Press, Philadelphia (2003)

Walsham, G.: Making a World of Difference: IT in a Global Context, 1st edn. Wiley, Chichester (2001)

Wilson, S., Tordoff, A., Beckett, G.: Pharmacy Professionalism: A Systematic Analysis of Contemporary Literature (1998-2009). Pharmacy Education 10(1), 27–31 (2010)

Zuboff, S.: In the Age of the Smart Machine: The Future of Work and Power. Basic Books, New York (1989)

About the Authors

Dimitra Petrakaki is a postdoctoral research officer at the London School of Economics and Political Science. Her research focuses on the relation between information technology, power, and knowledge, and its implication for organizational change. She is currently conducting research into the introduction of electronic health records and electronic transfer of prescriptions in the English NHS. She can be reached at d.petrakaki@lse.ac.uk

Tony Cornford is a senior lecturer in Information Systems at the London School of Economics and Political Science. He is interested in IT in health care, IS implementation, the open source software process, and socio-technical and socio-cognitive approaches to IS. His latest work has been in the area of electronic prescribing, electronic health records, and electronic transfer of prescriptions in the English NHS. He can be reached at t.cornford@lse.ac.uk

Ralph Hibberd is a research fellow at the School of Pharmacy, University London. His research focuses on safety and usability of complex (information) systems and on users' sense making and behavior. He is currently working as a project coordinator and researcher into the electronic yransfer of prescriptions initiative of the English NHS. He can be reached at ralph.hibberd@pharmacy.ac.uk

Valentina Lichtner is a postdoctoral research officer at the London School of Economics and Political Science. She is interested in adoption and adaptation of IT in healthcare, evaluation of systems, identity, and identification technology, human–computer interaction, and patient safety. She is currently conducting research into the introduction of electronic health records and electronic transfer of prescriptions in the English NHS. She can be reached at v.lichtner@lse.ac.uk

Nick Barber is Professor of the Practice of Pharmacy at the School of Pharmacy, University London. He held positions at the London School of Economics and Political Science and at Harvard Medical School. His research focuses on medication errors, technology evaluation, adherence, and the philosophy of prescribing and of pharmacy. He is a principal investigator for two research projects that evaluate the National Care Record Service and the Electronic Prescription Service in the English NHS. He can be reached at n.barber@pharmacy.ac.uk.

Section 5. The Future of Industrial–Institutional Practices and Outcomes through Information Technology

From Forestry Machines to Sociotechnical Hybrids: Investigating the Use of Digitally Enabled Forestry Machines

Daniel Nylén and Jonny Holmström

Umeå University, Department of Informatics, 901 87 Umeå, Sweden
{daniel.nylen,jonny.holmstrom}@informatik.umu.se

Abstract. Most forestry machines being produced today include a personal computer that monitors and controls the harvester head, and an information system that stores data on every action the driver or the machine performs. Information and communication technologies (ICTs) thus provide an opportunity to improve efficiency and competitiveness and possibly also opens up new ways of working for actors in the forestry industry. The purpose of this study is to investigate how ICT can enable the transformation from selling products to selling services in the forestry industry. We investigate such transformation through conducting a case study including a number of actors from the forestry industry in northern Sweden. First, we investigate the barriers for establishing an open innovation system in forestry. Then we describe how the use of ICTs can enable the establishment of such a system. The case study shows that the forestry industry as a whole is dominated by the salient traditional value chain where the raw materials are refined to paper products and that many of the actors are committed to a closed innovation paradigm. We argue that the ICT component in forestry machines constitutes a latent potential that can be fully captured in the context of an open innovation system.

Keywords: Open innovation, value constellations, materiality, forestry industry.

1 Introduction

Information and communication technologies (ICTs) enjoy a pervasive role in most societal contexts. In the past few decades, ICTs have come to play a major role in traditional industry settings (Jonsson et al. 2008; Holmström et al. 2010; Zuboff 1988). The forestry industry is no exception as it has become a high-tech industry in recent years. The mechanization of forestry in Sweden started in the 1960s, when woodsmen using chainsaws and log-driving and transports by horse were gradually replaced by tractors and lorries. During this decade, productivity increased drastically while the number of forestry workers was reduced by half. The first fully mechanical forestry machines were imported from Canada, the United States, and Russia and, in 1970, six percent of the timber was logged with forestry machines. This figure grew

M. Chiasson et al. (Eds.): Future IS 2011, IFIP AICT 356, pp. 199–214, 2011.

during that decade and was as high as 65 percent by 1980. During the 1990s, production was transformed from being of a bulk-character to being customer-oriented.

Continuous technical development has resulted in the harvesters and forwarders of today. Most machines today include a personal computer that monitors and controls the harvester head (the device in which the chainsaw is mounted) and an information system that stores data on almost every action the driver or the machine performs. ICT thus provides an opportunity to improve efficiency and competetiveness, and possibly opportunities for new ways of working. To this end, the use of ICTs in the forestry industry reflects patterns of usage found in other settings where ICTs have enabled the transformation of organizational collaboration (Holmström and Boudreau 2006; Leonardi 2009; Leonardi and Barley 2010), the transformation of business models (Jonsson et al. 2008), or flattening of organizational hierarchies to an open innovation ideal (Westergren and Holmström 2008).

While previous research has emphasized the mediating role of ICTs across multiple organizational contexts (Boudreau and Robey 2005; Rolland and Monteiro 2002), few empirical studies have demonstrated how ICT establish links between previously independent contexts (Vaast and Walsham 2009), thereby allowing for more distributed work practices (Pollock et al. 2009). Our study is inspired by these recent accounts, yet our empirical and analytical basis is different. The purpose of this study is to investigate how ICTs can enable the transformation from selling products to selling services in the forestry industry. Given the ways in which firms in the forestry industry are embedded in a wider innovation system, the analysis is guided by the following research question: How can the use of ICTs enable the establishment of open innovation systems in the forestry industry?

We use the open innovation lens in pursuing the research question. In the open innovation paradigm, firms do not try to protect their innovation processes to the same extent as in the closed innovation paradigm. Firms bring in knowledge from the research of other firms and share their own knowledge with other firms. This can be done through joint ventures, spin-ins, and spin-offs. This way of doing business often requires new business models aid in making sure that the firm captures some of the value it helped to create (Chesbrough 2006). The literature on open innovation is particularly silent on the role of ICTs in open innovation settings. To this end, we seek to contribute to this domain by paying close attention to the role of ICT in the transformation processes in forestry, and how a heterogeneous set of actors—human as well as nonhuman—forming sociotechnical hybrids (see Jonsson et al. 2009).

2   Related Research

We begin by outlining existing research on open innovation models. Building on how firms in the forestry industry are embedded in a wider innovation system, we proceed to present existing research on materiality, enabling us to be specific about the role of IT in open innovation contexts.

2.1   Open Innovation

The term *open innovation* was first coined by Henry Chesbrough. In the closed innovation model, the R&D staff develops products that might eventually reach the market—sold and distributed by the firm (Chesbrough 2006). What characterizes the open innovation paradigm, in contrast, is that firms do not try to protect their research to the same extent. Companies bring in knowledge from the research of other firms and share their own knowledge with other firms. Each firm will, of course, want to claim a certain amount of value from a given innovation, but it is not necessary that the innovation reaches the market through the internal path. Chesbrough (2006, p. 2) defines open innovation as

> the use of purposive inflows and outflows of knowledge to accelerate internal innovation, and expand the markets for external use of innovation, respecttively. Open innovation is a paradigm that assumes that firms can and should use external ideas as well as internal ideas, and internal and external paths to market, as the firms look to advance their technology.

The research on how to organize for open innovation is still very limited (Fredberg et al. 2008). Vanhaverbeke (2006) stresses the need to address a broader scope of analysis and argues that open innovation should be analyzed not only at the firm level, but also on the dyad-, intra-organizational, and interorganizational levels (Vanhaverbeke 2006).

In their 2002 article, Chesbrough and Rosenbloom set out to answer the question: Why do successful companies often fail to capture value from new technology that they helped to create? According to Chesbrough and Rosenbloom, there are two ways that firms can capture value from new technology:

1. Through incorporating the technology in their current businesses
2. Through launching new ventures that exploit the technology in new business arenas

The fundamental starting point for Chesbrough and Rosenbloom's theories is that a certain technology may have an inherent value, but it remains latent until it is enacted in some way. The value network created around the firm determines the role that suppliers, customers, and third parties play in influencing the value captured from the enactment of an innovation (Chesbrough and Rosenbloom 2002). The actors in the value-creating system produce value together through rethinking their roles and interrelationships. Hence, value creation is not just adding value step after step but reinventing it by means of a reconfiguration of the roles and relationships among actors of the value creating system (Vanhaverbeke and Cloodt 2006). In sum, value creation in constellations is determined by (Vanhaverbeke and Cloodt, 2006):

1. The resources it assembles
2. The way it can combine and govern those resources
3. The value of competing products and the competitive reactions of competing firms and constellations

Fair value distribution in a value constellation is important; it is crucial that all participants profit from their participation. Some actors are automatically better off in the new constellation compared to the old value creating system. Others might be worse off and have to be compensated to stay committed to the value constellation (Vanhaverbeke and Cloodt 2006).

2.2 Materiality

The open innovation literature is largely silent on the role of ICTs in an open innovation environment. This is perhaps not surprising; IS researchers have only recently started to conceptualize how ICTs influence multiple and previously independent work practices. In their study of how a packaged software producer provides customer support, Pollock et al. (2009) illustrate how new ICTs allowed the move to technical repairs online. In a similar vein, we believe that ICTs hold the potential to enable the establishment of open innovation systems in the forestry industry.

The focus in extant research on IT-enabled change is on changes caused by increased digitization, reflecting of the more general trend within information systems research to treat IT as a "black box," disregarding which IT attributes are used and how they are used (Orlikowski and Iacono 2001). To address this limitation, IS scholars have recently begun to pay attention to materiality issues associated with IT (Leonardi and Barley 2010; Orlikowski and Scott 2008; Zammuto et al. 2007).

Orlikowski (2007) has argued that even though new digital artifacts play a ubiquitous role in contemporary organizations, research "largely disregards, downplays, or takes for granted the materiality of organizations." She argues that "material artifacts" must be better addressed in management studies to show how they are fundamentally transformed by social practices and, subsequently, transform them:

> Consider any organizational practice, and then consider what role, if any, materiality may play in it. It should be quickly evident that a considerable amount of materiality is entailed in every aspect of organizing, from the visible forms—such as bodies, clothes, rooms, desks, chairs, tables, buildings, vehicles, phones, computers, books, documents, pens, and utensils—to the less visible flows—such as data and voice networks, water and sewage infrastructures, electricity, and air systems (Orlikowski 2007, p. 1436).

Discussing the physical and nonphysical matter of IT, Leonardi (2007, p. 816) notes how "the impact of its material features is transformed through the social action of collective appropriation." For example, as people confront a specific IT (human agency) that does specific things that are not completely in their control (material agency), they contend with the material agency of the technology and find ways to maneuver around it. Indeed, material agency comes in many forms and shapes and the material agency associated with IT is, for these reasons, fundamentally different from that associated with other artifacts. To this end, we need to be specific about IT while also being specific about the ways in which IT is implicated with social practices.

3 Research Methodology

This paper reports on an interpretive case study based on interviews with actors from the forestry industry in northern Sweden. The case study is single case, involving multiple firms. The case study approach was chosen due to its strengths in providing a way of collecting data and analyzing a contemporary phenomenon (Yin 2003).

The case study aimed at gaining an understanding for how work is organized in the forestry industry, which roles the different actors play, and how they are interrelated.

The actors studied are mainly located in one county. A total of 11 organizations were selected for participating in the case study (see the Appendix).

Data were collected in two phases. In the first phase, four interviews were conducted. The aim was to explore how work is organized in the forestry industry in northern Sweden. The authors needed to gain an understanding for the context and to start identifying key actors. To achieve this, interviews in this phase were of an open and unstructured character. After the first round of interviews the data were analyzed. The analysis provided a deeper understanding of the phenomenon and served as input for the next round of interviews. An interview guide was created based on these insights. Nine semi-structured interviews were conducted in the second phase.

Most of the interviews were conducted in offices and meeting rooms at the client's premises. The exceptions were two interviews conducted by telephone. In both phases, the duration of the interviews varied from 50 minutes to 1 hour, 45 minutes. The interviews were digitally recorded and later transcribed. An iterative process commenced, where the transcriptions were read several times. Emerging patterns were identified and coded with an open-ended approach, allowing grouping into themes. These themes built the foundation for the results and analysis presented in the paper.

When writing up the results and analysis sections, our ambition was to tell the story in its diversity, rather than summing up (Flyvbjerg 2006). All informant and firm names have been fictionalized in order to protect and respect privacy. Ultimately an interpretive case study seeks to contribute to theorizing (Holmström 2005; Truex et al. 2006; Walsham 1995), which in this particular case is focused on contributing back to the extant research on IT-enabled change. As outlined by Truex et al. (2006), an ambitious research program will also seek to contribute back to the "mother discipline" from which the analytical lens is borrowed. In this case, we will make an effort to contribute back to open innovation.

4   Case Study

We now present the data collected through interviews with a number of actors from the forestry industry in northern Sweden. In what follows, we will present the forestry machine supply chain, its key actors, and how the ICT component in the logging process holds the potential for radically restructuring the supply chain.

4.1   Forestry in Northern Sweden

Forestry has historically employed a large number of people in northern Sweden. As the mechanization of forestry began in the 1960s, firms producing vehicles and machines to be used were also founded in the area. Timbercut and one of its suppliers was founded in the 1960s. More start-up firms soon followed. Since then, Timbercut has gone through a number of changes in ownership as well as a number of name changes. In 2003, the firm was acquired by a large multinational enterprise. Today, Timbercut is one of the largest forestry machine manufacturers in the world. The headquarters are still located in the northern Swedish town were the original firm was founded. The site contains one of two worldwide manufacturing plants as well as the research and development (R&D) department. Among the products produced are harvester and forwarder machines.

4.2 Forestry Machines Supply Chain

Timbercut's customers exist on a global market. Apart from their Swedish customers, most machines are sold to customers in Brazil, Canada, Finland, and Great Britain. As forestry is organized in varying ways in different countries, the customers are a heterogeneous set of actors. In northern Sweden, however, Timbercut's customers are either logging contractors or forest owning companies. The firms range from a single person owning one machine to large forest-owning companies owning several hundred machines that are operated by as many employees.

As Timbercut has expanded its operations in the area over the last five decades, firms supplying them with components have not only remained in the area, but expanded their operations as well. Supplying firms S1, S2, and S3 are all located in the same county as Timbercut.

Our interviews with Timbercut and its suppliers (S1, S2, and S3) illustrate a tightly knit community. Many of the managers have moved between at least two of the firms. The CEOs at Timbercut, S1, and S2 all know each other through having worked together. The chairman at S1 was hired by the firm in the 1970s. Since then, he has had a long career in different firms around the world, including Timbercut, before coming back to S1 through acquiring shares and becoming the chairman. Today, S1 and Timbercut still closely collaborate on the product development of their component.

> We hire S1 as contract manufacturers of certain components...they are sub-contractors to us....Those components are our design....but S1 are a subcon-tractor—[they] draw on or they build from our drawings....S3, I do not think is a supplier of anything so far. We do not really have cooperation with S3. They are pretty closely linked to the other big forestry machines manufac-turer instead. So that's a bit trickier....Yeah, that's when they are suppliers to other brands of machines that they have to try being a bit cautious. Of course, they don't want to jeopardize their relationships with them. S2 don't want to come to us and say, hey, now you should...do this and like this. They have to be a little cautious. [TPM/Timbercut]

The connections between the firms are many, as in fact suppliers S1 and S2 also collaborate with each other.

> And with S2, they have their product and we buy it and of course...they are a supplier to us on that product and we do some welding work for them. We have close cooperation. [CEO/S1]

S3 is also located in the area, but delivers components to the all of the major forestry machines manufacturers apart from Timbercut. The CEO shares his thoughts on where in the supply chain innovation takes place and whose needs S3 should satisfy.

But they [the forestry machines manufacturers] are the ones controlling what the machine should look like. It's their machine, their brand, their marketing, and so on and so forth. So being an inventor but not being able to determine what the machine should look like, it's a bit of a tricky position. We can be sitting on a bunch of great ideas as we go knocking on their door. They will say, sure, that's interesting, but we do not want to change ours, we have already invested in this production line. [CEO/S3]

He also shares his thoughts on the role of the logging contractors.

The contractors who use the machines are weak. I mean, they are very weak. It is small family businesses, often with huge financial difficulties. So, therefore, we have to work with the one's who, in the end, actually pay. And that's the forest owning companies. [CEO/S1]

4.3   The Logging Process

Today, the logging process is close to being completely automated. Like most machines today, Northlog's harvester machine includes a PC that monitors and controls the harvester head. It also contains an information system that picks up data from sensors located on the harvester and forwarder heads. The data covers the length, dimensions and quality of the trees that are logged. This data is fed into software installed on the PC that is mounted on every machine. The PC stores data on almost every action the driver or the machine performs. Although some manual quality controls are performed, the main focus of the driver is operating the machine and monitoring the process.

For the contractor to be able to run a well-functioning organization, the computers in the forestry machines have to be in a serviceable condition at all times. When they are not, it is practically impossible to get any work done.

Yes, it really has accelerated. Nowadays the situation is that if something breaks, for example the computer in the harvester machine, then that's it! We're at a total standstill, since we can't log at all. Everything is totally dependent on computer activity in the machine. It has to work, otherwise you can't use the machine....At best you can move it from its location. [Owner/Logging contractor]

The rural areas of northern Sweden are sparsely populated. Distances between the towns are far. For the logging contractor, this means that the nearest service technician is still 55 kilometers away.

This local guy will come out and help us....He connects a PC laptop to the machine. He has software that we don't have access to. That's because, you know, everyone can't be allowed to play around with that. I mean, you can cause major disorder if you open up files and you don't know what you're doing. The machine will be unusable, it can even nearly become dangerous. [Owner/Logging contractor]

When preparing for the logging of a new area, Northlog receives an *apt-file* from the customer. The apt-file specifies the length and diameter that is required by the sawing mills. The file also controls how the harvester cuts, calculates price, and detects the optimal length for a certain dimension. When the logging activities operate at normal conditions, timber is logged and forwarded to a landing point. A carrier continually picks up the timber at the landing point. The communication between the driver of the harvester machine and the lorry driver is mainly done through mobile phones and com radio.

At the end of each night shift, logging statistics are sent to the Skogsbrukets Datacentral (SDC) server. The data is transferred through a Mobitex system. The Mobitex device is connected to the PC in the harvester machine. A prd-file (production file) is saved on the PC and transferred to the Mobitex device. The data contains information about the timber harvested during the day, amounts of timber located on the clear-cut area, and amounts of timber that have been conveyed to the road.

> *But then of course we have a Mobitex system. And it is an old technology really....I guess you could discuss that back and forth, but it is a functioning technology. And it has coverage everywhere....They're trying NMT now and they think it seems to work fine, but I have said that the question [is] whether you should jump on every technology step....Well, I guess that I'm thinking along the lines that in this technological march that is going on, maybe there are some steps you probably have to sit out and keep the old technology for a while. [Owner/Logging contractor]*

The product manager (TPM) is aware of the fact that there are still logging contractors out there using Mobitex. He recognizes its advantage of providing full coverage in remote forest areas in the inland of northern Sweden where the customers are often located. However, he points out that

> *It is at a lousy transmission rate, so you can only send short text messages. And you can't use it at all for remote desktop or to send e-mails, browse the web—it is in fact worthless. [TPM/Timbercut]*

At Alpha Forest Corp., the logging manager (TLM) is responsible for making sure that the amount of timber logged corresponds to the amount that is supposed to be delivered to a number of saw mills and pulp mills each month. The teams report the volumes logged and forwarded to the landing to TLM on a daily basis. The volumes are then reported to SDC's server. TLM can download the files containing this data from SDC's system and transfer them to her system. These files help her to maintain control over where recently logged timber is located at the moment. She can also get an overview of the amount of timber in the forest warehouse and in the road warehouse.

The logging teams all have access to the web-based information system *mapleweb*, developed by Alpha. The teams can log-on to mapleweb from home. In the system, a time line visualizes the objects they are to log during the coming month. TLM has estimated the time consumption based on how many cubic meters of forest should be logged in each area and the average performance of the logging team in that type of forest.

The logging team can download information about each object from mapleweb. One of the things they download is the logging directive which contains all of the information about the type of forest in the area, etc. They can also download map files from mapleweb. This is done continuously and as soon as the logging team has finished logging an object, they log on to mapleweb from home and download all the information they need to move on and start working with the next object. In practice, the movement from one object to the next often does not happen according to the time line. TLM points out that the deliveries required by the mills often change. This means that she has to reschedule and change the order of the objects on the time line.

When logging has taken place, the timber stays approximately five to six weeks at the landing before it is transported to the mills by the carriers. According to TLM, she can at any time log on to her systems and see how much timber is in the road stock and the forest stock. This information is based on the reports that are uploaded from the harvester and the forwarder.

4.4 Knowledge and Capabilities

As the logging process has become automated and partly digitalized, the capability requirements of the drivers have changed. A key competency required of the driver is to be able to assess the terrain and have a high level of driving technique. The driver also needs knowledge of basic forestry such as assessing damage on the stem, skewness, and so forth. Apart from these skills, the driver of today also needs to have skills in computer and mechanical engineering. The driver needs to able to remove, change, and repair files when the computers are not working properly. On mechanical matters, the driver needs to be able to do trouble shooting, basic problem solving, and service on the mechanical parts of the machine. According to the contractor, there are, unfortunately, a lot of drivers that have a negative attitude toward the increased computerization. When asking the contractor which training he prefers the people he hires to have completed, his answer is no such formal training really exists. He acknowledges that there are forestry schools, but his goal when recruiting is to find a full-fledged driver that doesn't have an effect on the overall productivity. According to the contractor, however, they are few and far between. He also concludes that he doesn't really believe that any training program can produce a fully qualified professional.

4.5 Digitally Enabled Vehicles

The 1960s and 1970s saw the establishment of forestry machine manufacturers and mechanical suppliers in northern Sweden. In the first decade of the new millennium, as forestry machines started becoming increasingly digitalized, actors focused on ICT emerged and got involved in forestry.

4.5.1 Digital Services

Timbercut's core business is currently in selling forestry machines. Apart from selling entire machines, they sell spare parts. The services they offer are troubleshooting, technical support, and servicing when the machines break down. Timbercut is also working on a new product that only has a preliminary release date which has not yet been announced. The product is an integrated artifact and service called eTimber. It will enable Timbercut to offer remote support to their customers through a subscription-based support contract. The long-term plan is that the eTimber platform, including the hardware, will be installed in all new machines that are manufactured.

Mobile Internet coverage has been scarce in the inland areas of northern Sweden. However, this changed during 2009 as a new ISP emerged, delivering a theoretical speed of 3.1 Mbits downlink and 1.8 Mbits uplink in these areas. The eTimber hardware is ready to be connected to the PC in the forestry machines. To be able to use eTimber, the customer needs to sign up for a 3G mobile Internet service. The 3G USB modem is then plugged-in to the eTimber hardware. Although the eTimber platform will be installed in all machines, service is not activated until the customer signs up for the subscription-based support contract. Once this is done, the service technician adds the customer's machine(s) to his support system.

4.5.2 Remote Operation and Digital Training

In the local area, there are also other types of actors with whom Timbercut , S1, S2, and S3 collaborate. One of these actors is the simulation firm ICT firm 2 (ICT2); another is the research center (TRC). The CEO at S1 provides an account of his role in the start-ups of these firms.

> *And then, among other things, I got in contact with the Partnership Vice-Rector at the University and I got involved in starting ICT2. The Vice-Rector and I also started the Research Center.* [CEO, S1]

Although ICT2 received some help from Timbercut and S1, S2, and S3 in its start-up phase, it is today an established firm with customers outside the forestry industry as well. Reflecting on ICT2's activities with the forestry actors so far, the CEO stresses one area where he would like to see more work get done.

> *I have thought that we should have done more with the simulation, including this idea of automated systems. I mean, not autonomous vehicles, but remote operation, where you sit in a different location than the vehicle when driving it. We have done such a project with a port cranes manufacturer. We have tried in a simulated environment, where the operator has moved out of the cabin and sits in a control room and runs the vehicles through the monitors.* [CEO/ICT2]

The CEO stresses that their simulation gives an opportunity to evaluate if the operator can perform equally well, even though he does not sit inside the vehicle. TRC has performed activities with Timbercut, S1, S2, and ICT2, and has been working with Timbercut on a project with autonomous forestry machines, where the vehicle is programmed to be able to drive itself and detect and avoid obstacles. However, the research manager at TRC expresses some disappointment.

> *I've felt that the interest from Timbercut has been rather lukewarm almost from the very start....I think it's interesting in terms of research, but it is far ahead of the time when they can really translate it to anything. So...they have provided access to the machines, and made it possible to run it on the field and do tests on the machines. And it's not a bad thing for the research team to have access to such an experimental platform. But really, you also want them to be pushing things forward.* [Research manager/TRC]

One of the projects that TRC has been working on is a remotely operated harvester machine. It is operated from two manned forwarding machines. However, the research manager's view is that Timbercut does not seem to be ready for the project yet. He explains these are such high risk investments that Timbercut chooses to rather wait and monitor their competitors' moves before going ahead with such a product.

Another actor located in the area, which has had discussions with Timbercut, is ICT1. The firm started out serving mainly as a product supplying unit, designing and producing hardware for remote monitoring and communication. Today, the firm focuses on product development in a wider sense through selling software and services. ICT1 has taken on a number of Swedish industrial companies, helping them with the transition from selling products to selling services. This has mostly been done trough installing their sensors which allows, for example, an elevator to order a service technician automatically when needed.

5 Discussion

This paper has focused on the ways in which ICTs enable the establishment of open innovation systems in the forestry industry. The digital capabilities embedded in forestry machines have rapidly changed forestry. The move from forestry machines to sociotechnical hybrids has opened up possibilities for changes in industry structure, partnership relations, and business models.

In this paper, we have presented an argument for the utility of the concept of *open innovation* in the forestry industry. In particular, we have examined how ICTs can enable open innovation practices in the forestry industry. The contribution of this work is two-fold.

First, it initiates discussion about the possibility of innovation at a level that transcends and encompasses the firm level. Indeed, we have argued that ICT innovation will eventually be better understood when it can be placed in an open innovation context. Clearly, as our case illustrates, ICTs have become increasingly critical in the daily work in the forestry industry. However, the digitally enabled forestry machine can also serve as a means by which organizations can tap into and make use of the knowledge embedded in an open innovation system. Organizations and clusters of organizations can achieve long-term competitive advantage by developing and deploying core capabilities which in turn requires developing an overarching strategic intent and core values (see Tushman and O'Reilly 2006). Having said this, the possibilities for such capability-building efforts in forestry must be approached by focusing on what the barriers are for establishing an open innovation system in forestry, and how the use of ICTs could help to enable such open innovation systems. As we have seen, establishing an open innovation system in forestry involves a long journey for some of the actors involved. Our case study tells the story of the traditional value chain in the forestry industry, and in order to identify the barriers for establishing an open innovation system, we need to understand the traditional value chain that has long dominated the forestry industry.

The salient value chain is the one where the raw material—trees in a forest—are refined to paper products through passing a number of links. The first link in the chain consists of forest owning firms and private forest owners that decide to sell a certain amount of trees on their grounds. They purchase the services of the logging contractors in the next link. The logging contractors cut down the trees and branches are taken away. The trees are turned into timber and are transported to a landing point. Carriers, which constitute the next link in the value chain, pick up the timber and transport it to a saw or pulp mill. The timber is turned into planks or paper. The mills pass on the finished product to resellers in different industries.

The process illustrates how the product to be passes through the activities in the value chain in a certain order. The product gains value at every activity, a way of doing business that indicates a traditional way of creating value. It is also clear that forestry machine manufacturers are not an actual link in this value chain. Their role is that of a supplier to the first two links in the chain—the forest owners and the logging contractors on which we have chosen to focus. This way of doing business and the industry culture that is likely to come with it is in itself an important barrier to overcome in order to be able to work in an open innovation system where forestry machine manufacturers and ICT specialists take an active and leading role.

There was thus a limited amount of cooperation between the links in the chain other than those directly connected. The innovation that took place in the chain is likely to be closed to influence from actors other than the previous and the next link in the chain, if open to any actor at all. The open innovation ideal was thus far from realized.

Second, we promote the understanding of digitally enabled forestry machines as hybrids. To this end, we build on the materiality discourse in information systems, specifically addressing how technological agency plays a part in the open innovation processes and outcomes. Indeed, while the open innovation literature is largely silent on the role of ICTs in open innovation environments, IS researchers have recently started to conceptualize how ICTs influence work practices (Jonsson et al. 2008; Leonardi 2007; Pollock et al. 2009).

The way that Timbercut and its mechanical suppliers S1 and S2 collaborate today in some respects illustrates an open approach to innovation. However, the actors actively taking part in the actual logging process are not organized according to a traditional value chain only; they are also committed to a closed innovation paradigm.

We found that Timbercut is aligned with the traditional value chain, acting as a supplier to forest owners and logging contractors, listening to their needs and turning these needs into better products. At the same time, we provided an account for how new types of actors, focusing on ICT services and solutions, have emerged and started to participate in forestry projects. However, ICT2 as well as TRC expressed disappointment with the lack of commitment from Timbercut in pushing those projects.

We argue that the way in which Timbercut is embedded in a peripheral position in the current value chain constrains their possibility of fully capturing value from the technology in their forestry machines. Although an open approach to innovation is found in the design and manufacturing of the mechanical technology, to some extent it is the use of this mechanical technology that contributes in holding the traditional value chain together. A possibility for overcoming Timbercut's peripheral position in the current value chain is making an effort to employ an open innovation approach to working with the ICT components of the forestry machines.

With Timbercut's new service, eTimber, their forestry machines not only store data valuable in analyzing the usage, but are also connected to the Internet. Apart from the possibility of remote support, there are arguably other latent potentials in a digitally enabled forestry machine connected to the Internet. The access to stored data and the fact that the machine is online holds the potential to enable knowledge sharing between the actors that was not possible previously.

Following Chesbrough and Rosenbloom (2002), if Timbercut wants to fully capture the value in their digitally enabled forestry machines, there are two alternatives: incorporating the technology in their current business or setting up new ventures. The projects with ICT2 and TRC are examples of their work on new technologies together with new types of actors. However, in order to exploit that new technology and eventually translate it into new product offerings, Timbercut may consider setting up a venture with ICT1. In order to capture value in a open innovation system, new types of value constellations can be set up around Timbercut. One option is for Timbercut and ICT1 to invite customers to discuss, assess, and address their needs. A wider definition of the customer in this context could include other actors in the value chain, such as saw and pulp mills. For Timbercut to set up a venture with ICT1 would demand a high degree of openness in terms of access to data and an opening up the protocol of the ICT component in the machines. Another actor that could participate in such interorganizational knowledge sharing is Alpha, providing that they are willing to open up some parts of their system, mapleweb. This would also enable Timbercut and ICT1 to be able to determine how to design and integrate new services. Access to data from the harvester and forwarder that Northlog uses may serve the same purpose.

6   Conclusions

This study has addressed the following research question: How can the use of ICT enable the establishment of open innovation systems in the forestry industry?

In order to answer this question, we conducted a case study including key actors from the forestry industry in the northern part of Sweden.

The case study shows how the forestry industry as a whole is dominated by the salient traditional value chain where the raw materials are refined to paper products and that many of the actors are committed to a closed innovation paradigm. We argue that the forestry industry in northern Sweden is currently organized in a very traditional manner, in the value chain arrangement that has characterized business relations in the forestry industry for decades. This way of doing business reveals what we refer to as a traditional way of thinking about value creation, and a limited capability to see beyond the existing value chain.

The barriers identified to working in an open innovation system are hampering the evolution of the forestry industry. It should be noted that informed use of ICTs can be an aid in overcoming them. We argue that the ICT component in Timbercut's forestry machines constitutes a latent potential that can be fully captured through a joint venture with ICT1. Further, we argue that a favorable way of doing this is through the creation of an open innovation system. ICT can enable this transition through the interorganizational knowledge sharing that it makes possible.

References

Boudreau, M.-C., Robey, D.: Enacting Integrated Information Technology: A Human Agency Perspective. Organization Science 16(1), 3–18 (2005)

Chesbrough, C.: Open Innovation: A New Paradigm for Understanding Industrial Innovation. In: Chesbrough, H.W., Vanhaverbeke, W., West, J. (eds.) Open Innovation: Researching a New Paradigm, pp. 1–12. Oxford University Press, Oxford (2006)

Chesbrough, C., Rosenbloom, R.S.: The Role of the Business Model in Capturing Value from Innovation: Evidence from Xerox Corporations Technology Spinoff Companies. Industrial and Corporate Change 11(3), 529–555 (2002)

Flyvbjerg, B.: Five Misunderstandings about Case-Study Research. Qualitative Inquiry 12(2), 219–245 (2006)

Fredberg, T., Elmquist, M., Ollila, S.: Managing Open Innovation–Present Findings and Future Directions. Vinnova, Stockholm (2008)

Holmström, J.: Theorizing in IS Research: What Came Before and What Comes Next? Information Resources Management Journal 17(1), 167–174 (2005)

Holmström, J., Boudreau, M.-C.: Communicating and Coordinating: Occasions for Information Technology in Loosely Coupled Organizations. Information Resources Management Journal 19(4), 23–38 (2006)

Holmström, J., Wiberg, M., Lund, A.: Industrial Informatics: Design, Use and Innovation. IGI Global, Hershey (2010)

Jonsson, K., Holmström, J., Lyytinen, K.: Turn to the Material: Remote Diagnostics Systems and New Forms of Boundary-Spanning. Information and Organization 9(4), 233–252 (2009)

Jonsson, K., Westergren, U., Holmström, J.: Technologies for Value Creation: An Exploration of the Remote Diagnostics Challenge in Ubiquitous Computing Environments. Information Systems Journal 18(3), 227–245 (2008)

Leonardi, P.M.: Activating the Informational Capabilities of Information Technology for Organizational Change. Organization Science 18(5), 813–831 (2007)

Leonardi, P.M.: Crossing the Implementation Line: The Mutual Constitution of Technology and Organizing Across Development and Use Activities. Communication Theory 19(3), 278–310 (2009)

Leonardi, P.M., Barley, S.R.: What's Under Construction Here? Social Action, Materiality, and Power in Constructivist Studies of Technology and Organizing. The Academy of Management Annals 4, 1–51 (2010)

Orlikowski, W.J.: Sociomaterial practices: Exploring Technology at Work. Organization Studies 28, 1435–1448 (2007)

Orlikowski, W.J., Iacono, C.S.: Research Commentary: Desperately Seeking the "IT" in IT Research–A Call to Theorizing the IT Artifact. Information Systems Research 12(2), 121–134 (2001)

Orlikowski, W.J., Scott, S.V.: Sociomateriality: Challenging the Separation of Technology, Work and Organization. Academy of Management Annals 2(1), 433–474 (2008)

Pollock, N., Williams, R., Grimm, C., D'Adderio, L.: Post Local Forms of Repair: The Case of Virtualised Technical Support. Social Science Research Network, working paper series (2009)

Rolland, K.H., Monteiro, E.: Balancing the Local and the Global in Infrastructural Information Systems. The Information Society 18(2), 87–100 (2002)

Truex, D., Holmström, J., Keil, M.: Theorizing in Information Systems Research: A Confessional Tale of the Adaptation of Escalation Theory to Information Systems Research. Journal of the Association of Information Systems 7(12), 797–821 (2006)

Tushman, M.L., O'Reilly, C.M.: Managing Evolutionary and Revolutionary Change. In: Mayle, D. (ed.) Managing Innovation and Change. Oxford University Press, Oxford

Vaast, E., Walsham, G.: Trans-Situated Learning: Supporting a Network of Practice with an Information Infrastructure. Information Systems Research 20(4), 547–564 (2009)

Vanhaverbeke, W.: The Interorganizational Context of Open Innovation. In: Chesbrough, H.W., Vanhaverbeke, W., West, J. (eds.) Open Innovation: Researching a New Paradigm, pp. 205–219. Oxford University Press, Oxford (2006)

Vanhaverbeke, W., Cloodt, M.: Open Innovation in Value Networks. In: Chesbrough, H.W., Vanhaverbeke, W., West, J. (eds.) Open Innovation: Researching a New Paradigm, pp. 220–240. Oxford University Press, Oxford (2006)

Walsham, G.: Interpretive Case Studies in IS Research: Nature and Method. European Journal of Information Systems 4, 74–81 (1995)

Westergren, U., Holmström, J.: Outsourcing as Open Innovation: Exploring Preconditions for the Open Innovation Model in the Process Industry. In: Proceedings of 29th ICIS, Paris, France (2008)

Yin, R.: Case Study Research: Design and Methods, 3rd edn. Sage Publications, Thousand Oaks (2003)

Zammuto, R.F., Griffith, T.L., Majchrzak, A., Dougherty, D.J., Faraj, S.: Information Technology and the Changing Fabric of Organization. Organization Science 18(5), 749–762 (2007)

Zuboff, Z.: In the Age of the Smart Machine: The Future of Work and Power. Basic Books, New York (1988)

About the Authors

Daniel Nylén is a Ph.D. student at the Department of Informatics, Umeå University. His research examines the digitalization of a number of contexts and industries. A particular focus is investigating emerging digital innovation processes in the media industry.

Jonny Holmström is a professor of Informatics at Umeå University, Sweden. His research interests include the organizational consequences of information technology, digital innovation, and open innovation methods for university–industry collaboration. Holmström's larger research program has examined how organizations innovate with IT, and he is currently investigating how organizations in the process industry sector can develop sustainable competitive advantages through mindful use of IT, and how media organizations make use of a heterogeneous media portfolio. His research has been published in *Communications of the AIS, European Journal of Information Systems, Information and Organization, Information Resources Management Journal, Information Technology and People, International Journal of Actor-Network Theory, Technological Innovation, International Journal of Systems Assurance Engineering and Management, Journal of Information Technology Management, Journal of the AIS, Journal of Global Information Technology Management,* and *Scandinavian Journal of Information Systems.*

Appendix: Description of the Actors Included in the Study

Organization	Description	Role
Logging contractor (Northlog)	Logging contractor firm. Our informant owns and manages the firm. Northlog has three employees. Including the contractor, the total of four persons work shifts on one harvester machine and one for-warder machine. Northlog currently has a 5-year contract with one of Sweden's largest forest owners.	Owner
Forest owning company (Alpha)	One of the largest forest owners in Sweden. The firm manages its own forest through logging and selling timber to sawmills and pulp mills. Alpha also acquires timber from private land owners. The firm has over 700 employees.	Purchaser Logging manager (TLM) R&D manager
Forestry machines manufacturer 1 (Timbercut)	Founded in the 1960s as a local firm, developing and manufacturing forestry machines. Since then, a number of changes in ownership also resulted in a number of name changes. Timbercut is today a division within a multinational enterprise. The firm is today one of the worlds largest manufacturers of forestry machines. The headquarters are still located in the northern Swedish town were the original firm was founded in the 1960s.	Product manager (TPM)
Forestry machines manufacturer 2	Recently started manufacturer of smaller forestry machines	CEO
Supplier 1 (S1)	Produces components to forestry machines.	Chairman
Supplier 1 (S2)	Produces components to forestry machines.	CEO
Supplier 1 (S3)	Produces components to forestry machines.	CEO
Research center (TRC)	Conducts research on intelligent off-road vehicles. More specifically on autonomous forestry machines.	Research manager
ICT1	The firm started out serving mainly as a product supplying unit, designing and producing hardware for remote monitoring and communication. Today, the firm focuses on Product Development in a wider sense through selling software and services.	CEO
ICT2	Formed in the late 1990s as a spin-off from the University. Produces training simulators for forestry machines. The firm is co-owned by Timbercut, but has a row of other multinational customers. End-customers are either training organizations or fleet owners.	CEO
Municipality	Local municipality of a small town where some of the suppliers are located.	Trade and industry director

Lessons from Volunteering and Free/Libre Open Source Software Development for the Future of Work[*]

Kevin Crowston

Syracuse University School of Information Studies
crowston@syr.edu

Abstract. In this paper, we review research on voluntary organizations to identify key features of and problems in volunteer work and organizations. We then use the example of free/libre open source software (FLOSS) development teams to examine how those features and problems apply in this situation and how they might be affected by the use of information and communications technologies (ICT). We suggest that understanding volunteer organizations can illuminate the changing nature of all knowledge work, paid as well as unpaid.

Keywords: Free/libre open source software, volunteering, motivation, coordination, visibility of work.

1 Introduction

In this paper, we discuss the features of volunteer work and organizations to gain insight into the future of work, in particular, information and communications technology (ICT) supported work. Our analysis focuses initially on organizations that seek to incorporate volunteer contributors. This approach is increasingly common as many organizations seek to profit from "the wisdom of crowds" (Suroweicki 2002) or from user-led innovation (von Hippel and von Krogh 2003), forms of work that depend on unpaid voluntary contributions as well as ICT-enabled online community spaces and shared information resources to channel the efforts of geographically dispersed volunteer contributors. Wikipedia is the most dramatic, although not unique, example of this mode of work. This online encyclopedia has expanded rapidly (over 15 million articles in more than 270 languages), incorporating billions of contributions from voluntary contributors (more than six million account holders and 91,000 active contributors) who develop and edit content for the site. There are many similar but smaller-scale collaborations, ranging from blogs and discussion groups on a wide variety of topics, evaluations of products or posts on sites like Amazon or Slashdot, and free/libre open source software (FLOSS) projects that bring together teams of programmers and users who contribute software and documentation.

Such efforts have been surprisingly successful—surprising in light of known difficulties of working across distance and with potentially unreliable collaborators.

---

[*] This work was supported in part by US National Science Foundation Grant 07–08437.

M. Chiasson et al. (Eds.): Future IS 2011, IFIP AICT 356, pp. 215–229, 2011.

FLOSS, for example, has become a significant industry force, with leading market share in numerous categories. The apparent success of technology-enabled and volunteer-based organizations has sparked much interest among both researchers and practitioners, again leading to speculation on the future of work. Indeed, predictions have even been made that such forms of voluntary organizations will replace conventional organizations in some fields (e.g., bloggers replacing journalists or FLOSS replacing proprietary developers). While these predictions seem overblown, they reflect the perceived potential of this mode of work.

In this paper, we specifically use the lens of volunteering to examine the organization of FLOSS development. We address the following research questions:

1. Which features of FLOSS development practices and structures result from reliance on volunteer workers?
2. How does extensive use of ICT work-support affect the impact of the reliance on volunteer workers?

This analysis shows that certain features of FLOSS (such as a core–periphery group structure) are a consequence of the reliance on volunteer contributors. This analysis also indicates points where the use of ICT can mitigate observed problems with volunteer work and organizations (such as reduced real-time coordination and lack of knowledge of other workers).

But the implications of this analysis are potentially much broader: understanding volunteer organizations illuminates the changing nature of all knowledge work, paid as well as unpaid (a point made by Pearce 1993). Indeed, in an interview, Peter Drucker stated, "increasingly employees are going to be volunteers, because a knowledge worker has mobility and can go pretty much every place, and knows it.... Businesses will have to learn to treat knowledge workers as volunteers" (Collins and Drucker 1999). In other words, simply offering money and then telling people what to do might not be enough to attract the best and brightest, nor hold onto them or ensure that they do their best work. But to "treat knowledge workers as volunteers" requires a better understanding of the nature of such work.

The rest of the paper is structured as follows. We start by examining the literature on volunteer organizations to describe a range of issues that arise in managing volunteers. We then examine what is known about these issues from research on an extreme example of technology-supported volunteer organizations, namely free/libre open source software (FLOSS) development teams. Finally, we discuss how the lessons of volunteer organizations and FLOSS teams can be applied to ICT-supported work in employee-based organizations of the future and raise a series of questions for future research.

Before we start, we clarify a point of terminology. Butler (2004) suggested analyzing online communities as volunteer associations. However, in this paper, we draw on research on volunteer organizations, specifically, on purposive and utilitarian organizations. While volunteer associations and organizations have many similarities, they differ in that associations primarily serve their members while organizations create a valued good or service to serve those beyond the organization. Consider as an example the difference between a bridge club (an association that serves its members) and a volunteer fire department (an organization that serves a community) (Pierce 1993).

The presence of an external customer to be served makes the volunteer contributions a kind of work.

2   Volunteer Organizations: A Review

In this section, we discuss findings from research on volunteer work and organizations. The key feature that distinguishes volunteer work from conventional work is that volunteers are unpaid. Motivation for volunteers has been a major concern of those researching volunteer organizations, understandably, as organizations are eager to identify factors that attract volunteers. But researchers have identified a number of other issues for which the work of volunteers differs from that of traditional employees. We will discuss in turn clarity of job definitions, core–periphery organizational structure, organizational understaffing, reduced opportunities for coordination and knowledge of coworkers, and organizational control of volunteer workers. These issues are shown graphically in Figure 1.

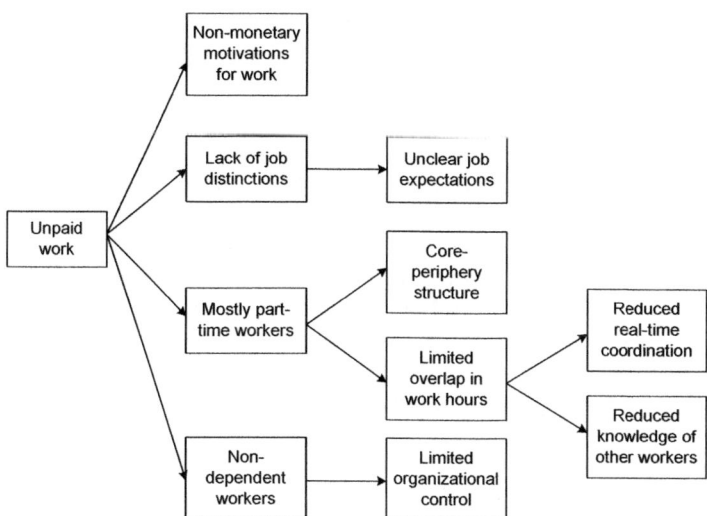

Fig. 1. Effects of Volunteer Work

Nonmonetary motivation for work. We start by considering motivations for work. Because volunteers receive no monetary compensation for their work, they must be assumed to have other motives for their contributions. The nature of volunteer motivations is an important question for organizations hoping to attract volunteer contributions and, as a result, the question has been a major focus of the volunteer research literature and research has identified a wide range of possibilities. Clary et al. (1988) suggested a combination of selfish and unselfish motives as the basis of sustained voluntarism. With respect to selfish motivations, they suggested that individuals volunteer as a method of self-education, as a social activity, or to assuage feelings of guilt concerning entitlement or privilege. Individuals also want to feel appreciated and needed; indeed, Pearce (1993) notes that leaders of volunteer organizations often stress the importance of volunteers' contributions, in part to contradict the impression that their work is valueless since it is unpaid. Volunteers may agree with the organization's goals or want the organization's outputs (Pierce 1993) and so be motivated to contribute. Individuals also volunteer on an unselfish basis, springing from what Clary et al. identify as a combination of altruistic and humanitarian values. Finally, Clary et al. suggested that group-related motivations emerge when people volunteer to identify with or to maintain their status as a member of a valued group.

Unclear job expectations. A second implication of zero pay for true volunteers is that the lack of distinction in pay (all are equal) often leads to a lack of formal job distinctions among volunteers and unclear job definitions in general (Pierce 1993). As a result, new members are often left to work out for themselves how best to contribute, but unfortunately often have trouble determining exactly what they should be doing. Other volunteers may be too busy working to be able to assist with this process. Furthermore, volunteers may have an ambiguous relationship with the organization, since many volunteer organizations are governed by their members, meaning that volunteers are simultaneously workers and directors. This role ambiguity again makes it difficult for a volunteer or those working with volunteers to assess what work performance is expected.

Organizational understaffing. A further implication of low or zero pay is that most volunteer organizations have trouble attracting sufficient numbers of workers and so are generally understaffed (Pierce 1993). Research on volunteer organizations suggests that understaffing in turn leads to lower requirements for job performance. Since every contribution is needed, the organization cannot afford to be overly selective or demanding: low levels of performance are better than none and so are tolerated. Understaffing also leads to a perceived need for constant recruitment to attract new volunteers, although the stream of new volunteers actually exacerbates the problem of lack of orientation for new members. Finally, the combination of understaffing and unclear job expectations can lead to overloading of active volunteers and burnout. When an individual is found who is willing to work, there is a temptation to ask that person to do more and more; without clear job definitions, it is not obvious what the limit should be.

Core–periphery structures. A third implication of work being unpaid is that most volunteers only work for the organization part time. Reliance on part-time employees has several implications for the structure of volunteer organizations and the conduct of work (Pierce 1993). First, the fact that most members are only contributing part time has been found to lead to a core–periphery organizational structure. A few members, perhaps those with higher commitment to the group or more free time, work more. As a result, these core members have a greater opportunity to learn about the organization and each other, and thus build up a higher level of skills and knowledge, both about the tasks performed and the state of the organization. On the other hand, the majority of volunteers are peripheral, contributing at a low level and with a lower level of knowledge of the task and organization. These members have contact with core members, but likely not with each other. The organization likely has porous boundaries and fluid membership for such volunteers. New volunteers join with little fanfare. Dropping out is also unmarked: if a volunteer has not been seen in a while, is this because they have left the organization, or are they just busy at the present time and will contribute again later? On the one hand, this fluidity can be an advantage, as the organization can tailor the available workforce to the immediate need. On the other hand, at an organizational level, there may be uncertainty as to volunteers' skills, interests, capabilities, or even their exact number.

Reduced real-time coordination and knowledge of coworkers. Reliance on part-time workers has a second implication, namely, a lack of overlap in work hours among volunteers. Peripheral members in particular are likely to have only limited contact with other peripheral members. A lack of opportunities for regular contact between volunteers reduces the ability to coordinate work directly. As well, the lack of contact makes it difficult for workers to know what to expect from coworkers or for what contributions they can rely on them. As a result, many volunteer organizations find the need for formal coordinator roles (Pierce 1993). Such limited contact also reduces the likelihood of building social relations that motivate further contributions to the organization.

Limited organizational control of volunteers. A final issue is the question of control (or lack of control) over volunteer workers and its inverse, the reliability of their work. Research on volunteer organizations suggests that because volunteers are unpaid and do not depend on the organization for their living, the organization has reduced ability to control their behaviors. Rather than giving orders and expecting them to be carried out in return for pay, in volunteer organizations, authority is more often indirect. Furthermore, as noted above, volunteers may play mixed roles in the organization (workers and directors), again reducing a manager's formal authority.

One strategy is for managers to appeal to shared goals and values. Such a strategy is powerful but limited: appeals have to be credible to carry weight—the link from the goals to the actions must make sense to the volunteer. A further limitation is that goals do not specify means (Pearce 1993, p. 119). As a result, reliance on this mode of motivation can lead to organizational schisms, as different subgroups advocate different means to achieve the common goals. Alternately, leadership may be personal. Leaders can derive authority from knowledge and experience, rather than from normative power of a position or title. Being a recognized core member of the group can carry more weight than any title. Leading by example provides authority and helps set job expectations. Finally, volunteer organizations can motivate contributions through personal relationships and feeling of solidarity. As Pearce (p. 162) puts it, "volunteers worked for one another" and felt a commitment to the organization's leaders and to fellow volunteers.

Summary. In summary, the literature on volunteer organizations identifies a set of issues stemming from reliance on unpaid workers, specifically the need to identify other sources of motivation for contribution, possible lack of job distinctions leading to unclear job expectations, a core–periphery structure with reduced opportunities for real-time coordination and reduced knowledge of other workers, and reduced organizational control of volunteers. These issues in turn require a different approach to managing volunteer workers, including personal contributions and development of personal relations.

3 Volunteering and Free/Libre Open Source Software Teams

In this section, we examine how the features of volunteer work and organizations described above apply to free/libre open source software (FLOSS) development teams. FLOSS is a broad term used to embrace software developed and released under a license allowing inspection, modification, and redistribution of the software's source code. While there are important differences between free software and open source software, their software development practices are similar, hence our use of an umbrella term in this paper. The goal of this analysis is first to identify features of FLOSS work and organization that can be explained by the reliance on volunteer work and second to identify issues with volunteer work that are affected by use of ICT to support the work.

We focus in particular on what have been called "community-based" rather than company-sponsored projects (e.g., Apache rather than MySQL). These projects are developed by dynamic self-organizing teams comprising software professionals and users (von Hippel and von Krogh 2003). Although often informally organized, FLOSS project teams are teams. The core members of these projects have a shared goal of developing a product, a user base to satisfy, and a shared social identity. Team members are interdependent in their tasks and core members know and acknowledge each other's contributions. Furthermore, as in volunteer organizations, FLOSS developers are not paid by their projects. Some may be paid by other organizations to contribute to projects (e.g., IBM pays a number of its employees to work on Linux or Apache projects), but others contribute without any direct compensation. As a result, findings from prior research on volunteer work and organizations should be directly relevant to FLOSS project teams, and consideration of the issues discussed above should, therefore, help explain them.

In addition, FLOSS has attracted great interest among information systems researchers because it provides an accessible example of virtual work. FLOSS teams are virtual, as developers contribute from around the world, meet face-to-face infrequently, if at all, and coordinate their activity primarily by means of ICT (Raymond 1998; Wayner 2000). Discontinuities among team members make any kind of consistent process seemingly harder to attain, yet effective teams seem to have developed productive ways of working together, making their work practices of interest to those interested in virtual work. Thus, examination of this research setting will provide insight into how the known features of volunteer work are affected by the use of ICT to support that work.

In the remainder of this section, we consider in turn the factors of volunteer work identified above.

Nonmonetary motivation for work. One of the most striking features of FLOSS development is that developers are largely volunteers. As a result, many researchers have examined developer motivations for participation. Their studies have found heterogeneous individual motivations that are largely consistent with the research on volunteer organizations. Researchers have described three types of motives: extrinsic motivations, internalized extrinsic motivations, and intrinsic motivations. Reputation (Hann et al. 2004) and reward motives such as career development (Hann et al. 2002; Orman 2008) are the two most frequently mentioned extrinsic motivations. User needs (Lerner and Tirole 2002; Lu et al. 2006) are the most commonly mentioned internalized extrinsic motivations. Enjoyment-based motivations such as fun (Ghosh 1998) and sharing or learning opportunities (Shah 2006; Ye and Kishida 2003) are the two most commonly mentioned intrinsic motivations. Another frequently cited benefit of working on FLOSS projects is the freedom to work on a task entirely of one's own choosing (Kuznetsov 2006). While employees are assigned work, volunteers choose it. Xu et al. (2009) further identified project community factors such leadership effectiveness, interpersonal relationships, and community ideology. Kavanagh (2004) noted that part of the motivation for some to contribute to FLOSS was identification with a narrative of resistance to proprietary software, an example of motivation from shared values.

Unclear job expectations. A lack of formal roles and the need to self-define contribution, as found in volunteer organizations, also seems to apply to FLOSS teams. A frequent comment in the literature is the difficulty of new members getting socialized into teams (Ducheneaut 2005). As might be seen in the volunteer organizations described above, Dahlander and Magnusson (2005) found that a common reason for not contributing to a FLOSS project is that there did not seem to be a need. A further limitation of the FLOSS model is that the onus for socialization falls almost entirely on the would-be developer, rather than the team (von Krogh et al. 2003).

Organizational understaffing. Understaffing does seem to be an issue in FLOSS teams. A few projects attract a lot of attention, while the majority have only a small number of core developers. As a result, for most projects there is more work that could be done than developers to do it. Some FLOSS projects do engage in some amount of recruiting to attract new developers, especially those with the time to become core developers. However, most seem to rely on developers self-identifying and overcoming the barriers to joining.

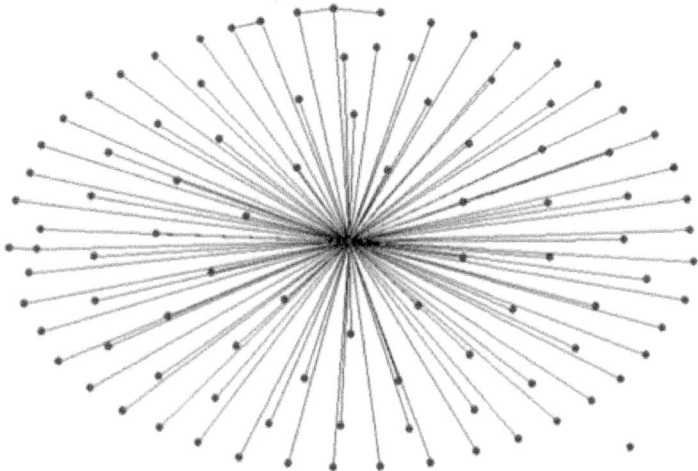

Fig. 2. Interactions in Bug Reports for the Curl Project (from Crowston and Howison 2006)

Core–periphery structures. A core–periphery structure is seen quite commonly in FLOSS teams. Academic case studies of FLOSS projects (e.g., Gacek and Arief 2004; Mockus et al. 2000, 2002; Moon and Sproull 2000) suggested a model of FLOSS development with a hierarchical structure. The focus of these studies has largely been on the contribution of code. For example, Mockus et al. (2002) studied the Apache httpd project and found that development was quite centralized, with only about 15 developers contributing more than 80 percent of the code for new functionality. Bug reporting, on the other hand, was quite decentralized, with the top 15 reporters submitting only 5 percent of problem reports in the Apache project. They summarize this finding by hypothesizing that, "In successful open source developments, a group larger by an order of magnitude than the core will repair defects, and a yet larger group (by another order of magnitude) will report problems" (p. 329). Crowston and Howison (2006) examined interactions around bug reports and found a strong core–periphery structure, such as shown in Figure 2.

Overall, FLOSS teams exhibit an onion-like structure as shown in Figure 3. At the center of the onion are the core developers, who contribute most of the code and oversee the design and evolution of the project. In the next ring out are the codevelopers who submit patches (e.g., bug fixes), which are reviewed and checked in by core developers. Further out are the active users who do not contribute code but provide use cases and bug reports as well as testing new releases. Further out still, and with a virtually unknowable boundary, are the passive users of the software, those who use the software but who do not contribute to the project's lists or forums. Even if the passive users do not contribute directly, they are still important, as the existence of a user base with needs for the software provides one motivation for further development.

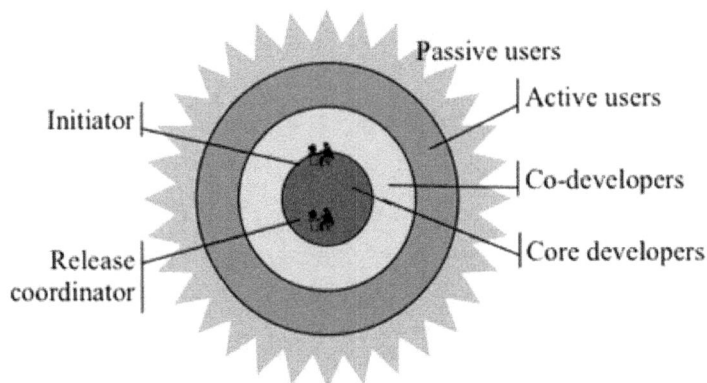

Fig. 3. Core–Periphery Structure in FLOSS Project Teams

Reduced real-time coordination and knowledge of other workers. FLOSS teams resemble other volunteer organizations in that members cannot rely on real-time coordination—members contribute at their leisure and from many different time zones. However, few FLOSS teams seem to address this gap with appointed coordinators. Instead, many FLOSS teams eschew real-time communications and rely instead on asynchronous communication technology that can span discontinuities of time. This mode of interaction enables group members to stay in touch without seeing each other or having to work at the same time. In other words, the use of ICT provides a mechanism for addressing this particular aspect of volunteer work. Another explanation for the low level of explicit coordination observed in FLOSS teams is increased reliance on modular job design that minimizes the need for coordination (e.g., by making source code highly modular). Work can be designed so that an individual can complete a task without needing extensive interaction with others. FLOSS teams have also been described as relying on self-assignment of work (Crowston and Scozzi 2008), again eliminating the need for task coordinators. Finally, an interesting possibility recently described in FLOSS teams is the use of stigmergic coordination (Bolici et al. 2009; Robles et al. 2005), that is, coordination performed through the work itself. Developers in FLOSS teams can determine the current state of work by examining the shared code base; detailed discussion with other programmers may, therefore, be unnecessary for coordination.

In volunteer organizations, a lack of face-to-face contact means that volunteers often do not get to know coworkers other than core members. However, the fact that FLOSS work is mostly done online means that members can review the contributions of others and thus understand their background. Similarly, all members can follow discussions held on email, which can provide an avenue for joining and understanding the group. Furthermore, the coordination and work assignment practices noted above reduce the need for close coordination between members and so make development of mutual knowledge less critical. Again, this particular aspect of volunteer work is one that might be mitigated by the use of ICT.

Organizational control of volunteers. As with other volunteer organizations, FLOSS projects have few means of controlling volunteer contributors, making project leadership difficult. The nature of leadership in such teams has recently been examined. Consistent with the research described above, the main duties of leaders in FLOSS projects have been described as providing a vision, attracting developers to the project, and keeping the project together and preventing forking (i.e., schisms) (Giuri et al. 2008; Lerner and Tirole 2002), rather than giving directions or assigning work.

Research has also addressed who can become a leader in FLOSS development teams. First, leaders are usually not appointed, and in most cases not formally identified, but rather emerge from participation in FLOSS development. Individuals are perceived by others as leaders based on their sustained and strong technical contributions (Scozzi et al. 2008) and diversified skills (Giuri et al. 2008). A novel feature of FLOSS teams is that they often exhibit shared leadership instead of having a single leader (Sadowski et al. 2008). According to Fielding (1999), shared leadership enables these teams to continue to survive independent of the participation of particular individuals, and enables them to succeed in a globally distributed and volunteer organizational environment. However, Heckman et al. (2007) suggested that while virtual teams are characterized by shared leadership in the form of substantive task contributions, group maintenance, task coordination, and boundary spanning, leadership functions related to vision and norm setting are more likely to be centralized.

Summary. In summary, the research on FLOSS teams suggests that they embody many of the same features described in research on volunteer organizations (our first research question): reliance on nonmonetary motivations, unclear job expectations, organizational understaffing, and a core–periphery structure with reduced real-time coordination and reduced organizational control. FLOSS teams also have been characterized as exhibiting shared leadership on some aspects, such as task contribution and boundary spanning. However, the use of technology as the prime conduit for interactions among group members seems to enable new approaches for addressing two of these issues (our second research question): educed real-time coordination and lack of knowledge of other workers. In particular, FLOSS teams seem not to rely on formal coordinator roles, but rather use the technology to enable asynchronous communications and to make work visible across the team.

4 Discussion

In this paper, we have examined research on volunteer organizations and on free/ libre open source software development teams to identify features of FLOSS work and organization that stem from a reliance on volunteer workers and how the use of ICT to support work changes this relationship. We conclude by drawing from this analysis to identify issues that might confront ICT-supported knowledge work in the future in general, and discussing managerial implications and opportunities for future research.

4.1 Managerial Implications

The analysis presented above offers several implications for managers of volunteer organizations in particular, but of all organizations to some degree.

Recognize additional motivations for work. First, managers should recognize motivations for work beyond financial. For example, as employees can be motivated in particular by their evaluation of the organization's goals, managers should strive to make these values explicit. The research on FLOSS on the inherent interest of tasks suggests that there are benefits to allowing employees to self-select some of their work. For example, companies like 3M and Google reportedly allow some employees to spend up to 20 percent of their time working on projects of their choice, both for the possible benefit of the projects as well as the increased motivation of the employee.

Expect core–periphery structures. Second, a common characteristic of volunteer organizations is their reliance on part-time workers. Even though flexible job arrangements are becoming more common for employees, we would not expect to see all employees become part-time. However, some organizations now routinely assign workers to multiple teams simultaneously (Chudoba et al. 2005; Lu et al. 2006), a practice called multi-teaming. Employees assigned to multiple teams work full-time for the organization, but from the perspective of any particular team, they are essentially part-time. As a result, extensive use of multi-teaming can lead to a core–

periphery structure for each team, as each member picks a few teams to contribute to at a higher level, while participating only peripherally in the others. Pearce (1993) noted that increased use of contract workers can have a similar impact: the contractors are likely to have only minimal contact among themselves and so to be peripheral to the group.

In the face of developments like flexible work, contracting, and multi-teaming, managers should recognize that employees may make different levels of contribution to projects. Organizations need to adjust their evaluation schemes to address the contributions of employees who are shared across multiple teams. Managers should recognize core members who contribute at a higher level and develop expertise with models of authority based on contribution. Perhaps more importantly, they should appreciate the importance of contributions from peripheral members, and ensure that their work is also recognized.

Clarify job expectations. Third, managers should clarify job expectations and provide examples of good work. This clarification is of particular importance for peripheral members and those who are true volunteers, as they often have little knowledge of the organization and so lack clarity about how they can contribute. For example, it may be useful to provide new volunteers specific tasks to perform, as with the lists of bugs published by many FLOSS projects. In general, allowing employees to self-select some or all tasks may lead to ambiguity about appropriate roles, making role setting important in these cases as well. Finally, managers should identify routes to becoming a core member for those who are interested, while recognizing that not all will be.

Enhance knowledge of other workers. Fourth, managers may want to pay close attention to the kinds of connections formed between team members. Findings from volunteer organizations suggest that a core–periphery structure, brought on by increased multi-teaming or use of contract employees, may lead to problems for team members and leaders in not knowing how much members can be counted on or even exactly who is in the team. For example, contractors may only know their contact and so be unable to directly coordinate their work with other team members; other team members may not be fully aware of the contractor's role. These trends would be expected to lead to an increased need for formal coordinator roles to connect workers who do not have opportunities to interact for coordination or to develop mutual knowledge. The use of ICT may provide tools for distributed team members to get to know each other, but research suggests that forming strong ties over these media can be challenging.

To address this problem, particular attention should be paid to socialization of new members. For example, a welcoming ceremony can help new volunteers to identify their place in the organization and to feel more valued as members, and also provide an opportunity for current members to learn or establish what role the new members will play. Finally, managers should promote continuity of membership to enable development of social ties (Pearce 1993, pp. 124-126), which are the basis for better job performance as well as a source of motivation.

Make work visible. Fifth, the research on FLOSS teams suggests further opportunities to use ICT to support virtual work. A recurrent theme is the value of making individual work visible to the entire team. Research on FLOSS teams suggests that it may be beneficial to use interaction media that enable all team members to see the status and contributions of others. Enabling team members to see each others' contributions provides new venues for coordinating work and for building mutual knowledge of skills and interests. Furthermore, the use of asynchronous media and shared work products may enable effective coordination even in the absence of face-to-face interaction.

Develop alternative modes of leadership. Finally, organizations that seek to employ true volunteers might expect to face problems in control. However, organizations may face these problems more broadly, as the problem of getting more than minimal work from employees parallels the reluctance of volunteers to simply follow orders. For example, Howell and Dorfman (1986) noted that teams of highly trained individuals would resist and in fact might not need hierarchical direction, while Organ et al. (2006) described organizational citizenship behavior, acts beneficial to the organization but not directly a requirement of the job, as essentially voluntary.

A virtual team setting in particular seems likely to exacerbate difficulties for leadership. In the absence of face-to-face contact, appointed leaders may lack influence over team members due to organizational or physical separation: Kerr and Jermier (1978) described distance as a leadership neutralizer, while Howell and Dorfman said that it makes leadership practices "nearly impossible to perform." These authors wrote before the extensive use of ICT for team interactions, but it is apparent that use of ICT does not completely ameliorate the problems of distance and separation. Hoegl et al. (2007) noted that leadership is less effective in dispersed groups. Team leaders often cannot directly observe member behavior or performance, which makes it difficult for them to manage task and social dynamics. Social interaction is reduced, making it difficult to moderate team process. Traditional forms of social control such as direct supervision, physical proximity, and shared experiences are largely absent in virtual team environments (Pinsonneault and Caya 2005). Opportunities to receive feedback are reduced, as are opportunities to assess perceived commitment to project or team goals (Kondradt and Hock 2007). These effects of distance make traditional methods of leadership less effective and suggest the need for reliance on modes similar to volunteer organizations: setting an example, providing a vision, attracting effort to the project, and keeping the project together, rather than giving directions or assigning work.

Summary. In summary then, work, in particular technology-supported work, appears increasingly to take on some of the characteristics of volunteer work. In part, these changes are due to attempts to include volunteers in the organization, but other developments suggest that the features will apply more broadly. In particular, employees may be motivated by more than pay, with implications for leadership, and organizations may have teams with a core–periphery structure, with implications for coordination.

4.2 Implications for Research

The work above also provides some implications for future research. A major methodological implication to consider is that teams may have unequal participation from members, in contrast to the typical tacit assumption that all members contribute equally and full-time. The participant's role and level of contribution should be assessed when sampling members, especially given that there are likely to be many more peripheral members than core members.

The work reviewed above suggests that the relevant model for studying online interaction may be volunteer management (Butler 2004). Example questions for future research include

1. What kind of motives are most effective in eliciting job performance from knowledge workers?
2. For what kinds of work does the motivational gain from allowing employees to choose their own tasks outweigh the possible reduction in effort on core tasks or increased coordination cost?
3. What kinds of tasks will volunteers be willing to take on in employee organizations?
4. What are the implications of multi-teaming for work performance? How should such work be evaluated?
5. What is the role of visible work in coordinating group work?
6. What is the nature of effective leadership in voluntary and ICT-supported organizations?

This shift in focus provides a good opportunity for further work, since there has been relatively little research about the nature of volunteer work beyond the focus on motivation. As a result, future research on technology-supported work, viewed as volunteering, may make basic contributions to our understanding of the future nature of work.

References

Bolici, F., Howison, J., Crowston, K.: Coordination Without Discussion? SocioTechnical Congruence and Stigmergy in Free and Open Source Software Projects. In: 2nd International Workshop on Socio-Technical Congruence, ICSE, Vancouver, Canada, May 19 (2009)

Butler, B.S.: When Is a Group Not a Group: An Empirical Examination of Metaphors for Online Social Structure. In: OCIS Division, Academy of Management, New Orleans, LA (2004)

Chudoba, K.M., Wynn, E., Lu, M., Watson-Manheim, M.B.: How Virtual Are We? Measuring Virtuality in a Global Organization. Information Systems Journal 15(4), 279–306 (2005)

Clary, E.G., Snyder, M., Ridge, R.D., Copeland, J., Stukas, A.A., Haugen, J., Miene, P.: Understanding and Assessing the Motivations of Volunteers: A Functional Approach. Journal of Personality and Social Psychology 74, 1516–1530 (1998)

Collins, J., Drucker, P.: A Conversation between Jim Collins and Peter Drucker. Drucker Foundation News 7(2), 4–5 (1999)

Cox, A.: Cathedrals, Bazaars and the Town Council (October 13, 1998),
  http://slashdot.org/features/98/10/13/1423253.shtml

Crowston, K., Howison, J.: Hierarchy and Centralization in Free and Open Source Software Team Communications. Knowledge, Technology & Policy 18(4), 65–85 (2006)

Crowston, K., Scozzi, B.: Bug Fixing Practices Within Free/Libre Open Source Software Development Teams. Journal of Database Management 19(2), 1–30 (2008)

Dahlander, L., Magnusson, M.G.: Relationships between Open Source Software Companies and Communities: Observations from Nordic Firms. Research Policy 34(4), 481–493 (2005)

Ducheneaut, N.: Socialization in an Open Source Software Community: A Socio-Technical Analysis. Computer Supported Cooperative Work 14(4), 323–368 (2005)

Fielding, R.T.: Shared Leadership in the Apache Project. Communications of the ACM 42(4), 42–43 (1999)

Gacek, C., Arief, B.: The Many Meanings of Open Source. IEEE Software 21(1), 34–40 (2004)

Ghosh, R.A.: Interview with Linus Torvalds: What Motivates Free Software Developers? First Monday 3, 3 (1998)

Giuri, P., Rullani, F., Torrisi, S.: Explaining Leadership in Virtual Teams: The Case of Open Source Software. Information Economics and Policy 20(4), 305–315 (2008)

Hann, I.H., Roberts, J., Slaughter, S.: Why Developers Participate in Open Source Software Projects: An Empirical Investigation. In: Proceedings of the 25th International Conference on Information Systems, pp. 821–830 (2004)

Hann, I.H., Roberts, J., Slaughter, S., Fielding, R.T.: Economic Incentives for Participating in Open Source Software Projects. In: Proceedings of the 23rd International Conference on Information Systems, pp. 365–372 (2002)

Heckman, R., Crowston, K., Misiolek, N.: A Structurational Perspective on Leadership in Virtual Teams. In: Crowston, K., Seiber (eds.) Proceedings of the IFIP Working Group 8.2/9.5 Working Conference on Virtuality and Virtualization, pp. 151–168. Springer, Portland (2007)

Hoegl, M., Ernst, H., Proserpio, L.: How Teamwork Matters More as Team Member Dispersion Increases. J. of Product Innovation Management 24(2), 156–165 (2007)

Howell, J.P., Dorfman, P.W.: Leadership and Substitutes for Leadership among Professional and Nonprofessional Workers. J. of Applied Behavioral Science 22(1), 29–46 (1986)

Kavanagh, J.F.: Resistance as Motivation for Innovation: Open Source Software. Communications of the AIS 13, 615–628 (2004)

Kerr, S., Jermier, J.M.: Substitutes for Leadership: Their Meaning and Measurement. Organizational Behavior and Human Performance 22(3), 375–403 (1978)

Konradt, U., Hoch, J.E.: A Work Roles and Leadership Functions of Managers in Virtual Teams. Int'l. J. of E-Collaboration 3(2), 16–35 (2007)

Kuznetsov, S.: Motivations of Contributors to Wikipedia. ACM SIGCAS Computers and Society 36, 2 (2006)

Lakhani, K.R., von Hippel, E.A.: How Open Source Software Works: "Free" User-to-User Assistance. Research Policy 32, 923–943 (2003)

Lerner, J., Tirole, J.: Some Simple Economics of Open Source. J. of Industrial Economics 2(1), 197–234 (2002)

Lu, M., Watson-Manheim, M.B., Chudoba, K.M., Wynn, E.: How Does Virtuality Affect Team Performance in a Global Organization? Understanding the Impact of Variety of Practices. J. of Global Information Technology Management 9(1), 4–23 (2006)

Mockus, A., Fielding, R.T., Herbsleb, J.D.: A Case Study of Open Source Software Development: The Apache Server. In: Proceedings of the International Conference on Software Engineering (2000)

Mockus, A., Fielding, R.T., Herbsleb, J.D.: Two Case Studies of Open Source Software Development: Apache and Mozilla. ACM Transactions on Software Engineering and Methodology 11(3), 309–346 (2002)

Moon, J.Y., Sproull, L.S.: Essence of Distributed Work: The Case of Linux Kernel. First Monday 5, 11 (2000)

Organ, D., Podsakoff, P., MacKenzie, S.: Organizational Citizenship Behavior: Its Nature, Antecedents, and Consequences. SAGE Publications, Thousand Oaks (2006)

Orman, W.H.: Giving it Away for Free? The Nature of Job-Market Signaling by Open-Source Software Developers. Advances in Economic Analysis & Policy 8, 1 (2008)

Pearce, J.: Volunteers: The Organizational Behavior of Unpaid Workers. Routledge, London (1993)

Pinsonneault, A., Caya, O.: Virtual Teams: What We Know, What We Don't Know. International J. of e-Collaboration 1(3), 1–16 (2005)

Raymond, E.S.: Homesteading the Noosphere. First Monday 3, 10 (1998)

Robles, G., Merelo, J.J., Gonzalez-Barahona, J.M.: Self-Organized Development in Libre Software: A Model Based on the Stigmergy Concept. In: 6th International Workshop on Software Process Simulation and Modeling (2005)

Sadowski, B.M., Sadowski-Rasters, G., Duysters, G.: Transition of Governance in a Mature Open Software Source Community: Evidence from the Debian Case. Information Economics and Policy 20(4), 323–332 (2008)

Scozzi, B., Crowston, K., Eseryel, U.Y., Li, Q.: Shared Mental Models among Open Source Software Developers. In: Proceedings of the 41st Hawai'i International Conference on System Sciences. IEEE Computer Society Press, Los Alamitos (2008)

Shah, S.K.: Motivation, Governance, and the Viability of Hybrid Forms in Open Source Software Development. Management Science 52(7), 1000–1014 (2006)

Surowiecki, J.: The Wisdom of Crowds. Doubleday, New York (2005)

von Hippel, E.A., von Krogh, G.: Open Source Software and the "Private–Collective" Innovation Model: Issues for Organization Science. Organization Science 14(2), 209–213 (2003)

von Krogh, G., Spaeth, S., Lakhani, K.R.: Community, Joining, and Specialization in Open Source Software Innovation: A Case Study. Research Policy 32(7), 1217–1241 (2003)

Wayner, P.: Free for All. HarperCollins, New York (2000)

Xu, B., Jones, D.R., Shao, B.: Volunteers' Involvement in Online Community Based Software Development. Information & Management 46(3), 151–158 (2009)

Ye, Y., Kishida, K.: Toward an Understanding of the Motivation of Open Source Software Developers. In: Proceedings of the International Conference on Software Engineering (ICSE), Portland, OR (2003)

About the Author

Kevin Crowston is a professor in the School of Information Studies at Syracuse University. He received his Ph.D. (1991) in Information Technologies from the Sloan School of Management, Massachusetts Institute of Technology. His research examines new ways of organizing made possible by the extensive use of information and communications technology. Specific research topics include the development practices of free/libre open source software teams and work practices and technology support for citizen science research projects, both with NSF support.

Investigating Open Innovation and Interorganizational Networks in the IT Industry: The Case of Standard Software Customization

Karlheinz Kautz[1], Deborah Bunker[2], Sameen M. Rab[1], and Michael Sinnet[1]

[1] Informatics, Copenhagen Business School, Howitzvej 60, DK-2000 Frederiksberg, Denmark
Karl.Kautz@cbs.dk, Smr@kmd.dk, Michael@Sinnet.dk
[2] Faculty of Economics and Business, University of Sydney, NSW2006, Australia
Deborah.Bunker@sydney.edu.au

Abstract. This research presents and analyzes an empirically grounded account of a new trend, open innovation, in the IT industry. The case depicts another new trend, innovation through customization of standard software as a business model, and we investigate the open innovation activities of an interorganizational network which consists of a small customizing company, a large global software producer, and other companies involved in the innovation process. We contribute to the development of a theory of open IT innovation with a theoretical framework that integrates formally separate aspects of open innovation and interorganizational networks. We extend the literature on open innovation by broadening the view from one focal firm to the relations in a network of companies that mutually contribute to innovation which occur in the different companies. Our research underlines the importance of balanced formal and informal relations, and coopetive and opportunistic behavior for the open innovation process.

Keywords: Open innovation, interorganizational networks, software customization.

1 Introduction

The research presented here investigates a new trend in the information technology industry. Open innovation is a novel way to create innovation where organizations open their innovation processes and cooperate with others to develop new products and services (Chesbrough 2003; Kautz et al. 2009). However, beyond work on open source development (see, for example, West and Gallagher 2005) and in extension of these efforts, Ågerfalk and Fitzgerald's (2008) research on open sourcing—they study from an individual psychological contract perspective the use of the open source development model where commercial companies and open source communities collaborate on the development of software innovations—little insight on open IT innovation exists. We study open innovation by taking another future trend into account, namely innovation through customization of standard software as a business model (Pollock et al. 2003).

M. Chiasson et al. (Eds.): Future IS 2011, IFIP AICT 356, pp. 231–246, 2011.

Interorganizational relationships and networks are both decisive for open innovation and software customization. The latter has mostly been described in the literature as a general development activity which takes place within the organization that has developed the software. There is another view that looks at customization as a specialized business activity performed by an independent business: the software customizer. This view implies some interaction in interorganizational networks between the customizer and the developer to effectively customize the software (Pollock et al. 2003).

Open innovation takes place in interorganizational networks (Vanhaverbeke 2006). Feller et al. (2009) provide a categorization of interorganizational relationships in open innovation based on whether these relationships are mediated or direct, and whether they seek to exchange intellectual property or innovation capability. On this basis, they call for more research that takes an interorganizational perspective on facilitating open innovation into account.

On this background, we empirically investigate the open innovation activities of an interorganizational network which consists of a small customizing company, a large global software producer, and other companies involved in the innovation process. Our research question, then, is how does open innovation take place in interorganizational networks in the IT industry?

Table 1. A Framework for Open Innovation in Interorganizational Networks: Key Concepts

Open Innovation	Interorganizational Networks
Idea and Knowledge Flow Knowledge Sharing Opportunities Product Access and Flow Adaptable Development Context Active Partner Search Inducements	Formal Relations • Market • Product life • Shared destiny • Minority share holding • Strategic alliance • Joint venture • Merger/Acquisition Informal Relations/Social Capital • Commitments, expectations, trust • Performance of favors, reciprocity • Admission to less accessible information through personal relations to other organizations • Norms, sanctions, behavior governed by unwritten rules Coopetition/Opportunistic Behavior • Close integration/open innovation process • Rules/caring for cooperation

The remainder of the article is structured as follows: in the next section we provide the theoretical background for our research and present a theoretical framework which integrates concepts of open innovation with concepts of interorganizational networks (summarized in Table 1) to study standard software customization as an instance of open innovation in our case setting. We then introduce our interpretive case study research approach and the case description. This is followed by our case analysis and the presentation and discussion of our findings. We finish with a summary of our contributions and some conclusions.

2 Theoretical Background

2.1 Open Innovation

Open innovation (Chesbrough 2003) means that valuable ideas can come from inside or outside a company and can go to the market from inside and outside the company. Organizations committing to open innovation view the outside world as a source of inspiration and accept the strategic potential of letting other organizations contribute to the innovation process. Grassman and Enkel (2004) distinguish between an outside-in process where external knowledge and technologies are acquired from outside a company, but the locus of innovation is within the company, an inside-out process where unused knowledge and technologies are introduced to the market, but mostly exploited inside the company, and a coupled process where these two processes are joined and the company works in alliance with others in various forms of cooperation; the locus of innovation lies both inside and outside the company. Heavy exchange of ideas and easy access to products is a prerequisite for open innovation (Vanhaverbeke and Cloodt 2006).

Open innovation is linked to openness with regard to access to a product, but it is also an overall strategy to improve the conditions for companies, which contribute to the innovation process (Vanhaverbeke and Cloodt 2006); this can mean to provide inducements such as capital for start-up companies that want to further develop their products and might function as laboratories for large organizational sponsors in the innovation process.

When engaging in open innovation, companies have to understand their role with regard to other involved parties (Vanhaverbeke and Cloodt 2006). This includes searching for new partners, providing opportunities for innovators to effectively share their knowledge and their ideas (Vanhaverbeke and Cloodt 2006), for example, knowledge sharing forums in which the developers use each other as mutual inspiration to support the creation of innovations (von Hippel 2005), and providing an appropriate development context, for example, suitable development tools and a product of high quality with a flexible product architecture, as well as providing further incentives in the form of new markets (Chesbrough 2003) where the customized solutions attract attention, but also create additional business value for the original product.

Nursing and steering an open interorganizational innovation network is significant to develop or use innovations (Vanhaverbeke and Cloodt 2006). Interorganizational relations facilitate organizations' capabilities and willingness to open their innovation process and let innovation happen across organizational boundaries (Simard and West 2006). The composition of the network has an impact on the innovative processes (Vanhaverbeke 2006). It is important not to be satisfied with tying together some established interorganizational cooperation partners, but to build up a network that consists of many broad relationships instead of a network with a few and deep relations (Simard and West 2006). This approach utilizes innovative opportunities better as the generation of ideas becomes much more unpredictable. But open innovation networks can take many forms. Organizations can participate in the research and development of an innovative product, resell the product, promote the product, or build upon the existing product (Chesbrough 2006). The knowledge and product flow between organizations in open innovation does not necessarily have to occur in the unrestricted public domain, but can take place in hierarchical relationships (Feller et al. 2009) or on a dyadic level (Vanhaverbeke and Cloodt 2006). The advantages of letting other organizations contribute to the development of new products mostly outweigh the difficulties of coordinating interorganizational processes (Chesbrough 2003).

2.2 Interorganizational Networks

Interorganizational networks are a specific type of relation that binds organizations closely together through communication, interaction, and cooperation (Harland 1996; Håkasson and Snehota 1995). These features provide a competitive advantage that could not have been achieved by organizations on their own (Dyer and Singh 1998). A network reduces the transaction costs for the exchange of information, minimizes uncertainty, and limits opportunistic behavior (Williamson 1991).

Interorganizational relations depend on the degree of formal cooperation between the organizations (Harland 1996) where organizations may have no shared objectives, deal with each other on the market, and communicate through purchase orders, to situations where organizations merge or where one organization acquires or influences others through joint ventures, strategic alliances, and minority shareholdings. Shared destiny and product life relationships see partners sharing their vision and cooperating either with regard to the organizations as a whole or with regard to individual products.

When problems arise, formal contracts are often inhibiting; informal and emergent approaches are often more usable, but organizations that know each other well and have mutual trust achieve the most effective outcomes (Håkansson and Snehota 1995). Coleman (1988) has defined the concept of social capital which contributes to an organization's competitive capacities. Interorganizational networks consist of a social structure of relations of employees across the different organizations. This consists of three elements: (1) commitments, expectations, and trust, which relate to the performance of favors and services without payment based on reciprocity, (2) information channels, which provide access to less accessible information through personal relations to trusted employees in other organizations, and (3) norms and sanctions, which are the unwritten rules which exist between people and which govern how they act and behave.

An important aspect in such networks is relations that can take a form where organizations might simultaneously cooperate and compete with each other, called *coopetition* (Ganguli 2007). The objective of coopetive relations is to achieve a joint competitive advantage by competing while at the same time jointly striving for better quality in other areas. The informal knowledge exchanged in these relationships can often benefit coopetive partners; however, such relationships are difficult to manage and control and invite opportunistic behavior (von Hippel 1987). Opportunistic behavior can be reduced through close integration and nursing the cooperation between partners. Defining the scope and the rules for innovation and cooperation is one way to achieve this; another way is opening up the innovation process and letting interested parties contribute to this process.

2.3 Standard Software Customization

Standard software has existed since the 1960s (Sawyer 2000), with the aim of creating a common comprehensive business software solution which can be implemented for a broad range of businesses. Standard software hardly ever satisfies all business needs (Scott and Kaindl 2000) and organizations want to adapt or customize the standard software for their own needs (Simard and West 2006).

Light (2001, p. 416) argues that

> Customization is meant to describe changes or additions to the functionality available in the standard software. It does not refer to the switching on and off of functionality that is part of the blueprint of the software, sometimes referred to as software configuration.

Software customization as a creative task goes beyond adjusting pre-defined settings; while including simple configuration practices such as the creation of reports, amendment of existing reports and/or displays, automation of existing processes, a greater effort is expended in changing existing functionality and addition of functionality (Kuitunen et al. 2005).

In this research, we consider customization as a specialized business activity performed by an independent business (Pollock et al. 2003) which is distinct from tailoring and modifying information systems through users (Germonprez et al. 2007). Software customization businesses can then be categorized according to two parameters (Kuitunen et al. 2005): (1) how tailored or standardized are a software company's products and services (tailored offerings versus standardized offerings) and (2) are the company's earnings primarily based on the sales of products or performance of services (product-based business versus service based business)?

3 Research Approach

Our research follows the approach of engaged scholarship (Van de Ven 2007), a participative form of research for seeking advice and perspectives of key stakeholders in order to understand and theorize about a complex problem. Given the limited research literature concerning our topic, our investigation is based on an exploratory, qualitative, single case study (Creswell 2003) of open innovation activities in an interorganizational network that consists of the small Danish software company Alpha, which customizes a software product, the large global software company Zeta, the producer of the original software product, and other companies involved.

Our research approach is inspired by Eisenhardt (1989) and Walsham (1995), who stress that in all types of research, including case study research, theory is important as an initial guide to data collection, during the iterative process of data analysis, and as a final product of the research. While it is often stated that it is not possible to generalize and certainly not to theorize from a single case study, it is possible to generalize case study findings among others in the form of a contribution of rich insight (Walsham 1995). We thus used our theoretical framework to guide our data collection and analysis in order to contribute to the existing body of knowledge with rich insight about open innovation in interorganizational networks.

The empirical data for the case study was collected in semi-structured, open-ended interviews conducted by a team of two researchers. The team focused on Alpha and performed six interviews with its founders and key personnel, covering more than half of the organization's staff, and with their partner account manager at Zeta. The interview data was supplemented with publicly available and internal company documents, especially about Zeta's partnership program. The interviews were tape-recorded and transcribed. Subsequently the data was coded independently by the two researchers. The few differences in the researchers' conceptions were discussed and resolved in collaboration with a third researcher. To move from surface observations toward theory building and from description to explanation, a detailed narrative of the case was written. In a narrative theory, the story builds a conceptual model where the story provides a progress or sequence of events (Van de Ven 2007) which serves as an additional frame of reference for the further analysis and interpretation of the data (Fincham 2002). In this process, the third and fourth members of the team acted as facilitators and carefully scrutinized the narrative. The combination of interpretation and collaboration between the four researchers with different levels of involvement brought interpretive rigor to the project.

4 The Case

In this section, we describe the case setting and take as a point of origin company Alpha. As the basis for the subsequent analysis, we describe how relations were formed, changed, and disbanded in the different phases which the organization went through. We identified seven such phases and our description is a narrative in seven acts (see Table 2).

Table 2. The Seven Phases of the Case Narrative

Freelance	Launch	Partnership	Product Development	Growth	Outsourcing	Merger

4.1 Freelance

Alpha has its origins in the company Omega. Omega, established early in 2005 as a consultancy company, focuses on a CRM (customer relationship management) product developed in 2004 by the software producer Zeta. Omega's founders are former Zeta product managers. Omega is a Zeta partner and resells Zeta's CRM product, but to do this they must have the technical skills for implementing the product. As they lack these skills in the summer 2005, Omega hires a freelance IT professional for technical support and product configuration. Subsequently, the business develops very quickly and another freelancer is hired. In this phase, Omega and the freelancers have an informal relationship without any direct payment for the work. Assignments are largely related to system configuration and customer-specific adjustments where some customers wish to import data from other systems into the CRM.

4.2 Launch

In the fall of 2005, Alpha is created by the freelancers focusing on consultancy tasks and adjusting the CRM for their customers, obtained through Omega's contacts. Importing customer data for different customers is their main focus with Omega as their strategic partner.

This phase is dominated by informal guidelines and development methods. Low cost solutions are the order of the day and the informal agreements create stability which provides Alpha with a firm base for their first standard product offering. As the assignments from different customers become similar, the founders of Alpha decide to develop a standardized solution, which Omega resells to their customers and which creates most of Alpha's initial earnings.

4.3 Partnership

The product satisfies the certification requirements in Zeta's partnership program. In the beginning of 2006, Alpha becomes a certified partner, as an independent company officially offering Zeta-based IT-services, products, and know-how. In April 2006, Alpha becomes a Gold Zeta partner, receiving more attention, support, licenses and knowledge from Zeta. They can also preview, experiment with, and test the beta versions of products much earlier. Zeta sets up the relationship through a Partner Account Manager, but this limits Alpha's access to Zeta's technical knowledge which they need to adapt the CRM product.

Alpha feels that the formal communication with Zeta is longwinded, so they look for new possibilities to get information about the CRM product. The Omega founders create a number of informal relations between Alpha and some Zeta developers, where those involved support each other by mutually exchanging information on the CRM product. These informal relations are advantageous for Alpha as they no longer need to utilize Zeta's communication channels to get information on their products, thus enhancing the relationship with Zeta.

In June 2006, Alpha appears at the annual Zeta conference in the United States to present their standardized product to Zeta partners. This is the first of many international conferences Alpha uses to strengthen its network and to develop partnerships with other Zeta partners. The new partnerships consist primarily of distribution contracts with existing CRM vendors who see an advantage in including Alpha's solutions in their portfolio. In the fall of 2006, Alpha succeeds in interesting several local Danish CRM vendors which increasingly take over contact with potential customers. This leads to the end of Omega's role as the link between Alpha and new partners. Alpha now takes over contact with these partners and, although customers still can buy Alpha's products from the company's web site, Alpha chooses to change their focus from customers to distribution partners who thus become links in Alpha's network.

4.4 Product Development

The new partner focus is an opportunity for Alpha to sell their products to a larger range of customers. Until the end of 2006, Alpha's work assignments consist both of consultancy services and the development of their own standardized solutions. The success of their first product leads to an understanding of the large potential in dedicated product development and standardized solutions. A number of new off-the-shelf products are developed of which both the new version of their first product and a system to import business data from the yellow pages achieve Zeta certification. During 2007, the company develops a further three products based on the CRM system. All three solutions meet the demands of a broad user group and fill gaps in the original CRM product.

Lacking legal protection of their ideas, however, Alpha is forced to continuously develop new products, among others yet another new version of their first product, their major product.

4.5 Growth

As Alpha products are limited in lifespan, in January 2007, Alpha starts to develop more products leading to an increased need for resources to supply technical products with user-friendly descriptions that support their positive reputation.

To further improve this reputation, over the next few months Alpha hires a sales and promotions person as well as a couple of developers to take care of their home page—used to distribute promotion materials, offer products and handle customer enquiries—as well as of their important first product. In September 2007, the founders decide to headhunt their Zeta partner account manager, who has been very enthusiastic about the company. He is employed as a sales manager, a business domain so far given low priority, and assumes an important role bringing both knowledge about the industry sector and more of Zeta's contacts and partners with him.

4.6 Outsourcing

In the fall of 2007, more international companies start to show interest in Alpha's primary product. Alpha chooses to cooperate with the largest CRM vendor in the United States. Delta, and launches a specific Delta product version. As Delta insists on using its own software testers in India, this collaboration becomes Alpha's first step toward outsourcing. The positive experience with these IT professionals results in the decision to continue to use their services instead of performing tests internally.

In November 2007, Alpha contacts the Danish company Gamma, which specializes in outsourcing of IT related work tasks. Gamma offers them a solution where three highly educated developers from Pakistan with CRM experience and low salaries are assigned to product development. Despite some challenges related to the different time zones, culture, and communication, Alpha's founders state that the decision to outsource has been favorable for the company.

At first, Alpha experiences problems with the further development of software without technical documentation, which was not an issue when developers had the necessary knowledge for this task. This leads to an effort to help the foreign developers understand and adopt the way Alpha customizes Zeta's CRM. At the same time, all code developed abroad is reviewed by Danish developers to ensure that the developers in Pakistan follow Alpha's guidelines. A focus is put on documentation and governance to ensure development quality.

4.7 Merger

Finally, in spite of a historically happy relationship, in March 2008, Alpha and Omega opt to merge. Alpha sees an advantage in the merger as they want to increase their market share and extend their network and the merger provides access to more than 100 new partners worldwide.

5 Analysis and Discussion

The case description provides highlights of a company's successful business model of customizing standard software in an open innovation context by closing gaps in an original CRM product through additional functionality. Alpha has moved from tailoring individual solutions for customers to the development of standardized, customized products (Kuitunen et al. 2005). Their primary product represents a classic functional extension of the original CRM product. The other products either fall in this category or are process automations or amendments of existing reports (Light 2001).

Since the early 1990s, Zeta has focused on opening up their innovation processes. Valuable ideas and knowledge enter and leave the organization in the research and development stages where external companies contribute with competence, suggestions, and newly developed products. To gain rich insight about open innovation in our case setting, we focus on the relation between Alpha and Zeta on a dyadic level (Vanhaverbeke and Cloodt 2006).

We find an open innovation process where external knowledge and technologies are acquired from outside a company, and where internal knowledge and technologies are introduced to the outside. This is a coupled process; Gassman and Enkel (2004) put forward that the locus of innovation in such a case is often outside the company. We find that both focal companies innovate as a result of their mutual relationship; innovation takes place inside both companies and analogically outside of them as well.

The launch of Alpha is a direct consequence of the development and diffusion of Zeta's CRM product; Alpha can thus be considered a spin-off company. From its start, Alpha focused on this standard product. Through Omega's customer network, they got ideas for customizations and adjustments that were lacking in the original product. Omega's close relationship to Zeta contributed to that development knowledge from Zeta was shared with Alpha across Zeta's boundaries. This knowledge then contributed to Alpha's idea of building their first product. This had decisive influence on Alpha's certification as Gold Partner, which gave Alpha access to knowledge that is produced in Zeta's research process.

Yoo et al. (2008) classify open source innovation as a type of innovation network that is based on homogeneous knowledge sources and a distributed mode of control and coordination. Our case innovation network shows many of these traits, but we can also argue that Zeta is to a large extent controlling the network, thus showing traits of a centralized market with heterogeneous knowledge sources, or that Alpha much more independently follows its own path to innovation pointing toward a doubly distributed network with heterogeneous sources and distributed control.

Feller et al. (2009) distinguish four types of interorganizational relationships in open innovation; these are solution hierarchy, a direct relation with a focus on intellectual property; solver market, a direct relation with a focus on innovation capabilities; solution brokerage, a mediated relation with a focus on intellectual property; and solver brokerage, a mediated relation with a focus on innovation capabilities. We find a complex mesh of multiple relations which cannot be categorized so neatly; both focal companies seek knowledge in hierarchical and market relations and brokers such as Omega provide knowledge of potential solvers and solutions.

As Alpha has detailed knowledge about the CRM product, they contribute with development ideas which they believe are important to be implemented in the original product. Alpha has promoted the idea that the CRM product should interact with other vendors' data base systems. Zeta is interested in these kinds of ideas and collects them through interviews with their partners, who in the research phase put their stamp on the future product.

Zeta has created forums where people who innovate their products can ask technical questions and extend their product knowledge. Zeta has an online forum for developers who customize their standard software. The online forum only plays a small role in Alpha's work, but it evinces Zeta's efforts to create an information flow between its own and external developers. In Alpha's case, the Zeta conferences played a more important role for building competences and relationships.

Zeta provides a flexible product architecture so that the innovating companies can reduce their resources; they easily can adjust and adapt components of the original product. For Alpha, it was critical that Zeta made the technical architecture more flexible so they could host their customers' solutions and thus make it much easier to maintain the software. The modular architecture of the CRM product allowed Alpha to change, add, and remove functionality without larger compatibility problems.

To attract new markets, Zeta supports the promotion of their partners' customized products. Alpha has secured that their products satisfy Zeta's perquisites and quality criteria for product promotion and has permission to promote their products on Zeta's home page, where Zeta's customers seek new products and product information. Promotion at conferences has been decisive for Alpha in finding new customers.

As ideas enter Zeta's open innovation environment, Zeta also provides inspiration to Alpha's product development early in the process. Alpha has been accepted as a member of Zeta's early-adopter program, which provides them in the research and the development stages with leading-edge information about new CRM product features and versions that are a source of inspiration for their own innovations. Alpha's participation in the beta tests has the same effect. Beyond improving the original product, Alpha's solutions ensure better utilization of the CRM product and contribute to its further sale to new markets. This is in line with Vanhaverbeke's (2006) claim that a focus on open innovation emerges often when companies such as Zeta try to promote and sell their products in new markets.

Zeta is relying and dependent on other companies' contributions to their product as they cannot cover all markets; this, in particular, is valid for niche markets with special needs. They continuously provide new versions of the original product as inspiration which their partners can customize and further develop.

Zeta works actively to identify companies interested in innovating their standard software. Beyond a significant effort to promote their partnership program with a minimal participation fee, Zeta helps minor, non-certified companies by providing free support and technical advice to develop solutions that will allow them to achieve partner certification. Zeta, Alpha, and Omega use this program and build an inter-organizational network where they draw from each other's knowledge.

The formal relations in the interorganizational network are mostly made up by partners and less by customers. They have entered a number of partnerships and close alliances. Their first mutual links are created with the launch of Alpha's primary product. Alpha becomes a registered partner, which eases their customization of Zeta's CRM solution. This is beneficial for Zeta, which gets its product promoted through an increase of its business value. The partnership with Zeta is advantageous for Alpha, but initially far from as profitable as their relation to Omega. Their shared aims and strategic cooperation have been decisive for both partners' success on the CRM market through the creation of Alpha's first product.

Alpha's cooperation with Zeta on the CRM product exhibits a shared destiny based on both companies' mutual dependency (Harland 1996). Alpha's product development also leads to partnerships with two of Zeta's Danish CRM vendors. Alpha has entered these relationships to secure an increased sale of licenses for their products, which are distributed through these two partners. The partnerships are primarily a sales channel. In a similar way, Alpha has a relationship to the Zeta partner and U.S. distributor Delta, which is limited to their first product. Delta has been interested in the product and opens the US market for them.

Alpha forms a partnership with Gamma to satisfy the company's need for more competent staff who are sourced from Pakistan. The partnership forms a reciprocal dependency and can be considered as shared destiny where both partners have an interest in a mutual progress. Alpha finally merges with Omega, strengthening the organizations' positions in their individual networks. This is an important strategic reason for a merger (Harland 1996).

Alpha has, with Omega's support, created strong personal links to some Zeta employees. The company's sales manager, who has been a Zeta employee, has contributed and created a number of informal relations and commitments which Alpha carefully nurtures; for example, they are committed to providing technical help in situations where Zeta employees are not able to solve tasks themselves. This facilitates easier access to different kinds of information (Coleman 1988) and, for Alpha, their personal links to Zeta employees means that they no longer need to go through bureaucratic information channels, but can contact the relevant people when they need knowledge about certain things in the development process, thus building their core competencies about the CRM product.

Alpha's social structures with other organizations are strongly marked by the informal relations and personal bonds to Omega. Omega has been an important source of information and provided free advice to Alpha in its start-up phase concerning business and customer needs, and Alpha helped Omega to overcome technical problems with their CRM product. They thus strengthened their mutual trust to pool resources, knowledge, and competence. This has increased the social capital between the two organizations and decreased the need for formal rules and regulations in their cooperation.

Informal agreements typify social structures and it is difficult to identify the unwritten laws that define cooperation (Coleman 1988). Alpha's founders felt that they had to earn Zeta personnel's trust by rendering themselves visible by conference attendance. They also felt that they had to constantly meet Zeta employees' expectations. By satisfying these expectations, they are in a stronger position than other Zeta partners as they can better source technical information. These activities point to a social norm where a partner profits from the unwritten rule that its activity is rewarded in the form of easy access to product information.

Trusted relationships have been identified by Ågerfalk and Fitzgerald (2008) as a premise for open sourcing as a particular form of open innovation. A broad innovation network, as in our case, with many partners in many forms of relations carries the risk of superficial, insufficient trust; still, it is considered as having the best potential for innovation by Simard and West (2006). We find a network where the central partners evidently found the right level of trust.

In the relationship between Zeta and Alpha, we discover some examples for coopetive behavior. Zeta has defined the boundary between cooperation and competition, where opportunistic behavior might appear, in a formal, written contract that provides both sides with some certainty. Alpha is placed under these rules which determine the parts of the software they are allowed to customize and change in the original product. However, no formal agreement exists which describes what Alpha can customize to avoid Zeta copying their customized solution, a serious problem in open innovation environments (Graham and Mowery 2006). Only an informal agreement exists that Zeta try to avoid updating their software with identical solutions already developed by Alpha. Zeta's attempt to not immediately develop matching solutions is essential for Alpha's survival and creates some trust, which characterizes informal contracts (Ganguli 2007). Still, most of Alpha's products have a life span of 18 to 24 months so they are pushed to constantly develop new innovative customizations. Simultaneously, Zeta expects that Alpha will promote Zeta's products and contributes to Zeta's good reputation as a brand.

Opportunistic behavior and the right balance is thus a predicament for the relationship of Zeta and Alpha. Zeta does not always stay within the limits of their

Table 3. Characteristics of Open Innovation in the Case

Open Innovation	
Idea and Knowledge Flow	Coupled Process—outside-in/inside-out
Knowledge Sharing Opportunities	Developer communities conferences Online developer forums
Product Access and Flow	Access (e.g., through beta tests)
Development Context	Flexible product architecture
Partner Search	Proactive search for partners Technical counseling for non-certified partners
Inducements	Spin-off support Cheap partner program Partner solutions promotion on company page

announced changes when they update the original product. This creates a challenge as Alpha has to put extra effort into their customized solutions. Alpha is aware of this risk, but does not feel negative about the situation. They accept it as they are conscious of the power balance that exists when they customize a larger software producer's product and see this as a part of their living conditions. Alpha also has a dilemma: deficiencies in the CRM product are opportunities for new customized solutions, which are the basis for their business. Thus, at times they delay and limit their feedback about the product which Zeta asks for before they release a new version to customers. However, given the power balance, mutual opportunistic behavior will have more serious consequences for Alpha; thus, cooperation prevails. The results of our analysis are summarized in Tables 3 and 4.

Table 4. Findings Related to the Interorganizational Open Innovation Network in the Case

Interorganizational Networks		
Formal Relations	**Informal Relations and Social Capital**	**Coopetition and Opportunistic Behavior**
Mostly formal partnerships Product life: Alpha/ Zeta partners (Delta and other CRM vendors) Shared destiny: Zeta/ Alpha/Gamma Strategic alliance: Alpha/Omega Merger/Acquisition: Alpha Omega Market: Customers	Commitments, trust, performance of favors • Alpha/Omega/Zeta: Personal, trusting relationships based on friendly turns Admission to less accessible information • Alpha/Omega: Omega staff provides information about customer and business needs • Alpha/Zeta: Zeta staff provides access to product information Norms and sanctions • Alpha/Zeta: Continuous proof of worthiness of Zeta's staff trust	Close integration/open innovation process Rules/caring for cooperation • Formal contract • Defined scope of customization/ innovation Rules are broken • Updates and compatibility • Copying of solutions • Limiting feedback on functionality in original product

6 Conclusions

Most research on open innovation focuses on the firm (Grøtnes 2009) and research on interorganizational networks has either investigated regional innovation networks or network characteristics (Vanhaverbeke 2006; Vanhaverbeke and Cloodt 2006) from the perspective of one firm with the notable exception of Grøtnes (2009), who has studied the phenomenon in the neutral arena of standardization outside a firm.

Despite the fact that results from single case studies are not generalizable, we contribute to the development of a theory of open IT innovation with a theoretical framework that integrates formally separate aspects of open innovation and interorganizational networks. We extend the literature on open innovation as an interorganizational phenomenon by broadening the view from one focal firm to the relations in a network of companies that mutually contribute to the innovations which occur in the different companies.

This research presents and analyzes an empirically grounded account of open innovation in the IT industry. We confirm and convincingly demonstrate that initiatives such as proactive search for new partners, providing occasions for developers to share knowledge and build communities, affording a suitable development context and an accommodating product architecture, as well as making inducements available in the form of financial support and promoting innovation partners (Chesbrough 2003; Simard and West 2006; Vanhaverbeke and Cloodt 2006; von Hippel 2005) are all schemes that successfully support open innovation undertakings.

We also substantiate that interorganizational networks have a significant influence on open innovation processes of the cooperating organizations (Vanhaverbeke 2006). Extending the investigation of the formal relations with the analysis of the informal relations is a contribution of our work. The network in our case primarily builds on formal partnerships with a number of different companies, but the informal relations are invaluable sources of knowledge. We thus recommend that companies involved in open innovation should support and nurture the informal relations of their employees both within and beyond organizational boundaries.

We find an extensive network with numerous collaborators in various relations. In line with Simard and West (2006), we corroborate this as one viable strategy in open IT innovation. We also find a network in which, despite formal contracts, opportunistic behavior occurs, influencing the case companies' interorganizational innovation processes. Because of the limited life of its products, the smaller company constantly seeks and collaborates with new partners which provide information about new business opportunities. This enables the company to continuously further develop their solution to be one step in front of the original software producer. A last lesson from our case is, therefore, to monitor the balance of formal contracts, informal relations, and opportunistic behavior, and to intervene, if necessary, to not jeopardize otherwise supportive open innovation initiatives.

As we have only studied one particular instance of an open innovation in an interorganizational network, further research is needed to confirm our results and understand and support other forms of the phenomenon.

References

Ågerfalk, P., Fitzgerald, B.: Outsourcing to an Unknown Workforce: Exploring Opensourcing as a Global Sourcing Strategy. MIS Quarterly 32(2), 385–410 (2008)

Chesbrough, H.: Open Innovation: A New Paradigm for Understanding Industrial Innovation. In: Chesbrough, H., Vanhaverbeke, W., West, J. (eds.) Open Innovation: Researching a New Paradigm, pp. 1–14. Oxford University Press, Oxford (2006)

Chesbrough, H.: Open Innovation: The New Imperative for Creating and Profiting from Technology. Harvard Business School Publishing, Boston (2003)

Coleman, J.S.: Social Capital in the Creation of Human Capital. American J. of Sociology 94(6), 95–120 (1988)

Creswell, J.W.: Research Design–Qualitative, Quantitative and Mixed Methods Approaches. Sage Publications, Thousand Oaks (2003)

Dyer, J.H., Singh, H.: The Relational View: Cooperative Strategy and Sources of Interorganizational Competitive Advantage. Academy of Management Review 23, 660–679 (1998)

Eisenhardt, K.M.: Building Theories from Case Study Research. Academy of Management Review 14(4), 532–550 (1989)

Feller, J., Finnegan, P., Hayes, J., O'Reilly, P.: Institutionalizing Information Asymmetry: Governance Structures for Open Innovation. Information Technology & People 22(4), 297–316 (2009)

Fincham, R.: Narratives of Success and Failure in Systems Development. Brit. J. of Management 13, 1–14 (2002)

Ganguli, S.: Coopetition Models in the Context of Modern Business. J. of Marketing Management 6, 4 (2007)

Gassmann, O., Enkel, E.: Towards a Theory of Open Innovation: Three Core Process Archetypes. In: Proceedings of The R&D Management Conference, Lisbon, Portugal, July 6-9 (2004)

Germonprez, M., Hovorka, D.S., Collopy, F.: A Theory of Tailorable Technology Design. JAIS 8, art. 21, 351–367 (2007)

Graham, S.J.H., Mowery, D.C.: The Use of Intellectual Property in Software: Implications for Open Innovation. In: Chesbrough, H., Vanhaverbeke, W., West, J. (eds.) Open Innovation: Researching a New Paradigm, pp. 184–204. Oxford University Press, Oxford (2006)

Grøtnes, E.: Standardization as Open Innovation: Two Cases from the Mobile Industry. Information Technology & People 22(4), 367–381 (2009)

Håkansson, H., Snehota, I.: Developing Relationships in Business Networks. Routledge, New York (1995)

Harland, C.M.: Supply Chain Management: Relationships, Chains and Networks. Brit. J. of Management 7, 63–80 (1996)

Kautz, K., Serrano, G.L., Barbolla, A.B., Corredera, J.R.C.: Guest Editorial Special Issue on Open IT-Based InnovationCMoving Towards Cooperative IT Transfer and Knowledge Diffusion. Information Technology & People 22(4), 293–296 (2009)

Kuitunen, H., Jokinen, J.-P., Lassila, A., Mäkelä, M., Huurinainen, P., Maula, M., Ahokas, M., Kontio, J.: Finnish Software Product Business: Results from the National Software Industry Survey 2005. Centre of Expertise for Software Product Business, Tekes, Helsinki, Finland (2005)

Light, B.: The Maintenance Implications of the Customization of ERP Software. J. of Software Maintenance and Evolution: Research and Practice 13, 415–429 (2001)

Pollock, N., Williams, R., Procter, R.: Fitting Standard Software Packages to Non-Standard Organizations: The 'Biography' of an Enterprise-Wide System. Technology Analysis and Strategic Management 15(3), 317–332 (2003)

Sawyer, S.: Packaged Software: Implications of the Differences from Custom Approaches to Software Development. European J. of Information Systems 9, 47–58 (2000)

Scott, J.E., Kaindl, L.: Enhancing Functionality in Enterprise Software Package. Information and Management 7, 111–122 (2000)

Simard, C., West, J.: Knowledge Networks and the Geographic Locus of Innovation. In: Chesbrough, H., Vanhaverbeke, W., West, J. (eds.) Open Innovation: Researching a New Paradigm, pp. 220–240. Oxford University Press, Oxford (2006)

Van de Ven, A.H.: Engaged Scholarship: A Guide for Organizational and Social Research. Oxford University Press, New York (2007)

Vanhaverbeke, W.: The Interorganizational Context of Open Innovation. In: Chesbrough, H., Vanhaverbeke, W., West, J. (eds.) Open Innovation: Researching a New Paradigm, pp. 205–219. Oxford University Press, Oxford (2006)

Vanhaverbeke, W., Cloodt, M.: Open Innovation in Value Networks. In: Chesbrough, H., Vanhaverbeke, W., West, J. (eds.) Open Innovation: Researching a New Paradigm, pp. 258–284. Oxford University Press, Oxford (2006)

von Hippel, E.: Cooperation between Rivals: Informal Knowhow Trading. Research Policy 16(6), 291–302 (1987)

von Hippel, E.: Democratizing Innovation. MIT Press, Cambridge (2005)

Walsham, G.: Interpretive Case Studies in IS Research: Nature and Method. European J. of Information Systems 4, 74–81 (1995)

West, J., Gallagher, S.: Patterns of Open Innovation in Open Source Software. In: Chesbrough, H., Vanhaverbeke, W., West, J. (eds.) Open Innovation: Researching a New Paradigm, pp. 82–108. Oxford University Press, Oxford (2006)

Williamson, O.E.: Comparative Economic Organization: The Analysis of Discrete Structural Alternatives. Administrative Science Quarterly 37(2), 269–296 (1991)

Yoo, Y., Lyytinen, K., Boland, R.J.: Distributed Innovation in Classes of Networks. In: Proceedings of the 41st Annual Hawaii International Conference on System Sciences (2008)

About the Authors

Karlheinz Kautz is Professor in Systems Development and Software Engineering at the Department for Informatics at Copenhagen Business School. His research interests are in the diffusion and adoption of information technology innovations, systems development and system development methodologies for advanced application areas, the organizational impact of IT, knowledge management and software quality and process improvement. He has published widely in these areas. Karl is a founding member and past Chairman of the IFIP TC 8 WG 8.6 on the adoption and diffusion of IT.

Deborah Bunker is an associate professor in the Business Information Systems discipline at the University of Sydney. She is also president of the Australasian Association of IS and vice chair of IFIP Working Group 8.6 (Innovation, Diffusion, Transfer and Implementation of IS). She holds a Ph.D. in Information Systems Management. Her research interests are in IS philosophy, IS management, IS adoption and diffusion, and e-Commerce/e-Business. She has published widely in these areas.

Sameen M. Rab has been a student for the degree of Computer Science and Business Administration at Copenhagen Business School and has been a researcher for the project, which builds the basis for the research described here.

Michael Sinnet has been a student for the degree of Computer Science and Business Administration at Copenhagen Business School and has been a researcher for the project, which builds the basis for the research described here.

Section 6. The Future of Critical Realism in IS Research

Systems of Innovation, Multidisciplinarity, and Methodological Pluralism: A Realist Approach to Guide the Future of Information Systems Research and Practice

Arturo Vega[1] and David Brown[2]

[1] Canterbury Christ Church University, Canterbury, United Kingdom
arturo.vega@canterbury.ac.uk
[2] Lancaster University Management School, Lancaster, United Kingdom
d.brown@lancaster.ac.uk

Abstract. Information systems (IS) are complex phenomena. For instance, the diffusion of IS in small and medium enterprises (SMEs) depends on various levels of networked, localized, and changing determinants, such as the ones related to the adopter organizations, decision makers, technologies, complementary innovations, business partners, professional groups, universities, and government policies. This complex view of IS implies the use of different disciplines and methodologies to study the diffusion process. The objective of this empirical research is to demonstrate how the systems of innovation approach (SIA), for addressing the institutional and evolutionary determinants of diffusion, and the philosophical stance of critical realism (CR), for guiding the research process, are compatible and meet the multidisciplinarity and methodological pluralism required to move on the field of complex IS and recommend meaningful actions to practice. To exemplify our arguments, we focus the study on one relevant determinant that affects the diffusion of IS in SMEs, namely government programs.

Keywords: Information systems research and practice, systems of innovation approach, critical realism, multidisciplinarity, methodological pluralism, information systems and SME policies.

1 Introduction

There has been strong criticism regarding the low impact of the research produced by the IS community. For example, Hirschheim and Klein (2003) argued that mainstream IS research does not address relevant topics and its results are not usable for practitioners. A related debate in the IS research community concerns the core of the IS discipline. Benbasat and Zmud (2003) proposed that the core is the information technology artifact. Alter (2003) went further, suggesting that the core should be the systems in organizations. In general, the acceptance of the existence of a core implies narrowing the IS field to fundamental concepts. Conversely, the position of Myers (2003) is that the IS field is far from ready to define a core. Myers argues that the core has been modified many times given the rapidly changing environment of the field,

M. Chiasson et al. (Eds.): Future IS 2011, IFIP AICT 356, pp. 249–268, 2011.

and that a concrete core would not consider research that has proved to be extremely valuable, for example information economics (e.g., Bakos and Kemerer 1992) and IS research on institutions (e.g., King et al. 1994; Robey and Boudreau 1999), industries (e.g., Crowston et al. 2001), and countries (e.g., Ein-Dor et al. 1997; Watson and Myers 2001). We completely agree with Myers' view.

Accordingly, the diffusion of IS in SMEs is a complex process that requires the coordinated activity of numerous participants far beyond the adopter organization (Vega et al. 2008, 2010b), as well as the adoption of complementary innovations by many of these participants (Vega et al. 2010a). A simplified example is an SME that operates in the human resource sector and wants to adopt a transactional website to serve employers and applicants. Clearly, the success of the SME will depend on the adoption of this system by employers and applicants. The SME will also depend on its initial adoption of broadband and the availability of the system in application service provider technology. The owner-manager of the SME might need the assistance of several public programs to accomplish all stages of the adoption process, for instance for the selection of the system, technologies, and providers, for the design of a marketing plan to launch the website, and to get soft funding for the entire process. Moreover, program organizations will depend on external factors that are determined in the policy system in order to deliver proper services to SMEs, such as the evaluation mechanisms and the access to resources determined by the funding bodies at the highest levels of public governance. Noticeably, this hypothetical scenario differs depending on the location of the participants. For example, the providers of broadband could be reluctant to operate in isolated regions. Finally, the scenario should also change over time. For instance, the owner-manager could learn about marketing after taking a course in a university.

However, mainstream IS research has basically focused on the accounting of discrete factors of the organization and micro-environment that directly impact the adoption in the SMEs (e.g., Chitura et al. 2008; Fichman 2004; Jeyaraj et al. 2006; Parker and Castleman 2007; Williams et al. 2009). For example, the characteristics of the SME, the decision maker, the IS, customer power, and competitor initiatives. Fichman (2004, p. 315) described this predominance as the "dominant paradigm" and the "economic-rationalistic model." Accordingly, Chitura et al. (2004, p. 1) concluded that "researchers should stop reinventing the list of adoption barriers but instead focus their efforts on how SMEs can overcome these barriers."

Under this context, we argue that the diffusion of IS in SMEs should be researched using the SIA in order to explain the institutional and evolutionary complexity that goes much further than the organization and its micro-environment. Similarly, it would be productive to study the diffusion of IS in SMEs using the deep ontological perspective of CR to guide every iteration of the research process. As we will demonstrate, the compatibility between the SIA and CR stresses the need of using multiple disciplines and methodologies with the aim of researching complex IS in a comprehensive way and improving the value given to practitioners. In general terms, we postulate an end-to-end research approach to address the practical problems and opportunities of IS phenomena. In our view, mainstream IS research is limited in many cases and represents only the initial stage of a research process.

The SIA has been expressly and properly applied very few times to study the diffusion of IS. For example, Mansell and Wehn (1998) addressed the diffusion of IS in developing countries. They called for tailored strategies depending on national or regional technological strengths and development priorities. They gave recommendations mostly concentrating on the supply side. Oyelaran-Oyeyinka and Lal (2006) did a cross-country comparison in the export sector to develop a typology of SMEs based on technological and learning capabilities. They identified systemic determinants and potential interventions for the internationalization and take-up of IS by SMEs. Finally, the work of Vega et al. (2008, 2010a, 2010b) attempts to emphasize the relevance of the SIA in IS diffusion, exemplifying this with case studies of IS adoption by SMEs, explaining a series of systemic barriers affecting the adoptions, and recommending interventions in the system with the aim of improving the coordinated work of its parts and ultimately the diffusion process.

Although slowly increasing, the use of CR in the IS literature is very limited. Radically, Carlsson (2005, p. 97) stated that "CR is almost invisible in the IS field." Similarly, Dobson et al. (2007, p. 138) said that there is a "dearth of practical examples of research in the area." In general terms, we could classify the CR works in IS into three groups. The first are the calls to the IS research community to realize the underlaborer value of CR in IS research (e.g., Carlsson 2004; Dobson 2001; Mingers 2004; Mutch 2002; Smith 2006). Most of these works have been conceptual discussions on how CR can overcome the inconsistencies of the positivist, interpretivist, and postmodernist research practices. The second group is composed of conceptual discussions about the appropriateness of CR to study specific IS topics such as IS evaluation (Carlsson 2003), IS design (Carlsson 2005), organizational use of information (Mutch 1999), IS functions to address operational risks (Rotaru et al. 2009), and information seeking behavior (Wikgren 2005). The third are basic empirical attempts to use CR in order to show its suitability to research particular IS issues, for example the implementation of IS (Dobson et al. 2007), IS investment decisions (Fox 2009), the life cycle of strategic IS plans (Morton 2006), and the perception of users on the impact of IS on practice (Oroviogoicochea and Watson 2009). Most of the explanations and usage of CR in IS has been at the organizational level.

There were also few efforts to connect the SIA and CR from a generic perspective (e.g., Castellacci 2006; Iliev 2005), and not in terms of IS. Basically, the discussion has centered on the critics of CR proponents to the reduction of the reality and the simplistic research approach used in neoclassical economics to study industrial development. There is also recognition of the relevance of heterodox economics as a pillar of the SIA. However, a core conclusion is that there has been a simultaneous coexistence and tension between the diverse philosophical assumptions declared by SIA scholars, which has been caused in large part by a lack of clarity of the SIA concepts. This controversy has proved to be counterproductive for the development of the field. However, CR resolves this divergence and provides a solid grounding to the SIA research practice.

This paper addresses the application of the SIA and CR on complex IS. We focus on one highly relevant determinant of the system of innovation for the diffusion of IS in SMEs, namely government programs (e.g., Berkeley et al. 1996; Cuadrado and Garcia 2004; Gengatharen et al. 2005; Lebre 1995; Simpson and Docherty 2004). Importantly, there is a general concern regarding the quality of the government support to SME innovation (Johnson 2005; Martin and Matlay 2001; Mole 2002; Nugent and Yhee 2002). The topic is even more relevant if we consider that our empirical work demonstrated that there is a negative and enduring context affecting programs. This comprehensive research inquires from the micro aspects of IS innovation in SME organizations to the macro structures in the policy system. The paper starts with a revision of the foundations of the SIA and CR. We continue with an explanation of how CR solves some deficiencies in the SIA research practice, as well as the conceptual commonalities between them. We then explicate the aim, theories, research design, and findings of each level of our empirical research process. We conclude by summarizing the correspondence between the IS phenomenon under study and the systemic and realist perspectives, as well as defining a roadmap for the future research of complex IS.

2   Systems of Innovation Approach

The SIA (see Freeman 1987; Lundvall 1992; Nelson 1993) was developed under the foundation of innovation research and institutional and evolutionary economics (e.g., Lundvall and Borras 2005). In addition, it is related to general systems theory (e.g., Edquist 2005). The SIA is a conceptual device, which includes "all important economic, social, political, organizational, institutional, and other factors that influence the development, diffusion, and use of innovations"(Edquist 1997, p. 14). From a dynamics perspective, the SIA defines innovation as an open, interactive, and non-linear learning process (Lundvall 1992), which is affected by the capabilities (e.g., laws, common practices, power distribution, and trust) and accumulated knowledge in communities, business networks, and organizations (Asheim and Isaken 2000). Reciprocally, the capabilities and accumulated knowledge change locally as a result of learning trajectories, which are driven by societal actors (Asheim and Isaken 2000). Thus all this complexity creates uncertainty around innovation activities (e.g., Meyer et al. 2006). Finally, private or public interventions should be based on the detection of visible problems and the subsequent identification of causal explanations at any part of the system, namely system failures (Edquist 2002, 2008). System failures can occur given the inappropriateness or missing of activities, actors, institutions, or linkages (Edquist 2002, 2008). The activities are the factors that influence innovation, the actors are the individuals or organizations that perform the activities, the institutions determine the capabilities to carry out activities, and the linkages are the connections between activities, actors, and institutions.

3   Critical Realism

CR (see Archer et al. 2001; Bhaskar 1989; Danermark et al. 2001; Sayer 1992) was developed based on the general philosophy of science called transcendental realism (Bhaskar 1997) and the more specific human science philosophy named critical naturalism (Bhaskar 1998). Basically, CR states that there is a concrete and mind-independent reality that has real consequences on the perceptive and cognitive functions of social actors. It means that CR is a compromise between the two extreme philosophical positions, namely positivism and interpretivism (e.g., Easterby-Smith et al. 2008). For critical realists, the world operates at multiple levels, and each level has the capacity to affect other levels in diverse and localized ways (Archer 1995; Bhaskar 1997). For example, an individual can be affected by the characteristics of the organization in which he or she works, the organization can be affected by its industrial sector, and all of them can be affected by the regional policy system, the national culture, and the global economy. Also, the real world is open and changes relatively fast given human agency in the reproduction and transformation of social structures and causal mechanisms (Archer 1995; Bhaskar 1998). Given this complexity, both the knowledge-creation process and research become on-going and time-dependent activities. Consequently, in order to explain and control the tendencies of events in the social world, we have to understand the underlying processes of often temporal, counteracting, and contingently related structures and mechanisms that give rise to these events. According to Pawson and Tilley(1997), there are mechanisms that cause problems in a social setting and mechanisms that can be applied to block or neutralize the problems.

4 The SIA Research Practice and CR

The SIA places the object of study (i.e., innovation processes) at the center of focus (e.g., Edquist 1997, 2005; Lundvall 1992), leaving methodologies and techniques open to the pragmatic criteria of researchers (Iliev 2005). Certainly, we have not identified any substantial philosophical discussion among SIA scholars in order to guide their methodological choices. While the commitment to methodological pluralism is positive, it has a negative connotation if we consider that the conceptual base of the SIA is still evolving and confusion exists about some of its components (e.g., Edquist 2005; Radosevic 1998).

For instance, it is up to the researcher to decide the boundaries of a system, which could be as diverse as the country, the region, the sector, the technology, or a mix of them (e.g., Edquist 1997, 2005). Another example is multiple definitions of institutions, which for some researchers could mean brick-and-mortar organizations such as government departments and industry associations and for others softer aspects such as national culture and social norms (e.g., Edquist 2005; Radosevic 1998). As a result, SIA researchers have been presenting very different, too descriptive, and superficial accounts of the systems, probably based on their personal preferences on specific methodologies and theories, as well as the limitations to access more diverse data.

Whereas the choice of SIA researchers to address different aspects of the systems could be considered specific entry points to the innovation processes under investigation (Hommen and Edquist 2008), excessively superficial descriptions are a serious constraint to properly explain innovation processes (Radosevic 1998) as well as to determine system failures and formulate relevant advice for practitioners. Against this situation, the adoption of the CR paradigm allows the reconciliation of a variety of systems given the identification of the underlying causal mechanisms that generate and integrate them (Iliev 2005). For this reason, the focus of research should be on deeper structures and mechanisms using multiple methodologies more than accounting the visible and discrete factors that directly affect innovation processes.

In fact, CR can act as a disciplining device and underlaborer of SIA research efforts. However, before claiming this, we have to be sure that the SIA and CR are compatible in terms of more fundamental and comprehensive concepts. The next section explains this compatibility and reinforces the arguments presented here about the role of CR to address some deficiencies of the SIA's research practice.

5 Similarities and Gaps

The pragmatic and *ad hoc* attempts to define an ontological foundation to the SIA have been divergent. However, we can appreciate that the conceptual base of the SIA strongly supports the view of the adequacy of CR as a general ontological framework to explain innovation processes. Basically, an innovation process is complex because it depends on a stratified and intricate array of determinants. Adding to this difficulty, an innovation process is dynamic, given the openness of its causal constituents and the transforming effect of human activity. An innovation process is also localized because of the contained character of the factors affecting the process. Finally, there is correspondence between the definitions of system failures and interventions of the SIA (Edquist 2002, 2008) and the problematic and corrective mechanisms of CR (Pawson and Tilley 1997).

SIA researchers have been making restrictive and varying choices to study innovation processes. From the epistemological perspective, there are concepts of the SIA and CR that are compatible. However, there are missing concepts in the SIA framework which can be supplied by CR in order to guide and improve its research practice. We turn next to explain four aspects that support this view.

5.1 Focus of Study

Both the SIA and CR are expressly committed to research the underlying generative structures and mechanisms (e.g., system of activities, actors, institutions, and linkages) that determine the surface events (e.g., innovation outcomes). The imperative is to go to deeper levels by searching the processes that provoked the observed evidence. Therefore, the aim of research is to identify the root complexity of the object of study as a means to recommend strategic actions to practitioners in order to improve social conditions.

5.2 Research Approach

The SIA and CR need a starting point for analysis. Lawson (1997) calls the partial regularity of an observable event which at first sight indicates the occasional, but less-than-universal, state of generative processes over a specific time and space, demi-regularity. The SIA uses appreciative theorizing (Nelson and Winter 1982) to explain innovation processes through theoretical abstract reasoning. This approach focuses on relevant points of entry to the innovation processes under investigation (Hommen and Edquist 2008, p. 445) with the aim of producing typological theory. This kind of explanations is idiosyncratic but developed in terms of general variables (Christensen 2006). Typological theory enables practitioners to make discriminating diagnoses under emerging situations (George 1979; Hommen and Edquist 2008). However, the SIA does not expressly specified how to become immersed in the different levels of systems in order to explain the underlying determinants or system failures affecting innovation processes. In contrast, CR scholars name retroduction to the movement from the observable events to the buried generative processes (Sayer 1992).

5.3 Multidisciplinarity

According to the SIA and CR, reality is driven by networked, stratified, and open systems. Therefore, the social realm is an intricate, interconnected whole. As a consequence, the explanation of innovation processes necessarily requires an understanding of the formation and simultaneous effects of different interacting determinants, which can be constitutive elements of different disciplines. For example, psychology and business studies are relevant at the company level. Microeconomics and network theories explain much sector behavior. Similarly, institutions and political science deal with aspects at higher levels of society.

5.4 Methodological Pluralism

Both the SIA and CR focus on objects of study (e.g., innovation processes) instead of a methodology of study. Accordingly, SIA researchers have used diverse methodologies based on a variety of entry points to systems. However, as many individual researchers may have been biased in terms of points of entry and levels of analysis, their studies have used mono-methodologies. CR can contribute to overcoming this undesired research practice. If the metatheoretical stance of CR were the guide for the whole research process, the selection of data collection and analytical methods would be based on a deep ontological perspective. This implies that a study could employ various methods, derived from various ontological assumptions of the parts of the innovation process under investigation.

6 The Diffusion of IS in SMEs and Public Programs

This section explains the aim, theories, research design, and findings of each stage of the research process. The research on IS diffusion in SMEs should begin with the detection of the factors that affect the diffusion in a particular context. The context could include a specific IS, companies of a specific size, a sector of the economy, and a particular region—for example, the diffusion of transactional websites for employers and applicants in the small enterprises of the human resource sector in the northeast of England. This could be done using surveys and statistical analysis, as well as employing widely used theories in the IS field such as the diffusion of innovations (Rogers 2003), the technology acceptance model (Davis et al. 1989), or the absorptive capacity (Zahra and George 2002). As a finding of this exercise, we could determine several barriers affecting diffusion, for instance the knowledge to select the system, technologies, and providers, the knowledge to design a marketing plan to launch the website, or the lack of funding. As mentioned, this kind of research represents in many cases the entire research done on the diffusion of IS in SMEs. We argue that this approach is an excellent way to define important demi-regularities or entry points to guide the research, but it must not be the final objective.

Alternatively, the research approach should try to find underlying causes and determine potential initiatives at any part of the system in order to accomplish the ultimate objective, namely, the massive and proper diffusion of IS in SMEs. This kind of research approach takes several stages in order to address every level affecting the diffusion process, with each stage guiding the next in a retroductive way. As an illustrative example, we will focus on the public programs that support IS innovation in SMEs. These programs are aimed at overcoming many of the diffusion barriers detected at the beginning of the research process, such as any lack of knowledge in the SMEs. We start with an exploration with the purpose of identifying a deeper and relevant demi-regularity (i.e., the poor assistance to IS initiatives in SMEs). After this, we address the issue of discretion at the program implementation level. Then we develop a typology of program contexts in order to explain the choice of goals of their workers and the potential for success in terms of service quality and evaluative targets. Finally, we exemplify the numerous systemic issues to better explain the underlying structures and mechanisms affecting programs and, consequently, the diffusion of IS in SMEs.

6.1 Exploration

The aim of the exploration was to define the specific research topic and questions. At this stage, the research approach was purely inductive and based on three organizations delivering public assistance to IS adoption in SMEs. We conducted unstructured interviews with the program managers and read secondary data about the programs, the policy system around the programs, and a few of their interventions. We appreciated that some contextual aspects could have negatively influenced both programs and SMEs, including the excessive discretion of program workers, poor evaluation mechanisms, scarcity of resources, low demand for program services, and the complex characteristics of the adoptions that were assisted. As most of these aspects are determined in the system, and not within program organizations, we suspect that these conditions are common and enduring. For these reasons, we considered a relevant demi-regularity to the potential poor assistance of this kind of program. This caused the research on IS diffusion in SMEs to go deeper into the system as suggested by the realist approach to program evaluation (e.g., Henry et al. 1998; Kazi 2003; Pawson and Tilley 1997). The consequent research questions were as follows:

- What is the nature of program interventions?
- What are the nature and consequences of program contexts?
- How could program contexts be improved?

6.2 Nature of Program Interventions

This stage of the research addressed a long-standing debate in the political science and public administration fields, namely the existence and effect of discretion at policy implementation. On the one hand, we have the view of the defenders of the existence of discretion (e.g., Ellis et al. 1999; Lindblom and Woodhouse 1993; Lipsky 1980; Long 1999; Maynard-Moody and Musheno 2003). Basically, they argue that discretion has its origins in the political decisions at the highest levels of government, the dependency of policy makers and program managers on program worker activity, as well as poorly defined goals, policies, and procedures. In this situation, public policies tend to be made as much by program workers as by policy makers. On the other hand, we have the view of the advocates of a shift in power in favor of policy makers and managers over bureaucrats (i.e., the new managerialism stance) (e.g., Clarke and Newman 1997; Howe 1991; Jones 1999; Langan 2000). New managerialism sees a change in the distribution of power as having occurred because of the centralization of strategic political direction and the inclusion of competition in the delivery of services. This demanding structure would have generated a drastic cultural change in terms of supervision and management responsibilities.

We initially used a deductive approach based on the replication of six case studies (Yin 2009) of program assistance and on the pattern matching analytical method (Trochim 1989). In doing so, we discarded soon the reductionist stance because excessive discretion was present in practically all of the cases. For example, instead of delivering high-level knowledge transfer from academics in a computing department to IT SMEs, a program delivered traditional IS services using third-party service providers to a non-IT SME. After that, we went deeper into the context with the purpose of understanding the underlying causes that gave rise to excessive discretion. Our findings are illustrated in Figure 1.

We defined three levels of activity in order to differentiate the macro and micro ambits of contextual influence (Archer 1995). The first level is the political, which is characterized for the decisions of policy makers at the highest levels of governance (e.g., European Union, national government, and regional authorities). The second level is operational. Here, the political ideology defined at the first level is materialized by funding bodies, auditors, program managers, and program workers. The third level is the street level. Program workers exert discretion when implementing innovation policies, which is permitted by the context initially outlined by policy makers and then realized by the actors of level two.

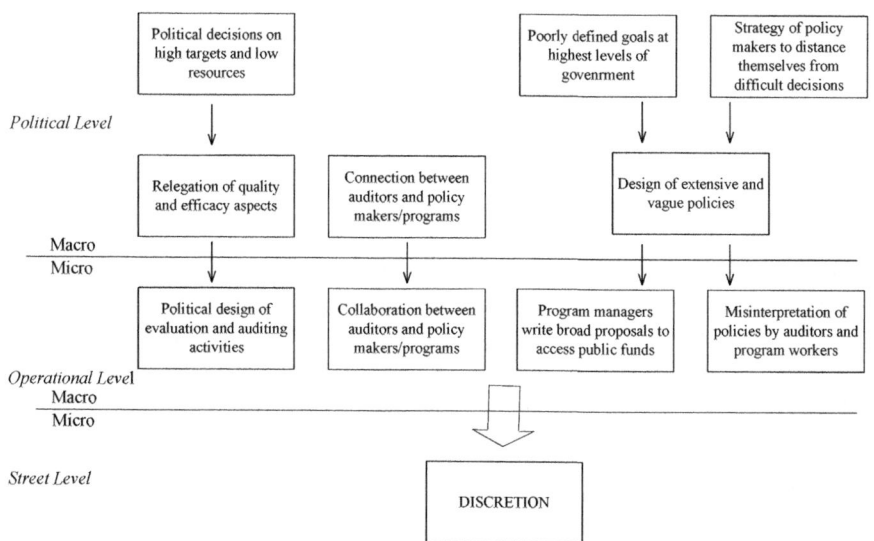

Fig. 1. Contextual Influence on Discretion

In principle, there is a policy-making imperative of delivering a high quantity of services but being very efficient in the use of resources (e.g., Lewis and Glennester 1996). In this situation, the quality and efficacy of the services would be relegated to a secondary level of relevance. Accordingly, the evaluation and auditing activities were designed to focus on politically relevant issues. For example, a typical indicator was the ratio between funding and SMEs assisted. Another probable cause for discretion is the bottom-up collaboration of auditors with policy makers and programs (e.g., Storey 2006). Basically, funding bodies commissioned the administration of the deployment of funds, including program auditing and control, to organizations with important roles in designing the policies or that were connected to the program organizations; for instance, a university association audited the programs implemented by their members.

Discretion could also be facilitated from top to bottom if the fact that some policy statements were very extensive and vague is taken into account; for example, one long policy had many contradictory statements, including the extremes of "advanced research and development and knowledge transfer" and "websites." This could be a consequence of poorly defined goals at the highest levels of government (e.g., Hasenfeld and English 1974). Policy makers could also use broad policies as a strategy to distance themselves from the consequences of the decisions to balance demand, needs, and resources (e.g., Wells 1997). We found evidence that the broadness in policy definition was exploited by program organizations to formalize discretion when they wrote broad proposals for the selection process to access public funds. Finally, another risk is that auditors and program workers could misinterpret the numerous and unclear phrases of the policies, which could have allowed public interventions to escape even broad policy statements (e.g., Lewis and Glennerster 1996).

Given the excessive discretion identified in the cases, it is important to research in detail the work context and potentially competing priorities of program workers.

6.3 Nature and Consequences of Program Contexts

The aim of this level of the research was to explain the macro context and its causal powers (Archer 1995) to the performance of public programs. This stage of the study was based on a collective structure (Stake 2005) of six case studies of program assistance and the abductive analytical method (Bergene 2007; Danermark et al. 2001). The collective structure required the selection of a varied and balanced group of cases that were believed to offer the greatest potential to learn and develop theoretical constructs, for example, cases with program organizations with different operating structures, programs funded by different funding bodies and offering different types of services, as well as assistance to different types of SMEs and IS.

We defined a typological classification of program contexts based on modification and grouping of the Lipsky's (1980) contextual components of public services. These interrelated components include the formal evaluation mechanisms of program assistance, power between programs and SMEs, access to resources by programs in terms of time, knowledge, information, and budget, level of demand for program services, program worker alienation due to any job monotony or limitation, and competition between SME, social, and program goals. This part of the study represents an abductive research approach because there was an initial guiding theoretical framework but the development of our theoretical construct was completely dependent on the data.

To begin, we defined two determinants to classify program contexts, namely evaluation result and goal moderator. Evaluation result is determined by the interaction of evaluation and power. A positive influence occurs when the result shows what actually happened in the adoption and assistance processes. A negative influence occurs when the evaluation does not show what happened. For instance, let us consider that the formal evaluation is the quantification of the increase in sales in SMEs after program interventions. Clearly, the increase in sales could be caused by different changes in the SMEs or the market, not necessarily by the program assistance. Additionally, if the SMEs depend on further public assistance to carry out their strategic activities, there would be an imbalance of power in favor of programs. In this case, the evaluation will tend to please programs independently of the quality of the interventions. We argue that the evaluation result influences the focus of program workers on SME, social, or program goals. In our example, there would be a tendency to address program goals (i.e., quantitative targets).

The goal moderator is defined by the situation of the resources, demand, and alienation. A positive influence occurs when none of the contextual components that form the goal moderator present problems. A negative influence occurs when at least one of these components presents problems. For instance, let us consider that because of financial restrictions a program has a short time to service each SME. In this case, the goal moderator will be a negative influence because this problem compromises the delivery capacity of the program. We argue that the goal moderator can determine the extent in which non-focused goals are addressed. Continuing with our example, and assuming a focus on program goals, we can make more concrete inferences regarding program worker behavior, for instance at the selection of SMEs. As the focus is on program goals, the tendency would be to select SMEs with ambitious growth plans in order to reach the quantitative targets. The selection of an SME would not depend on the match between the SME needs and program capacities. However, it would be a matter of coincidence if the program could deliver proper services to some of these SMEs in order to address SME or social goals. The probability of this coincidence will be low because the program has a poor delivery capacity (i.e., a negative goal moderator).

With the combination of the two determinants and their two values, we constructed a classification of four types of program contexts, shown in Table 1. The objective is to explain the choice of goals of program workers and the potential for success of programs in terms of service quality and evaluation targets. We have already exemplified the type *chaotic*. With regard to the type *misleading*, the predominance would be for program goals. This is because of the freedom of action allowed by negative evaluation results and because program workers would try to surpass the quantitative targets to have the greatest chance of succeeding in the next public funding rounds. Given the better response situation of this type of programs in terms of the goal moderator, there would be more coincidences among goals in comparison to the type chaotic. The type *optimum* is the best condition, in which positive evaluation results force program workers to choose social goals and programs are well-prepared to face this challenge. Finally, in the type *unsustainable*, positive evaluation results oblige program workers to opt for social goals. However, given the poor goal moderator, there would be low probabilities to select a great number of SMEs to deliver proper services.

We found that the type chaotic could be the most common program context given the causal effects of the macro context. The reasons for this worrying situation are (1) that most funding bodies set flawed evaluation mechanisms (e.g., the European Regional Development Fund, the Regional Development Agency Fund in England, and the Higher Education Innovation Fund in England), (2) that SMEs tend to depend much on external support given their characteristic lack of resources, (3) that there is a policy-making imperative of providing few resources but setting high targets (e.g., Lewis and Glennester 1996), (4) that there is a low inherent demand for SME innovation services precisely because of the innovative character of these services, and (5) that there is the possibility of alienation of program workers as an indirect consequence of using insufficient resources and poor evaluation mechanisms (Lipsky 1980). In fact, these reasons can explain the deficient outcomes that we found in the IS adoption and assistance processes, as well as confirm the increasing general concern regarding SME policies. These arguments emphasize the relevance of immersing even more in the system in order to research how to improve program contexts.

Table 1. Program Context Types and Behavior

Evaluation Result	Goal Moderator	Type	SME Goals	Social Goals	Program Goals
Negative	Negative	Chaotic	If it coincides with the program goals, very few times	If it coincides with the program goals, very few times	Tendency
Negative	Positive	Misleading	If it coincides with the program goals, sometimes	If it coincides with the program goals, sometimes	Tendency
Positive	Positive	Optimum	If it coincides with the social goals, sometimes	Tendency	If it coincides with the social goals, sometimes
Positive	Negative	Unsustainable	If it coincides with the social goals, very few times	Tendency	If it coincides with the social goals, very few times

6.4 Improvement of Program Contexts

As pointed out by Archer (1995), agents could continually reproduce or transform the structures that condition their actions. This interaction between structures and agents is called *morphogenetic cycle*. In the previous section, we explained how program worker activity is affected by its macro context. Accordingly, the aim of this section is to define an initial framework to elaborate a systemic structure that improves program worker conditions. This structure is represented by the system of activities denoted in Table 2. Consequently, the agents in capacity of modifying the structure are the actors identified in the table.

This stage of the research was another exploration. Doing so, we gathered additional information, for example via semi-structured interviews with regional IS

Table 2. Systemic Initiatives Affecting the Program Context Components

Context Component	Suggested Initiative	Explanation	Actors
Evaluation	Adoption and assistance process evaluations	In order to improve the evaluation design, the methods should include qualitative approaches and the focus should be on the outcomes of adoption processes and the analysis of program actions and inactions	Funding bodies
Evaluation	Third-party evaluators	In order to avoid conflict of interests, the evaluators should not be connected to the policy-making teams, the program organizations, or contracted by any of them	Non-departmental public body, which could sub-contract private evaluators
Power	SME empowerment	In order to have an influencing presence at all levels, SME representatives should improve their involvement in the design, administration, and evaluation stages of the policy process	SME associations
Power	Marketing competetion simulation for programs	In order to avoid the dependency of SMEs on a single program organization, a group of program organizations should offer similar services in the same geographical area	European and national entities in charge of SME policies Funding bodies and their regional delegates
Resources	Sector and functional area focused services	In order to get knowledge and expertise, program organizations should continually deliver services to the same sectors and functional areas	European and national entities in charge of SME policies Funding bodies and their regional delegates
Resources	Consultancy accreditation	In order to guarantee knowledge and expertise, program organizations could opt to accredit their practices through rigorous academic and practical assessments	Professional associations or public–private partnerships
Demand	Awareness campaigns	In order to trigger the agenda-setting in SMEs, coordinated IS policies should include campaigns to increase the demand for IS and program services	Regional entities in charge of SME policies
Demand	Simplification of contractual procedures	In order to start program operations on time and have better chances to reach targets, the procedures of the policy administrators to sign contracts should be shortened	Funding bodies and their regional delegates
Alienation	More comprehensive set of services	In order to make program workers to participate more in each SME adoption process, programs should deliver services that cover most of the SME's needs	European and national entities in charge of SME policies Funding bodies and their regional delegates
Alienation	Modification and reduction of numerical targets	In order to make program workers participate more in each SME adoption process, the targets should be more qualitative and any numerical indicator should be reasonably ambitious	European and national entities in charge of SME policies Funding bodies

policy managers and program managers, as well as by reading diverse academic research, IS policy initiatives of different regions and sectors, and economic policy documents.

It is relevant to state that all of the initiatives presented in Table 2 must be carried out in the system of innovation, and not in the program organizations. For instance, funding bodies are in charge of defining the evaluation design. Another example is the issue of SME empowerment, which should be tackled directly by the SME associations. The systemic initiatives could also be interrelated, which creates even more complexity. For instance, correctly empowered SME groups could influence funding bodies with the aim of changing the evaluation design. Importantly, all of these systemic issues have their own underlying generative structures and mechanisms. This implies that, to study each of them, we would have to consider their particular ontologies, theoretical fields, and research methods.

7 Conclusions

We developed a research cycle to show an example of how CR is compatible and supports the SIA research practice to study complex IS. To do so, our early exploration uncovered a relevant demi-regularity, namely the poor program assistance to IS adoption processes in SMEs. After this, we found excessive discretion at the program implementation level. The excessive discretion made relevant the study of the context and priorities in programs. Therefore, we constructed a typological classification of contexts to explain the choice of goals and the potential for success of programs in terms of service quality and evaluative targets. As the type chaotic seems to be the most common context, we decided to explore ways to improve program contexts. Thus we identified a list of interrelated systemic initiatives that could contribute to this end.

In general, the research gives a clear vision about the networked, stratified, and open nature of public programs and, consequently, of the diffusion of IS in SMEs. In fact, the diffusion processes do depend on systemic issues as distant as consultancy accreditation led by professional groups or the decisions on program targets made by funding bodies. In addition, these issues can be complexly interconnected; for example, any focus on sector and area services, initially aimed at improving program resources, could also positively impact the demand for program services.

We used theoretical components that are not utilized in mainstream IS research, specifically the frameworks to explain discretion and program contexts, which come from the political science and public administration fields. In addition, we used a combination of inductive, deductive, and abductive research approaches to carry out the multiple levels of the study, which reflects a deep ontological variety and metatheoretical retroductive reasoning. The multidisciplinarity and methodological pluralism become more diverse if we take into account the detection of the factors of adoption in particular contexts, or initial demi-regularities, which is normally done using mainstream IS theories, surveys, and statistical analysis. More importantly, the study of IS diffusion in SMEs becomes much more complex if we continue researching the systemic issues recommended to improve program contexts.

This study is an illustration of a meaningful way of how complex IS should be researched. In a particular context, there could be many demi-regularities which must be researched in detail. The lack of knowledge for the planning and implementation of IS, the lack of complementary marketing knowledge to support the company web presence, and the lack of funding to carry out adoption processes are only a few examples of visible factors affecting adoption. Similarly, the underlying causes of the factors can be very diverse, as well as the potential private and public initiatives to address them. This kind of study should take several research iterations and each of them should guide the next.

This research calls for the IS research community to approach IS as a complex social phenomenon, and not as a discrete discipline tied to specific preferences of methodologies and techniques. The most common studies oriented to organizational and micro-environment factors are absolutely relevant as entry points of longer and higher impact research processes, which could contribute significantly more to theory and practice. These research processes, or programs, could be developed forming teams composed of researchers from different disciplines. However, IS researchers should have a leadership role because they are knowledgeable of the organizational processes and micro-environment elements directly affecting the IS phenomenon. For this reason, IS researchers are instrumental in the determination of relevant demi-regularities, as well as the initiation, planning, execution, and evaluation of complex IS research efforts.

References

Alter, S.: Sidestepping the IT Artefact, Scrapping the IS Silo, and Laying Claim to Systems in Organizations. Communications of AIS 12(2), 494–526 (2003)

Archer, M.: Realistic Social Theory: The Morphogenetic Approach. Cambridge University Press, Cambridge (1995)

Archer, M., Bhaskar, R., Collier, A., Lawson, T., Norrie, A. (eds.): Critical Realism: Essential Readings. Routledge, London (2001)

Asheim, B., Isaken, A.: Localized Knowledge, Interactive Learning and Innovation: Between Regional Networks and Global Corporations. In: Taylor, E., Taylor, M. (eds.) The Networked Firm in a Global World: Small Firms in New Environments, pp. 163–198. Ashgate Publishing Group, Aldershot (2000)

Bakos, J., Kemerer, C.: Recent Applications of Economic Theory in Information Technology Research. Decision Support Systems 8(5), 365–386 (1992)

Benbasat, I., Zmud, R.: The Identity Crisis Within the IS Discipline: Defining and Communicating the Discipline's Core Properties. MIS Quarterly 27(2), 183–194 (2003)

Bergene, A.: Towards a Critical Realist Comparative Methodology: Context-Sensitive Theoretical Comparison. J. of Critical Realism 6(1), 5–27 (2007)

Berkeley, N., Clark, D., Ilbery, B.: Regional Variation in Business Use of Information and Communication Technologies and the Implications for Policy: Case Study Evidence from Rural England. Geoforum 27(1), 75–86 (1996)

Bhaskar, R.: Reclaiming Reality: A Critical Introduction to Contemporary Philosophy. Verso, London (1989)

Bhaskar, R.: A Realist Theory of Science, 2nd edn. Verso, London (1997)

Bhaskar, R.: The Possibility of Naturalism: A Philosophical Critique of the Contemporary Human Sciences, 3rd edn. Routledge, London (1998)

Carlsson, S.: Advancing Information Systems Evaluation (Research): A Critical Realist Approach. Electronic J. of Information Systems 6(2), 11–20 (2003)

Carlsson, S.: Using Critical Realism in IS Research. In: Whitman, E., Woszczynski, B. (eds.) The Handbook of Information Systems Research, pp. 323–338. Idea Group Publishing, Hershey (2004)

Carlsson, S.: Developing Information Systems Design Knowledge: A Critical Realist Perspective. The Electronic J. of Business Research Methodology 3(2), 93–102 (2005)

Castellacci, F.: A Critical Realist Interpretation of Evolutionary Growth Theorizing. Cambridge J. of Economics 30(6), 861–880 (2006)

Chitura, T., Mupemhi, S., Dube, T., Bolongkikit, J.: Barriers to Electronic Commerce Adoption in Small and Medium Enterprises: A Critical Literature Review. J. of Internet Banking & Commerce 13(2), 1–13 (2008)

Christensen, C.: The Ongoing Process of Building a Theory of Disruption. J. of Product Innovation Management 23(1), 39–55 (2006)

Clarke, J., Newman, J.: The Managerial State. Sage, London (1997)

Crowston, K., Sawyer, S., Wigand, R.: Investigating the Interplay between Structure and Information and Communications Technology in the Real Estate Industry. Information Technology & People 14(2), 163–183 (2001)

Cuadrado, J., Garcia, A.: ICT Policies for SMEs and Regional Disparities: The Spanish Case. Entrepreneurship and Enterprise Development 16(1), 55–75 (2004)

Danermark, B., Ekstrom, M., Jakobsen, L., Karlsson, J.: Explaining Society: An Introduction to Critical Realism in the Social Sciences. Routledge, London (2001)

Davis, F., Bagozzi, R., Walshaw, P.: User Acceptance of Computer Technology: A Comparison of two Theoretical Models. Management Science 35(8), 982–1003 (1989)

Dobson, P.: The Philosophy of Critical Realism: An Opportunity for Information Systems Research. Information Systems Frontiers 3(2), 199–210 (2001)

Dobson, P., Myles, J., Jackson, P.: Making the Case for Critical Realism: Examining the Implementation of Automated Performance Management Systems. Information Resources Management Journal 20(2), 138–152 (2007)

Easterby-Smith, M., Thorpe, R., Lowe, A.: Management Research: An Introduction, 3rd edn. Sage, London (2008)

Edquist, C.: Systems of Innovation Approaches: Their Emergence and Characteristics. In: Edquist, C. (ed.) Systems of Innovation: Technologies, Institutions and Organizations, pp. 1–35. Pinter, London (1997)

Edquist, C.: Innovation Policy: A Systemic Approach. In: Archibugi, D., Lundvall, B. (eds.) The Globalizing Learning Economy, pp. 219–238. Oxford University Press, Oxford (2002)

Edquist, C.: Systems of Innovation: Perspectives and Challenges. In: Fagerberg, J., Mowery, D., Nelson, R. (eds.) The Oxford Handbook of Innovation, pp. 181–208. Oxford University Press, Oxford (2005)

Edquist, C.: Design of Innovation Policy through Diagnostic Analysis: Identification of Systemic Problems (or Failures). Working paper, Centre for Innovation, Research and Competence in the Learning Economy (CIRCLE), Lund University, Lund, Sweden (2008), http://circle-lund.net/UploadedPublications/200806Edquist.pdf (accessed November 15, 2009)

Ein-Dor, P., Myers, M., Raman, K.: Information Technology in three Small Developed Countries. J. of Management Information Systems 13(4), 61–89 (1997)

Ellis, K., Davis, A., Rummery, K.: Needs Assessment, Street-Level Bureaucracy and the New Community Care. Social Policy and Administration 33(3), 262–280 (1999)

Fichman, R.: Going Beyond the Dominant Paradigm for Information Technology Innovation Research: Emerging Concepts and Methods. J. of the Association for Information Systems 5(8), 314–355 (2004)

Fox, S.: Applying Critical Realism to Information and Communication Technologies: A Case Study. Construction Management and Economics 27(5), 465–472 (2009)

Freeman, C.: Technology Policy and Economic Performance: Lessons from Japan. Pinter, London (1987)

Gengatharen, D., Standing, C., Burn, J.: Government Supported Community Portal: Regional E-Marketplaces for SMEs–Evidence to Support a Staged Approach. Electronic Markets 15(4), 405–417 (2005)

George, A.: Case Studies and Theory Development: The Method of Structured, Focused Comparison. In: Lauren, P. (ed.) Diplomacy: New Approaches in History, Theory and Policy, pp. 43–68. The Free Press, New York (1979)

Hasenfeld, Y., English, R. (eds.): Human Service Organizations. University of Michigan Press, Ann Arbor (1974)

Henry, G., Julnes, G., Mark, M. (eds.): Realist Evaluation. Jossey Bass, San Francisco (1988)

Hirschheim, R., Klein, H.: Crisis in the IS Field? A Critical Reflection on the State of the Discipline. J. of the Association for Information Systems 4(5), 237–293 (2003)

Hommen, L., Edquist, C.: Globalization and Innovation Policy. In: Edquist, C., Hommen, L. (eds.) Small Country Innovation Systems: Globalization, Change and Policy in Asia and Europe, pp. 442–484. Edward Elgar Publishing, Cheltenham (2008)

Howe, D.: Knowledge, Power and the Shape of Social Work Practice. In: Davies, M. (ed.) The Sociology of Social Work, pp. 202–220. Routledge, London (1991)

Iliev, I.: Addressing the Methodological Anxieties of the Systems of Innovation Approach: Complementarities with the Critical Realist Project. In: Proceedings of the Danish Research Unit for Industrial Dynamics (DRUID) Academy of Winter 2005 Conference, Aalborg, Denmark (2005),
http://www2.druid.dk/conferences/viewpaper.php?id=2536&cf=17
(accessed January 15, 2010)

Jeyaraj, A., Rottman, J., Lacity, M.: A Review of the Predictors, Linkages and Biases in IT Innovation Adoption Research. J. of Information Technology 21(1), 1–23 (2006)

Johnson, S.: SME Support Policy: Efficiency, Equity, Ideology or Vote-Seeking? In: Proceedings of the Institute of Small Business and Entrepreneurship (ISBE) Conference, Blackpool, UK (2005)

Jones, C.: Social Work: Regulation and Managerialism. In: Exworthy, M., Halford, S. (eds.) Professionals and the New Managerialism in Public Services, ch. 4. Open University Press, London (1999)

Kasi, M.: Realistic Evaluation in Practice. Sage, London (2003)

King, J., Gurbaxani, V., Kraemer, K., McFarlan, F., Raman, K., Yap, C.: Institutional Factors in Information Technology Innovation. Information Systems Research 5(2), 139–170 (1994)

Langan, M.: Social Services: Managing the Third Way. In: Clarke, J., Gewirtz, S., McLaughlin, E. (eds.) New Managerialism, New Welfare?, pp. 152–168. Sage, London (2000)

Lawson, T.: Economics and Reality. Routledge, London (1997)

Lewis, J., Glennerster, H.: Implementing the New Community Care. Open University Press, New York (1996)

Lindblom, C., Woodhouse, E.: The Policy-Making Process, 3rd edn. Prentice Hall, Englewood Cliffs (1993)

Lipsky, M.: Street-Level Bureaucracy: The Dilemmas of Individuals in Public Service. Russell Sage Foundation, New York (1980)

Long, N.: The Multiple Optic of Interface Analysis. UNESCO background paper on interface analysis, Wageningen University, Wageningen, Netherlands (1999), http://lanic.utexas.edu/project/etext/llilas/claspo/ workingpapers/multipleoptic.pdf (accessed August 5, 2010)

Lundvall, B.: National Systems of Innovation: Towards a Theory of Innovation and Interactive Learning. Pinter, London (1992)

Lundvall, B., Borras, S.: Science, Technology and Innovation Policy. In: Fagerberg, J., Mowery, D., Nelson, R. (eds.) The Oxford Handbook of Innovation, pp. 599–631. Oxford University Press, Oxford (2005)

Mansell, R., Wehn, U. (eds.): Knowledge Societies: Information Technology for Sustainable Development. Oxford University Press, Oxford. Commissioned by the United Nations Commission on Science and Technology for Development, Geneva, Switzerland (1998), http://www.sussex.ac.uk/spru/1-4-9-1-1-2.html (accessed June 10, 2009)

Martin, L., Matlay, H.: Blanket Approaches to Promoting ICT in Small Firms: Some Lessons from the DTI Ladder Adoption Model in the UK. Internet Research 11(5), 399–410 (2001)

Maynard-Moody, S., Musheno, M.: Cops, Teachers, Counselors: Stories from the Front Lines of Public Service. University of Michigan Press, Ann Arbor (2003)

Meyer, I., Hekkert, M., Faber, J., Smits, R.: Perceived Uncertainties Regarding SocioTechnological Transformations: Towards a Framework. Int. J. Foresight Innovation Policy 2(2), 214–240 (2006)

Mingers, J.: Real-izing Information Systems: Critical Realism as an Underpinning Philosophy for Information Systems. Information and Organization 14(2), 87–103 (2004)

Mole, K.: Business Advisers Impact on SMEs. International Small Business J. 20(2), 139–162 (2002)

Morton, P.: Using Critical Realism to Explain Strategic Information Systems Planning. J. of Information Technology Theory and Application 8(1), 1–20 (2006)

Mutch, A.: Critical Realism, Managers and Information. British J. of Management 10(4), 323–333 (1999)

Mutch, A.: Actors and Networks or Agents and Structures: Towards a Realist View of Information Systems. Organization 9(3), 477–496 (2002)

Myers, M.: The IS Core – VIII: Defining the Core Properties of the IS Disciplines: Not Yet, Not Now. Communications of the AIS 12(38), 580–588 (2003)

Nelson, R. (ed.): National Innovation Systems: A Comparative Study. Oxford University Press, Oxford (1993)

Nelson, R., Winter, S.: An Evolutionary Theory of Economic Change. The Belknap Press, Boston (1982)

Nugent, J., Yhee, S.: Small and Medium Enterprises in Korea: Achievements, Constraints and Policy Issues. Small Business Economics 18(1/3), 85–119 (2002)

Oroviogoicochea, C., Watson, R.: A Quantitative Analysis of the Impact of a Computerized Information System on Nurses' Clinical Practice Using a Realistic Evaluation Framework. International J. of Medical Informatics 78(12), 839–849 (2009)

Oyelaran-Oyeyinka, B., Lal, K.: SMEs and New Technologies: Learning E-Business and Development. Palgrave Macmillan, Basingstoke (2006)

Oztel, H., Martin, S.: Local Partnership for Economic Development: Business Links and the Restructuring of SME Support Networks in the United Kingdom. Economic Development Quarterly 12(3), 266–278 (1998)

Parker, C., Castleman, T.: New Directions for Research on SME E-business: Insights from an Analysis of Journal Articles from 2003 to 2006. J. of Information Systems and Small Business 1(1), 21–40 (2007)

Pawson, R., Tilley, N.: Realistic Evaluation. Sage, London (1997)

Radosevic, S.: Defining Systems of Innovation: A Methodological Discussion. Technology in Society 20(1), 75–86 (1998)

Robey, D., Boudreau, M.-C.: Accounting for the Contradictory Consequences of Information Technology: Theoretical Directions and Methodological Implications. Information Systems Research 10(2), 167–185 (1999)

Rogers, E.: Diffusion of Innovations, 5th edn. Free Press, New York (2003)

Rotaru, K., Wilkin, C., Ceglowski, A., Churilov, L.: Towards Operational Risk-Aware Information Systems: A Critical Realist Perspective. In: Proceedings of the 17th European Conference on Information Systems, Verona, Italy (2009),
http://is2.lse.ac.uk/asp/aspecis/20090140.pdf
(accessed August 15, 2010)

Sayer, A.: Method in Social Science: A Realist Approach, 2nd edn. Routledge, London (1992)

Simpson, M., Docherty, A.: E-commerce Adoption Support and Advice for UK SMEs. J. of Small Business and Enterprise Development 11(3), 315–328 (2004)

Smith, M.: Overcoming Theory-Practice Inconsistencies: Critical Realism and Information Systems Research. Information and Organization 16(3), 191–211 (2006)

Stake, R.: Qualitative Case Studies. In: Denzin, N., Lincoln, Y. (eds.) The SAGE Handbook of Qualitative Research, 3rd edn., pp. 443–466. Sage, Thousand Oaks (2005)

Storey, D.: Evaluating SME Policies and Programmes: Technical and Political Dimensions. In: Cason, K., Yeung, B., Basu, A., Wadeson, N. (eds.) The Oxford Handbook of Entrepreneurship, pp. 248–278. Oxford University Press, Oxford (2006)

Trochim, W.: Outcome Pattern Matching and Programme Theory. Evaluation and Program Planning 12(4), 35–366 (1989)

Vega, A., Chiasson, M., Brown, D.: Extending the Research Agenda on Diffusion: The Case of Public Program Interventions for the Adoption of E-Business Systems in SMEs. J. of Information Technology 23(2), 109–117 (2008)

Vega, A., Chiasson, M., Brown, D.: The Effects of Innovation Process and Programme Contexts on the Implementation of Public Services: The Worrying Case of Enterprise Innovation. In: Proceedings of the 14th International Research Society for Public Management Conference, Berne, Switzerland (2010a),
http://www.irspm2010.com/workshops/papers/
G_theeffectsofinnovation.pdf (accessed August 15, 2010)

Vega, A., Chiasson, M., Brown, D.: Setting Up University Support to Small and Medium Enterprise Innovation: Managerial, Policy and Research Implications. In: The Engage HEI (Higher Education Institutions) 2010 Conference, Bradford, UK (2010b)

Watson, R., Myers, M.: IT Industry Success in Small Countries: The Cases of Finland and New Zealand. J. of Global Information Management 9(2), 4–14 (2001)

Wells, J.: Priorities, Street-Level Bureaucracy and the Community Mental Health Team. Health and Social Care in the Community 5(5), 333–342 (1997)

Wikgren, M.: Critical Realism as a Philosophy and Social Theory in Information Science. J. of Documentation 61(1), 1–22 (2005)

Williams, M., Dwivedi, Y., Lal, B., Schwarz, A.: Contemporary Trends and Issues in IT Adoption and Diffusion Research. J. of Information Technology 24(1), 1–10 (2009)

Yin, R.: Case Study Research: Design and Method, 4th edn. Sage, London (2009)

Zahra, S., George, G.: Absorptive Capacity: A Review, Reconceptualization and Extension. Academy of Management Review 27(2), 185–203 (2002)

About the Authors

Arturo Vega is a senior lecturer at Canterbury Christ Church University in the Faculty of Business and Management. He has more than 10 years of a varied international experience in the United Kingdom, Spain, Mexico, and Peru in corporations such as Oracle, IBM, Philips, and Red Unicard. Arturo's research is on the development, diffusion and use of innovations in the economic system. Doing so, he uses multiple disciplines and research approaches, including management information systems, critical realism, innovation, entrepreneurship, institutions, public policies, public administration, SMEs, and higher education institutions.

David Brown is Chair of Strategy and Information Systems at Lancaster University Management School. His research interests have two separate but linked strands. First, strategic studies including strategic information systems and e-business, and second the application of these strands internationally, especially in transitional economies. The majority of his work is strongly organizationally based and includes action research and soft systems methodology. He has published widely including three coauthored edited books and over 40 research articles. Current research includes ICT policy, planning and implementation as well as enterprise systems in Chinese SMEs.

Critical Realist Information Systems Research in Action

Sven A. Carlsson

Informatics, School of Economics and Mangement, Lund University,
Ole Römers väg 6, 223 63 Lund, Sweden
sven.carlsson@ics.lu.se

Abstract. There is a growing interest in critical realism (CR) in Information Systems (IS) research. This paper presents and discusses how critical realism can be an alternative philosophical underpinning for IS research. It briefly presents critical realism and how it can be used in IS research. Contemporary examples of how CR have been used in IS research are presented and discussed. The future use of CR in IS research is also discussed.

Keywords: Critical realism, empirical research, theory development, design science research, theory testing, evaluation research.

1 Introduction

There is a growing interest in critical realism (CR) in Information Systems (IS) research. Scholars have pointed out major weaknesses and limitations in positivism and constructivism, see, for example, Archer et al. (1998) and Lòpez and Potter (2001). CR is an alternative to the different strands of positivism and constructivism currently dominating IS research. CR argues that social reality is not simply composed of agents' meanings, but that there exist structural factors influencing agents' lived experiences. CR starts from an ontology that identifies structures and mechanisms, through which events and discourses are generated, as being fundamental to the constitution of our natural and social reality.

This paper presents and discusses how critical realism can be an alternative philosophical underpinning for IS research. It briefly presents critical realism and how it can be used in IS research. Contemporary examples of how CR have been used in IS research are presented and discussed. The future use of CR in IS research is also discussed.

2 Critical Realism

Different philosophies of science have different ontological views. Idealists have the view that reality is not mind-independent. Idealism comes in different forms, reflecting different views on what is man-created and how it is created. Realists have the view that reality exists independently of our beliefs, thoughts, perceptions,

M. Chiasson et al. (Eds.): Future IS 2011, IFIP AICT 356, pp. 269–284, 2011.

discourses, etc. As for idealism, realism comes in different forms. Bhaskar says that it is not a question of being a realist or not, but what type of realist (Bhaskar 2000).

Critical realism was developed as an alternative to traditional positivist models of social science as well as an alternative to constructivism. The most influential writer on CR is Roy Bhaskar. Good summaries of CR are available in Archer et al. (1998), Dean et al. (2005), Sayer (2000), and Chapter 1 in Bhaskar (2002); key concepts and main developments are presented in Hartwig (2007). In Archer et al. (1998) and Lòpez and Potter (2001), chapters focus on different aspects of CR, ranging from fundamental philosophical discussions to how statistical analysis can be used in CR-based research.

CR was primarily developed as an answer to the positivist crisis. In 1975, Bhaskar's work *A Realist Theory of Science*, with "transcendental realism," was published. In *Possibility of Naturalism* (1998), Bhaskar focused on the social sciences and developed "critical naturalism." These two major works present a thorough philosophy of science project and later critical realism and critical naturalism were merged to "critical realism," a concept also used by Bhaskar. Through the 1980s, Bhaskar primarily developed his position through sharpening arguments. The late 1970s and early 1980s saw a number of other CR scholars publishing influential works, for example, Margaret Archer's *Social Origins of Educational Systems* (1979) and Andrew Sayer's *Method in Social Science* (1992). Most early critiques of CR targeted positivism, but later critique is targeting alternatives to positivism, for example, constructivism and structuration theory.

Critical realism can be seen as a specific form of realism:

> To be a realist is to assert the existence of some disputed kind of entities such as gravitons, equilibria, utility, class relations and so on. To be a scientific realist is to assert that these entities exist independently of our investigation of them. Such entities, *contra* the post modernism of rhetoricians, are not something generated in the discourse used in their investigation. Neither are such entities, *contra* empiricists, restricted to the realm of the observable. To be a *critical* realist is to extend these views into social science (Fleetwood 2002, p. 29).

The manifesto of CR is to recognize the reality of the natural order and the events and discourses of the social world. It holds that

> we will only be able to understand—and so change—the social world if we identify the structures at work that generate those events or discourses.... These structures are not spontaneously apparent in the observable pattern of events; they can only be identified through the practical and theoretical work of the social sciences (Bhaskar 1989, pp. 2-3).

Bhaskar (1978) outlines what he calls three domains: the *real*, the *actual*, and the *empirical* (see Table 1).

Table 1. Ontological Assumptions of the Critical Realist View of Science (from Bhaskar 1978. X's indicate the domain of reality in which mechanisms, events, and experiences, respectively reside, as well as the domains involved for such a residence to be possible)

	Domain of Real	**Domain of Actual**	**Domain of Empirical**
Mechanism	X		
Events	X	X	
Experiences	X	X	X

The *real domain* consists of underlying structures, mechanisms, and relations; events and behavior; and experiences. The generative mechanisms residing in the real domain exist independently of, but capable of producing, patterns of events. Relations generate behaviors in the social world. The *domain of the actual* consists of these events and behaviors. Hence, the actual domain is the domain in which observed events or observed patterns of events occur. The *domain of the empirical* consists of what we experience; hence, it is the domain of experienced events.

Bhaskar (1978, p. 13) argues that

> real structures exist independently of and are often out of phase with the actual patterns of events. Indeed it is only because of the latter we need to perform experiments and only because of the former that we can make sense of our performances of them. Similarly it can be shown to be a condition of the intelligibility of perception that events occur independently of experiences. And experiences are often (epistemically speaking) "out of phase" with events—e.g., when they are misidentified. It is partly because of this possibility that the scientist needs a scientific education or training. Thus I [Bhaskar] will argue that what I call the domains of the real, the actual and the empirical are distinct.

CR also argues that the real world is ontologically stratified and differentiated. The real world consists of a plurality of structures and generative mechanisms that generate the events that occur and do not occur. From an epistemological stance, concerning the nature of knowledge claim, the realist approach is non-positivistic, which means that values and facts are intertwined and hard to disentangle.

Critical realism is a well-developed philosophy of science, but on the methodological level, it is less well-developed. The writings of Kazi (2003), Layder (1993, 1998), Pawson (2006), Pawson and Tilley (1997), and Robson (2002), as well as some of the chapters in Ackroyd and Fleetwood (2000) and Fleetwood and Ackroyd (2004), can serve as guidelines for doing critical realist research. Unfortunately, from an IS perspective, the writings on CR have not focused on artifacts like IS/IT and it has been only in the behavioral science paradigm.

CR has influenced a number of disciplines and fields, for example, economics, management, and organization studies. There is a growing interest in CR in the IS field. Scholars have argued for the use of CR in IS research (Carlson 2004; Dobson 2001; Mingers 2004; Mutch 2002). CR-based empirical research can be found in Dobson et al. (2007), and DeVaujany (2008), Morton (2010), Strong and Volkoff

(2010)m and Volkoff et al. (2007). CR has also critical and emancipatory components (Bhaskar 2000). Wilson and Greenhill (2004) and Smith (2005) address how CR in IS research can work critically and be emancipatory. CR's potential for IS design science research has been argued by Carlsson (2010) and Lyytinen (2008). CR-based IS design science can be found in Clarson et al. (2011) and Hrastinski et al. (2010). A sign of the growing interest and importance of CR-based research is a recent call for paper for an *MIS Quarterly* special issue on "Critical Realism in Information Systems Research." Having briefly presented CR, we will now focus on how it has been used in IS research and discuss strengths and weaknesses in the presented studies.

3   Using Critical Realism in IS Research

Gregor (2006) argues that five interrelated types of IS theories can be distinguished: (1) theory for analyzing, (2) theory for explaining, (3) theory for predicting, (4) theory for explaining and predicting, and (5) theory for design and action. The five types can be clustered into two main types: traditional natural/social research (first four types) and design science research (fifth type). Next, we examine how CR can be used in both main types of research. Theory developing studies (3.1), evaluation research (3.2), and design science research (3.3) are presented.

3.1   CR-Based Development of IS Theories

Two theory-generating IS studies are briefly presented. The first is the development of a CR-based theory of technology-enabled organizational change. The second study develops an explanation of the causes of the outcomes of attempts to develop and implement strategic IS plans in organizations.

Volkoff et al. (2007) addressed the classical concern: How does technology mediate organizational change? They did this by developing a new theory based on the philosophy of CR. They longitudinally studied the implementation and use of an enterprise resource planning (ERP) system. Their specific view on technology-mediated organizational change is based on Archer's (1995) morphogenetic approach, which is conceptualized as a cycle consisting of three phases: (1) structural conditioning, (2) social interaction, and (3) structural elaboration. The "concept *morphogenesis* indicates that society has no preferred form...but is shaped and re-shaped by the interplay between STRUCTURE and AGENCY" (Archer 2007, p. 319). The middle phase of social interaction is the one which may appear to be where human agency has its greatest role, but this is not the case, as human agency is implicated in and embedded within all phases of the cycle. The structural conditioning phase incorporates the critical realist assumption that structure predates action(s) which transforms it. Structural elaboration postdates those actions. The structural elaboration phase of the model, which flows out of the social interactions in phase two can have one of two characteristics: structural elaboration/morphogenesis, where people and structures are transformed, and structural reproduction/morphostasis, where people and structures are largely reproduced. As Archer states, "Although, all three lines [phases] are in fact continuous, the analytical element consists in breaking up the flows into intervals determined by the problem in hand" (2007, p. 319).

Volkoff et al. (2007, p. 835) view ERP as

> a source of structural conditioning that is relatively independent and enduring, existing materially in the real domain, rather than primarily as a malleable structure, existing only in the empirical domain at the moment of instantiation. Using a critical realist perspective, we can discuss the interplay between structures and human agents, and examine the generative mechanisms or mediators through which agents affect structure and, of greater importance for this study, how structures shape agency.

Volkoff et al. based their study on Pentland and Feldman's (2005) work on organizational routines and especially their distinction between ostensive (structural) aspects of routines and the performative (agentic) aspects of routines. Volkoff et al. found that "in addition to ostensive and performative aspects, routines also have a material aspect that is embedded in the technology....[and] material aspect of routines plays a critical and direct role in the change process" (p. 833). Their study resulted in a new technology-mediated organizational change theory.

The study by Volkoff et al. illustrates how their theory overcomes some of the problems with previous theories. Previous theories can be categorized as having a deterministic view or an emergent view. They can also be classified as having an agency view or a structural view (including a technology view). In line with CR, Volkoff et al.'s study and theory focuses both on structure and agency and has an emergent view. It separates structure and agency, whereas some other theories either ignore agency (i.e., theories based on institutional theory), ignore structure (i.e., theories based on behavioral approaches), or conflate the two (i.e., theories based on structuration theory and ANT). A similar study is Strong and Volkoff (2010); it is a CR-based longitudinal study of an ERP system focusing on organization–ERP system fit. Strong and Volkoff and Volkoff et al. use a qualitative approach and their analyses are based on grounded theory (their coding process generally followed a grounded theory approach). It should be noted that retroduction, which is adopted by critical realism and refers to the inference from a description of some phenomenon to a description of something that produces it or is a condition for it, is not used or mentioned.

The second CR-based theory generating study by Morton (2010) addresses the research question: What are the causes of the outcomes of attempts to develop and implement strategic IS plans in organizations? Achieving the vision of the strategic IS plan is difficult and Morton's literature review shows that both private and public sector organizations having used SISP had problematic experiences. This motivates the research question for his thesis.

Morton argues that CR is useful for establishing causal explanations of phenomenon where closed system conditions (controlled experiments) are difficult to apply, such as in organizational settings where complex interactions occur between people and technology and outcomes are not predictable. The methodology used by Morton is consistent with CR and he uses a multiple case study research design.

Morton reviewed the SISP literature and an immanent critique was undertaken to establish a conceptualization of SISP consistent with the open systems view of social reality set out by CR. An immanent critique is an examination of existing theories about the phenomenon of interest using CR as a meta-theory to critique the theories' ontological presuppositions (Hesketh et al. 2006). The two dominating models of SISP, the comprehensive, formal, and systematic model and the incremental, informal, and opportunistic model, were the targets of the immanent critique. The immanent critique finds significant theory–practice inconsistencies in relation to both the comprehensive and informal models of SISP. On the basis of the immanent critique, a new reconceptualization of the phenomenon was offered: SISP as an intervention into the open systems social reality of the organization with unpredictable outcomes. In this view, SISP is itself a collection of causal mechanism that activate other causal mechanisms in the setting which originate in the agency of participants, the prevailing social structures, and the use by agents of a range of ideational elements from the cultural system. Morton used the reconceptualization as a framework to analyze each of four case studies to identify a set of causal mechanisms responsible for the outcomes of SISP projects contingent on organizational conditions.

Morton's research design follows Robson's (2002) four-part structure for CRbased research comprising (1) purpose, (2) methods, (3) theory, and (4) sampling strategy. Morton's aim was not to test specific propositions or hypotheses about SISP; rather it was to generate theory, by a process of retroducing the form and constitution of causal mechanisms, that could have produced and hence explain the empirical effects in the case studies. The theorization of causal mechanisms was supported by reference to the literature for corroboration of their existence. Four case studies, drawn from organizations either developing or implementing a strategic IS plan, were used as the primary source of empirical data for. A multiple case study design allows for the corroboration of findings across case studies via a comparative approach (Bergene 2007), although the effects of causal mechanism are always subject to contingent conditions. Four methods of data collection were used: (1) participant observation (case one), (2) non-participant observation (case two), (3) interviewing (all cases), and (4) document review (all cases).

Comparative analysis of the 4 case studies revealed a set of 13 causal mechanisms that had a significant impact on the outcomes in each case and 9 contingent factors that affected their activation and interaction. The mechanisms complete the CR-based reconceptualization of SISP and explain the varied outcomes of the SISP projects by showing how they result from the contingent interaction of these mechanisms.

Morton's study is primarily a qualitative study. Morton's work is interesting because of his use of immanent critique (Hesketh et al. 2006) and his use of Bergene's (2007) comparative approach. The use of immanent critique can be viewed as one way to address that CR rejects judgmental relativism (the inability to judge the merits of theories). An alternative approach would have been to use the three theories on the four cases and compared how they were performing in terms of describing and explaining the phenomenon that are the causes of the outcomes of attempts to develop and implement SISP in organizations.

3.2 CR-Based Information Systems Evaluation Research

IS evaluation and IS evaluation research have been stressed as critical means in advancing the IS field. Generally, IS evaluation is concerned with the evaluation of different aspects of real-life interventions in the social life where information systems are critical means in achieving the anticipated goals of the intervention. IS evaluation research can be considered a special case of evaluation research.

Driving CR-based IS evaluation research, which here is called *realistic IS evaluation*, is the aim to produce ever more detailed answers to the question of why an IS initiative—IS, types of IS, or IS implementation—works for whom, in what circumstances, and why. This means that evaluation researchers attend to how and why an IS initiative has the potential to cause (desired) changes.

A realistic evaluation researcher works as an experimental scientist, but not according to the logic of the traditional experimental research. According to Bhaskar (1978, p. 53),

> The experimental scientist must perform two essential functions in an experiment. First, he must trigger the mechanism under study to ensure that it is active; and secondly, he must prevent any interference with the operation of the mechanism. These activities could be designated as "experimental production" and "experimental control."

Realistic evaluation researchers do not conceive that IS initiatives "work." It is the action of stakeholders that makes them work, and the causal potential of an IS initiative takes the form of providing reasons and resources to enable different stakeholders and participants to "make" changes. This means that a realistic evaluation researcher seeks to understand why an IS initiative works through an understanding of the action mechanisms. It also means that a realistic evaluation researcher seeks to understand for whom and in what circumstances (contexts) an IS initiative works through the study of contextual conditioning.

Realistic evaluation researchers orient their thinking to context–mechanism–outcome pattern configurations—called CMO configurations (Pawson and Tilley 1997). In IS evaluation research, a CMO configuration is a proposition stating what it is about an IS initiative (IS implementation) that works for whom in what circumstances (Carlsson 2003). A refined CMO configuration is the finding of IS evaluation research—the output of a realistic evaluation study.

Realistic IS evaluation based on the above may be implemented through a realistic effectiveness cycle. The starting point is theory. Theory includes propositions on how the mechanisms introduced by an IS invention into pre-existing contexts can generate outcomes. This entails theoretical analysis of mechanisms, contexts, and expected outcomes. The second step consists of generating hypotheses. Typically the following questions would be addressed in the hypotheses: (1) What changes or outcomes will be brought about by an IS intervention? (2) What contexts impinge on this? (3) What mechanisms (social, cultural, and others) would enable these changes, and which one may disable the intervention? The third step is the selection of appropriate data collection methods. In this step, it might be possible to provide evidence of the ability of the IS intervention to change reality. Based on the result from the third step, one may return to the program (the IS intervention) to make it more specific as an intervention of practice. Next, but not finally, one returns to theory. The theory may be developed, the hypotheses refined, the data collection methods enhanced, etc.

To illustrate realistic IS evaluation, two studies are presented. The first is an evaluation study of enterprise systems implementations. The second is a study of the impact of a computer-based IS on clinical practice.

The first study focused automated performance measurement systems (APMS). APMS are a fairly recent evolution within the context of enterprise information systems. APMS deliver information (values for key performance indicators) to senior managers through automatically collecting operational data from integrated information systems. APMS are a consequence of the Sarbanes–Oxley Act (SOX) and similar legislation. The study investigated a number of APMS implemenations with varying degree of success. In reflecting on their research, Dobson et al. (2007, p. 143) say,

> In the context of the APMS research, it became evident that contextual issues were paramount in explaining the success and failure of the implementations....This emphasis on context impacted the underlying research focus. The critical realist focus on retroductive prepositional-type questioning led to a contextual basis for the study seeking to answer "Under what conditions might APMS implementation prove successful?" rather than "What are the (predictive) critical success factors for an APMS implementation?" A simplistic critical success factors approach tends to deny the heavy contextuality and complexity of large-scale systems implementation.

Dobson et al.'s study had six major phases. The first phase was a literature review. The purpose of the review was to develop an APMS success model. The literature review followed Pawson's (2006) suggestions on how to conduct systematic reviews to make sense of a heterogeneous body of literature. The review was driven by a focus on CMO and how outcomes can be "produced." Using Pawson's approach means that it is possible to move away from the many one-off studies and instead learn from fields such as medicine and policy studies on how to develop evidence-based IS knowledge and theory. In order to guide practitioners, researchers should analyze previous research based on the assumption that one can draw more powerful conclusions from the collective wisdom of previous research.

In the second phase, the developed success model was used as the basis for generating questions for semi-structured, qualitative interviews. In the third phase, the generated questions were used in a focus group interview. The focus group was composed of IS industry experts, active in the performance measurement system area. The generated data and the first developed model were analyzed and a revised model (Model 1) was developed. In the fourth phase, this model was be tested against a case study with further refinements to the model resulting in Model 2. In the fifth phase, a number of reviews and case interviews were done. These led to the refinements of the model (Model 3 and 4). A final model was synthesized and presented by Myles (2008).

Dobson et al.'s study illustrates the realistic IS evaluation research well. The study has a focus on unpacking the mechanisms of how complex IS implementations work in particular settings and contexts. The focus is on what is it about this IS implementation that works for whom in what circumstances and why. With the study's emphasis on deep understanding of contexts, settings, and mechanisms, it shows how realistic IS evaluation research can be a very good alternative to simplistic critical success factors studies.

It is also possible to use a quantitative approach for CR-based IS evaluation. Oroviogoicoechea's (2007) study is an example of a primarily quantitative CR-based evaluation study (see also Oroviogoicoechea and Watson 2009). The aim of Oroviogoicoechea's study was to explore nurses' perceptions of the impact on clinical practice of the use of a hospital information system. Computer-based information systems are increasingly being introduced in clinical practice.

Oroviogoicoechea used a realistic IS evaluation design based on Pawson and Tilley 1997) and Carlsson (2003). It was used across all phases of the study. Oroviogoicoechea used a questionnaire containing both closed and open-ended questions. Descriptive statistics were used for an overall overview of nurses' perceptions. Inferential analysis, including both bivariate and multivariate methods (path analysis), was used for cross-tabulation of variables searching for CMO relationships. Content analysis of open-ended questions was used to identify major themes in nurses' responses. Overall satisfaction with the IS was positive. Mechanisms and outcomes are highly correlated. Comparisons with context variables show how users' characteristics, with the exception of attitude toward the introduction of technology, did not have a significant influence on perceptions while the nursing unit context had greater influence. Path analysis illustrated that the influence of unit context variables are on outcomes and not on mechanisms. Six main themes emerged from open-ended questions. Some differences in relation to the unit context were observed.

The two studies are different in that one is primarily a qualitative study and the other is primarily a quantitative study. Although most CR-based IS evaluation studies are qualitative studies, the two studies exemplify how CR is committed methodological pluralism. At the same time it should be noted that few studies have really taken advantage of CR's methodological pluralism.

Both studies are driven by the equation context + mechanism = outcome. As pointed out by Houston (2010), time is also relevant in shaping outcome and human agency certainly can play a critical role in shaping outcome. Hence, the extended equation is context + mechanism + time + human agency = outcome. Future IS evaluation studies could explore the use of the extended equation as the driver for IS evaluation research.

3.3 CR-Based Information Systems Design Science

This section addresses Gregor's (2006) fifth type of theory: theory for design and action. Research generating this type of theory is solution-driven and called IS design science research. Two major IS design science research schools have emerged (El Sawy 2006): (1) information systems design theory (see Walls et al. 2004), and (2) design science research (Hevner et al. 2004). The schools share a focus on the IT artifact. Some scholars argue for a third "school" based on IS as a socio-technical discipline and that

> design science and the research that builds that body of knowledge must acknowledge that IS is fundamentally about human activity systems which are usually technologically enabled, implying that *the context of design and use* is critical, and that research paradigms, practices and activities must embrace such a worldview (McKay and Marshall 2005, p. 5).

A number of projects have been developed in the past several years on IS design knowledge for "IS use and management" and an approach developed for socio-technical IS design science research (STISD) (Carlsson et al. 2011; Hrastinski et al. 2010). The approach is underpinned by CR and has four major research activities (Figure 1): (1) identify problem situations and desired outcomes, (2) review extant theories, knowledge, and data, (3) propose/refine design theory and knowledge, and (4) test design theory and knowledge. The figure reveals that IS design science research is not only about doing or designing. An important part of this research approach is to continuously test design theories.

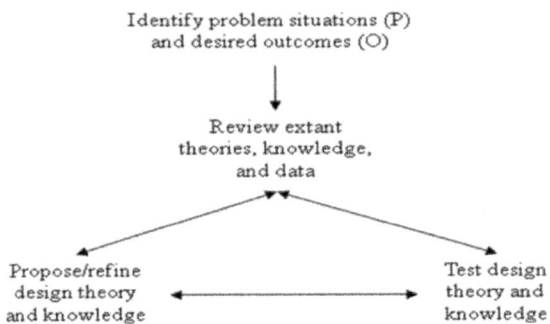

Fig. 1. IS design knowledge development (from Carlsson et al. 2011; Hrastinski et al. 2010)

Research Activity: Identify Problem Situations and Desired Outcomes. Design theories and design knowledge aim to support solving practical problems in such a way that desired outcomes are reached. Hence, such theories and knowledge are goal- and outcome-oriented, which means that, when used, they should increase the likelihood of reaching desired outcomes.

Research Activity: Review Extant Theories, Knowledge, and Data. Design theories and design knowledge should be enhanced through grounding in previous research. A design theory should be enhanced by continuously interacting with what is currently known, that is, grounding in extant theories, knowledge, and data. Gregor (2006) argues that other types of theories can inform design theory and that design theory and explanatory and predictive theories are strongly interrelated. Van Aken (2005) maintains that design knowledge in the form of design propositions can be developed through cross-case analyses of previous case studies (see also Carlsson et al. 2003; Gregor 2009; and Hrastinski et al. 2010). This means that design knowledge is abstracted from cases. Van Aken refers (2004) to this as "extracting case studies" and shows how it has led to a number of useful and actionable design propositions, for example, Kanban systems and just-in-time.

In general, design theories and design knowledge can be enhanced through systematic reviews of previous research—see, for example, Pawson's (2006) CR-based approach for conducting systematic reviews. Such reviews should be driven by PIMCO configurations and should have a specific focus on outcome(s) and how outcome(s) can be produced or enhanced (in the next activity, PIMCO configurations are explained). Using this approach for review of relevant literature means that it is possible to move away from the many one-off studies and instead learn from fields such as medicine and policy studies on how to develop evidence-informed IS design knowledge.

Research Activity: Propose/Refine Design Theory. Researchers orient their thinking to problem situation (P), IS initiative (I), mechanisms (M), context (C), outcome (O) pattern configurations (PIMCO configurations). A PIMCO configuration is a proposition stating what it is about an IS initiative that works for whom in what circumstances. When proposing a design theory, for example, in the form of design propositions, it is important to provide thick descriptions to aid the reader in understanding the theory, which may support practitioners in translating a theory to specific contexts and situations (van Aken 2005). A design proposition can be expressed as: In problem situation (P) and context (C), to achieve outcome (O), then design and implement IS initiative (I). The "design and implement IS initiative I" includes three different types of designs: (1) object-design, (2) realization design, and (3) a process design.

A field-tested and grounded design proposition has been tested empirically and is grounded in science. The latter means primarily grounding in results and theories from the behavioral science paradigm. Field-tested and grounded design propositions will in most cases be in the form of heuristics. This is consistent with critical realism's view on causality and means that the indeterminate nature of a heuristic design proposition makes it impossible to prove its effects conclusively, but it can be tested in context, which in turn can lead to sufficient supporting evidence.

Research Activity: Test Design Theory. After having formulated an initial design theory, the next step is empirical tests, which include the selection of appropriate data collection methods (Carlsson 2010; Carlson et al. 2011). In doing this, it can be examined whether the design theory may be used as support when trying to change reality. Based on the results, the outcome may be reflected on and the design theory may be refined. Through multiple studies, one can accumulate supporting evidence iteratively and continuously move toward evidence saturation. To strengthen the validity of design theories, test triangulation may be beneficial (i.e., to combine two or more complementing ways of conducting tests, such as focus groups and field experiments).

The approach has been used in a number of projects for developing socio-technical design theory and knowledge, for example, for the development of a design theory for synchronous e-learning (Hrastinski et al. 2010) and a design theory for IS integration management in mergers and acquisitions (Carlsson et al. 2011; Henningsson and Carlsson forthcoming).

4 Discussion

Above, some CR-based IS studies have been presented. Most of CR-based IS studies identified have been done as "traditional" behavioral science research and there is a domination of qualitative theory generation studies and qualitative evaluation studies. Given this picture, a few areas where CR-based research can move the IS-field forward and how CR-based studies can be improved are pointed out.

As noted above, CR rejects judgmental relativism (the inability to judge the merits of theories). This means that it should be possible to compare different theories. This will also open up for possibilities for theory testing. Currently, there are few, if any, CR-based theories testing IS studies. Miller and Tsang (2010) present a four-step approach for theory testing. Their approach is based on CR and provides guidance for deploying established research methods to test theories. Their approach is worthwhile to explore in CR-based IS research where the aim is to test theories—in behavioral science as well as in design science research. Their approach calls for the use of a diversity of research methods. I agree with their call for using a diversity of research methods in CR-based studies, not only for testing theories but also in research aiming at generating theories (see also Downward and Mearman 2007; Easton 2010; Zachariadis et al. 2010). Miller and Tsang's approach would, in most cases, require collaboration between researchers trained in different fields. In terms of comparing theories, Mole and Mole (2010) compare the use of Gidden's (1984) structuration theory and Archers (1995) morphogenesis theory in the entrepreneurship field and conclude that a CR perspective, like Archer's morphogenesis, may be more appropriate. Similar types of studies are needed in the IS field.

There is also a need for researchers using CR to be more cautious in their use of methods and techniques, for example, some studies use induction or deduction instead of critical realism's retroduction.

Most CR-based IS studies focus only one or two of Layder's (1993, 1998) domains of social life (self, situated activity, setting, and context). Future CR-based IS studies could address a larger number of domains and also incorporate that the domains are interlocking and mutually dependent on each other—on this issue, see, Houston (2010).

CR-based studies could also have critical and emancipatory aims. Bhaskar does not view the role of the social scientist as one that is value free and he views "facts" as having moral implications. This means that there is certainly a need for CR-based studies aimed at discovering mechanisms that led to harmful effects. If researchers find such mechanisms, then there is an obligation to expose the mechanisms and facilitate the conditions or contexts whereby emancipatory mechanisms can be activated. As Houston (2010, p. 76), states, "It is only by understanding the deep causes of oppression that we can develop ways of dismantling it."

5 Conclusion

Although CR has influenced a number of disciplines and fields, there has until recently been very little CR-based research. CR's potential for IS research has been argued by a number of scholars. In this paper, we have seen that CR can be useful as an underpinning philosophy for behavioral IS research as well for IS design science research. The examples presented in the paper can function as exemplars for how to do different types of IS research underpinned by CR. It should be noted that doing CR-based IS research is not without problems. For example, due to its open system view and that it recognizes social systems' complexity, CR-based IS research will generate theories that are provisional, fallible, incomplete, and extendable. In other words, CR-based IS research will not produce simple theories and "quick fix" results. Some weaknesses in current CR-based IS research have also been pointed out and ways to move forward suggested.

References

Ackroyd, S., Fleetwood, S. (eds.): Realist Perspectives on Management and Organizations. Routledge, London (2000)
Archer, M.S.: Social Origins of Educational Systems. Sage, London (1979)
Archer, M.S.: Realist Social Theory: The Morpohogenetic Approach. Cambridge University Press, Cambridge (1995)
Archer, M.S.: Morphogenesis/Morphostatis. In: Hartwig, M. (ed.) Dictionary of Critical Realism, p. 319. Routledge, London (2007)
Archer, M., Bhaskar, R., Collier, A., Lawson, T., Norrie, A. (eds.): Critical Realism: Essential Readings. Routledge, London (1998)
Bhaskar, R.: A Realist Theory of Science. Harvester Press, Sussex (1978)
Bhaskar, R.: Reclaiming Reality. Verso, London (1989)
Bhaskar, R.: Philosophy and the Idea of Freedom. Basil Blackwell, Oxford (1991)
Bhaskar, R.: The Possibility of Naturalism, 3rd edn. Routledge, London (1998)
Bhaskar, R.: Reflections on Meta-Reality. Sage, London (2002)
Bergene, A.C.: Towards a Critical Realist Comparative Methodology: Context-Sensitive Theoretical Comparison. J. of Critical Realism 6(1), 5–27 (2007)
Carlsson, S.A.: Advancing Information Systems Evaluation (Research): A Critical Realist Approach. Electronic J. of Information Systems Evaluation 6(2), 11–20 (2003)
Carlsson, S.A.: Using Critical Realism in IS Research. In: Whitman, M.E., Woszczynski, A.B. (eds.) The Handbook of Information Systems Research, pp. 323–338. Idea Group Publishing, Hershey (2004)
Carlsson, S.A.: Design Science Research in Information Systems: A Critical Realist Approach. In: Hevner, A., Chatterjee, S. (eds.) Design Research in Information Systems, pp. 209–233. Springer, New York (2010)
Carlsson, S.A., Henningsson, S., Hrastinski, S., Keller, C.: Socio-technical IS Design Science Research: Developing Design Theory for IS Integration Management. Information Systems and e-Business Management 9(1), 109–131 (2011)
Dean, K., Joseph, J., Norrie, A.: Editorial: New Essays in Critical Realism. New Formations 56, 7–26 (2005)
De Vaujany, F.-C.: Capturing Reflexivitiy Modes in IS: A Critical Realist Approach. Information and Organization 18, 51–71 (2008)
Dobson, P.J.: The Philosophy of Critical Realism–An Opportunity for Information Systems Research. Information Systems Frontier 3(2), 199–201 (2001)
Dobson, P., Myles, J., Jackson, P.: Making the Case for Critical Realism: Examining the Implementation of Automated Performance Management Systems. Information Resources Management Journal 20(2), 138–152 (2007)
Downward, P., Mearman, A.: Retroduction as Mixed-methods Triangulation in Economic Research: Reorienting Economics into Social Science. Cambridge Journal of Economics 31, 77–99 (2007)

Easton, G.: Critical Realism in Case Study Research. Industrial Marketing Management 39, 118–128 (2010)

El Sawy, O.A.: Personal communication (August 2006)

Fleetwood, S.: Boylan and O'Gorman's Causal Holism: A Critical Realist Evaluation. Cambridge Journal of Economics 26, 27–45 (2002)

Fleetwood, S., Ackroyd, S. (eds.): Critical Realist Applications in Organization and Management Studies. Routledge, London (2004)

Giddens, A.: The Constitution of Society. Polity Press, Cambridge (1984)

Gregor, S.: The Nature of Theory in Information Systems. MIS Quarterly 30(3), 611–642 (2006)

Gregor, S.: Building Theory in the Sciences of the Artificial. In: DESRIST 2009, Malvern, PA, May 7-8 (2009)

Hartwig, M. (ed.): Dictionary of Critical Realism. Routledge, London (2007)

Henningsson, S., Carlsson, S.A.: The DySIIM Model for Managing IS Integration in Mergers & Acquisitions. Information Systems Journal (forthcoming)

Hesketh, A., Fleetwood, S.: Beyond Measuring the Human Resources Management Organizational Performance Link: Applying Critical Realist Meta-Theory. Organization 13(5), 677–699 (2006)

Hevner, A.R., March, S.T., Park, J., Ram, S.: Design Science in Information Systems Research. MIS Quarterly 28(1), 75–105 (2004)

Hrastinski, S., Keller, C., Carlsson, S.A.: Design Exemplars for Synchronous e-Learning: A Design Theory Approach. Computers & Education 55, 652–662 (2010)

Houston, S.: Prising Open the Black Box: Critical Realism, Action Research and Social Work. Qualitative Social Work 9(1), 73–91 (2010)

Kazi, M.A.F.: Realist Evaluation in Practice. Sage, London (2003)

Layder, D.: New Strategies in Social Research. Polity Press, Cambridge (1993)

Layder, D.: Sociological Practice: Linking Theory and Social Research. Sage, London (1998)

Lòpez, J., Potter, G. (eds.): After Postmodernism: An Introduction to Critical Realism. Athlone, London (2001)

Lyytinen, K.: Design: Shaping in the Wild. Keynote speech at the Third International Conference on Design Science Research in Information Systems & Technology (DESRIST 2008), Atlanta, GA, May 7-9 (2008)

McKay, J., Marshall, P.: A Review of Design Science in Information Systems. In: Proceedings of the 16th Australasian Conference on Information Systems, Sydney, November 29-December 2 (2005)

Miller, K.D., Tsang, E.W.K.: Testing Management Theories: Critical Realist Philosophy and Research Methods. Strategic Management J. 32, 139–158 (2010)

Mingers, J.: Re-establishing the Real: Critical Realism and Information Systems. In: Mingers, J., Willcocks, L. (eds.) Social Theory and Philosophy for Information Systems, pp. 372–406. Wiley, Chichester (2004)

Mole, K.F., Mole, M.: Entrepreneurship as the Structuration of Individual and Opportunity: A Response Using Critical Realism. J. of Business Venturing 25, 230–237 (2010)

Morton, P.A.: Explaining Outcomes of Strategic Information Systems Planning Using a Critical Realist Approach. Unpublished Ph.D. Thesis, School of Business IT and Logistics, RMIT University, Melbourne (2010)

Mutch, A.: Actors and Networks or Agents and Structures: Towards a Realist View of Information Systems. Organizations 9(3), 477–496 (2002)

Myles, J.F.: Discovering Critical Success Factors for Implementing an Automated Measurement System: A Case Study Approach. Unpublished Ph.D. Thesis, Faculty of Business and Law, School of Management, Edith Cowan University (2008)

Oroviogoicoechea, C.: A Realistic Evaluation of the Impact of a Computerized Information System on Clinical Practice: The Nurses' Perspective. Unpublished Ph.D. Thesis, School of Nursing and Midwifery, University of Sheffield (2007)

Oroviogoicoechea, C., Watson, R.: A Quantitative Analysis of the Impact of a Computerized Information System on Nurses' Clinical Practice Using a Realistic Evaluation Framework. International J. of Medical Informatics 78, 839–849 (2009)

Pawson, R.: Evidence-Based Policy: A Realist Perspective. Sage, London (2006)

Pawson, R., Tilley, N.: Realistic Evaluation. Sage, London (1997)

Pentland, B.T., Feldman, M.S.: Organizational Routines as a Unit of Analysis. Industrial and Corporate Change 14, 793–815 (2005)

Robson, C.: Real World Research, 2nd edn. Blackwell, Oxford (2002)

Sayer, A.: Method in Social Science: A Realist Approach, 2nd edn. Routledge, London (1992)

Sayer, A.: Realism and Social Science. Sage, London (2000)

Smith, M.L.: Overcoming Theory-Practice Inconsistencies: Critical Realism and Information Systems Research. Working Paper 134, Department of Information Systems, London School of Economics (2005)

Strong, D.M., Volkoff, O.: Understanding OrganizationBEnterprise System Fit: A Path to Theorizing the Information Technology Artifact. MIS Quarterly 34(4), 731–756 (2010)

van Aken, J.E.: Management Research as a Design Science: Articulating the Research Products of Mode 2 Knowledge Production in Management. British J. of Management 16(1), 19–36 (2005)

van Aken, J.E.: Management Research Based on the Paradigm of Design Sciences: The Quest for Field-tested and Grounded Technological Rules. J. of Management Studies 41(2), 219–246 (2004)

Volkoff, O., Strong, D.M., Elmes, M.B.: Technological Embeddedness and Organizational Change. Organization Science 18(5), 832–848 (2007)

Walls, J.G., Widmeyer, G.R., El Sawy, O.A.: Building an Information Systems Design Theory for Vigilant EIS. Information Systems Research 3(1), 36–59 (1992)

Wilson, M., Greenhill, A.: Theory and Action for Emancipation: Elements of a Critical Realist Approach. In: Kaplan, B., Truex III, D., Wastell, D., Wood-Harper, T., DeGross, J. (eds.) Information Systems Research: Relevant Theory and Informed Practice, pp. 667–675. Kluwer, Amsterdam (2004)

Zachariadis, M., Scott, S., Barrett, M.: Designing Mixed-Method Research Inspired by a Critical Realism Philosophy: A Tale from the Field of IS Innovation. In: ICIS Proceedings, paper 265 (2010)

About the Author

Sven Carlsson is Professor of Informatics at Lund University School of Economics and Management (LUSEM). His current research interests include the use of IS to support management processes, knowledge management, enterprise systems, techno-change, enterprise 2.0, and the use of social media in business processes. He has published more than 125 peer-reviewed journal articles, book chapters, and conference papers and his work has appeared in journals such as *Journal of Management Information Systems, Decision Sciences, Information Systems Journal,*

Information & Management, Journal of Decision Systems, International Journal of Technology Management, Knowledge and Process Management, Knowledge Management Research & Practice, Information Systems and e-Business Management, and *Scandinavian Journal of Information Systems.* Sven has been a visiting scholar/professor at University of Arizona, Tucson, National University of Singapore, University College Cork, University of Southern California, Monash University, Melbourne, and Università della Calabria, Rende. He is a regional editor for *Knowledge Management Research & Practice.*

Section 7. Panels and Workshop

The Social Design of Information Systems

Steve Sawyer[1], Murali Venkatesh[2], Juhani Iivari[3],
Cathy Urquhart[4], and Ben Light[5]

[1] School of Information Studies, Syracuse University, Syracuse, NY 13244-4100 U.S.A.
ssawyer@syr.edu
[2] School of Information Studies, Syracuse University, Syracuse, NY 13244-4100 U.S.A.
mvenkate@syr.edu
[3] Department of Information Processing, Oulu University, Linnanmaa, Oulu 90570 Finland
iivari@rieska.oulu.fi
[4] Digital Business and Management Information Systems Division, Manchester Metropolitan
University Business School, Mancheste M1 3GH, U.K.
c.urquhart@mmu.ac.uk
[5] School of Media, Music and Performance, University of Salford, Salford M3 6EN U.K.
B.Light@slaford.ac.uk

1 Introduction

This panel focuses on issues of designing information systems to both account for, and better support, the increasingly social functions that computer-based technologies play. The goal of this panel is to serve as a forum to advance and discuss initial principles for what we are calling the *social design of information systems*. By social design we mean to emphasize that the presence and uses of information systems play an often significant role in supporting the reshaping social relations, social structures, social boundaries, and social norms. Many such aspects of this reshaping are highlighted in the scholarship of IFIP 8.2 members, and with this panel we seek to focus the collective attention of the assembled scholars to shift attention from "problematizing" the issues with designing information systems toward advancing socially relevant design principles (e.g., Iivari et al. 1998).

Issues with information systems design and development have always been a core concern of the IFIP 8.2 community. Since the 1970s, much of the IFIP 8.2 scholarship has focused on illuminating issues and the assumption of organizationally oriented information systems design—often with a critical stance (e.g., Hedberg 1975). This critical stance is certainly embodied in the rich tradition of critical theoretic research. However, the critical stance found in much IFIP 8.2 scholarship means, more broadly, questioning assumptions—conceptually and empirically—and challenging orthodox or taken-for-granted stances (e.g., Boland 1987).

We observe, like many, that contemporary information systems are increasingly expected to span organizational boundaries and the design of information systems is no longer a functional focus or even a unilateral organizational issue (Benkler and Nissenbaum 2006). The interorganizational focus of contemporary information systems calls into question some of the taken-for-granted design principles and practices of more organizationally focused approaches such as the importance of a production-oriented purpose, the need for top management support, or even the

M. Chiasson et al. (Eds.): Future IS 2011, IFIP AICT 356, pp. 287–290, 2011.

explicit involvement of organizational actors in the system design, development, and deployment. Departures (with both positive and negative effects) are commonly identified in the literature regarding large-scale interorganizational information systems such as interconnected national identity card and passport systems, digital health-care records, and cooperative information-sharing and e-commerce systems such as Amazon.com. Concurrent with the shift toward interorganizational systems is the rise of Internet-based social media applications that involve more socially oriented functionality. Certainly contemporary web-based social media platforms/applications like Twitter, Flickr, and Facebook are contemporary examples of such systems.

This trend toward explicitly social functionality is seemingly profound: organization leaders are increasingly more aware that social functionality must be embedded in information systems—and organizational workers are coming to expect this to be the norm. Organizational leaders are, however, struggling with how best to accommodate socially relevant (and often divisive) requirements. For example, what are the proper ways to model social behavior? Given that these information systems are *designed* to always span organizational boundaries (becoming interorganizational systems and demanding new collaborative forms of governance), what sorts of cross-boundary social interactions are to be supported (or made more difficult)? Certainly the design needs for such socially complex systems are likely to differ from the set of what we are labeling *organizational design principles*, which are focused on a particular functional or cross-functional aspect of an organization.

Given these trends, what are the basics of social design (versus organizational design) of an information system? For this panel, we consider two aspects of this issue.

1. How do designers grapple with the tensions of developing for role-based organizational uses and users versus . the more socially complex users of social software?
2. How do designers grapple with the issues of social needs for users in their work?

2 Panelists

To do this, we bring together four scholars who have, through their work, focused on various aspects of social design (with Sawyer serving as moderator).

Juhani Iivari will focus on aspects of social design and social use by drawing from three streams of his research: (1) philosophical bases of information systems development approaches, (2) comparative analyses of information systems development methodologies (e.g., Iivari et al. 1998), and (3) some recent empirical material on individual's uses of Facebook.

Ben Light will draw upon two ethnographic projects of online communities to illuminate social design issues. Study one is based on an Internet dating site (Light 2007; Light et al. 2008). Study two concerns digital gaming experiences on and beyond the screen (Fletcher and Light 2008). By considering sets of socio-technical arrangements that, as yet, have not been subject to much scrutiny within information systems, these ethnographies help frame what social design will need to consider.

Cathy Urquhart will build on her work in the areas of information and communication technologies (ICTs) and social inclusion. ICTs are increasingly seen as a means for social inclusion (e.g., Urquhart et al. 2008). She will discuss how, in a world where we assume that everyone is accessing the Internet in the same way, one design of a web site may not fit all communities and can exclude people as well as include them. These issues of design can cover language (Diaz Andrade and Urquhart 2009) and cultural and visual aspects (Ornelas and Gregory 2009; Tan et al. 2006). She will also discuss how the design of some mainstream websites such as Facebook might shape social interactions and make assumptions about their users, who are in fact extremely varied.

Murali Venkatesh will build from his ongoing work in community networks research (Venkatesh 2003) and influences of Simon (1996). While many in information systems point to Simon's guidance on design science, few note that he spends an equal amount of time discussing social design.

3 Panel Structure

The panel is structured in four distinct phases. Two of the phases rely on participation with the audience. Principles guiding this design are to

1. Draw on the panelist's expertise and experience to provide initial principles and issues with social design
2. Fully engage participants in advancing these principles and surfacing issues

For the first phase, panelists will provide one or more tentative social design principles and one or more social design issues. This set of tentative principles and issues will serve as the basis for discussions in the second phase. The first phase will take 20 minutes (including introductions).

The second phase of the panel time will be done in concert with the audience and last for about 30 minutes. The members of the panel audience will work together (or alone; it will be their choice) to respond to the initial positions outlined by the panelists. These responses can come in one of three forms: (1) extension— modifying or extending a current principle with additional insight, specificity, or direction, (2) challenge—providing argumentation or guidance which challenges or seeks to refute the initial position, and (2) addition—providing additional principles or issues that were not provided initially. To enact this phase, panelists and the moderator will help to organize groups and provide support. The *ad hoc* groups formed among audience members will be given a set of colored note cards (green for extension, red for challenge, and orange for addition). These note cards will be collected at the end of the second phase.

The third phase will last 10 minutes and will have two parallel activities. The panelists will use this time to reflect on what they have learned by working with various audience groups. In parallel to this, the moderator will organize the responses to provide some initial feedback from what the audience generated and to highlight provocative or insightful feedback for further discussion in the final phase.

In the fourth phase, the panelists and audience will participate in a more open discussion of the selected feedback generated in phase two and summarized in phase three. In this phase, the goal is to begin identifying common positions and to identify areas of distinct differences regarding social design principles and issues.

Following the panel, a full summary of the discussion, responses, and points will be posted to LOCATION so that participants can have access to the material they helped to cocreate.

References

Benkler, Y., Nissenbaum, H.: Commons-Based Peer Production and Virtue. The Journal of Political Philosophy 14(4), 394–419 (2006)

Boland, R.J.: The In-formation of Information Systems. In: Boland, R.J., Hirschheim, R.A. (eds.) Critical Issues in IS Research. John Wiley, New York (1987)

Diaz Andrade, A., Urquhart, C.: ICTs as a Tool for Cultural Dominance: Prospects for a Two-Way Street. Electronic Journal of Information Systems in Developing Countries 15(2), 108–132 (2009)

Fletcher, G., Light, B.: Making the Game Work? Lessons from Ethnographies of SingStar. In: CITASA Workshop, American Sociological Association, Boston (2008)

Hedberg, B.: Computer Systems to Support Industrial Democracy. In: Mumford, E., Sackman, H. (eds.) Human Choice and Computers. North Holland, New York (1975)

Lamb, R., Kling, R.: Reconceptualizing Users as Social Actors in Information Systems Research. MIS Quarterly 27(2), 197–235 (2003)

Light, B.: Introducing Masculinity Studies to Information Systems Research: The Case of Gaydar. European Journal of Information Systems 16(5), 658–665 (2007)

Light, B., Fletcher, G., Adam, A.: Gay Men, Gaydar and the Commodification of Difference. Information Technology and People 21(3), 300–314 (2008)

Iivari, J., Hirschheim, R., Klein, H.K.: A Paradigmatic Analysis Contrasting IS Development Approaches and Methodologies. Information Systems Research 9(2), 164–193 (1998)

Ornelas, Y., Gregory, J.: Design for Social Inclusion and Social Sustainability. Special Session Organizers. In: Proceedings of IASDR 2009: Design Rigor & Relevance, Seoul, Korea, October 18-22 (2009)

Simon, H.A.: The Sciences of the Artificial, 3rd edn. MIT Press, Cambridge (1996)

Tan, F.B., Lin, H.J., Urquhart, C.: An Exploratory Study of the Design Preferences of U.S. and Chinese Virtual Communities. International Journal of E-Business Research 2(3), 47–69 (2006)

Urquhart, C., Liyanage, S., Kah, M.: ICTs and Poverty Reduction: A Social Capital and Knowledge Perspective. Journal of Information Technology 23(3), 203–213 (2008)

Venkatesh, M.: Public Participation in Broadband Network Development. In: Day, P., Schuler, D. (eds.) Community Networks and the Public Sphere. Routledge, London (2003)

Teaching Foresight and the Future

Erran Carmel[1], Michel Avital[2], Paul Gray[3], Jannis Kallinikos[4],
and John Leslie King[5]

[1] American University, Washington, DC U.S.A.
carmel@american.edu
[2] University of Amsterdam, Amsterdam, The Netherlands
avital@uva.nl
[3] Claremont Graduate University, Claremont, CA U.S.A.
paul.gray@cgu.edu
[4] London School of Economics, London, UK
j.kallinikos@lse.ac.uk
[5] University of Michigan, Ann Arbor, MI U.S.A.
jlking@umich.edu

Abstract. We train students as retrospective observers who specialize in evidence-based *post hoc* analysis. Building on action research and a cry for relevance, we witness the emergence of engaged scholarship and focus on the present and ongoing affairs. However, the future appears to be virtually neglected in the IS management curricula and organizational studies. In keeping with the theme of the meeting, the objective of the panel is to demonstrate the relevance of foresight and future in our curriculum and its critical role in nurturing the next generation.

Keywords: Futures studies, strategic foresight, prospective thinking, curriculum development, teaching information systems.

1 Introduction

Based in the sciences, we train students as retrospective observers who specialize in evidence-based *post hoc* analysis. Building on action research and a cry for relevance, we witness the emergence of engaged scholarship and focus on the present and ongoing affairs. However, the future appears to be virtually neglected in information systems management curricula and organizational studies. Dealing with the future is considered by many to be something between speculation and reading tea leaves. In keeping with the theme of the meeting, the objective of the panel is to tear down the myth and demonstrate not only the relevance of foresight and analysis of the future in our curriculum but also its critical role in nurturing the next generation.

We live the future. Students love dabbling in it. Faculty members in other disciplines thrive teaching it. Futures Studies is a discipline with its own methodologies that is taught in social science programs around the world. Sometimes it is its own discipline, as is the case with Turku's Finland Futures Research Centre. The Institute for Alternative Futures (in the United States) lists 18 futures or foresight graduate programs around the world (see **http://www.fernweb.org**). Many of us

M. Chiasson et al. (Eds.): Future IS 2011, IFIP AICT 356, pp. 291–293, 2011.

teach information systems in business schools, where teaching futures thinking has been remarkably sparse[1], perhaps because IS faculty assume that futures thinking is part of the epistemology of business strategy and the IS capstone courses. In general, the discipline of Futures Studies never progressed beyond a niche discipline.

2 Controversy

The panelists will take opposing yet complementary positions with respect to the role of futures studies in the IS curriculum. They will argue that

1. Futures studies should be taught in independent courses.
2. The area of futures should be best infused into other courses, such as IS strategy and as a tool for doctoral research.
3. Futures techniques have advanced to the point where they are taken seriously as a scholarly environment in other fields but technology transfer has not yet reached the point where these techniques can be widely adopted in the IS field.

3 Panel Structure

The panel topic is intended to generate responses to several specific questions. After a brief introduction by the panel moderator, the panelists will present short overviews in response to guiding questions that aim to contextualize the discussion and raise core issues. Specifically, panelists will be asked to draw on their experience in both the futures and IS fields to answer two initial questions:

- Why should we deal with the future in the IS curriculum?
- What methodologies can be used in the classroom environment for learning about the IS future and the effect of ICT on possible futures?

Then the discussion will move to a forward-looking perspective. Questions for this portion of the panel discussion are

- What IS research topics and domains would best be illuminated by futures research?
- Should we entrust only Forrester and Gartner with forecasting and understanding future technologies and environments?

The panel will conclude with a deliberation among the panelists and facilitated discussion with the audience. Examples of expected questions and topics include

- Are we seriously suggesting gut feel, crystal balls, tea leaves, and palm reading as appropriate approaches?
- Since futures studies are both quantitative and qualitative, should they be part of a course in analytics, or one about the social side of information systems, or both?
- How should we infuse or mesh futures studies in current IS courses?
- Should we deal with the future in a standalone course? Can it be done? Should the course be interdisciplinary in business schools?
- What is the future of Futures Studies as a discipline?

---

[1] With some notable exceptions, for example, in 2009 the University of Notre Dame became the first undergraduate business program requiring all business students to take a foresight course.

4 Panelists

Michel Avital, Associate Professor at the University of Amsterdam and Visiting Professor at Viktoria Institute. Building on his interest in how information technology promotes innovation and extraordinary outcomes, Michel has studied and published articles on topics such as design, creativity, innovation, generative systems, collaboration and competition, green IT and sustainable value, positive organizational scholarship, and appreciative inquiry. In lieu of prediction, he relies on a constructive approach that links *positive image* with *positive action*. That is, the more collectives or individuals accustom to dealing with the future and to nurturing desired scenarios, the more likely they are to realize them. Michel designs courses with a prospective orientation and regularly incorporates elements of envisioning and future thinking into his graduate and post-graduate classes.

Erran Carmel (panel moderator), Professor of Information Technology and International Business Research Professor at the Kogod School of Business, American University. He is a recognized thought leader on the globalization of technology work and offshoring. He began teaching the MBA course Future & Foresight in 2010.

Paul Gray, Emeritus Professor at Claremont Graduate University, is one of the early members of the Association for Information Systems, and a recipient of the LEO Award for Lifetime Achievement. Before retiring, Paul taught Futures as part of courses and IS doctoral seminars. He was a member of the Center for Futures Research at the University of Southern California from 1972 to 1980 where he conducted several futures studies. He has published on the future of IS. He is particularly concerned with IS researchers taking a futures perspective on the field so that we lead the thinking about the information systems future rather than depending on the opinions of consulting firms.

Jannis Kallinikos, Professor in the Department of Management at the London School of Economics. Recent publications include the *The Consequences of Information: Institutional Implications of Technological Change* (Elgar, 2006), and *Governing through Technology: Information Artefacts and Social Practice* (Palgrave, MacMillan, 2010). Both of his books and other recent writings deal extensively with the technological and social processes that shape the future, paying attention to how the diffusion of information and digital content are negotiating the functional habitat of organizations and the patterns of everyday living.

John Leslie King, Vice Provost for Strategy, and W. W. Bishop Professor in the School of Information at the University of Michigan. His research focuses on the relationship between technical change and social change, especially the transforming role of information technology in highly institutionalized production sectors such as transport, health, education, financial services, and government. The best predictor of the future *is* the past, for the simple reason that it is the *only* predictor. But as Marx said, people don't create the future as they please. The trick lies in seeing the persistent features of the world, the patterns, and figuring out where things are likely to go. The great ice hockey star Wayne Gretzky summed it up well: skate to where the puck is going to be. It's easier said than done, but it can be done.

Will Current Trends in Information Systems Development Lead to More Visible Usage of Socio-technical Approaches?

Steven Alter[1], Mikko Korpela[2], Doncho Petkov[3], and Nancy Russo[4]

[1] University of San Francisco, U.S.A.
alter@usfca.edu
[2] University of Eastern Finland, Finland, and Cape Peninsula University of Technology and Nelson Mandela Metropolitan University, South Africa
mikko.kropela@uef.fi
[3] Eastern Connecticut State University, U.S.A.
petkovd@easternct.edu
[4] Northern Illinois University, U.S.A.
nrusso@niu.edu

1 Background and Goals

There is broad agreement that socio-technical approaches to systems analysis and design have not been used to their full potential in the information systems field. There are also a number of trends in information systems development (ISD) that might generate opportunities for greater usage of socio-technical approaches.

The panel has several overlapping goals related to current ISD trends and the adoption of socio-technical approaches. The goals include

1. Providing an interesting way of exploring the strengths and limitations of current versions of several socio-technical methods.
2. Identifying ways to extend those methods to make them more useful.
3. Discussing current ISD trends and trying to identify the characteristics and methods from a socio-technical viewpoint that would best support the development environments implied by these trends.

The assumption underlying the entire discussion is that every socio-technical approach has some advantages and some disadvantages, and that much of the value of the panel session is in clarifying those advantages and disadvantages and combining ideas from multiple approaches to come up with a multifaceted method for a particular situation. This discussion can contribute to the evolution of information systems development methods by highlighting the growing importance of socio-technical approaches in emerging development environments.

2 Structure and Time Line

The panel is structured to allow the presenters to explain their initial views, to allow them to interact around practical ISD issues, and to allow the audience to participate

M. Chiasson et al. (Eds.): Future IS 2011, IFIP AICT 356, pp. 295–297, 2011.
© IFIP International Federation for Information Processing 2011

extensively in the discussion during the last 30 minutes of the panel. The panel will proceed as follows.

Nancy Russo will set the stage by summarizing **current ISD trends** that might generate greater opportunities for using socio-technical methods in ISD. These trends include more collaboration, along with the breakdown of organizational boundaries to allow greater interaction with external influences; explosive growth in the distributed cocreation of structures and content, often through what are considered Web 2.0 technologies; increased focus on issues of sustainability and social responsibility; and the continuing movement toward a services model of delivery (Bughin et al. 2010).

Mikko Korpela will briefly provide background about activity theory, originally a psychological theory of purposeful human activity mediated by tools and signs, which has been applied widely in educational studies and increasingly in socio-technical design. He will summarize how **activity-driven methods for ISD** have been used, particularly addressing citizen and community centered service models, codesign, social responsibility, sustainability, and use in Finland, China and Africa (Korpela et al. 2004; Luukkonen et al. 2010). He will also mention some of the limitations of activity theory in relation to possible use in practical ISD situations, especially those in which current ISD trends apply.

Steven Alter will briefly provide background about the **work system method**, a socio-technical approach that emphasizes evaluation and planning by business professionals who are facing questions about whether a work system operates well enough, and how it can be improved. He will summarize how the work system method has been used in teaching; and its potential value as a tool for business professionals trying to evaluate and analyze IT-reliant systems in organizations (Alter 2010; Truex et al. 2010). He will mention some of its limitations in relation to possible use in practical ISD situations, especially those in which current ISD trends apply.

Don Petkov will explore several issues in using a third socio-technical approach, Checkland's **soft systems methodology**, in combination with traditional *IS development approaches*. These include their different epistemological assumptions; the degree of support for stakeholder participation; any potential support for decisions to take a particular action; difficulties in transitioning from SSM analysis to traditional IS development models; degree of support for analyzing of both the technical and social aspects of a work system; and availability of means to promote learning (Petkov et al. 2008; Petkov et al. 2007). Then he will explore whether similar conclusions may apply to Alter's *work system method* or the *activity driven methods* for IS development by Korpela and his group.

An interactive discussion by the panel members will focus on the question giving title to the panel: Will current trends in information system development lead to more visible usage of socio-technical approaches? After the panel members have provided their comments, audience members will be welcomed to join the discussion with their own observations and suggestions.

3 Panelists

Steven Alter is a Professor of Information Systems at the University of San Francisco, San Francisco, California. His research for over a decade has concerned developing systems analysis concepts and methods that can be used by typical business professsionals and can support communication with IT professionals. His publications include a 2006 book, *The Work System Method: Connecting People, Processes, and IT for Business Results*, and many related articles in journals and conference proceedings.

Mikko Korpela is a Research Director in Health Information Systems Research and Development, School of Computing, at the University of Eastern Finland, in Kuopio, Finland, as well as an Adjunct Professor at Cape Peninsula University of Technology, Cape Town, and an Honorary Professor at Nelson Mandela Metropolitan University in Port Elizabeth, South Africa. He has studied ISD with an activity-theoretical approach since the late 1980s, collaborating with several African universities. He has published in IFIP WG 8.2 and WG 9.4 conferences and elsewhere.

Don Petkov is a Professor of Information Systems at Eastern Connecticut State University, Willimantic, Connecticut. His research explores the application of SSM and other systems approaches in software engineering, telecommunications planning, and environmental management. His papers have appeared in *The Journal of Systems and Software, Decision Support Systems, Information Resources Management Journal, Telecommunications Policy,* and elsewhere.

Nancy L. Russo is a Professor of Information Systems in the Operations Management and Information Systems Department at Northern Illinois University, DeKalb, Illinois. She studies information systems development and implementation, and is the co-author of *Information Systems Development: Methods-in-Action.* Her work has appeared in *Information Systems Journal, Communications of the ACM, European Journal of Information Systems,* and *Information Technology & People*

References

Alter, S.: Bridging the Chasm Between Sociotechnical and Technical Views of Systems in Organizations. In: 31st International Conference on Information Systems (2010)

Bughin, J., Chui, M., Manyika, J.: Clouds, Big Data, and Smart Assets: Ten Tech-Enabled Business Trends to Watch. McKinsey Quarterly, August 1-14 (2010)

Korpela, M., Mursu, A., Soriyan, A., Eerola, A., Häkkinen, H., Toivanen, M.: Information Systems Research and Development by Activity Analysis and Development: Dead Horse or the Next Wave? In: Kaplan, B., Truex III, D.P., Wastell, D., Wood-Harper, A.T., De Gross, J.I. (eds.) Information Systems Research: Relevant Theory and Informed Practice. IFIP TC8/WG 8.2 20th Year Retrospective, pp. 453–471. Kluwer Academic, Boston (2004)

Luukkonen, I., Korpela, M., Mykkänen, J.: Modelling Approaches in the Early Phases of Information Systems Development. In: IT to Empower – 18th European Conference on Information Systems (2010)

Petkov, D., Edgar-Nevill, D., Madachy, R., O'Connor, R.: Information Systems, Software Engineering and Systems Thinking? Challenges and Opportunities. International Journal on Information Technologies and the Systems Approach 1, 62–78 (2008)

Petkov, D., Petkova, O., Andrew, T., Nepal, T.: Mixing Multiple Criteria Decision Making with Soft Systems Thinking Techniques for Decision Support in Complex Situations. Decision Support Systems 43, 1615–1629 (2007)

Truex, D., Alter, S., Long, C.: Systems Analysis for Everyone Else: Empowering Business Professionals Through a Systems Analysis Method that Fits Their Needs. In: IT to Empower – 18th European Conference on Information Systems (2010)

Methods for Studying the Information Systems Future

Paul Gray[1] and Anat Hovav[2]

[1] Claremont Graduate University, School of Information Science and Technology,
Claremont, CA
paulgray@cgu.edu
[2] Korea University, Business School, Seoul, Korea
anatzh@korea.ac.kr

Abstract. Information Systems studies involve the present and the future. Although data can be obtained on the present, the future can only be estimated. In Information Systems, a rapidly changing intellectual and technological field, simply extrapolating the present to the future is likely to be wrong. This paper presents and explains three proven research methods for studying the IS future and describes the role of Futures Research methods as a tool for academic research.

Keywords: Modeling the future, environmental scanning, Delphi, scenarios, role of futures in academic research.

1   Introduction

> A research method is a strategy of inquiry which moves from the underlying philosophical assumptions to research design and data collection.
>
> Michael Myers (1977)

Historically, the study of the human and organizational aspects[1] of management information systems (MIS) adopted the methodologies of social science. This view of research permeated IS as early as the Minnesota experiments (Dickson et al. 1977). The majority of work published at the time used surveys or quasi-experiments. Over time, the field recognized the need for a "pluralism of methodologies" (Robey 1996; Walsham 1995). At the IFIP 8.2 working conference in 1997, Markus pointed out that qualitative research methods were becoming acceptable in MIS research. These methods, including case studies, action, ethnographic, and grounded research, are now a routine part of the IS tool kit. These methodologies encompass positivist, and critical work. One cannot say that a given methodology is better than another (Markus 1997). The choice depends on the research question and the context being studied.

---

[1] Although IS research is primarily concerned with systems, people, and the policies involved in managing IS, those aspects change as the technology changes. Hence IS research also needs to consider the impact of future technologies.

M. Chiasson et al. (Eds.): Future IS 2011, IFIP AICT 356, pp. 299–316, 2011.

1.1 The Conference Theme

The theme of this conference is "Researching the Future." The future is a dynamic environment and is fraught with uncertainty. Because the future will differ from the present, simple extrapolation of current trends into the years ahead is not enough. Policies, organizational business practices, science and technology, and tastes can and will change Information Systems and their use. The occurrence of events and the direction of trends are unknown in advance. Often the best that can be done is assigning probabilities to outcomes. As a result, conventional methods of research are no longer sufficient when considering the long-term future.

Consider, for example, the future of the Internet and its security. At this writing, the United States government proposes to allow the President to shut down domestic Internet providers in an emergency (e.g., foreign cyber-attack). What is the probability this law will pass in 2011? If passed, will the authority be used? How severe must an attack be to declare an emergency? If an emergency is declared, how long will the Internet be down in the United States? In other countries? What will be the effect on the economy as a function of shutdown period?

Another example: The conventional wisdom is that the trend of security incidents is rising. Will this trend continue? Stabilize? Decrease? Alternate between increasing and decreasing? Are there inflection points? How will security be improved by specific policies? By enforcement? By government investment? By private sector investment? For each of these alternatives, when (if ever) will they be introduced? If one of them is introduced, how much will it affect other options? Will its security be perceived so poor that significant numbers will stop using the Internet? What are the economic implications if the Internet collapses? If alternative future situations are possible, what is the probability of each? If a particular unfavorable outcome is highly likely under one set of assumptions, are there policies, actions, or technologies that can ameliorate or eliminate that outcome?

Note that in these examples the scope is much broader than the IS field's conventional studies of individual organizations or industries. The impact of IS is moving from the organizational context to society and beyond. Furthermore, the research questions being asked by the MIS discipline have expanded from the operational and strategic to societal policies and issues. To address these questions, MIS researchers need to expand their methodology toolkit.

Although futures research methodologies are used extensively in such disciplines as policy analysis, strategy, competitive intelligence, and forecasting, and are widely used by industry, government, and centers for studying the future, they are rarely used in IS research. Studies about the future of information technology itself have appeared from time to time. Herbert Simon (1969) forecast design science and artificial intelligence. Dahlbom (1997; Dahlbom and Mathiassen 1997) discussed the future of IT in conceptual terms but did not use a futures methodology to address ICT research questions.

1.2 What This Paper Is About

This paper introduces three well-established futures research methodologies, and shows how these methodologies can be applied to rigorous IS academic research. The goal of this paper is technology transfer; that is, to familiarize IS researchers with these methodologies and explore some of the institutionalization mechanisms needed to incorporate them into the IS research tradition. The discussion is exploratory to initiate dialogue among IS researchers.

Section 2 briefly describes three standard futures methodologies (environmental scanning, Delphi, and scenarios) and illustrates how they can be incorporated into IS research. Using scenarios as an example, Section 3 discusses futures methodology as an academic method for IS research. This section includes epistemology, research design (research questions, unit of analysis, setting propositions and criteria for interpreting results), and issues such as construct and internal validity and generalizability. The conclusions (Section 4) present our views of what can best be accomplished with conventional and futures methods. Appendices A and B expand the descriptions of the Delphi and scenarios methodologies, Appendix C suggests guidelines for futures research in information systems, and Appendix D lists 37 methods used in futures research.

2 Futures Research Methods

This section describes three futures research methodologies: environmental scanning, Delphi, and scenarios. These methods were selected for this paper because they are relatively simple to implement and are widely used.

Futures research methods have been used actively since the 1950s. Methods such as Delphi, cross-impact analysis, and scenarios were discussed by this paper's authors in their IS research since the 1990s (Gray and Hovav 1999, 2002, 2007, 2008). Attempts to predict the future of IS by using extrapolations were also published in the 1990s (Cule and Grover 1994; Ein-Dor and Segev 1993). Most recently, Crespo et al. (2010) reference six Delphi studies on IS topics published since 2002.

2.1 Assumptions of Futures Research

The three methods and their variations described in this section share a common set of assumptions. First, the future is not prewritten nor is it wholly determined by the past. Second, present conditions and trends will continue along evolutionary lines unless natural limits are approached (e.g., speed of light) and/or extreme external changes occur (e.g, PC, Internet, iPhone, iPad).

External changes are inherently uncertain. Some aspects cannot yet be explained scientifically and some aspects (e.g., policy) depend on human choice. Attempts to guide the future through policy are based on (1) assessment of present and past conditions, (2) possible future changes, and (3) the extent to which future conditions can be altered by social resources. The desirability of social conditions is a value judgment, not based on fixed criteria of economic rationality.

Futures research methods should be undertaken when[2]

1. Uncertainty about the future is high
2. Historical data is limited

---

[2] These criteria were enumerated by Olaf Helmer (personal communications).

3.   The number of stakeholders (e.g., IT and communications vendors, users, companies, government) is large
4.   The issue is important for decision makers
5.   Major impact on IS is involved and the issue is more than just technical
6.   The analysts involved are knowledgeable about the problem

2.2   Environmental Scanning/Collective Intelligence

Environmental scanning[3] involves observing the present and using the results to infer the future. Glenn and Gordon (2009) trace the method back to the crow's nest on ancient sailing ships. Environmental scanning is also a way to gain the input needed for SWOT (strength, weaknesses, opportunities, threat) analysis.[4]

Environmental scanning is used to create databases that serve as the foundation for futures studies. The objective is to distinguish among constant, slow, continuous or potentially disruptive change. Scanning involves analyzing multiple sources of information (public and private) and identifying early change indicators. Such indicators are used to provide managers the required lead-time necessary to respond to future events and trends. Public sources include database searches, executive speeches and interviews, papers at meetings, and employment advertisements. Much analysis and skill are involved in filtering information (i.e., deciding what is important and what is irrelevant). Of particular interest, for example, are finding disruptive technologies and obtaining reliable estimates of when they will reach the market. Environmental scanning is often used in business intelligence.

2.3   Delphi

The Delphi method (Linstone and Turoff 2002) combines the wisdom of crowds (Surowiecki 2004) to estimate, as a function of time, the probabilities of events (e.g., an invention) and the evolution of trends (ongoing phenomena) when there is no source of factual data and a basis for opinion exists. The information sought usually affects decisions and policies.

In Delphi, questions are presented to a panel of subject experts on a topic of interest. For example, what is the earliest, most likely,and latest time when the Google.com market share for businesses equals Microsoft's? How many PCs will be sold in Africa in 2015? In 2020? In 2025? (Input provided to the respondents might include 2000–2009 sales.) Respondent anonymity prevents undue influence, groupthink, or biased judgment under uncertainty (Tsohou et al. 2008). The panelists are typically dispersed in space and time, and communication is often facilitated by information and communication technologies (e.g., email, GDSS, Web 2.0 applications).

A Delphi survey is administered in loop-back rounds, usually by a facilitator. Each round's responses are tabulated and fed back to the group. Panelists who provided extreme estimates (smallest and largest values) are asked to state their reasons. Their opinions are also used as inputs to the next round. The rounds stop when either

---

[3] Also called collective intelligence, futures scanning systems, and early warning systems.

[4] SWOT analysis is taught in business schools as a way of assessing present and future competition.

consensus or dissensus occurs. Consensus is measured with traditional statistical tools (cluster analysis or distance from the mean). Desired betas[5] are predetermined. Experimental results indicate that good forecasts can be obtained and that accuracy can be improved by asking people to state their expertise for each item. Dissensus on a question indicates that expert opinion on the subject is divided. At present, Delphi is the most commonly used futures research methodology in published IS research. Appendix A explains the method further.

The cross-impact model (e.g., Glenn and Gordon 2009) is the next step of sophistication beyond Delphi. Delphi assumes events and trends are mutually independent and all other things are equal (i.e., *ceteris paribus*). These assumptions are rarely valid in the real world. For example, the probability of occurrence of a particular innovation may be more likely if another innovation occurs or if a trend reaches a threshold level. That is, event probabilities and trends do interact with one another. An additional set of inputs is therefore required: the estimated change (i.e., the impact) in the probabilities of every other event if a particular event occurs.

Cross-impact analysis is run as a multi-period stochastic simulation. The first period (e.g., 2 years) is examined. A random number generator is used to determine which events "occurred." That is, if the random number for an event is less than or equal to the probability of an event during that period, the event is declared occurred. For each occurred event, its impact on events that have not yet occurred is used to update the future probabilities of events with which it interacts. Given the updated probabilities, the next period is run. The process is repeated until the entire time being studied is completed. To keep the updated probabilities in the range 0 to 1, the calculations involve the use of likelihood ratios. The output of a single run is a scenario that has a low probability of occurrence. The aggregate of all the runs—that is, the complete simulation—provides expected values and variances.

If the foregoing sounds complex, it is. Cross-impact requires many more inputs and calculations than Delphi. In terms of physical effort by researchers and expert panels, it takes much longer to perform than a Delphi. However, the results obtained provide a much richer understanding of the problem studied.

2.4 Scenarios

Scenarios are a way of communicating about the future. They are stories that describe the future in terms that managers and other nonspecialists can understand. That does not mean that they are arbitrary. They are carefully developed to reflect the logical implications of assumptions and forecasts about the future (Gray and Hovav 2007). Scenarios are an end product of a prudent analysis, not the workings of the imagination of a novelist or a science fiction writer. Scenario building is a discipline that involves a number of stakeholders and typically describes future events and trends within a given set of assumptions and constraints.

Why Scenarios? Organizations use scenarios to forecast alternative futures they may face. Scenarios examine the issues to be resolved, time relations, interactions, and logical consequences. Scenarios are most powerful when several are used to present alternative views of the future as seen from the present. They are often used as a

---

[5] That is, the acceptable probability of Type II error.

policy analysis tool (Boroush and Thomas 1992). For example, if a scenario indicates a high probability of an undesirable future, actions can be taken to reduce that probability (e.g., lobbying, merging, changing business practices, innovating).

Scenarios are most valuable when: (1) the external environment is highly uncertain, (2) the environment could take plausible alternative trajectories, or (3) specific indicators measure the driving forces and their likely impacts if they occur.

Scenario Development. Six principles in creating high quality scenarios are described in Boroush and Thomas (1992) and Morrison (1994).

1. Establish assumptions and constraints in advance.
2. Identify the critical (or possible) choices likely to be faced.
3. Identify key drivers.
4. Model or create the scenario space (see below). Select the values to be associated with each variable in the scenario space. The values should lead to a range of outcomes that cover the scenario space.
5. Analyze the implications of alternative contingency policies and strategic plans that cope with each scenario.
6. Use Delphi, qualitative discussion, or cross-impact analysis as inputs.

To use scenarios for long-term strategic planning, iterate steps 3, 4, and 5 to identify the impact of various actions.

Scenario Principles. Scenarios must adhere to three principles. They must be possible, plausible, and internally consistent .

Possible: No barriers to the events described can occur (e.g., speeds faster than light)
Plausible: The described events are believable (e.g., isolating all corporate computers from the Internet to ensure privacy is possible but not plausible)
Internally consistent: All parts of the scenario are consistent with one another (e.g., that a firm relies on law enforcement for cyber protection but personnel rarely report hacking attempts is internally inconsistent)

The Scenario Space. Scenarios are embedded in a scenario space. The space is defined by dimensions with prespecified values. For example, the scenario space in Figure 1 is based on two dimensions: technical software security and identity theft and privacy breaches, with each assigned a high and a low. These two dimensions create four scenarios, one for each combination.

The practicalities of scenarios and an example from our previous work are presented in Appendix B.

High Technical Security Level	Trusted	Social Engineering
Low Technical Security Level	Status Quo	Chaos
	Low Identity Theft Level	High Identity Theft Level

Fig. 1. Sample Scenario Space

3 Futures as an Academic Method

The theme of this conference indicates that investigating the future of ICT and ICT-based practices is ready to become a new, viable part of mainstream IS research. Researchers who want to establish new paradigms generally overcome the inevitable gatekeeper objections by mobilizing a community of supporters to achieve the convergence of opinions required to introduce new ways of thinking. To gain mainstream acceptance, futures research methodologies should have the characteristics of a scientific methodology so they can be applied with academic rigor.

This section presents exploratory ideas for making futures research methodologies viable for IS. The section is framed in terms of a specific methodology, *scenarios*, discussed in Section 2.4 and Appendix B. It is also framed in terms of the sequence of steps usually followed in IS research. The initial step is to explore whether existing IS research designs can incorporate established futures research methods to create rigorous and relevant results.

3.1 Epistemology

The epistemology of futures research methods can be either positivistic or interpretive. In positivistic research, the assumptions lead to propositions which are then investtigated using, for example, Delphi or cross-impact analysis. Alternatively, they could be interpretive, where subjective processes lead to various outcomes (scenarios). In both qualitative and interpretive research, the role of the researcher is instrumental. The researchers' values and beliefs help shape their investigation. It is rare for two futures studies to arrive at identical solutions. Yet, by determining the necessary dimensions and driving forces in advance, the researchers can justify their assumptions and the logical progression of their arguments.

3.2 Theoretical Foundations and Research Design

Research Design Components. A proper design for both quantitative and quailtative research should include at least the following five distinct components[6]:

1. Research question
2. Propositions or hypotheses (if applicable)
3. A defined unit of analysis
4. The logic linking data to the propositions
5. Criteria for interpreting the results

Each of these components is discussed in turn for futures research methodologies and additional considerations are presented. A set of guidelines based on this section are given in Appendix C.

Research Questions. The first issues considered are

1. What type of research questions are Futures Research methods able to address?
2. Can futures research methods be used in conjunction with theoretical underpinnings?

---

[6] Although, this list is based on Yin (1994), who centers his research on case studies, the basic steps also apply to other methodologies.

It is our contention that futures research methodologies are well suited to study what Markus and Robey (1988) termed "process theories."[7] Process theories are longitudinal and dynamic. Process theories are defined as "causation consists of necessary components in sequence" (Markus and Robey 1988, p. 590) where chance and random events play a role. Future methodologies can be used to incorporate interactions (e.g., through cross impact) and unexpected events (e.g., through scenarios). In process theories, the dependent variable is a set of discrete outcomes rather than a continuous variable. Outcomes depend on the nature of the process as well as the levels of the predictors. Conventional variance theory, on the other hand, assumes that a change in the independent variables will result in a predicted change to the dependent variable. In addition, process models are event-driven (Tsohou et al. 2008). Process theories assume that the dependent variable can change over time and that the sequence and duration of events matter.

Process studies aim to answer research questions such as, "How does a particular issue emerge, develop, increase/decrease/cease over time?" (Tsohou et al. 2008). Futures methodologies are well positioned to answer such questions. For example, a scenario can describe the process by which an issue will emerge and the events that could lead to its development. Cross impact analysis can be used to estimate the probability distribution that an issue becomes salient over time or ceases to exist.

Setting Propositions and Linking Data to Propositions. Gregor (2006) defines five types of IS theories based on their structure. Theories for predicting (Gregor's Type III), address the question "what will be" rather than why something is. Such theories should be used to predict outcomes from a set of relevant factors. Predictive theories can be used to define a set of alternative propositions. Unlike in traditional research, the assumption is that the future cannot be predicted and that propositions should be formulated as discussed above, under "Research Design Components" and their formulation depends on the methodology used. For example in a study of the future of academic e-journals (Hovav and Gray 1999), the authors used Eisenhard's (1994) framework to develop two propositions: the future of academic e-journals depends on user acceptance and on economic viability. A subsequent paper developed a scenario space and created four possible scenarios (Hovav and Gray 2002). The scenarios were used to link the data collected about six types of e-journals in support of the two propositions.

Gregor also states that predictive theories, although used in econometrics and finance, are rarely used in IS. She suggests using traditional research methods designed for studying the present and the past (e.g., correlations, regression, and data mining) to address Type III problems. We disagree. Futures research methodologies are more suitable to the study of these type of problems.

Unit of Analysis. Most futures studies tend to be broad, looking at topics that span societies, countries, organizations, and technologies.

Selecting Criteria for Interpreting Results. The methods illustrated in this paper depend on the selection of a set of assumptions. In their classification of current and future information systems, Ein-Dor and Segev (1993) argued that selecting the

---

[7] This contention is an example and does not negate the use of futures research methodologies to answer other type of research questions.

dimensions for classifying the systems is crucial and difficult. A different set of dimensions can lead to different results. Sommer and Sommer's (1991) guideline for ethnographic research also highlights the need to separate the selection of criteria from data collection. Separation is especially important due to the involvement of the researcher and his/her possible subjectivity in data collection. These assertions also apply to futures research. By determining the dimensions along which the future is described in advance, research subjectivity can be lessened. For example, one of the critical and more difficult steps in scenario building is identifying the driving forces that shape one potential future from others (Morrison 1994).

Quality of the Design. Construct, internal, and external validity are important in research design. Quantitative research has well-defined mathematical methods to measure internal and external validity. Qualitative research also has a set of requirements (e.g., Yin 1994), although these guidelines are less defined and are often subjective. The following subsections explore the content, internal, and external considerations for futures research methodologies.

Construct Validity. Construct validity refers to the ability to ensure that the measures used correlate with the theorized construct. Quantitative research uses methods such as convergent and discriminant analysis. Qualitative research uses triangulation, multiple sources of information, chain of evidence, and participant review (Yin 1994). Futures research methodologies could use multiple sources of data and methods, converging expert review and the "wisdom of crowds." The implementation depends on the specific method used, the question studied, and the availability of data. Consider a simple example. A research project investigating the long-term relationships between Internet security and e-commerce might use both environmental scanning (Section 2.2) and Delphi (Section 2.3). If the two methods lead to similar forecasts, the validity of the relations found between security and e-commerce are assumed to be stronger.

Internal Validity. Internal validity refers to the validity of the causal relationships between constructs. In traditional quantitative research, internal validity is measured statistically. In futures studies as in qualitative research, internal validity guidelines need to be developed. These guidelines are likely to vary among methodologies. For example, in scenarios, the relationships among various outcomes need to be plausible, possible, and internally consistent (Section 2).

Generalizability. Generalizability (i.e., external validity) to a range of situations is the hallmark of a good theory. However, generalizability has to be examined from two aspects: (1) the methods and (2) the problems. The methods of futures research are generalizable in that they can be used in most studies about the "future of..." including both the future and the impact of IS. However, the results obtained from these methods rarely extend beyond the specific problem being considered.

Comparison of Methodologies. Table 1 shows an initial comparison of a futures research methodology (the creation of scenarios) with conventional qualitative and quantitative methodologies. This comparison provides illustrative examples and is intended to stimulate discussion.

Table 1. Comparison of Quantitative, Qualitative and Scenarios Methodologies

Item	Scenarios	Quantitative	Qualitative*
	Dynamic	Static	Static
Time	Longitudinal	Cross sectional	Mixed
Theory type	Process	Variance	Variance/process
Research question	Prediction	Analysis Explanation	Analysis Description
Construct and internal validity	Possible, plausible, internally consistent	Statistical	See Tsohou et al. 2008
Antecedents	Past events, trends	Quantifiable dependent variables	Descriptive or quantifiable dependent variables
Consequences	Alternative or unforeseen outcomes	Quantifiable independent variables	Descriptive or qualitative independent variables
Postulations	Scenario space	Hypotheses	Propositions
Unit of analysis	Society, policy, organization	Individual, group, organization	Individual, group, organization
Generalizability	Classification, analytical, bounded by cases	Statistical, classification	Analytical but not statistical
Role of the researcher	Researcher beliefs and values help shape the investigation	Neutral, objective	Weak or strong constructionist views
Role of theory	Dimensions of the scenario space, driving forces and possible directions	Define variables and quantifiable relationships, suggest models	Define variables and descriptive relationships

* Although qualitative methodologies range from positivistic case studies to critical theory building, the entries in the table refer to positivistic case studies, the most common qualitative method used in MIS research.

4   Conclusions

Information Systems is a field that changes rapidly. It is subject to disruptions in both technologies and social norms. If IS researchers are to do more than speculate about change, they need to ensure that their analyses about the future rest on solid ground. Fortunately, by learning about existing, well-established methodologies, such as the ones presented in this paper and in Coates (2000), Glenn and Gordon (2009), Gray and Hovav (2008), and Linstone and Turoff (2002), researchers do not need to reinvent them. Rather, they can use them to gain insight into what lies ahead.

The results of applying any of the futures research methods cannot and does not forecast the future precisely. Because they do reduce the uncertainly, they can improve decision-making at the firm, country, and societal levels.

References

Boroush, M.A., Thomas, C.W.: Scenarios for the Defense Industry after 1995. Planning Review 20(3), 24–29 (1992)

Coates, J.: Scenario Planning. Technological Forecasting & Social Change 65, 115–123 (2000)

Crespo, A.G., Colomo-Palacios, R., Soto-Acosto, P., Ruano-Mayoral, M.: A Qualitative Study of Hard Decision Making in Managing Global Software Development Teams. Information Systems Management 27, 247–252 (2010)

Cule, P.E., Grover, V.: Prospective on the Next Twenty Five Years. Into the Next Millennium: Some Thoughts on IS Practice and Research. Data Base 25, 15–23 (1994)

Dahlbom, B.: Going to the Future. In: Berleur, J., Whitehouse, D. (eds.) An Ethical Global Information Society: Culture and Democracy Revisited. Chapman and Hall, London (1997)

Dahlbom, B., Mathiassen, L.: The Future of Our Profession. Communications of the ACM 40(6), 80–90 (1997)

Dalkey, N., Helmer, O.: An Experimental Application of the Delphi Method to the Use of Experts. Management Science 9, 458–467 (1963)

Dickson, G.W., Senn, J.A., Chervany, N.L.: Research in Management Information Systems: The Minnesota Experiments. Management Science 23, 913–934 (1977)

Ein-Dor, P., Segev, E.: A Classification of Information Systems: Analysis and Interpretation. Information System Research 4, 166–204 (1993)

Eisenhart, D.: Publishing in the Information Age: A New Management Framework for the Digital Era. Quorum Books, Westport (1994)

Glenn, J.C., Gordon, T.J.: Futures Research Methodology, Version 3.0. The Millenium Project, Washington (2009)

Gray, P., Hovav, A.: Using Scenarios to Understand the Frontiers of IS. Information Systems Frontiers 1, 15–24 (1999)

Gray, P., Hovav, A.: The IS Organization of the Future: Four Scenarios for 2020. Information Systems Management 24, 113–120 (2007)

Gray, P., Hovav, A.: From Hindsight to Foresight: Applying Futures Research Techniques in Information Systems. Communications of the AIS 22, 211–234 (2008)

Hovav, A., Gray, P.: Electronic Publishing: A Framework. In: Proceedings of the 5th Americas Conference on Information Systems, Milwaukee, WI (1999)

Hovav, A., Gray, P.: Future Penetration of Academic Electronic Journals: Four Scenarios. Information Systems Frontiers 4, 229–244 (2002)

Gregor, S.: The Nature of Theory in Information Systems. MIS Quarterly 30, 611–642 (2006)

Linstone, H. A., Turoff, M.: The Delphi Method: Techniques and Applications (2002), http://is.njit.edu/pubs/delphibook/index.html

Markus, L.: Writing Up "Intensive" Research in the "Standard Article Format" Enablers or Constraints. Working Paper, Claremont Graduate University, Claremont, CA (1992)

Markus, L.: The Qualitative Difference in Information Systems Research and Practice. In: Lee, A.S., Liebenau, J., De Gross, J.I. (eds.) Proceedings of the IFIP TC8 WG8.2 International Conference on Information Systems and Qualitative Research, pp. 11–27. Chapman & Hall, London (1997)

Markus, L., Robey, D.: Information Technology and Organizational Change: Causal Structure in Theory and Research. Management Science 34, 583–598 (1988)

Myers, M.: Qualitative Research in Information Systems. MIS Quarterly 21(2), 241–242 (1997)

Morrison, J.: The Future Tool Kit. Across the Board 3, 18–25 (1994)

Robey, D.: Research Commentary: Diversity in Information Systems Research: Threat, Promise, and Responsibility. Information Systems Research 7, 400–408 (1996)

Simon, H.A.: The Sciences of the Artificial. MIT Press, Cambridge (1969)

Sommer, B., Sommer, R.: A Practical Guide to Behavioral Research: Tools and Techniques. Oxford University Press, New York (1991)

Surowiecki, J.: The Wisdom of Crowds. Anchor Books, New York (2004)

Tsohou, A., Kokolakis, S., Karyda, M., Kiountouzis, E.: Process-Variance Models in Information Security Awareness Research. Information Management & Computer Security 16, 271–287 (2008)

Walsham, G.: The Emergence of Interpretivism in IS Research. Information Systems Research 6, 376–394 (1995)

Yin, R.K.: Case Study Research Design and Method, 2nd edn. Sage Publications, Thousand Oaks (1994)

About the Authors

Paul Gray is Professor Emeritus and Founding Chair of the School of Information Systems and Technology at Claremont Graduate University. His interests in studying the future started in the 1970s when he was a professor at The University of Southern California. He was previously a professor at Stanford University, the Georgia Institute of Technology, the University of Southern California, and Southern Methodist University. Prior to his academic career, he worked for 16 years in research and development organizations including nine years at SRI International. He received his Ph.D. from Stanford University.

Anat Hovav is an associate professor at Korea University Business School in Seoul, South Korea. She holds a Ph.D. in Management and Information Systems from Claremont Graduate University and has over 15 years of industry experience in information systems management and strategic planning. Her research interests include the socio-technical aspects of organizational information security, studies of the future, risk assessment, Internet standards, and electronic scholarship.

Appendix A. Delphi

In the 1950s, the Air Force regularly convened expert civilian panels to obtain technical and/or policy advice about future directions. They found the advice they received was typically from one or two dominant participants, rather than the whole group. The dominant individuals were the most respected or most vocal. The Air Force hired RAND Corporation to develop a method to overcome group-think. The RAND researchers, led by Olaf Helmer and Norm Dalkey, decided the problem was the face-to-face interaction because inevitably the dominant voices prevailed. Therefore, they recommended the panels should be anonymous and unaware of who favored which policy.

The Approach. Delphi is a method that uses anonymity of opinion to obtain forecasts from a group of experts. A group is needed if the scope of the problem is too broad for any one expert or so new that there are few experts. The group cross-fertilizes ideas and ensures that all aspects of the problem are covered.

Delphi involves multiple rounds. During the first round, the experts are asked to give their estimates and their reasons for making those estimates. The resulting data is analyzed. If there is consensus on a particular question, there is no need to continue on that question. However, if there is dissensus, the distribution of answers (without attribution to individual respondents) is fed back to the group as are the rationales given for the outliers. The group is asked to re-estimate. This is round 2. Usually a number of rounds is needed to reach consensus or to conclude that there is dissensus.

The relatively straight forward steps in a perfect Delphi are[8]

1. Specify the subject and the objective
2. Specify all outcomes you want to know about
3. Specify how the results will be used if achieved
4. Include only precisely phrased judgmental questions that cover topics of interest
5. Assemble respondents who can answer questions creatively, in depth, and on schedule
6. Provide respondents with relevant historical data so that they anchor their answers based on reality
7. Collate the group's responses consistently and promptly
8. Make sure respondents are explicit about the reasons for their estimates, interpretations, and recommendations
9. Analyze the data
10. Identify any important needed improvements in methodology and results
11. Write and publish a report

Research Results. Experiments were undertaken by Delphi co-inventors Dalkey and Helmer (1963). UCLA graduate students and RAND analysts were asked questions, (e.g., number of telephones in Uganda) for which correct answers were available. However, only a few subjects were likely to know the answers. In general, the subjects made reasonable "estimates" for these questions. The major findings were

1. The spread of opinion narrows after the second round and the median usually shifts toward the true answer.
2. Delphi interactions generally produce more accurate estimates than face-to-face meetings.
3. Usually, the narrower the range of opinion, the more accurate the answer.
4. Self-appraised expertise is a powerful indicator of accuracy.

Variations on Delphi. Variations on the standard Delphi process include

*   *Round 0.* In round 0, the panel members define the subject, using open-ended questions, rather than the organizer selecting the questions. This approach expands and refines the range of topics covered (e.g., in a Delphi on computer security, a panelist introduces a new physical form of identification or a different encryption algorithm).

---

[8] Source: Personal communication with Olaf Helmer.

- *Self-rating.* Rather than accepting all responses as equal, panelists rate their own expertise on each question. These ratings become weights when tabulating responses. Self-ratings are not perfect (e.g., a small fraction rates themselves low on almost everything but their specialty whereas others claim expertise on almost everything).
- *Permanent Panel.* For running many Delphi sessions over time, recruiting panelists for each inquiry becomes a major task. Helmer (personal communication) proposed setting up a large permanent panel (called D-net) from which people are chosen for a particular Delphi. Such a panel might include broadly knowledgeable, computer-literate, retired people.
- *Mini Delphi.* Distributed technologies used in real time allow the panel to work simultaneously. For each round, the participants enter their responses anonymously into the computer and give reasons for their values. For each question, two or more participants (typically those with extreme answers) are asked to discuss their views briefly. Panelists then revise their estimates anonymously. This approach is particularly useful for gaining closure.

Delphi Advantages. Delphi brings together knowledgeable people to work on a problem and maintains their attention on the issues. The set of questions provides a framework in which to work. Anonymity minimizes barriers to communication. Delphi provides people the opportunity to be heard as individuals rather than as labels (e.g., affiliation, field, reputation). It produces precise, documented records.

Delphi Disadvantages. Anonymity and separation from other panelists removes the face-to-face stimulation of interactions. When invented, the process was paper and pencil. A round took considerable time because questionnaires and results of previous rounds involved reproduction, mailing, and waiting for responses. Panel size decreased with each round because of a lack of timely response. Much changed with email and the Internet. Although rounds run more quickly, the attrition problem still exists.

Conclusions on Delphi. Delphi is well established. It incorporates expert opinion into forecasts, providing insights for scenarios and input to cross-impact analysis. Occasionally, Delphi is easy to discount given the history of expert opinion failure and the many pitfalls in running it. Yet, the use of the wisdom of crowds, where the crowd knows about the subject, commends it where other approaches fail.

Appendix B. Scenarios

Practicalities. The sequence of steps in scenario development are

1. Select system variables of interest
2. Forecast system parameters
3. Develop scenario space
4. Perform a consistency check
5. Develop measurements
6. Write the scenarios
7. Analyze the scenarios and develop relevant policies

Scenarios for a given time horizon can be written from three points of view (Coates 2000):

1. A *newspaper story* written on some date in the future (e.g., July 1, 2020) describing the situation that day with no history or motivation. Assumes everyone knows what happened previously.
2. A *history* written on say, July 1, 2020, that describes the events that led to the future situation.
3. A *forecast* that starts in the present and shows the evolutionary path which results from the assumptions in the scenario space. This approach leads forward into the future rather than working backward from the end-point. This evolutional approach is the one most often used for strategic planning and is the one the authors recommend.

In creating scenarios, it is import to discuss (1) the stakeholders involved, (2) the effects on the stakeholders, and (3) the assumed values of the parameters.

The parameter values must be consistent with the scenario space element being discussed. For example, a scenario for coping with security issues by making software an outsourced service results in a different role, size, and technical composition of the IS department than one based on technological advances and preventive tools.

Number of Scenarios. Because each scenario takes considerable time to create, only a few can be generated in a particular study. Select a small number of scenarios (e.g., four or six) from a scenario space which together represent diverse future outcomes. Present an even number of scenarios; an odd number leads managers to select the middle scenario as most likely and avoid considering the others (Morrison 1994). With two scenarios, managers select only the more favorable one.

Scenario Pitfalls. Coates (2000) suggests five pitfalls scenario builders should avoid:

1. Confusing the scenario and the outcome
2. Confusing the scenario with a forecast
3. Assuming that scenarios are static
4. Relying on extrapolation as THE scenario
5. Creating scenarios where everything is maximum or minimum or average

Example: In the 1990s, companies like Digital Equipment Corporation disappeared because they assumed the mainframe or minicomputer would continue to be the only future. They did not plan for microcomputers or Intel architecture.

Conclusions on Scenarios. Scenarios are stories used for communicating and are a basis for policy discussions. They help in understanding the implications of different outcomes and the range of possibilities as well as in developing alternatives that can react to or influence whichever future occurs. Scenario building is both art and science. Although it involves experts that follow the processes described here, rarely do two scenario builders create the same scenarios for a given problem (Coates 2000).

Example: Figure B1 and Table B1 summarize the findings of a study published by the authors in *Information Systems Frontiers* in 1999. Four scenarios were considered in a two- dimensional scenario space. The details are shown in Table B1. The shadings show the outcomes as of 2011. Much of the status quo remains but only three of the Dystopian elements exist and many of the Utopian and Technological outcomes came true. Recognize that scenarios rarely occur as forecast.

Social Acceptance	Limited Telecommunications	Ubiquitous Telecommunications
High	Status Quo	Utopian
Low	Dystopic	Technology

Fig. B1. Scenario Space for 1999 Study

Table B1. Scenarios on the Future of IS***

Variable	Utopian	Dystopian	Status Quo	Technology
Technological				
Internet diffusion*	Internet III****	Internet II****	Internet II****	Internet III****
Rate of technological change*	Constant	Decreasing	Constant	Increasing
Y2K problem*	Solved	Unsolved	Partly solved	Solved
Moore's law*	Continues	Ends	Continues	Speeds up
Socioeconomic				
Economic crisis*	No	No	No	No
Energy crisis*	No	No	No	No
Globalization*	Continues	Stops	Continues	Stops
Computer literacy	Everyone	Constant	Everyone	Techies only
Privacy*	Medium	High	Medium	Low
Luddite reaction	No	Yes	No	No
Information Systems				
Systems	ERP	Systems Integration	Mix**	ERP
Centralization	Decentralized	Centralized	Mix**	Decentralized
Sourcing	Outsourcing	Insourcing	Mix**	Insourcing
Software	Standards	Proprietary	Proprietary	Standards
Software	Packages	Custom	Mix**	Package

Source: Updated from Gray and Hovav (1999)
*   See Gray and Hovav (1999) for assumptions.
**   Mix implies both options included.
***   These scenarios were created in 1999. The shaded areas show which elements were correct as of 2011.
****   The term Internet II refers to a next generation Internet infrastructure using IPv6. Internet III refers to the version after IPv6. This terminology is not to be confused with Web 2.0, which refers to existing 2011 Web-based services.

Appendix C. Suggested Guidelines for Futures Research in Information Systems

1. **Proper process:** Define the philosophical assumptions for the study based in theory, research design, data collection, data analysis based on preset criteria, and conclusions. Each step needs to be well defined, self-contained, and justified.

2. **Research design:** Use a structured research design, following the five steps described in Section 3.

3. **Triangulation:** Use several methods or several sources of data. Triangulation is particularly difficult when data is scarce. For example, a study can incorporate and compare results from a Delphi study and environmental scanning in selecting events and trends (i.e., multiple sources of data). Similarly, researches can use cross impact and scenario analyses when estimating the probability of future outcomes (i.e., multiple methods). This process is similar to the triangulation used in case studies that involve multiple cases and multiple investigators (Yin 1994).

4. **Content validity:** The definition of content validity in futures studies differs from the one used in other IS methodologies. However, much as in traditional research, content validity can be obtained by using a panel of experts. For example, the discussion of scenario building in Section 2.3 stresses that events described in a scenario should be possible, plausible, and internally consistent. The results of a well-designed Delphi can be used to achieve these criteria (Section 2.2).

5. **Standard formats of reporting** (Markus 1992) result in making the reviewing process easier and in engaging the reader.

6. **Consistency in the unit of analysis:** Avoid mixing units of analysis in defining events and trends. It is too easy to shift from one level of analysis (e.g., the organization) to another (e.g., society). For example, if the unit of analysis is the level of technology over time, the Delphi questions presented to the experts should first ask them to provide not only a baseline estimate of the technology over time but also estimates of the technology's impact on society and suggested policies.

7. **The set of characteristics** or dimensions should be selected prior to the data collection or analysis (Sommer and Sommer 1991). Researchers should not confuse the subject of the analysis with its attributes.

Appendix D. Futures Research Methodologies

Table D1 lists 37 futures research methodologies described in great detail in Glenn and Gordon (2009).

Table D1. Futures Research Methodologies

1. Environmental Scanning	14. Substitution Analysis	26. Using Vision in Futures
2. The Delphi Method	15. Statistical Modeling	27. Normative Forecasting
3. Real Time Delphi	16. Technology Sequence Analysis	28. Science and Technology Road Mapping
4. Scenarios	17. Morphological Analysis	29. Field Anomaly Relaxation
5. Cross-Impact Analysis	18. Systems Perspectives	30. Agent Modeling
6. Trend Impact Analysis	19. Robust Decision Making	31. Multiple Perspective Concept
7. Interactive Scenarios	20. Participatory Methods	32. Heuristics Modeling
8. Scenario Planning	21. The Futures Polygon	33. Causal Layered Analysis
9. Wild Cards	22. The Futures Wheel	34. Personal Futures
10. Decision Modeling	23. Structural Analysis	35. State of the Future Index
11. Text Mining for Technology Foresight	24. Genius Forecasting, Intuition, and Vision	36. SOFI Software System
12. Relevance Trees	25. Prediction Markets	37. Chaos and Nonlinear Dynamics
13. Simulation and Games		

Source: Glenn and Gordon (2009)

Author Index

GPSR Compliance

*The European Union's (EU) General Product Safety Regulation (GPSR)
is a set of rules that requires consumer products to be safe and our
obligations to ensure this.*

*If you have any concerns about our products, you can contact us on
ProductSafety@springernature.com*

In case Publisher is established outside the EU, the EU authorized
representative is:

Springer Nature Customer Service Center GmbH
Europaplatz 3
69115 Heidelberg, Germany

Batch number: 09490835

Printed by Printforce, the Netherlands